CRITICISM AND COUNTER CRITICISM

Essays in honour of the doyens of English Studies at Aligarh Muslim University, Aligarh – Asloob Ahmad Ansari, Masoodul Hasan, and Zahida Zaidi

Editors
Mohammad Asim Siddiqui
Abdur Raheem Kidwai

Viva Books
New Delhi | Mumbai | Chennai | Kolkata | Bengaluru | Hyderabad | Kochi | Guwahati

Publisher's note

Every possible effort has been made to ensure that the information contained in this book is accurate at the time of going to press, and the publisher and author cannot accept responsibility for any errors or omissions, however caused. No responsibility for loss or damage occasioned to any person acting, or refraining from action, as a result of the material in this publication can be accepted by the editor, the publisher or the author.

Every effort has been made to trace the owners of copyright material used in this book. The author and the publisher will be grateful for any omission brought to their notice for acknowledgment in the future editions of the book.

First Published 2013
Reprinted 2015, 2017, 2024

Viva Books Private Limited

- 4737/23, Ansari Road, Daryaganj, New Delhi 110 002
  Tel. 42242200, 23258325, 23283121, Email: vivadelhi@vivagroupindia.net
- 76, Service Industries, Shirvane, Sector 1, Nerul, Navi Mumbai 400 706
  Tel. 27721273, 27721274, Email: vivamumbai@vivagroupindia.net
- Jamals Fazal Chambers, 26 Greams Road, Chennai 600 006
  Tel. 28294241, 28290304, Email: vivachennai@vivagroupindia.net
- B-103, Jindal Towers, 21/1A/3 Darga Road, Kolkata 700 017
  Tel. 22816713, Email: vivakolkata@vivagroupindia.net
- 194, 1st Floor, Subbarama Chetty Road, Basavanagudi, Bengaluru 560 004
  Tel. 26607409, Email: vivabangalore@vivagroupindia.net
- 101-102, Moghal Marc Apartments, 3-4-637 to 641, Narayanguda,
  Hyderabad 500 029
  Tel. 27564481, Email: vivahyderabad@vivagroupindia.net
- First Floor, Beevi Towers, SRM Road, Kaloor, Kochi 682 018
  Tel. 0484-2403055, 2403056, Email: vivakochi@vivagroupindia.net
- 232, GNB Road, Beside UCO Bank, Silpukhuri, Guwahati 781 003
  Tel. 0361-2666386, Email: vivaguwahati@vivagroupindia.net

www.vivagroupindia.com

ISBN: 978-81-309-2302-4

Published by Vinod Vasishtha for Viva Books Private Limited, 4737/23 Ansari Road, Daryaganj, New Delhi 110 002.

Printed and bound by Replika Press, Kundli.

L0000 / L0135

Contents

Acknowledgements

To all contributors for writing for this volume; to Abrar Khan for his neat typing of many manuscripts and his excellent work at the computer; to Parvez Rafi Khan and Aqeel Ahmad for arranging for valuable back issues of the *Aligarh Journal of English Studies*; to Sahidul Islam and Sana Niazi for making countless rounds of the Maulana Azad Library for getting some books issued; to Zoya Zaidi for giving extremely useful and otherwise inaccessible information about Zahida Zaidi's publications; to Kaif Siddiqui for his computer wizardry and to the staff of UGC Academic Staff College, AMU Aligarh for being helpful as ever.

Mohammad Asim Siddiqui
Abdur Raheem Kidwai

About the Contributors

Ansari, Ameena Kazi. Teaches in the Department of English, Jamia Millia Islamia. Her areas of interest and publication are postcolonial literature and translation.

Asif, Mohammad. Teaches in the Department of English, Aligarh Muslim University, Aligarh. His areas of study include Continental fiction and literary theory.

Attri, Rashmi. Associate Professor, Department of English, Aligarh Muslim University, Aligarh. Her areas of specialization are modern British drama, Indian Writing in English and Indian aesthetics.

Ghauri, Shehla. Assistant Professor, Department of English, Aligarh Muslim University, Aligarh. She specializes in American fiction, literary autobiographies and Indian Writing in English.

Hasan, Nazia. Assistant Professor of English, Women's College, Aligarh Muslim University, Aligarh. Her areas of specialization include postcolonial literature, literary theory and Indian fiction in English.

Hasan, Seemin. Associate Professor, Department of English, Aligarh Muslim University, Aligarh. She specializes in Romantic literature, postcolonial literature and Translation.

Iqbal, Rubina, Assistant Professor of English, Women's College, Aligarh Muslim University, Aligarh. Her areas of interest are American fiction and Indian Writing in English.

Islam, Sajidul. Assistant Professor, Department of English, Aligarh Muslim University, Aligarh. His areas of interest include postcolonial fiction, contemporary British fiction and Cultural Studies.

Khan, Amirullah. Assistant Professor, Department of English, Aligarh Muslim University, Aligarh. His areas of interest are ESP, Materials Designing and Phonetics.

Khan, Samina. Associate Professor, Department of English, Aligarh Muslim University, Aligarh. Her areas of research and publication include British drama, modern Indian drama and comparative literature.

Kidwai, Abdur Raheem. Director, UGC Academic Staff College and Professor, Department of English, Aligarh Muslim University, Aligarh. His areas of interest and publications include Romantic writers, Literary Orientalism, ELT and the English Translations of the Quran.

Mehta, Rashmi, Assistant Professor of English, Nirma Institute of Law, Nirma University, Ahmedabad. Her areas of research and publication include Elizabethan drama and literary theory.

Mohammad, Taj. Teaches English at King Khalid University, Saudi Arabia. His area of interest is Indian Writing in English.

Nehal, Raashid. Associate Professor, Department of English, Aligarh Muslim University, Aligarh. His area of interest and publication is ELT with special focus on ESL writing and teacher education.

Parvez, Farha Hiba. Teaches English at Jamia Higher Secondary School, Jamia Millia Islamia, New Delhi. Her area of interest is Literary Orientalism.

Rafiq, Sami. Associate Professor, Department of English, Aligarh Muslim University, Aligarh. Her areas of research and publication include American drama, Translation, and Comparative literature.

Saquib, Shahabuddin. Teaches Urdu at the Department of Urdu at Aligarh Muslim University, Aligarh. He specializes in Urdu prose(non-fiction)

Sharma, Ankur. Senior Assistant Professor of English at Doaba College, Jalandhar, Punjab. His areas of interest in teaching and research include Comparative drama and theatre.

Siddiqui, Mohammad Asim. Associate Professor, Department of English, Aligarh Muslim University, Aligarh. His areas of interest include postcolonial fiction, Cultural Studies and Film Studies.

Suhaib, Madihur Rehman. Associate Professor, Department of English, Aligarh Muslim University, Aligarh. His areas of interest are American and Continental fiction, Marxist theory and Psychoanalysis.

Syed, Akbar J. A. Assistant Professor, Department of English, Aligarh Muslim University, Aligarh. His main interest is in the study of novels of different countries and periods.

Taj, Nikhat. Associate Professor of English, Women's College, Aligarh Muslim University, Aligarh. Her areas of research and publication include 18th and 19th century British fiction and literary theory.

Introduction

Mapping the Field of English Studies in India

Mohammad Asim Siddiqui

This book is a collection of essays on writers separated by time, place and technique. The subjects taken up in the book cover varied areas in literary studies. A question can be asked as to why one more book of a predictable variety. Why indulge in a game the rules, strategies and the outcome of which are known to everyone? Well, almost.

We are aware that in a volume of this kind which offers a lot of variety some parts may outshine the whole. But that is precisely the point because editors of the volume do not usually know which parts will receive that honour. What is beyond doubt is that the book has some distinct parts which justify the publication of 'one more book'. The parts include English classics, literature in translation, Continental literature, Indian literature, literature of the diaspora and the changing face of English criticism in India.

The book is written in the belief that meaning of a text is not fixed, standards of criticism change and that in matters of literature and criticism there is always space to accommodate one more opinion. Respecting the judgement of previous generations of critics—Western or Indian—does not mean following that judgement uncritically. Literary criticism thrives on discussion, dialogue, debate, disagreement and dissent. This book proposes to offer plenty of it.

The book can be faulted on another count too. In some parts it is two times or even three times removed from literature. A work is produced by Shakespeare or Hardy, critics like F.R.Leavis, Wilson Knight, and Kenneth Muir write on it and define the frontiers of literary criticism. Further, the likes of A.A.Ansari and M.H. Khan subject this literary criticism to a very thorough reading and in turn offer their bit to the discipline. Should things stop here? They do not, at least in this book. A need was felt to carry forward, what Helen Gardner calls in an ironic phrase 'business of criticism', to look critically at the work of critics themselves, critics of different order—the Leavises and Ansaris alike—in the belief that sometimes a thin line separates critics of the primary and the secondary rank, often ideology playing a role in creating the division. The reasons for this exercise are not mere critical indulgence or institutional duty but rather to identify and check the process of a caste hierarchy in literary criticism. This hierarchy operates at many levels. Though postcolonial criticism in its many avatars has dented this hierarchy a bit, in India we see a hierarchy of a different kind with critics from some metropolitan universities occupying a position of eminence denied to others who write from 'lesser universities'. It was never easy to find a mainstream publisher for a work of literary essays for an academic from a lesser known university. Probably things have changed now with publishing becoming a thriving industry. But many excellent works of literary criticism, not necessarily published by the celebrated Indian publishers, were produced from Aligarh and such places before the publishing boom. Many of these books of excellent and penetrative essays, published by small time publishers, sank without a trace. Many excellent essays have survived so far because they were first published in the pages of the *The Aligarh Journal of English Studies*. However, their chances of survival are slim because even finding a copy of all the issues of the journal even in the place of its origin and development was not an easy task. It is a pity that some outstanding essays on Shakespeare written by Aligarh scholars have suffered a state of oblivion. One will not be guilty of making a tall claim if one said that Aligarh has made its own contribution to Shakespearian criticism. The interest in Shakespeare has passed from generation to generation with the result that from the sixties to the nineties there developed in Aligarh a rich body of criticism. This is not to suggest that other major writers were not written about.

Alas! all this has not been preserved in publications with good distribution network. With the possible exception of Asloob Ahmad Ansar's writings on Blake which have been published from the U S and the U K, this body of knowledge did not reach out to a wider audience. It is also unfortunate that information about this does not appear in digitized form either. Many of the essays included in this book not only pay a tribute to the work of these doyens of English studies in India but they are also an effort to keep their work from suffering undeserved neglect.

The work of these persons, hard working scholars, inspiring teachers and effective bilingual communicators of their wisdom is an important thread in the matter of Aligarh.[1] Just as every country has a rich storehouse of myths, legends, folklores and above all memories of these entities articulated in different ways, on a smaller scale a region, maybe a city, or for that matter a university with a definite character and history may have its own reservoir of 'folklores', rich memories and associations. Aligarh, founded on a dream and vision, has been a fertile ground for nurturing many traditions, traditions deriving their sustenance from both Oriental and Western ethos. The mark of these Oriental and Occidental ethos can be felt in the many buildings of Aligarh, in many rituals which are religiously performed on both formal and informal occasions and in different traditions and customs which have acquired some sanctity in Aligarh University. Above all the matter of Aligarh is to be seen in its love of literature—poetry as a performing art , 'tall tales' narrated on an every day basis in different gatherings and the proverbial Aligarh wit—and respect for the Oriental and Occidental traditions in literature. Both Urdu and English literature have had a role in the formation of the idea of Aligarh University. The three scholars in whose honour these essays have been written typify both Oriental and Occidental traditions not only in their work—they have a substantial body of work in both English and Urdu—but also in their world view.

A lot of this 'evidence' of this love of literature is to be seen in the thousands of letters that Asloob Ahmad Ansari received from his many peers and contemporaries, important literary critics all, the

Northrop Fryes the F.R. Leavises, the Kenneth Muirs, their letters praising his work, discussing nuances of literary matters, promising articles and more articles for *the Aligarh Journal of Engish Studies*. These letters, often written in almost indecipherable writing,will become, have become, part of Aligarh folklore. It was a very reassuring feeling to learn that Asloob Ahmad Ansari is going to publish these letters in the near future. This publication will obviously be in line with many books that he has edited and written both in English and Urdu. The annotated bibliography of Ansari's writings, carefully prepared by Shahabuddin Saquib, Amirullah Khan and Sajidul Islam gives a fair indication of Ansari's range of interests. However, there is more to Ansari's writing than simply the number. Mohammad Asim Siddiqui reads his many essays published in *the Aligarh Journal of English Studies* to discover a point or two about his critical method. Siddiqui pays attention to Ansari's fondness for discovering existentialist patterns in Shakespeare's plays, his reliance on image and symbol school of criticism and the possible influence of Leavisite and New Criticism on his critical writings.

In another essay Siddiqui analyses the long history of literary criticism at the Aligarh Muslim University, a tradition that was given a big boost with the start of *the Aligarh Journal of English Studies* by Ansari. Some of the finest critical essays, contributed both by the foreign scholars including, among others, F.R.Leavis, Wilson Knight and Kenneth Muir, and the Aligarh academics like Maqbool Hasan Khan and S. Wiqar Husain were published in the pages of the journal. Siddiqui's piece gives a hint of the quality of this criticism especially the one on Shakespeare.

The literary-critical tradition and the humanist scholarship at Aligarh has been enriched in no small measure by the thoughts and writings of Masoodul Hasan. In his interview given to Mohammad Asim Siddiqui, Hasan speaks at length about the state of literary criticism in India, the dangers of theory-specific study of literature and the changing concept of literary studies in India. In his long career he has written on various authors and subjects ranging from Francis Quarles to John Donne to bibliographical research. More recently his interest in Sufi thought has yielded a very original study of Sufi images and echoes in English literature. Siddiqui's short bibliographic article on his writings was not out of place in this volume.

Another very informative bibliographic piece is written by Taj Mohammad .He has compiled a list of Zahida Zaidi's numerous books of poetry, drama, fiction and criticism. His annotated bibliography of her works is full of useful inputs about her work. Zahida Zaidi cannot be easily slotted. Her plays and poems capture the matter of Aligarh; her fiction is also immersed in the ethos of Aligarh; her criticism on drama and poetry is wide-ranging. All her writings, including her critical pieces are marked by a strong individualistic voice. The woman question in her writing is a muted presence but the political is very much pronounced.

However, in this entire exercise we have not concentrated on personalities but on literature and on literary criticism produced on literary texts, some canonical, some struggling to become canonical, some major forms of literature, some marginal but which never make one's interest flag. Most of these readings say something new on these texts. Nikhat Taj's reading of Thomas Hardy's *Return of the Native* offers a fresh perspective on the character of Clym Yeobright. She employs humanistic-existential model of Coleman and Hjelle which shares elements of psyschoanalysis, behaviourism and existentialism and which takes a very dynamic view of individuals recognizing their potentialities. One important characteristic of contemporary theory is that works originating in some other fields may have uses for literature students. In this piece Nikhat Taj gains a new perspective for character analysis which may have potential uses for the character study as such. Another character which does not cease to fascinate readers is that of Dr Faustus. In two different pieces Christopher Marlowe's great play yields different insights. Ankur Sharma looks at Faustus's search for godhead in the play and argues that Faustus's rejection of God makes him desperate to have godlike power. In many contemporary theories of power it is emphasized that power sees itself in the image of God. Despite

Dr Faustus's gaining immense power and knowledge his realization of his mortality keeps troubling him. His efforts to act in the manner of God also explain his usurpation of God's attributes. Rashmi Mehta's deconstructive reading of the play sees the divisions and differences in notions of Protestantism in the play. She also discovers a range of questions in the play which not only Christianity but all religions have tried to answer.

In any discussion of English literature the Romantic poets predictably occupy a pre-eminent position. Seemin Hasan's article, written in a very poetic prose, talks about heroines in Keats's odes. She recreates in her essay the mystery, beauty, romance as also the danger and pain in the world of Madeline, Angela, Isabella and Lamia. In her reading of "La Belle Dame Sans Merci" Hasan also subjects the archetype of femme fatale to a close scrutiny. A. R. Kidwai's short write-up on Wordsworth, on the other hand, deconstructs the very notion of romance and love unearthing their implied power dynamics and ideological contours. A blend of critical comment a la Said and an attempt at painstaking bibliographical research, Kidwai's piece not only inspects the Christian design of one of Wordsworth little talked about poem, but also relates Wordsworth's Orientalism to the Western tradition of creating Muslim stereotypes in works ranging from heroic poems of Medieval France to Shelley's and Southey's use of Orientalist tropes in their poetry. This tradition of Orientalism, as commentators like Edward Said and Ziauddin Sardar have so convincingly argued, can also be seen in related areas like films, administrative reports, dairies and letters. Farha Hiba Parvez has done an admirable job by reading the letters of Mary Wortley Montagu, written during her travel to Turkey, for their Orientalist content. Parvez discovers certain patterns of mind, what she appropriately terms Montagu's rhetorics, in these letters. Her essay indirectly hints at the danger involved in accepting the commonsense view of reality sanctioned by the dominant empiricist-rationalist tradition of the West. However, prejudice can assume many colours, Orientalist colour being just one, albeit of very powerful variety. These different colours also come on the surface when we make a broader survey of travel literature. Shehla Ghauri achieves this task by talking about the attitudes of Dr Johnson and James Boswell— the writer and his biographer are almost like 'Siamese twins' in popular imagination— towards the Scots. Ghauri not only presents a comparative picture of the writing styles and personalities of the two men and their work but she also communicates in her prose a feel of the joy she must have felt in reading the travel accounts of the two. This she does by capturing the fascinating details of their travel and their close interaction with each other extended over a long period of time.

In most universities today the syllabus of English literature at the postgraduate level includes not only an optional paper on American literature but also papers on Postcolonial literature{s} (the older term Commonwealth literature has long been discarded), Continental literature and ELT. The three papers on American authors Hawthorne, Mark Twain and Tennessee William are written from three different critical positions. Rubina Iqbal uses new historicist approach in her reading of *The House of Seven Gables*, a fine work which has suffered a relative neglect because *The Scarlet Letter* has appropriated all critical attention. In her effort to give a total picture of the context of representations in the novel Iqbal studies both the 17th century feudal American culture and notions of egalitarian society in the19th century. Her parallel readings include apart, of course, from a very close analysis of text, a peep into various relevant political documents, investigation of the history of various popular cults like mesmerism and attitudes of devotion and distrust towards them, inspection of some famous trials especially the trial and execution of one Matthew Maule and an interrogation of the rhetoric and machinations of many 19th century political figures. The other great nineteenth century writer Mark Twain is the subject of Madihur Rehman Suhaib's scrutiny. Like Iqbal he also focuses on a Twain novel which has suffered some neglect in comparision with *The Adventures of Huckleberry Finn.* He presents a fairly detailed view of the history of criticism of *The Prince and the Pauper.* His understanding of the issues of identity in the novel emerges from his very close reading of the text. His analysis of the actions of characters in the novel is expansive, exhaustive and totally free from reductionism. Moving on from fiction to American drama, Sami Rafiq uses an interdisciplinary approach to study Tennessee Williams's famous play *The Glass Menagerie*. She analyses Williams' use of the technique of impressionistic painting in *The Glass Menagerie* and discovers this pattern in the construction of the play especially the impressionistic style of colouring for presenting a picture of life. Another paper which roughly falls under the umbrella of American literature is on Ayn Rand's lesser-known works. Akbar Joseph reads Rand against the grain, discovering in her work a blatant celebration of patriarchy. His Marxist-feminist approach to Ayn Rand appears very liberating and it refuses to bow under the weight of Ayn Rand's cult status in capitalist world.

In the later decades of the twentieth century the notion of literature underwent a change. The paradigm shift from English literature to literature in English proved to be a new reading experience altogether. Suddenly the corpus of literature expanded phenomenally. The world 'discovered' excellent writings from not only the usual suspects like India and Africa but also from unlikely places such as Pakistan, Saudi Arabia and Afghanistan. Rashmi Attri analyses Indian English novelist Arun Joshi's novel *Foreigner* in existentialist perspective. Essentially a character study, it presents the protagonist Sindi Oberoi's sense of guilt and his rootlessness, which, inviting comparison with Camus' *Outsider*, transforms his experience into the experience of the modern man. Samina Khan, on the other hand, chooses to write on Zahida Zaidi's Urdu play entitled *Bahut Door Tak Raat Hogi*, a play inspired by the writer's sensitive reaction to Gujarat massacre of 2002. Khan finds the use of many Western theories of drama, especially of absurdist theatre, in Zaidi's play. However, Attri's good effort at universalist meaning in her study and Samina Khan's use of Western theatrical traditions in interpreting an Urdu play notwithstanding, literature other than English would usually promote different reading strategies, never losing sight of the local context. They in their turn would question the universalist manner in which English literature has traditionally been read. Postcolonial criticism and subaltern studies have proved their emancipatory potential. Quite a few essays in this volume touch aspects of literary studies that are the domain of postcolonial criticism. Ameena Kazi Ansari's fairly comprehensive and nuanced piece not only covers the trajectory, diachronic and synchronic, of Asian Diasporic Writing but also captures the new idiom of the postcolonial theory, its rhythm, its variety and above all its ideologically- positioned opacity. Her essay encapsulates some of the motifs of diasporic writing— among others, language, nation, resistance, displacement and angst--with reference to the work of writers as varied as Amitava Kumar, Anjana Appachana, Vassanji, Hanif Kureishi and Hindi poet Ved Prakash Vatuk. Understandably the voice of a poet like Vatuk can be heard by the outside world because of the English translation of his Hindi poetry and, it may be added, translation itself is an important site of debate in postcolonial writing. It is not for nothing that the twentieth century is also considered the century of translation. Nazia Hasan also gets to the core of postcolonial voices in Rabindranath Tagore's two plays in their English translation. Tagore's ambivalent stance on modernity in *Waterfall*, and his close look at colonialism in *The Red Oleanders* are substantiated by textual evidence by Hasan. Textual evidence is not lacking in the study of another translated text, namely *The Unbearable Lightness of Being*. Mohammad Asif's detailed study of Milan Kundera's magnum opus uses the twentieth century discourse on power to arrive at the issues taken up in the novel. Asif's ambitious article discusses, among other things, significance of Kundera's philosophical meditations, his critique of totalitarianism of all sorts, his depiction of uncertainties of life and the shrinking of individual space in our time and his analysis of pathological dimension of power.

In this entire discussion of the variety offered by literature in English the basic fact of the functional importance of English language can be ignored by Indian academics at their own peril. Raashid Nehal's long survey of the history of English Language Teaching at the Aligarh Muslim University comes as a reality check on our new role vis a vis the teaching of English. If the number of students studying literature does not show very encouraging signs, the students opting for the study of English language is growing phenomenally in universities and colleges. English language has now traveled outside the English Departments, to management, to mass communication and to engineering, to just name some new citadels it has conquered. Nehal's piece outlines not only the success story of the ELT at Aligarh but also subtly reminds the teachers of English not to forget an important dimension of their job i.e. to pay attention to the teaching of language not to serve the sinister project of linguistic imperialism but to prepare the students for the job market in the new era of globalization. And, ironically enough, this may probably ensure our own survival as teachers of English.

NOTE

1. I am indebted to Kathreen Raine's profound piece "The Sleep of Albion" for giving me this insight.

1

Doctrine in *Doctor Faustus*: A Deconstructionist Reading

Rashmi Mehta

Many critics have hailed Christopher Marlowe's *Doctor Faustus* as a great Christian tragedy in both conception and execution.[1] But this is to assume that Christianity in *Doctor Faustus* is a unified, unambiguous and univocal term. The fact, however, is that Christianity was a house divided against itself in Marlowe's as well as Faustus' time, and so it is in the play. One need hardly point out that it was during this time that Roman Catholicism, the oldest form of Christianity, began to be publicly ridiculed in Protestant countries like England and Germany. Marlowe's play also indulges in some blatant Catholic-baiting, whether it is in the scene of conjuration (I. iii), where Faustus asks Mephostophilis to "go and return as an old "Franciscan friar" because "That holy shape becomes a devil best" (ll.27-28),[2] or in Act III in which he, with the help of Mephostophilis, disturbs the Papal feast, plays practical jokes on the Pope of Rome, and frees the rival Pope Bruno from the papal custody.

More significantly, however, the divisions within Protestant Christianity, the dominant Christianity of the play, were no less sharp. C. L. Barber, for example, refers to the way Protestant bishops dispensed with the ritual of the Mass and yet retained its symbolic significance: "Semantic tensions were involved in this position; the whole great controversy centred on fundamental issues about the nature of signs and acts, through which the age pursued its new sense of reality" (Barber 97). To put it more crudely, the invisible ghostly presence of the signified was retained even as the signifier was obliterated!

A much greater tension within Protestantism, though, was the one created by what is known as Calvinism. The pre-Reformation, Medieval Christianity in England had, no doubt, presented man as frail, mutable and mortal. Simultaneously, however, it had emphasized man's free will to choose between good and evil, and offered him the hope of salvation through God's infinite mercy, which could be available to all human sinners. John Calvin's doctrine of predestination practically dealt a deathblow to the hope that one could always pray to God, beg forgiveness for one's sins and hope to be granted His mercy.[3] The theory of predestination meant in practice that one would never know whether one was an elect or a reprobate. As a result, there would always be uncertainty about salvation; for whatever free will a reprobate enjoyed could be exercised only in service of evil rather than good. Secondly, though Calvin does not deny the availability of God's grace to all sinners, he also makes it clear that this availability is only theoretical; for a reprobate will never repent and pray and thus benefit from God's mercy. Thus, the doctrine of predestination tended to put a limit on both man's free will and God's infinite mercy to pardon all human sins.

In the context of *Doctor Faustus*, the question becomes relevant because, like Faustus, a reader often wonders whether the learned theologian is an elect or a reprobate; for if he is an elect, he can always partake of God's infinite mercy until his very death—otherwise, this mercy would not be *infinite*. On the contrary, if he is a reprobate, he is predestined to suffer damnation regardless of whether or not he signs the bond with the devil and derives some real or illusory benefits from it. Indeed, several aspects of Christian doctrines dramatized in the play are either ambiguous or self-contradictory, and therefore continue to baffle the reader as much as, if not more than, they must have baffled Marlowe's hero; for these doctrines as well as the implied dramatized attitudes towards them continue to deconstruct one another. This paper will show how this self-deconstruction of the text goes on throughout the play, especially where it bears on the doctrinal issues.

The First Chorus tells us that Faustus "excelled" in divinity (ll. 15-19). Now according to Aquinas, the pursuit of divinity required God's grace (versefield 135). Since Faustus had found "sweet delight" in divinity, there is no reason to suppose that he was a reprobate. The devil's interest in his soul—"What will not I do to obtaine his soul?" (II. i. 462)—is a further proof that Faustus is not a reprobate but a fallen theologian. After all, the devil does not have to take special pains to secure the soul of a reprobate who, according to Calvin, has been damned even before he was born. Then, the appearance of the Old Man in V. i, his remark that he sees God's mercy hovering over Faustus' head, and the post-haste arrival of the devils to force Faustus to renew his bond—all these would be meaningless if Faustus were a reprobate. Furthermore, Faustus' hallucinatory visions in the last scene, where he sees Christ's blood streaming in the firmament, will be theologically meaningless if God's mercy were not available to Faustus during the last hour.[4]

As Faustus does not repent and save himself, we are left with another question to which no univocal answer can be found in the play: When Faustus' salvation in the play hinges on his ability to exercise his free will and ability to repent, why does he not repent when the reality about the bond and the devil becomes clear to him, especially toward the end of the play? It is precisely in this context that the theory of Faustus' free will and of his ability to repent becomes doubtful. When Faustus picks up two quotations from Jerome's Bible to arrive at his syllogism about man's tragic fate in this world, he ignores the full context of these quotations. Later Mephostophilis takes credit for turning the leaves of the scriptures, so that Faustus could be led to arrive at a wrong conclusion:

> I doe confesse it, Faustus, and rejoyce;
> 'Twas I that when thou wer't in' the way to heaven,
> Damb'd thy passage; when thou took's the booke,
> To view the Scriptures, then I turn'd the leaves
> And led thine eye. (V. ii. 1885-89)

This passage may be an addition since it is not found in the A-text, the 1604 quarto edition, of the play. In this and several other respects, the B-text, the 1616 quarto, does indeed make the play appear much more fatalistic than the A-text does. However, even if we ignore such passages as are found only in the B-text, both the texts have several common passages that allow the devil a real role, a role which tends to put a limit on Faustus' free will when he tries to exercise it in favour of good. Once he has signed the bond and obtained from the Devil a twenty-four year grace period during which the Devil will do and bring all that Faustus desires, the devils make their frequent appearances to cow Faustus down into submission whenever he tries to use his free will and repent. This happens when, for the first time, Faustus tries to repent and pray:

> O Christ my Saviour, my Saviour,
> Helpe to save distressed Faustus soule. (II. ii.634-35)

Ironically enough, it is not Christ who comes to save Faustus's soul; it is, instead, the diabolical trinity of Lucifer, Beelzebub and Mephostophilis that arrives on the stage and coerces Faustus into submission. It is one of the highly tense moments in the play and criticism of the play's doctrine fumbles and looks sideways. It is incorrect to say that Faustus' prayer is not sincere, or that Faustus has already become a spirit and therefore his prayer is not a prayer at all (Greg 99). Max Bluestone rightly recognizes that the situation is really double-edged:

> The heavenly prayer thus infernally answered enacts another oxymoron. Although Faustus has invoked the texts missing from his syllogism earlier, he has failed, or they have failed him. The ambiguity renders judgment impossible, for from one point of view Faustus has bravely struggled against the threat of being torn to pieces, but from another he has weakly succumbed to the divinity he earlier dismissed so scornfully (68).

We are made to wonder whether both heaven and hell have decided that Faustus must be damned. His prayer goes unanswered here, as it does in the last soliloquy. But is it the Devil who damns him or is it Heaven or God? If we go back to the First Chorus, where we are told of Faustus' achievements in theology, our suspicion about the role of "heavens" may legitimately increase.

> Till swolne with cunning of a selfe conceit,
> His waxen wings did mount above his reach,
> And melting, heavens conspir'd his over-throw. (ll. 20-22)

We may wonder whether God or Heaven plays an active role in Doctor Faustus' damnation. The use of "heavens" as the subject of the active verb "conspired" would suggest that God had a hand in Faustus' damnation. And if God had indeed conspired that the task would be undertaken by the Devil, then both the Devil and Doctor Faustus are fools in the hands of a "conspiring" God.

A similar ambiguity revolves round the fate of the Old Man who exhorts Faustus to repent and is, on Faustus' request, tormented by the devils. As he tells Faustus, Mephostophilis is clear in his mind that he cannot harm the Old Man's soul, but he can and does inflict physical torture, as the Old Man's speech indicates:

> Satan begins to sift me with his pride:
> As in this furnace God shal try my faith,
> My faith, vile hell, shall triumph over thee,
> Ambitious fiends, see how the heavens smiles
> At your repulse, and laughs your state to scorne,
> Hence hell, for hence I flie unto my God. (V. i. 1791-96)

The Old Man does triumph over the devil because of his faith, but there is some doubt as to whether he flies "unto my God" dead or alive. If the word "flie" suggests going to heaven, it also implies that the devil has at least succeeded in causing the Old Man's death. The doubt is not far-fetched because the Old Man does not appear in the play again after this speech, though it is also clear that his role in the play is over.

In Faustus' brief scene with the scholars just before his death and then in the last soliloquy, there is another unresolved issue. Does Faustus fail to repent because he is despaired about his salvation, or does the Devil prevent him from doing so? Secondly, does Faustus actually repent and is still punished because of the bond? In an episode in Act V, Faustus tells the scholars, "I would lift up my hands, but see they hold'em, they hold'em" (V. ii. 1852-53). In the last soliloquy, first we have this line: "O I'le leape up to my God: who puls me downe? (l. 1937). Then, after a gap of five lines, he says,

> Rend not my heart for naming of my Christ,
> Yet will I call on him: O spare me Lucifer. (A-text: ll. 16-42)

The punctuation and even the line arrangement for the first of these lines is not the same in the A- and the B-text. As for the second line, neither the A- nor the B-text has a comma before Lucifer. The result is that we cannot say with certainty whether it is Christ or Lucifer who is rending Faustus' heart. Secondly, it is difficult to say whether "Lucifer" at the end of the second line is a vocative or a dative[5]. If it is indeed a dative, then Faustus has succeeded in repenting at this last moment and, God's mercy being infinite, he should escape damnation. Perhaps it is this ambiguity that made it possible for George Santayana to say, "This excellent Faustus is damned by accident or by predestination; he is browbeaten by the devil and forbidden to repent when he has really repented" (Santayana 39).

Another aspect of Calvinism dramatized in *Faustus* is the hero's despair. Majority of Marlowe critics think that whenever Faustus tries to repent, his attempt results in remorse rather than repentance because he somehow believes that God's mercy is not available to him[6]. This is a state of despair with obvious Calvinistic overtones. Though this kind of despair is discernible even in Faustus' hasty rejection of divinity, it comes into sharp focus in the Bond Scene (II. i) and later in his scene with the scholars (V. ii). In II. i., Faustus is in his study, waiting for Mephostophilis to arrive. He says in a short soliloquy:

> Now Faustus, must thou needs be damn'd,
> And canst not now be sav'd.
> What bootes it then to thinke on God or Heaven?

> Away with such vaine fancies, and despaire,
> Despaire in God, and trust in Belzebub. (II. i. 389-93)

Significantly, Faustus is despaired about his salvation though he is yet to sign the bond with the devil and derive any benefit from it. When he wavers for a moment, he controls himself, saying that God does not love him (l. 398). One may ask him, somewhat querulously, what makes him think so? The answer is rooted in Faustus' belief that he is a reprobate whom God does not love and who must necessarily be damned. This is despair at its highest because it comes from his conviction that God is wrathful and implacable and that man, in this case Faustus, is irredeemably wicked and predestined to damnation.

This is also true of Faustus' short scene with the scholars on the eve of the expiry of the bond. When the two scholars try to assure Faustus that they will find some remedy for his melancholy, Faustus admits for the first time that he has signed a bond with the Devil, and that the period of twenty-four years allowed by the bond is going to expire in an hour or so. He says that even God cannot save him: "But Faustus' offence can nere be pardoned, the serpent that tempted Eve may be saved, but not Faustus" (V. ii. 1837-38). Then, speaking in the same vein, singing the same song of despair[7], if despair can indeed sing, Faustus says,

> On God, whom Faustus hath abjur'd? On God, whom Faustus hath blasphem'd? Ah my God, I would weepe, but the Divell drawes in my tears. Gush forth bloud instead of teares, yea life and soule: oh hee stayes my tongue: I would lift up my hands, but see they hold'em, they hold'em (ll. 1849-1853).

As they are seen only by Faustus himself and not the scholars, it is difficult to say whether the devils literally hold his hands and stop his tongue. It is also possible that what Faustus experiences is nothing but a hallucinatory vision caused in his mind by the fear of his impending death. Whatever the case, Faustus surely thinks at this point that his fate is sealed, even though the scholars are still hopeful.

Here once again, Faustus' Calvinistic bias comes into operation. As Faustus has by now made more than one attempt at repentance and failed, he is further convinced of his damnation. His Protestant conscience now tells him that, having sunk deep into sin and despair, he can never hope to come out of them again. What he needs at this moment is faith, but faith itself comes as a gift from God. As he is lacking in faith, his mind and will are controlled by the Devil—or so he seems to think.[8] It is no wonder, then, that he cannot believe in mercy and lapses into despair once again. If we argue that his thinking is misguided, we also know that he cannot help it. Pre-Reformation Christianity represented by the Old Man tells him that he can repent and save himself but the post-Reformation bias of his own mind says that it is too late. This is how David Kaula describes this paradoxical situation:

> The opportunity to renounce his bond and repent is genuinely available to Faustus to the very end, as the Old Man indicates. Nevertheless, a heavy element of spiritual predeterminism does appear in Faustus's conviction that even God's mercy is not so capacious as to embrace such a sinner as himself. Although the conviction may be illusory, it is still one of the most powerfully felt ingredients in the play (Kaula 11).

To put it differently, there is a basic incompatibility between the plot and the protagonist. While the plot appears to be informed by pre-Reformation theology and seems to leave ample scope for Faustus to repent, Faustus himself is a post-Reformation figure, who is convinced that his world is governed by Calvin's theories of predestination and reprobation, and that there is no escape for him, no matter how hard he tries at repentance and forgiveness.

The concept of hell, as presented in the play, is also marked by a certain duality; namely, that hell is both a state of mind and a geographical place where the damned souls are tortured forever. When Faustus wonders why and how Mephstophilis is out of hell, the devil presents hell as a state of mind:

> *Faustus*. Where are you damned?
> *Mephostophilis*. In hell.

Faustus. How comes it then that thou art out of hell?
Mephostophilis. Why, this is hell; nor am I out of it.

Think'st thou that I who saw the face of God,
And tasted the eternall Joyes of heaven,
Am not tormented with ten thousand hels,
In being depriv'd of everlasting blisse? (ll. 301-308)

What Mephostophilis says here is of course true, though he does not speak the whole truth as the church and Marlowe's contemporaries understood it. For orthodox as well as post-Reformation Christianity, hell was both a state of mind and a place of perpetual torment. According to the *Summa Theologica*,

[Hell] . . ., a twofold place of punishment is due to the demons: one, by reason of their sin: and this is hell, and another, in order that they may tempt men; and thus the darksome atmosphere is their due place of punishment. . . although the demons are not actually bound within the fire of hell while they are in this dark atmosphere, nevertheless their punishment is none the less; because they know that such confinement is in store for them. Hence it is said in the gloss upon Jac. I. ii. 6: "They carry the fire of hell with them wherever they go" (Kocher 117).

After Faustus has signed the bond, Mephostophilis admits that hell is a geographical place as well:

Faustus. First, I will question with thee about hell:
Tell me, where is the place that men call Hell?
Mephostophilis. Under the heavens.
Faustus. I, so are all things else; but whereabouts?
Mephostophilis. Within the bowels of these Elements,
Where we are tortur'd, and remaine for ever.
Hell hath no limits, nor is circumscribed,
In one self place: but where we are is hell,
And where hell is there must we ever be.
And to be short, when all the world dissolves,
And every creature shall be purifi'd,

> All places shall be hell that is not heaven.
> (II. i. 504-515)

Mephostophilis' description of hell here is, once again, consistent with the concept of hell in orthodox theology, but his words are somehow negative or at least circuitous. First he describes hell as a geographical place "within the bowels of these elements"; immediately thereafter, he returns to his earlier position that hell is primarily a state of mind, which pertains to any place "where we are." If hell is no more than a state of mind, Faustus can trust his own stoicism and not think of the joys he will never possess. As for the hell of picture books, which appears towards the end of the play in the B-text (but not in the A-text), it is no more than a "fable" or an "old wives' tale." We know that Faustus is tragically wrong here, but his error is understandable in terms of both his own character and the duality that characterizes the concept of hell in Christian theology. It is no wonder, then, that Faustus tries to have it both ways: that is, to sign a contract with a representative of hell and yet say that hell is a mere fable. This is how Wilbur Sanders explains Faustus' misguided thinking at this moment:

> But there's a deep consistency here—Hell is a fable only as long as it's place "where we are tortur'd for ever." If it affords all manner of delight, he [Faustus] believes in it. He'll scorn the joys he'll never possess only because he does not believe them to be joys. He'll willingly be damned provided he can have damnation on his own terms—"sleeping, eating, walking and disputing." The consistency resides in his determination to submit all moral categories to his personal convenience (Sanders 231).

It is this duality involved in the Christian concept of hell that enables Faustus to say that "Hell's a fable" (II. i. 516) and simultaneously prompts Mephostophilis to retort, "I, think so still, till experience change thy mind" (l. 517). Marlowe critics have focused on what they call Faustus' tragic blindness, saying that he does not accept the truth even when it comes from the mouth of Mephostophilis, who is "an instance to prove the contrary" (l. 525).[9] But the fact remains that despite these warnings, what Faustus sees in this scene is the power of the Devil represented by Mephostophilis. As for the suffering of Mephostophilis and of other devils, Faustus can always believe—until, of course, he himself experiences it personally—that it is spiritual rather than physical suffering, and that he can bear it with stoic indifference.

A related concept that suffers from a similar duality is the concept of evil, as it is presented and discussed in Christianity and as it is dramatized in *Doctor Faustus.* Just as Christian theologians from Augustine to Calvin believed that hell was both external and internal, a geographical place as well as a state of mind, they also believed that evil too was both external and internal. The Devil, the fountainhead of all external evil, enjoyed power to assume any shape and appear before any human being with worldly offers and baits to tempt his soul to damnation. If God embodies external good, the Devil is an embodiment of absolute evil. In *Doctor Faustus*, absolute external good is represented by God and Christ, whereas absolute external evil is represented by Lucifer and Beelzebub, and of course their emissary and agent provocateur, Mephostophilis. We cannot say that God, Christ and the devils in *Doctor Faustus* are merely poetic metaphors or symbols for representing certain internal characteristics of the hero; for even though it is only Faustus who refers to them several times and they do not appear as characters, their reality is not in doubt. This is exactly the role that the devils play in *Doctor Faustus.* Otherwise, Faustus' tragedy would make no sense, except perhaps at the purely psychological level.

When the devils find that Faustus is willing to choose necromancy, Mephostophilis appears before him and, at first, tries to dissuade him from choosing evil by speaking of his own suffering in hell; however, when he finds Faustus apt for going the primrose way, he begins to behave like a true devil and offers him all diabolical help to ensure his damnation. Not only that, whenever Faustus wavers and thinks of going back to God and Christianity, the devils make their appearance, threaten to tear Faustus' limbs to pieces if he tries to repent, and force him to renew his infernal bond. Toward the end, Faustus thinks that they hold his hands whenever he tries to repent and pray. No character in the play, whether it is Faustus himself, the Scholars, or the Old Man, dismiss the devils as mere hallucinations or as symbols of evil. As Robert H. West says, "... the devils in *Doctor Faustus* are devils. They behaved as the age thought devils did, and their dramatic power and meaning rest largely in the adequacy of their devilishness to the peculiar mystery of iniquity that is the play's subject. Marlowe has, I claim, made his devils adequate" (West 223).

Whatever external good is there in the play appears only in the form of omens and signs—otherwise, like Godot in Samuel Beckett's play, God and Christ do not turn up even when they are entreated. For example, when Faustus signs the bond with the Devil, his blood congeals and refuses to flow because, being Christian blood, it refuses to sign its own damnation. A few lines later, the inscription *homo fuge* appears on his stabbed arm, which Faustus tries to dismiss as a mere hallucination. In the last soliloquy, this absolute external good shows its fleeting appearance, first through Christ's blood streaming in the firmament and then through God's ireful brows threatening Faustus of extinction. In a way, both Christ and Lucifer, the antithetical fountainheads of good and evil in the play, are closely related figures of external, metaphysical authority in the play. It is no wonder, then, that Faustus cowers before both and sometimes confuses one for the other. His oscillation between them and his troubled prayer to Christ in the last soliloquy—"O, spare me Lucifer"—are indicative of the terror that he experiences in the real or imaginary presence of either of these metaphysical "bosses." And it is ironical that, but for the merciful God suggested by the Old Man briefly in Act V, the God that presides over the universe of the play does not seem to be a loving father, who looks with tenderness on his erring children on the earth, a God who can love them and be loved by them. Instead, he seems to be, or so Faustus thinks, a stern God of justice, the God of the Old Testament rather than of the New Testament.

The case of external good and evil, and of their fountainheads, God and the Devil, seems to be clear in the play. We know for certain that God and Christ in the play, as also the Old Man who makes his appearance in Act V, are not mere symbols or theatrical equivalents of the good and bad inside Faustus. This is also true of the supernatural representatives of external evil, the devils. The case for the internal good and evil, however, is not made so clearly in the play. We know that internal evil in Christianity is a legacy from the sin of Adam and Eve and a necessary condition of the postlapsarian man. This is known as the concept of inherited sin. When Faustus rejects divinity, he refers to this kind of evil, the inherited sin: "If we say that we have no sinne, we deceive our selves and there is no truth in us" (I.i.70). Subsequently, he begins to blame his own despair and lack of faith for choosing and clinging to necromancy.

Thus far there is no problem with internal evil in the play; the problem, however, lies with the way it is presented. The two principal representatives of this kind of good and evil in *Doctor Faustus* are the Good and the Bad angels. Sometimes dismissed as "a legacy from medieval drama that fits awkwardly into the Marlovian technique," (Boas 211) they are generally thought of as concrete, theatrical equivalents of the good and evil residing in Faustus' mind. Douglas Cole thinks that Marlowe's use of them is quite innovative: "The Angels, in emphasizing the conflict between good and evil, bring the issue to a heightened dramatic clarity, and reinforce the impression that not only does Faustus have the opportunity to choose between good and evil, but that the choice is his own and unconstrained" (Cole 202).

The problem with the Good and the Bad Angels, however, begins when we know that Christianity treats them not as mere symbols of the two contradictory characteristics inside the human mind but as external metaphysical forces representing good and evil. This is what Margaret O' Brien says about the theological position on the subject: "It is possible to understand these angels as externalizations of two tendencies within Faustus, but it would be heretical to consider them externalizations of two wills, as good will and bad will, within the man. Theology does, in fact, admit of the existence of angels and of their influence on the human will."[10] Needless to say, this duality, the simultaneously internal and external status of the two Angels, leads to difficulty in interpreting their role as well as their effect on the protagonist. It is clear that we cannot think of the two Angels as merely subjective, just as it would be erroneous to think of Mephostophilis as entirely objective. To the extent that the two Angels are externalizations of Faustus' internal characteristics, they emphasize Faustus' own responsibility for his ruin and make him appear as his own worst tempter. But when we think of them as objective representatives of metaphysical forces, Faustus appears to be an unwitting puppet in their hands. The problem is complicated by the fact that sometimes the play implies one attitude and sometimes another, with the result that there remains at the heart of the play an unresolved ambiguity and the resultant indeterminacy in its meaning. As the play stands, Doctor Faustus *is* and *is not* in control of the events that shape his life and future, and he is simultaneously *responsible* and *not responsible* for his own destruction.

We may deplore the fact that the play does not provide clear and univocal answers to some of the crucial questions that it raises. For example, is evil internal or external, or both? Are heaven and hell states of mind, or geographical places reserved for our afterlife—if there is indeed any life after death?—or are these merely old wives' tales? And finally, there is the question of all questions: Is man free or is he fated? It would be unfair to expect the play to provide precise answers to the questions which have been haunting mankind since the beginning of the human civilization. When the relevant Christian doctrines, shorn of jargon and technicalities, have no clear and univocal answers to any of these questions, it would be unfair to expect the play to provide any. It is enough that, like all great tragedies, *Doctor Faustus* draws our attention to such questions and makes us aware of the mystery that surrounds human life and death.

NOTES

1. The strongest proponent of this theory was the late Leo Kirschbaum, who wrote in "*Dr Faustus*: A Reconsideration," in *Critics on Marlowe*, ed. Judith O'Neill (London: George Allen and Unwin Ltd., 1969), p 80: "There is no more obvious Christian document in all Elizabethan drama than *Doctor Faustus*." Richard B. Sewall calls *Doctor Faustus* the first "Christian tragedy." See Sewall, *The Vision of Tragedy* (New Haven: Yale University Press, 1959), p.57.
2. All quotations from *Doctor Faustus* are from the old-spelling edition of *The Complete Works of Christopher Marlowe, Vol. II (Cambridge: At the University Press, 1973). Act and scene divisions and line enumeration are also from the same edition.*
3. John Calvin, in *A Compendium of the Institutes of Christian Religion by John Calvin*, ed. Hugh Thomas Kerr (Philadelphia: Presbyterian Board of Christian Education, 1939), p. 46, writes: "Man is not possessed of free will for good work, unless he be assisted by grace, and that special grace which is bestowed on the elect alone in regeneration."
4. See for example, Douglas Cole, *Suffering and Evil in the Plays of Christopher Marlowe* (1962). Rpt. New York: Gordian Press, 1972. p. 219: "Faustus' choice . . . does not become irrevocable until his death." See also, Joseph Westlund, "The Orthodox Christian Framework of Marlowe's *Faustus*," *Studies in English Literature*, 3 (1963), 205, and J. C. Maxwell, p.169.
5. My interpretation of these two lines is, in part, indebted to Max Bluestone, p. 77.
6. See, for example, J. C. Maxwell, "The Sin of Faustus," *Wind and the Rain*, rpt. in John Jump, ed., *Marlowe: Doctor Faustus*, a Casebook, p. 107-8; T. W. Craik, 196; Arieh Sachs, 626; Charles G. Masinton, *Christopher Marlowe's Tragic Vision: A Study in Damnation* (Athens: Ohio University Press, 1973), pp. 135-36; and Pauline Honderich, p. 4.

7. Commenting on Faustus' prose speeches in this scene, Wilbur Sanders says, "This is a piece of chamber music, finer, I think, than the symphonic grandeurs of the subsequent soliloquy—finer, because more assured, more poised, and less frenetic" (p. 237). *See Sanders, The Dramatist and the Received Idea: Studies in the Plays of Marlowe and Shakespeare* (Cambridge, Eng.: At the University Press, 1968).
8. If Faustus thinks so, he is not alone in this kind of thinking. For example, Sherman Hawkins, "The Education of Faustus." *Studies in English Literature*, 6 (1966), 208-09, writes, "Theologically, repentance never comes too late. But effective repentance requires some knowledge of good: a faith in the goodness of God which makes forgiveness possible, and an awareness of some surviving goodness in the soul, some vestige of God's image which can wish for forgiveness and receive it. But Faustus knows only evil."
9. See, for example, Robert Heilman, who has remarked on the irony involved in this situation in which "the nearly omniscient stealer of souls" urges "Faustus to save his soul," whereas Faustus, "the man with the soul, sneers "at both advice and adviser." See Heilman, "The Tragedy of Knowledge: Marlowe's Treatment of Faustus," *Quarterly Review of Literature*, 2 (1946), 321.
10. Margaret Ann O' Brien, "Christian Belief in Doctor Faustus," *ELH*, 37(1970), 6. See also, James Smith, "Marlowe's *Doctor Faustus*," in *Marlowe: Doctor Faustus*, a Casebook, ed. John Jump (London: Macmillan, 1969), who writes, "Yet obviously the Good and Evil Angel, Helen and the rest are not merely parts of Faustus. The two angels are emissaries of powers or representatives of orders, independent of himself" (p. 51).

WORKS CITED

Barber, C. L. "'The Form of Faustus' Fortunes: Good or Bad,'" *Tulane Drama Review*, 8, No. 4 (1964). Print.

Bluestone, Max "*Libido Speculandi*: Doctrine and Dramaturgy in Contemporary Interpretations of Marlowe's *Doctor Faustus*," in *Reinterpretations of Elizabethan Drama*, ed. Norman Rabkin. New York and London: Columbia University Press, 1969. Print.

Boas, Frederick S. *Christopher Marlowe: A Biographical and Critical Study* (1940) rpt. Oxford: At the Clarendon Press, 1966. Print.

Greg, W. W. "The Damnation of Faustus," first printed in *Modern Language Review*, 41 (1946); rpt. in *Doctor Faustus*, a Casebook, ed. John D. Jump. London: Macmillan, 1975. Print.

Kaula, David "Time and the Timeless in *Everyman* and *Dr. Faustus*," *College English*, 22 (1960). Print.

Kocher, Paul H. *Christopher Marlowe: A Study of His Thought, Learning, and Character*. New York: Russell & Russell, Inc., 1962. Print.

Santayana, George "Three Philosophical Poets," partially reprinted in *Doctor Faustus: a Casebook*. London: Macmillan, 1975, ed. John Jump. Print.

Versfeld, Martin "Some Remarks on Marlowe's *Faustus*," *English Studies in Africa*, 1 (1958). Print.

West, Robert H. "The Impatient Magic of Dr. Faustus," *English Literary Renaissance*, 4 (1974). Print.

2

The Search for Godhead in Marlowe's *Doctor Faustus*

Ankur Sharma

The dialectic between inherent human limitations and the never-ending human desire to transcend them seems to have haunted Christopher Marlowe all his life and accounts for much of the dramatic tension in all of his plays. In *Tamburlaine the Great*, the hero, burning with the desire for the "earthly crown," conquers one country after another until he dies, still wondering, ". . . shall I die, and this unconquered?" (2 *Tamburlaine*, V. iii. 158).[1] This longing for the infinite reappears in a small and different way in *The Jew of Malta* where Barabas the Jew gloats over his "infinite riches in a little roome" (*The Jew*, I. i.37). In *Edward II*, it is found in Mortimer's recognition that he had reached that point in the Wheel of Fortune "to which when men aspire,/They tumble headlong down" (*Edward II*, V. vi. 60-61). In *Massacre at Paris*, the Duke of Guise unequivocally asserts, "That like I best that flies beyond my reach" (I. ii. 99). In *Doctor Faustus*, his last and the greatest play, Marlowe returns to the same dialectic once again and makes his hero aspire for not only infinite knowledge, power, glory and wealth but, more significantly, God's central place in the universe.

The Prologue, spoken by the First Chorus, presents Doctor Faustus as a semi-transcendent figure who has already risen above most of the limitations imposed on him by his humble origin.

Extracted and shortened by the author, Mr Ankur Sharma, from a chapter in his Ph.D. thesis on comparative drama.

Now is he born, of parents base of stock,
In Germany within a town called Rhode:
At riper years to Wittenberg he went,
Whereas his kinsmen chiefly brought him up;
So much he profits in divinity,
The fruitful plot of scholarism graced,
That shortly he was graced with doctor's name,
Excelling all, whose sweet delight disputes
In th' heavenly matters of theology. (Prologue, ll. 11-19)[2]

When the play proper begins, Faustus himself speaks, in a soliloquy, of his own achievements. He says that he has already mastered several legitimate academic disciplines such as logic, philosophy, medicine and law. But he rejects all of them because none of them has helped him to transcend the limitations imposed on him by his human status or given him the kind of knowledge, greatness, glory and power that belong to God. Even his successful practice of knowledge in applied medicine has done little more than convince him that he cannot perform miracles as Christ did: to "raise the dead to life" or to "make men immortal." Ironically enough, his great regret at this stage is that, despite all his achievements, he still remains "but Faustus and a man" (l. 23). It is this realization that makes him embark on his search for godhead, a search which ultimately leads him to death and damnation. This becomes clear when he expresses his preference for magic, mistakenly believing that this forbidden art will enable him to get what the legitimate disciplines of study have failed to give him.

O what a world of profit and delight,
Of power, of honour, of omnipotence,
Is promised to the studious artisan!
All things that move between the quiet poles
Shall be at my command: emperors and kings,
Are but obeyed in their several provinces,
Nor can they raise the wind, or rend the clouds;
But his dominion that exceeds in this,

> Stretcheth as far as doth the mind of man:
> A sound magician is a mighty god;
> Here Faustus, try thy brains to gain a deity. (I. i. 52-62)

In other words, even as Faustus decides to reject God and divinity, he would usurp all the attributes of God and gain a new kind of "deity" for himself. Thus Faustus is no dispassionate scholar pursuing knowledge for its own sake; instead, he would like to use his knowledge to have godlike power, profit, and omnipotence in this very life, on this very earth. Indeed, his acquisition of knowledge has always been governed by the will to dominate. His rejection of divinity comes in the strongest terms—"Unpleasant, harsh, contemptible, and vile" (I. i. 108)—because he had hoped not only to become a "divine" in show but to possess divine attributes as well. And as divinity does not offer any worldly rewards and, instead, exhorts a Christian to lead a life of poverty and humility, Faustus finds it the "basest" of all legitimate academic disciplines.

Faustus' meeting with the two magicians in the Opening Scene confirms what is deep-seated in his mind. It would be incorrect to call the magicians the "devil's decoy" who "lure Faustus along the road to destruction" (Greg 74); for they appear in this scene at Faustus' invitation, when he has already made up his mind to opt for necromancy. The task given to them by him is to assist him in learning the "rudiments" of magic and the "words of art" as well as in the "ceremonies" related to it. Then they can leave him to "try his cunning by himself" (I. i. 157-60). And this is what they actually do; for after their brief off-stage meeting with Doctor Faustus in I. ii, they disappear from the play altogether. Marlowe shows that Faustus is not tempted by the two magicians. They only help him to give a practical shape to his own predilection for the black art after he has already decided to opt for it.

Faustus does not, in fact, need anyone to tempt him on to the primrose way; for he is his own worst tempter. This is true in respect of the role of the Bad Angel, too, who may be mistaken as the emissary of the Devil but who is hardly anything more than a theatrical equivalent of the internal evil in Doctor Faustus. Indeed the two Angels, who otherwise appear to be a legacy of medieval morality plays, are, to a great extent, the theatrical concretizations of Faustus' divided mind.[3] It is significant that they appear in the play only when Faustus is deeply perturbed, the Good Angel voicing Faustus' subconscious Christian inheritance while the Bad Angel expressing his infinite longings for power, dominion, and wealth. Douglas Cole says that Marlowe's use of the two Angels is quite innovative: "The Angels, in emphasizing the conflict between good and evil, bring the issue to a heightened dramatic clarity . . . and reinforce the impression that not only does Faustus have the opportunity to choose between good and evil, but that the choice is his own and unconstrained" (Cole 202).

The two angels, however, have an even more significant dramatic function than Cole and others would assign them. As they represent the two halves of Faustus' own mind, their very appearance in the play shows that, despite Faustus' apparently single-minded assertions, his mind is a house divided against itself. Faustus is caught in a tug-of-war between two mighty opposites: the lure of the new world introduced by the Renaissance and the strong subconscious hold of the orthodox world of medieval Christianity. As Arthur Mizner has aptly remarked,

> . . . if the Renaissance mind was aflame with thoughts of the splendour of life and of the knowledge and power which were the means to its realization, it was also, thanks to what Professor Farnham has called its "medieval heritage," imbued with the knowledge that these flames were the flames of hell and that Faustus would have done better merely to wonder at unlawful things, as the Epilogue says, than to be enticed "To practice magic and concealed arts . . . .(86).

Although Faustus rejects Christianity with a shrug of the shoulders, he cannot, with equal ease, throw away his strong subconscious Christian heritage. Similarly, though he rejects God, he tries to usurp the attributes traditionally associated with God:

infinite knowledge, infinite wealth, and infinite power. To put it differently, his revolt against God is not so much of a revolution in order to establish a new divine order in the universe but a kind of military coup in which he would like to take the place of the existing monarch, who in this case is none other than God. In this respect, he is more of a Lucifer than a Prometheus, and, like Lucifer again, he will never be able to forget what he has left behind once he has rejected heaven and God and opted for hell.

For the time being, however, Faustus believes that he is strong enough to pursue his quest for godhead with the help of the infernal powers. With this in mind, he goes to the solitary grove to abjure God and Christianity and raise the spirit of Mephostophilis. There is an ironical interplay between Faustus' belief in trying to obtain godlike power through magic and the limitations that govern his quest. When he stands at the centre of the magical circle, he thinks that he has occupied God's central place in the created universe by pushing God and the holy saints to a peripheral position:

> Within this circle is Jehovah's name,
> Forward and backward anagrammatized:
> Th' abbreviated names of holy saints,
> Figures of every adjunct to the heavens,
> And characters of signs and erring stars,
> By which the spirits are enforced to rise. (I. iii. 9-14)

This is close to a visual usurpation of godhead. The presence of the circle on the stage and of Faustus standing inside it, however, suggest a twofold illusion on his part. If we accept the B-text stage direction at the beginning of this scene[4], which is now followed by most editors of the play, the presence of "Lucifer and four Devils" on the upper stage (or balcony) will show the devils silently presiding over Faustus' abjuration of Christianity and thereby mocking his supposedly heroic revolt against God. That is to say, the spectacle on the Elizabethan stage would show an ironical interplay between what Faustus believes he is doing and what the audience sees as actually happening on the stage. While Faustus thinks that he has usurped

God's central place in the created universe, the audience in the theatre, who simultaneously sees Faustus on the main stage and the devils on the upper stage, can conclude that, instead of taking God's place, this misguided theologian is well on his way to becoming a mere puppet in the hands of the Devil.

Secondly, even if we do not follow the B-text stage direction and focus only on Faustus within the magical circle, we find that the circle is binding and limiting in yet another way. As it was a part of the magical rites of conjuring and was, according to popular belief, meant to protect the magician from harm from evil spirits as long as he did not step out of it, the circle points to the threat the devils really pose to the hero (Gill 15, fn). His effort to liberate himself from God's bondage will bind him to the Devil, and further limit his freedom; for, however we interpret it, the circle is after all an enclosure, which by its very nature encloses, restricts and circumscribes.

When Doctor Faustus goes through the magical rite of conjuration, which Levin has aptly called the "ceremonial of the Black Mass," (Levin 137) Mephistophilis appears in his true shape. Faustus cannot accept him as he is and asks him to appear before him in the shape of a Franciscan friar, because "that holy shape becomes a devil best" (I. iii. 25). Faustus' remark has often been dismissed as an anti-Catholic joke, which of course it certainly is. But there is more to it than a mere pandering to a Protestant bias against the Catholics. Faustus cannot accept reality as it is, be it the reality about God or the reality about the Devil; he must fashion both to suit his own convenience. So much blinded is he by his search for godhead at this moment that he refuses to face facts as they come before him. When he asks Mephostophilis whether he did not appear as a result of his conjuration, the devil says that it was only "*per accidens*":

> For when we hear one rack the name of God,
> Abjure the Scriptures, and his saviour Christ,
> We fly in hope to get his glorious soul. (I. iii. 47-49)

Again, when the Devil speaks the truth about the fall of Lucifer and other devils from heaven because of the sin of "aspiring pride and insolence" (I. iii. 67) and advises Faustus to "leave these frivolous demands/Which strike a terror to my fainting soul" (I. iii.), Faustus has the audacity to tender the devil the counter-advice of "manly fortitude" so that, like Faustus, the devil Mephostophilis too can learn to "scorn the joys thou never shalt possess" (ll. 86). Robert Heilman succinctly points out the irony involved in this situation of ". . . the nearly omniscient stealer of souls urging Faustus to save his soul; the man with the soul, thinking he is omniscient, sneering at both advice and adviser" (Heilman 321). Rejecting the advice of the devil, as he has earlier rejected the advice of the Good Angel, Faustus decides to go ahead with his choice of necromancy. He does not mind eternal damnation because he thinks that he can "confound hell in Elysium" and that he would like his soul to be with "the old philosophers'" (ll.59-60). With an irony which recoils on him later on, he asks Mephostophilis to leave "these vain trifles of men's souls" (l. 61) and convey to Lucifer his willingness to sign a bond with him.

Up to this point in the play and despite the appearance of the two Angels in the Opening Scene, Faustus appears single-minded in his quest for godhead. He thinks that he is going to hoodwink the devil into offering him so much in return for the "vain trifle" of a "soul," and that too after the expiry of twenty-four years. The trouble, however, begins in the next serious scene (II. i) when he is waiting in his study for Mephostophilis to return and inform him whether Lucifer is willing to accept his terms and conditions. Needless to say, there is a scathing irony in Faustus' attempt to transcend his limitations by signing a bond with the Devil; for by its very nature, a bond is that which binds the signatories to certain terms and conditions and thereby restricts and limits their freedom.

Of course, Faustus asks the Devil questions about hell once again, as he did in I. iii. But the Devil's answer that hell is both a state of mind and a geographical place makes him think that the picture-book hell of perpetual fire and brimstone is a mere "fable" (l. 127) and that any stories about pain and torture in hell after death are "mere old wives' tales" (l. 135). It is true that Faustus is wrong, tragically wrong here, because he cannot have it both ways: that is to say, sign a bond with Mephostophilis and yet deny the existence of hell. But Faustus is so much blinded by the prospect of power that he does not notice what he actually does by signing the bond with the Devil. Leaving the debate about hell, he asks Mephostophilis to give him a wife, the fairest maid in Germany. Instead of readily obliging him, Mephostophilis dismisses marriage as a "ceremonial toy" (II. i. 149) and tells Faustus not to ask for a wife, though he may get for him the "fairest courtesans" (l.151). Mephostophilis does not explain and Faustus is not keen enough to know at this moment why this is so. The simple fact, however, is that marriage is a sacrament, and by aligning himself with hell Faustus has cut himself off from all that belongs to God and heaven. To put it differently, Faustus has not found from the bond the freedom from limitations that he had hoped for; he has only exchanged one set of limitations for another.

Nevertheless, Faustus' subconscious Christian heritage continues to create problems for him. The next Faustus scene (II. ii) begins with his realization that, by signing the bond with the Devil, he has lost heaven forever. So when the devil refuses to answer his question "Who made the world?" Faustus does make one strong effort to repent:

> O Christ my saviour, my saviour,
> Help to save distressed Faustus' soul.(ll. 83-84)

Ironically, however, it is Lucifer, Beelzebub and Mephostophilis who enter the stage, "like party bosses in a totalitarian state before one guilty of thought-crime," and coerce Faustus into immediate submission (Steane 141). It would be incorrect to dismiss this Aristotelian *peripeteia* on technical grounds and say that Faustus' prayer is not sincere, or that it does not last long enough for heaven to intervene.[5] Whatever the theological or technical aspect of the case, the simple dramatic fact is that Faustus tries and fails in his attempt. The result is that he is made to renew the bond and then shown, as a reward for his ready compliance, a pageant of the Seven Deadly Sins. It is in such trivial ways that the Devil will let Faustus transcend his human limitations and keep him under his control.

The comic scenes that comprise the middle part of the play (Acts III and IV) demonstrate this kind of "transcendence" which the Devil willingly allows the learned Doctor and thereby keeps him bound to hell. Though universally condemned as inferior to the rest of the play and believed to suffer from textual corruption of the worst sort,[6] these two acts, along with the choral speeches that introduce them, are both structurally and thematically necessary for the play to show how Doctor Faustus spends the twenty-four year period allowed to him by the bond. For whatever the state of textual corruption, Acts III and IV, along with the choral speeches that introduce them, do reveal how far Doctor Faustus succeeds or fails in realizing his search for Godhead.

The Chorus who introduces Act III informs us of Faustus' eight-day tour in space, a tour during which Faustus has personally verified his knowledge of astronomy before he turns to cosmography. Here we have a glimpse of the earlier freethinking knowledge-seeker as well as of the empiricist that Faustus was until the end of Act II. In this speech of the Chorus, as Sanders has noted, there is a "fine enactment of the sweeping exhilaration of flight—the objective correlative of the Faustian aspiration," free from any kind of guilt feeling (Sanders 211). This is also true of Faustus' continental tour (III. i. 1-89) in the company of Mephostophilis, before both of them arrive in Rome to disturb the papal feast. The tour of the space as well as of the Continent does show Faustus receiving some benefits from the infernal bond because both these tours satisfy his curiosity. Nevertheless, what Faustus gets from the twin tours is no substitute for eternal salvation which is the price he will have to pay.

The Chorus that introduces Act IV describes once again the knowledge and power that Faustus continues to derive from his infernal contract. There is a reference to his space tour once again and the knowledge of "astrology" that he has acquired. Faustus, we are told, has become famous in "every land," and great kings and potentates are among his admirers. But Faustus' magical feats in the court of the Emperor of Germany, which follow the choral speech, show the illusory nature of the power that the Devil has given

Faustus. When the Emperor of Germany asks Faustus to raise the spirits of Alexander and his paramour, Faustus readily obliges but warns the Emperor that they are "shadows, not substantial" (IV. ii. 55), who must not be touched or spoken to. In IV. v, in which the horse-courser pulls out Faustus' leg, this great pilgrim of the absolute himself becomes a shadow without substance, whose limbs can be pulled out or restored to him as if they were the limbs of a robot. In the much-celebrated Helen episode in Act V, when Faustus speaks his famous apostrophe to the simulacrum of Helen and then takes this shadow to his bed, he himself mistakes the shadow for the substance. In fact, this is what he has been doing all along since the signing of the bond: mistaking the shadow for the substance.

The comic scenes of the play thus show not only what Faustus actually achieves from his infernal bond—and it is woefully so little—but also what he becomes in the process of his search for Godhead. According to Douglas Cole,

> In choosing the not-God in his desire to be as God, Faustus has provided not only for his own destruction, but also for his own degradation. Instead of reaching the stature of a demigod or even commander of the world, Faustus becomes an imperial entertainer. The restless scholar hemmed in by the limits of mortality gains his satisfaction by playing practical jokes on the Papal Court; the man who looked forward to controlling the lives and power of all earthly rulers becomes the magician of the Emperor, building castles in the air, and presenting spirits that resemble great men of the past.[7]

After the grace period of twenty-four years allowed by the infernal contract is over, Faustus' search for godhead comes to its deserved tragic end. The last soliloquy brings to a climax not only Faustus' anguish and spiritual disintegration but also the network of ironies woven carefully into the texture of the whole play. The man who had tried to possess things of time and signed a bond in time, now finds himself at the mercy of time. As the terrible clock begins to strike, he would like time to "cease" in the realm of time itself, so that the fateful midnight hour never comes. But he knows, to his horror, that "the stars move still, time runs" and "the clock will strike" (l. 141). The metaphysics of being and non-being, *on kai me on*, which he had dismissed as abstruse, begins to haunt him as he is troubled by the fact of being human–"Faustus and a man," as he had contemptuously said in the opening soliloquy. The man who wanted to transcend his human limitations in order to become God would now like to be much less than a man: he would prefer to be a brutish beast, a drop of water, or a vapour of mist, anything but a man. Ironically enough, having sought immortality through necromancy (an art or craft that deals with the dead rather than the living, because it enables a magician to raise the spirits of the dead), Faustus finds an immortality of a different kind staring him in the face: "O, no end is limited to damned souls" (l. 171). He had rejected Christ and Christianity and dismissed his chance of salvation through repentance, contrition and prayer as a fruit of lunacy, but now he sees a distant vision of "Christ's blood streaming in the firmament" and realizes that even a single drop of it would have saved his soul. Significantly, the man who had tried to transcend his inherent human limitations with the help of the Devil, ultimately goes to a hell, the eternal void, which has "no limits, nor is circumscribed to one self-place" (II. i. 121-22).

There is no doubt that Faustus' last soliloquy dramatizes, with unexampled immediacy, a deep spiritual experience in its highest intensity. But his cry of despair is also, in a way, the cry of all human beings who have been given the desire for the Infinite but deprived of the power to realize this desire. As Nicholas Brooke has written, "The dramatic tension of the Faustus story as Marlowe presents it lies primarily in the fact that Faustus is determined to satisfy the demands of his nature as God has made him—to be himself a deity—and that that is forbidden: it can only be achieved by a conscious rejection of the God who created him in his own image, but denied him (as much as Lucifer) the fulfilment of that image".[8]

What Brooke says may appear to be an extreme viewpoint, but it is not entirely extraneous to the play. Faustus' fall, as the moralistic Epilogue sums it up, may be a moral *exemplum* to exhort "the wise" only to wonder at "unlawful things,/Whose deepness doth entice such forward wits" (ll. 6-7). But the fact remains that these "unlawful things" are very much there on this earth, and that they are so beautiful, fascinating, and desirable that one may not simply stop by wondering at them. From a strict religious point of view, man should not attempt more than what "heavenly power permits" (l. 8). But if man had really followed this exhortation and not attempted what Icarus, the mythical prototype of Doctor Faustus, attempted long ago, there would not have been much progress. Faustus, like Icarus with his "waxen wings," thus becomes a martyr to the cause of building a rational, scientific and technological civilization. This is the civilization which has been trying since then to gain mastery over the elements of nature, over "all things that move between the quiet poles" (I. i. 55), and thereby trying to make man transcend all limitations that he is otherwise heir to. The godlike knowledge and power that science and technology have given the modern man are obviously a result of this ceaseless Faustian attempt at "more than what the heavenly power permits." But only time will tell what man will ultimately do with such knowledge and power.

NOTES

1. Quotations from all the plays of Marlowe except *Doctor Faustus* are from *The Complete Works of Christopher Marlowe*, Vol. 1 and 2, ed. Fredson Bowers. Cambridge, Eng.: Cambridge U.P., 1973. Line numbers and act and scene divisions are given in the text after each quotation.
2. All quotations from *Doctor Faustus* are from *The New Mermaids Doctor Faustus*, ed. Roma Gill. (1965); London: Ernest Benn, Ltd., 1973. Subsequent quotations are from this edition. So are line enumerations and act and scene divisions, which are given parenthetically in the text.
3. This is the general modern view. Christian commentators, however, insist that the two angels are representatives of external metaphysical forces of good and evil. Margaret O'

Brien, for example, says, "It is possible to understand these angels as externalizations of two tendencies within Faustus, but it would be heretical to consider them externalizations of two wills, as good will and bad will, within the man. Theology does, in fact, admit of the existence of angels and of their influence on the human will." See her "Christian Belief in *Doctor Faustus*," *ELH*, 37 (1970), 6.

4. As Roma Gill shows in a footnote (p.6) on the stage direction of this scene, the 1604 quarto does not have the entrance of the "devils above." The scene in 1604 begins simply with "Enter Faustus, to conjure." The B-text thus makes Faustus' fall into necromancy and damnation controlled more firmly by the Devils than the A-text.
5. In this connection, the comment of Max Bluestone is worth quoting: "The heavenly prayer thus infernally answered enacts another oxymoron. Although Faustus has invoked the texts missing from his syllogism earlier, he has failed, or they have failed him. The ambiguity renders judgment impossible, for from one point of view Faustus has bravely struggled against the threat of being torn to pieces, but from another he has weakly succumbed to the divinity he earlier dismissed so scornfully" (p. 68). See "*Libido Speculandi*: Doctrine and Dramaturgy in Contemporary Interpretations of Marlowe's *Doctor Faustus*," in *Reinterpretations of Elizabethan Drama*, ed. Norman Rabkin. New York and London: Columbia University Press, 1969.
6. It is largely in this part of the play where collaboration and corruption are found at their highest. This has led many critics to dismiss the comic scenes as pandering to the vulgar taste. See, for example, L. C. Knights, "The Strange Case of Christopher Marlowe," in *Further Explorations*, London: Chatto and Windus, 1965, p. 60. Knights says that any interpretation of these scenes as contrastively "presenting the gross stupidity of sins" is simply thought up.

7. Also see T. McAlindon, who has expressed a similar opinion: "What Faustus becomes with the aid of demons is not a god but a man who is allowed to play at being god; at the tail-end of his theological career he describes himself as "a divine in show" (I. i. 3), and in a sense that is what he remains (p. 125). See *English Renaissance Tragedy*. Vancouver: The University of British Columbia Press, 1986.
8. Nicholas Brooke, "The Moral Tragedy of *Doctor Faustus*," in John D. Jump, ed., *Marlowe: Doctor Faustus*, a Casebook. London, Macmillan, 1975, p. 112. Richard B. Sewall, *The Vision of Tragedy* (New Haven: Yale University Press, 1959), p. 67, says much the same thing when he writes, "...the final scene [of *Doctor Faustus*] gives a sense, not so much of the justice and goodness of the universe as of the transcendent human individual, caught in the consequences of a dilemma which, granted the conditions of his times, it was impossible for any imaginative man wholly to avoid."

WORKS CITED

Douglas Cole, *Suffering and Evil in the Plays of Christopher Marlowe* (1962); New York: Gordian Press, 1972. Print.

Greg, W. W. "The Damnation of Faustus," first printed in *Modern Language Review*, 41 (1946); rpt. in *Doctor Faustus*, a Casebook, ed. John D. Jump. London: Macmillan, 1975. Print.

Heilman, Robert B. "The Tragedy of Knowledge: Marlowe's Treatment of Faustus," *Quarterly Review of Literature*, 2 (1946), 321. Print.

Levin, Harry *Christopher Marlowe: The Overreacher* (1952; rpt. London: Faber and Faber Ltd., 1973. Print.

Mizner, Arthur "Marlowe's *Doctor Faustus*," in *Shakespeare's Contemporaries*, ed. Max Bluestone and Norman Rabkin (Englewood Cliffs, N. J.: Prentice-Hall, Inc., 1961. Print.

Steane, J. B. *Christopher Marlowe: A Critical Study*. Camb., Eng.: At the University Press, 1964.

Sanders, Wilbur *The Dramatist and the Received Idea: Studies in the Plays of Marlowe and Shakespeare*. Cambridge, Eng.: At the University Press, 1968.

3

"Too wide apart our faith has been": William Wordsworth's Orientalism

Abdur Raheem Kidwai

As compared with these Romantic writers, namely, Coleridge, Shelley, Byron, Southey, Moore, Landor, Hunt and Scott, the Oriental element in William Wordsworth's poetry is almost nominal. Yet his Orientalism stands out for its ambivalence and complexity.

Wordsworth's "Armenian Lady's Love" (Composed in 1830 and published in 1835) retains, rather resurrects some features of medieval Orientalism. In this poem the Saracen/Muslim Sultan's daughter is portrayed as enamoured of the Christian captive lodged at her father's palace. Exasperated with her "sensual creed" (l. 81) and "narrow world" (l. 78), she prevails on him to flee with her. She chooses this course of action, notwithstanding her knowledge that in the presence of his wife, she will have to lead the rest of her life on the margins, at best as his handmaid. Since in its conception, the poem follows the conventions of medieval Orientalism, it is concerned only with the conquest and conversion of a Muslim woman who readily abandons her tyrannical family and her false faith in order to embrace the true faith of Christianity after her first encounter with a Christian. It says nothing about the genesis of her love for him; it is merely a story of her self-surrender at the first opportunity. In being treacherous to both her family and faith, Wordsworth's Armenian lady is true to the stereotypical Saracen women of the heroic poems of medieval France, *Chansons de Geste*. For example, in the following *Chansons*, a daughter or wife of the Saracen is seen readily forsaking her faith, betraying her family, and falling instantly for a Christian knight : *Aiol, Aquin, Le Betrad de Bouillon, Blancandin, Bueve de Hamtoune, Codres, Elie de St Giles, L'entrée de Espagne, Galien de Restore, Gaufrey, Guibert d' Andrenas, Huon de Bordeaux, and Enfances Renier.*[1] Massinger's Donusa in *The Renegado* (1624) and Dryden's Morayama in *Don Sebastian* (1691) replicate the same.

The binary opposition in Wordsworth's representation of the "daughter of the proud Soldan"(l. 4) and the "gentle" and "generous Frank" (ll. 9 and 31) is unmissable. For it juxtaposes the darkness of Islam with the light of Christianity and a superior Westerner with an inferior Oriental. The Armenian lady in the poem is an "unfortunate" (l. 16) victim, reeling under her father's "rage" (l. 28) and her "sensual creed" (l. 81) which has "trampled/Woman's birthright into dust" (ll. 81 and 82). The Christian knight, even though in captivity, manages to secure her release from her "narrow world." (l. 78) More importantly, he ensures her redemption as her "dark night" (l. 119) is dispersed by "the Holy Church…by beams of gospel-light" (Stanza 20). Being "innocent, and meek" (l. 118) and bred with the "misbelievers" (l. 119), she stands in need of a redeemer. Not unsurprisingly therefore, in the very opening stanza she is found seducing the first Christian who comes her way by her "word, look, and deed." (l. 6) In doing so, she once again, conforms to the conventions of medieval Orientalism. For, as pointed out by C. Meredith Jones, the picture of Muslim woman in the *Chansons de Geste* is

> drawn largely from the imagination…She seems to have no other object in life than to fall in love at first sight…with a Christian knight whom she will eventually marry, and for whom she is eager to relinquish her religion.[2]

Little wonder then that this Armenian lady too, while "lifting up her veil" (l. 8) in her first encounter with that Christian addresses him adoringly as the "gentle gardener" (l. 9) who alone can take care of her or else she will "wither and grow pale" (l. 10). Her total and sudden self-surrender stuns him momentarily, as he admonishes her: "Tempt me not, I pray" (l. 49). Yet she stands in awe of him and regards him no less than an angel who alone can being about her deliverance. This otherwise "timid Maid" (l. 84) is so much carried away by such "higher and holier affections" (l. 79) that she abandons both her family and faith. She is applauded for her "boldness" (l. 84) and is promised deliverance, notwithstanding her breeding "with misbelievers" (l. 119). Her "path of life" is "smoothed" (l. 149) by Christianity. Eventually she is "Reverenced, like a sister" (l. 148) and draws this glowing homage:

> Mute memento of that union
> In a Saxon church survives,
> Where a cross-legged Knight lies sculptured
> As between two wedded Wives— (ll. 151-154)

Although she is acclaimed as the "Deliverer" (l. 112) in view of her role in securing the knight's freedom from captivity, it is actually she who attains real and abiding deliverance by having embraced Christianity.

Wordsworth's prescription of the redemptive power of Christianity assumes greater significance against the backdrop of the Evangelical incursions and the Clapham sect's call for the civilizing mission in the colonies, especially British India. Viewed thus, this poem of Wordsworth belongs to what Marilyn Butler brands as the "school of new politicized poetry."[3]

The Christian design of the "Armenian Lady's Love" brings to mind an almost identical stance adopted by Robert Southey in his *Thalaba the Destroyer* (1801), *The Curse of Kehama* (1810) and *Roderick, the Last of the Goths* (1814). These poems of Southey project a patently negative picture of Islam and Hinduism. These underline the need for taking up the civilizing mission in these degenerate societies. That Christianity should rise to the occasion in fulfilling its redemptive role in the Orient appears, for example, in the following passage in *Thalaba*, which records Southey's trenchant observations on the state of affairs in Baghdad, the capital of the Muslim world:

> Thou too art fallen, Baghdad! City of Peace
> . . .
> So one day may the Crescent from thy Mosques
> Be pluck'd by Wisdom, when the enlighten'd arm
> Of Europe conquers to redeem the East!
> (5, 72 and 83-85)

Not only Southey, Shelley too, upholds the same redemptive and enlightening role of Christianity, which is to the fore in Wordsworth's "Armenian Lady's Love". In his "Revolt of Islam" and "Hellas" Shelley portrays both Islam and Hinduism as devoid of spirituality or any positive feature. For him, Christianity may prove to be an effective instrument for bringing about gradual enlightenment and progress in the British India. Shelley's view is based on this premise:

> The zeal of the missionaries what is called the Christian faith, will produce beneficial innovation there [in India] even by the application of dogma and forms of what is here [in England] an outworn incumbrance.[4]

Wordsworth's revulsion towards the Sultan's "sensual creed" (l. 81) has its parallel in Southey's condemnation of the Muslim conception of Paradise, which he perceives to be sensual, and accordingly this "Paradise of Sin" is demolished in *Thalaba* (Books 6-7).

Common to both Wordsworth and Southey is their dubbing of Muslims as the "misbelievers". The latter recurrently employs this epithet in his *Roderick* (1, 35 and 179; 5, 126 and 185; 13, 38 and 23, 13). Both of them are consistent also in referring pejoratively to Muslims as "the turbaned ones". Another misperception shared by them is that the Muslim multitudes pose a menacing threat to Europe/West. Wordsworth gives vent to this alarmist view in his "Ecclesiastical Sonnet xxxiv, Crusades", in which Muslims appear as the enemy. "The turbaned race" (l. 1) is seen as the challenge to Europe. What is frightening is that already "the Crescent glitters on the towers of Spain" (l. 3). Moreover, "the thickening swarm" (l. 1) of the "Unbelievers" (l. 13) is huge. This description is closely similar to

Southey's in his *Roderick*, in which he alerts Europe against the hosts of "turbaned unbelievers"(1,258; 3,141; 20,7 and 23,13).

Amazingly, this uncharitable account of Islam and Muslims in Wordsworth's poetry is, however, offset by a refreshingly different and markedly positive representation of the Arab/Islam in his *Prelude* (V, 86-102). The Arab's dream underscores Wordsworth's acknowledgement of the rich Arab/Islamic legacy of knowledge. The Arab's "stone" and "shell" signify respectively books of science and poetry, alluding to the Arab preservation and transmission of Greek contribution to knowledge which otherwise would have been irretrievably lost. Wordsworth's Arab stands out as a culture-hero. He possesses answers to the dreamer's questions, signifying the opening of doors for dialogue and communication between the two great world civilizations -- the Islamic and Western. For pressing home this life-giving message, Wordsworth's Orientalism bears relevance and significance in our times.

Wordsworth's Oriental Reading:

Wordsworth's genuine interest in the Orient is borne out by his study of a wide range of books on various aspects of the Oriental history, travelogues, language and literature, as is evident from the following list of his Oriental reading[5]:

Arabian Nights Entertainments. Translated from the French of M. [Antoine] Galland. [Vol. 18 of the *Novelist's Magazine*].

Allan, John Harrison. *A pictorial tour in the Mediterranean: including Malta, Dalmatia, Turkey, Asia Minor, Grecian Archipelago, Egypt, Nubia, Greece, Ionian Islands, Sicily, Italy, and Spain.* 1843.

The Arabian Nights Entertainments, carefully revised … To which is added a selection of new tales, now first translated from the Arabic originals. Also, an introduction and notes… By Jonathan Scott. 6 vols. Oxford, 1811.

Arabian Tales or, a continuation of the Arabian Nights Entertainments... Newly translated from the original Arabic into French by Dom Chaves and Monsieur Jacques Cazottee. 3 vols. 1794.

Beveridge, William. *De linguarum orientalium*. 1664.

Bradford, John [Homely, Josias, pseudo.]. *Tales of the Moor*. London, Newton-Abbot, 1841.

Bruce, James. *Travels to discover the source of the Nile, in the years* 1768-73. 5 vols. Edinburgh, 1790.

Bruce, Peter *Henry. Memoirs of Peter Henry Bruce... containing an account of his travels in Germany, Russia, Tartary, Turkey, the West Indies*... Dublin, 1783.

Busbequius, Angierius Gislenius [i.e. Busbecq, Ogier Ghislain de]. *Travels into Turkey, containing the most accurate account of the Turks and neighbouring nations, their manners, customs, religion, superstition, policy, riches, coins* ... Translated from the original Latin of A.G. Busbequius, with memoirs of the illustrious author. 1744.

Carne, John. *Letters from the East*. 1826.

Clarke, Samuel, *The life of Tamerlane the Great; with his wars against... Bajazet the great Turk*... 1653.

Clapperton, Hugh. *Journal of a second expedition into the interior of Africa from the Bite of Benin to Soccatoo* by the late Commander Clapperton of the Royal Navy. 1829

Dubois, Jean Antoine. *Description of the character, manners, and customs of the people of India; and of their institutions, religious and civil*. Translated from the French manuscript. 1817.

Erpenius, Thomas. *Elementa linguae arabicae ex Erpenii rudimentis ut plurimum desumpta*. 1730.

---------------------. *Rudimenta linguae Arabicae*. Lutetiae

Parisiorum, 1638.

Hawkesworth, John. *Almoran and Hamet.*

Herbert, Sir Thomas. *A relation of some yeares travaile, begunne anno 1626 into Afrique and the greater Asia, especially the territories of the Persian Monarchie, and some parts of the oriental Indies*... 1634.

The History of the life of Tamerlane the Great... written in Arabic by Alhacen ... translated... from the French of J.du Bec by Lionel Vane. 1750.

La Curne de Sainte-Palaye, Jean Baptiste de. *Histoire litteraire des troubadours.* Edited by Claude Francois Xavier Millot. 3 vols. Paris, 1774.

La Vardin, Jacquies de. *The histories of George Castriot, surnamed Scanderbeg, King of Albania.* Newly translated into English by Zachary I. Jones. 1596

Malcolm, Sir John. *Observations on the disturbances in the Madras Army in 1809.* 1812.

Manu. *Institutes of Hindu Law; or, the ordinances of Manu.* Translated from... Sanscrit. With a preface by Sir William Jones. 1796.

Montagu, Lady Mary Wortley. *Letters of the Right Honourable Lady M--y W-----y M------e; written during her travels in Europe, Asia, and Africa... Which contains, among other curious relations, accounts of the policy and manners of the Turks* ... 3 vols. 1769.

Ockley, Simon. *The History of the Saracens.* 2 vols. London, 1718.

Park, Mungo. *Travels in the interior of Africa, in the years 1795, 1796, 1797, also in 1805 and 1806.* Compiled by ... John Campbell. Edinburgh, 1816.

Persons, Abraham. *Travels in Asia and Africa.* 1808.

Petis de la Croix, Francois, *The thousand and one days: Persian tales...* translated from the French by Mr. [Ambrose] Philips. Vol. 13 (1783) of the *Novelist's Magazine.*

Poiret, Jean Louis Marie, *Travels through Barbary, in a series of letters, written from the ancient Numibia in the years 1785 and 1786, and containing an account of the customs and manners of the Moors and Bedouin Arabs.* 1791.

Purchas, Samuel, *Purchas — his pilgrimage; or relations of the world and the religions observed in all ages.* 1617.

Ridley, James. *The Tales of the Genii: or, the delightful lessons of Horam, the son of Asmar.* Charles Morrell [i.e. James Ridley], London, 1764.

Sa'di. *The saint and the sinner, a tale from the Bostan of Sa'di* translated and accompanied by the original Persian, the various readings of twelve Mss., and notes, by Forbes Falconer. 1839.

_____________, *Selections from the Bostan of Sadi.* By Forbes Falconer. 1838.

Trench, Richard Chenevix. *Poems from Eastern sources; The steadfast prince; and other poems.* 1842.

Wilken, Friedrich. *Commentatio... de Bellorum Cruciatorum ex Abul Feda historia.* Gottingae. 1798.

Critical Writings on Wordsworth's Orientalism[6]
Articles:

- Bahti, Timothy, 'Figures of Interpretation, the Interpretation of Figures: A Reading of Wordsworth's Dream of the Arab', *Studies in Romanticism*, 18, 1979, 601-27.
- Chandler, David, 'Robert Southey and *The Prelude's* 'Arab Dream'', *Review of English Studies*, 54:214, 2003, 203-219.

- Haddad, Emily A., 'A Confederation of the Middle East and Art: Wordsworth', in Emily A. Haddad, *Oriental Poetics*, Aldershort, UK, Ashgate, 2002, 155-156.
- Haddad, Emily A., 'William Wordsworth and the Nature of the Middle East', in Emily A. Haddad, *Oriental Poetics*, Aldershort, UK, Ashgate, 2002, 103-108.
- Kelley, Theresa M., 'Deluge and Buried Treasure in Wordsworth's Arab Dream', *Notes and Queries*, 27, 1980, 70-71.
- Kelley, Theresa M., 'Spirit and Geometric Form: The Stone and the Shell in Wordsworth's Arab Dream', *Studies in English Literature 1500-1900, 22*, 1982, 563-582.
- Most, Glenn W., 'Wordsworth's 'Dream of the Arab' and Cervantes', *English Language Notes*, 22:3, 1985, 52-58.
- Ragussis, Michael, 'Language and Metamorphosis in Wordsworth's Arab Dream', *Modern Language Quarterly*, 36, 1975, 148-165.
- Tarawreh, Yousef, 'Islam Reflection: Revisionist Portrayals of Arab Civilization with Particular Reference to Wordsworth, Pope, Cervantes, and Dante', *International Journal of Islamic and Arabic Studies*, 4, 1987, 55-74.

Doctoral Dissertations

- Barker, C., 'The Stone and the Shell: The Image of the Arab and the Romantic Sublime in the Poetry of Wordsworth and Coleridge', University of Exeter, 2006.
- Khan, H.A., 'A Study of the Relationship Between the Sensuous and the Mystical in Wordsworth, with Some Oriental Parallels'.

NOTES AND REFERENCES

* Line 47 of William Wordsworth's "The Armenian Lady's Love".

1. See their plot summaries in Norman Daniel's *Heroes and Saracens: A Reinterpretation of the Chanson de Geste*, (Edinburgh, 1984) .pp. 328-339
2. C. Meredith Jones, "The Conventional Saracens of the *Songs of Geste*," *Speculum* 17(1942) , p.219
3. Marilyn Butler, "Byron and the Empire in the East", in *Byron: Augustan and Romantic*, Ed. Andrew Rutherford. (London, 1990), p.68
4. *Shelley and His Circle 1773-1822: Being an Edition of the Manuscripts in the Carl H. Pforzheimer Library*. Ed. K. N. Cameron, D.H. Reiman and D.D. Fischer. 10 vols (Cambridge, Harvard University Press, 1961-2002), VI, 987.
5. In compiling the list of Wordsworth's Oriental Reading the following sources have been used:
   i) *Wordsworth's Library: A Catalogue*, Eds. Chester L. Shaver and Alice C. Shaver. New York, 1979.
   ii) *Sale Catalogue of the Libraries of Eminent Persons: Poets and Men of Letters*, Ed. A. N. L. Munby, London, 1971. Vol.9.
6. Source: A. R. Kidwai, *Literary Orientalism: A Companion*. Delhi, Viva Books, 2009, pp. 167-168.

4

Unweaving a Rainbow: Heroines of Keats's Lyrics

Seemin Hasan

Writing was therapeutic for John Keats. Caught in a whirlwind of disease, death and despair, he turned to poetry for solace. His lyrics, ballads and medieval romances are often understated in comparison to his odes and epics. He wove tales of fantasy and also reworked legends and myths. Endo.wed with a rich imagination, he wrapped the old stories in dreams of a future he was not destined to have. Some of these poems are addressed to or inspired by Fanny Brawne, his beloved. In others she appears in one form or another depending on the intensity of the poet's passion.

The imagination serves as an alternate reality to Keats. Negative Capability levers him to experience the thrill of youth with Porphyro and Lycius, to pine for the evasive Belle Dame with the knight, to grow old and wise with Apollonius and to scheme and kill with Isabella's notorious brothers. The powerful medium spurs him on to bask in the purity of Madeline, to weep copiously with Isabella, to sink into a sinful entanglement with Lamia, and to shrivel under the emasculating aura of Belle Dame. The many-splendored moods capture sentiments defined by a psychoanalyst:

> When the starry sky, a vista of open seas, or a stained-glass window shedding purple beams fascinate me, there is a cluster of meaning, of colors, of words, of caresses, there are light touches, scents, sighs, cadences that arise, shroud me, carry me away, and sweep me beyond the things I see, hear, or think,

> The "sublime" object dissolves in the raptures of a bottomless memory. It is such a memory, which, from stopping point to stopping point, remembrance to remembrance, love to love, transfers that object to the refulgent point of the dazzlement in which I stray in order to be. (Kristeva 12)

The medieval narrative *The Eve of St. Agnes*, can be described as "a spontaneous expression of genius springing like Pallas Athena full grown from the forehead of the poet" (Finney 540-41). Steeped in eroticism, the fantasy is often considered to be an outcome of Keats's passion for Fanny Brawne (Ford 203). The young poet admired the charming girl next door but could not stake any claims "beyond tomorrow". (Ode to a Nightingale). The old romance of Porphyro and Madeline provided him with the perfect channel to dream and to write.

Every year, St. Agnes' Feast is celebrated on January 21. Keats acquired the material from John Brand's *Popular Antiquities* (1813 ed.):

> A Roman virgin and martyr, who suffered in the tenth persecution under the Emperor Dioclesian A.D. 306. She was condemned to be debauched in the common stews before her execution, but her virginity was miraculously preserved by lightening and thunder from Heaven.(Allott 452-53)

As legend has it, chaste maidens who maintained certain rituals on St. Agnes' Eve, would dream of their future husbands. Keats's version goes further to unite the lovers. Porphyro is on a love-quest, battling bitter chill and his beloved's hostile clan. Keats's Gothic rendering is enhanced by the use of the magical and the supernatural. Porphyro, the undaunted hero, succumbing to the enchanted St. Agnes' Eve, secretly enters the ancient castle. He is led by the old, faithful nurse Angela through winding, cold, tortuous corridors to Madeline's chamber. The lovers ultimately elope into the snowy, stormy night.

The mansion owned by Madeline's ferocious father is freezing cold. An old beadsman runs numb fingers over a rosary throughout the saint's night in the chapel of the castle. Old and weak, he huddles before the Virgin's picture:

> ...and soon among
> Rough ashes sat he for his soul's reprieve,
> And all night, kept awake, for sinners' sake to grieve.
> (Stz. III. ll. 25-27)

Patiently and uncomplainingly, the beadsman confines himself within "purgatorial rails". He willingly resists the temptations of "Music's golden tongue". He chooses to suffer for the sins of others through torture and self-denial. The inevitability of the beadsman's death is prophesied in the following lines:

> But no already had his death bell rung,
> The joys of all his life were said and sung;
> His was harsh penance on St. Agnes' Eve.
> (Stz. III. ll. 22-24)

Subtly, the 'Sculptur'd dead' of the chapel are replaced by the 'carved angles, ever eager-eyed' of the ballroom. The gush of warmth introduces the theme of desire. Madeline, innocent and dreamy-eyed, is engrossed in her plans for the rites she is about to perform under 'wing'd St. Agnes's Saintly Care'. The 'old dames' relive their own maidenhood as they guide the young girl:

> They told her now, upon St. Agnes' Eve,
> Young virgins might have visions of delight,
> And soft adorings from their loves receive
> Upon the honeyed middle of the night
> If ceremonies due they did aright;
> As, supperless to bed they must retire,
> And couch supine their beauties, like white,
> Nor look behind, nor sideways, but require
> Of Heaven with upward eyes for all they desire.
> (Stz. VI.ll. 46-54)

Madeline proceeds to her own chamber. In this duration her restless lover, "young Porphyro, with heart of fire", has slipped silently through the long passages behind old Angela, longing for a "sight of Madeline". He conceals himself in the shadows and secretly looks forward to a voyeuristic experience. He trembles and flushes in anticipation. The poet's own anxiety with regard to women becomes visible in Porphyro's alterations between fear and high-pitched excitement. He is fearful because his enemies are "more fang'd than wolves and bears". The element of danger heightens his senses and precipitates desire.

The 'one old beldame' Angela is destined to die on this eventful night. She is described as:

> A poor, weak, palsy – stricken churchyard thing,
> Whose passing-bell may ere the midnight toll;
> (Stz. XVIII. ll. 155-56)

Angela represents the eternal nurse. She calls Porphyro 'my child' and he looks at her like an 'urchin'. In contrast to the beadsman, she is well versed with the knowledge of the occult and she allows herself to be persuaded to assist him in this deadly venture. She advises him to accurately follow her directions:

> Thou must hold water in a witch's sieve,
> And be liege – lord of all the Elves and Fays
> To venture so;
> (Stz. XIV. ll. 120-21)

Under Angela's tutelage Porphyro gains confidence. He remains a mute spectator as Madeline enters her chamber. He watches her unclothe herself. In the grip of a lethal fascination, Porphyro is as helpless as the Knight ensnared by the Belle Dame. Madeline is simultaneously the pure virgin and the fatal enchantress. Madeline's chamber is an architectural variation of the regenerative green bower which is the usual Keatsian setting for mating:

> A casement high and triple-arch'd there was,
> All garlanded with carven-imag'ries
> Of fruits, and flowers, and bunches of knot-grass
> And diamonded with panes of quaint device,
> (Stz. XXIV. ll. 208-11)

The chamber is sensual and tempting. The "splendid dyes" highlighting the "diamond" panes are reminiscent of "the tiger moth's deep damask's wings" Unaware of Porphyro's growing apprehension and anticipation, Madeline says her prayers and falls asleep like a 'missal' in a pagan land. She sleeps cocooned by luxurious, sensual linen and Porphyro gazes at her with rapt devotion. Colour texture and metal combine with light and shade to lure him. He spreads out a sacramental feast. Angela, his benefactor in the context of the legend, had stored food in the closet. Porphyro lays out a banquet:

Of candied apple, quince, and plum, and gourd
With jellies soother than creamy curd,
And lucent syrops, tinct with cinnamon;
Manna and dates,
(Stz. XXX. ll. 265-68)

Manna has Biblical associations. It represents the purest form of nourishment. Food connects man with his elements. Feasting is associated with all important events. Porphyro's banquet is not consumed but it whets the appetite.

Into her dream he melted, as the rose
Blended its odour with the violet,--
Solution sweet;
(Stz XXXVI, ll 320-22)

Madeline responds and encourages him believing it to be her sacred dream. She is at once passive and powerful. When she wakes, she fears abandonment. Her turmoil is symbolized by a raging storm outside. Porphyro addresses her as "my bride" and persuades her to flee with him. The lovers disappear into the stormy night. Both the old beadsman and Angela die suggesting that the older cycle has reached its conclusion and has been supplanted by a new one symbolized by the union of Madeline and Porphyro.

Porphyro has often been treated by readers and critics as Keats's negative hero. One critic describes him as, "a young pagan ravisher with no regard for the religious taboo he is breaking" (Gilbriath

25). However, as the poem was inspired by Keats's own attraction to Fanny Brawne, it contains at times a certain youthful idealization of the beloved. In her sleeping form she appears angelic yet desirable. Her passiveness emboldens him and she becomes the subject of manipulation. Madeline is simultaneously controlled and controlling. She exudes a charm that he cannot resist. She turns manipulator when she realizes that she had not awakened from an erotic dream but emerged from a true experience. She laments that she is now a"dove forlon and lost" and solicits protection from Porphyro who valiantly promises to give her a home on the southern moor.

In a letter to Fanny Brawne, dated October 1819, Keats compared love and religion:

> I could be martyr'd for my Religion – Love is my religion – I could die for that – I could die for you. My Creed is Love and you are its only tenet – you have ravish'd me away by a Power I cannot resist. (Rollins 223-24).

Madeline's dual personality viz the chaste and innocent virgin of the first part and the passionate seductress of the later part represent the traditional, culture bound male perception of women. This is a common nineteenth century construct. This ambivalence can also be seen in Keats's attitude to his heroines and also to his beloved, Fanny Brawne.

Another dangerous romance that tackles notions of honour, manliness and desire is *Isabella, or The Pot of Basil.* Inspired by Boccaccio's narrative in *Decameron.* Keats derived the story from the fifth novel of the fourth day. Keats's construction of Isabella is, at a level, a construction of himself. He had been accused by critics of having a boyish imagination" and he feared that he did not "have the right feeling towards women." (Rollins 341-42) In *Isabella* the poet attempts to exonerate himself from effeminacy and boyish voyeurism and write convincingly for a mature audience.

Isabella appears as the only daughter of a wealthy mercantile family. She lives under the guardianship of two strict and ambitious brothers. They have plans to marry her off to "some high noble and his olive trees". Huge enterprises are expanded further as hundreds of employees slave under threat of the "bloody whip". The greed and cruelty of the brothers grows as their "red-lined accounts "increase. With the increase of profits they lose all human values and become mere "ledger men". Keats records the Romantic protest against industrialization and loss of agricultural values. Agriculture, to the Romantics, represented not just an occupation but a way of life. Isabella's brothers symbolize the evils of industrialization.

Isabella, however, is still bound to the land. She is simple and untouched by pride. She enhances the emotional element in the poem. The love story critiques rationality and material progress and creates space for personal, individual and the subjective. It challenges dominant social structures and values. It conducts an intense examination of the human personality and exalts intuition over reason. In her defiance of her brothers' arrogant patronage, Isabella is a rebel like Madeline. She rejects the impersonal, mechanical and artificial life at the mansion and embraces with emotional directness, the liberation of personal experience.

Midst the crowd of materialistic men, she identifies Lorenzo as a man with a good heart and becomes fascinated with him. She watches him at mealtimes and finds his presence soothing. Lorenzo, too, responds in a similar manner and the two fall in love. The poet describes this as a "malady" and anticipates deadly consequences. Even though the lovers remain acutely aware of each other, the poet is conscious of the class difference between them. Isabella and Lorenzo connect intuitively and the romance progresses through silent communication. Isabella instinctively perceives the magnitude of Lorenzo's love for her. The poet casts Lorenzo in the role of the noble savage. Though unlettered and uninformed in worldly terms, Lorenzo posseses wisdom learnt from nature and the natural world.

The romance of Isabella and Lorenzo follows the natural course of the cycle of the seasons and thus connects itself with the purity and perfection of nature .It flowers against all odds in a clandestine manner. The first consciousness of love occurs in May. Following the definition of Burton's love melancholy, the lovers pine or each other:

A whole long month of May in this sad plight
Made their cheeks paler by the break of June:
(Stz. IV. ll. 254-56)

The pallor associated with the malady casts the experience of love into a destructive mould. Fuelled by the power of new-born feelings, they finally communicate:

Love! thou art leading me from wintry cold,
Lady! thou leadest me to summer clime,
And I must taste the blossoms that unfold
In its ripe warmth this gracious morning time.
So said, his erewhile timid lips grew bold,
And poesied with hers in dewy rime.
Great bliss was with them, and great happiness
Grew like a lusty flower in June's caress
(Stz. IX. ll. 65-72)

The days grow warm and their passion grows intense. When the earth is drenched in warm, golden sunshine, the air doused with heavy fragrances and the colours and flavours of all nature are at their prime, the young lovers cannot help but respond to the call to mate:

All close they met, all eves, before the dusk
Had taken from the star its pleasant veil,
Close in a bower of hyacinth and musk
Unknown of any, free from whispering tale.
(Stz. XI. ll. 83-86)

In a symbolic connotation, the bower represents the traditional seed-bed of nature. It is the recurrent site for the union of lovers in Keats's poems. Isabella's departure from her brothers' control is now complete. The mating has been rendered with a certain reverence and seems to transcend reality. Isabella, like Madeline, has two facets. She is the chaste virgin as well as the sensual adulteress. She has a two pronged relationship with Lorenzo as well. Unlike Madeline or the Belle Dame, she is maternal and nurturing. At the first lush of love, her cheek:

Fell thin as a young mother's, who doth seek
By every lull to cool her infant's pain.
(Stz. V. ll. 35-36)

Lorenzo approaches his beloved with 'the meekness of a child'. Heart-broken at the news of his death, she rushes to his grave to sing to him 'one latest lullaby'. Later, she sits beside the pot of basil, which contains his severed head, 'patient as a hen-bird'. Obsessed with her treasure, she hurries back from the chapel 'as swift/As bird on wing to breast its eggs again'.

The lovers continue to meet and finally the realization that their sister is associating with," the servant of their trade" dawns on the two evil brothers. They fret and fume and lament the loss of honour and hatch a lethal plan to kill him before more damage is done to their reputation. The protectors turn into predators as they lure the innocent and trusting Lorenzo to his death:

So the two brothers and their murdered man
Rode past fair Florence, to where Arno's stream
Gurgles through straitened banks, and still doth fan
Itself with dancing bulrush, and the bream
Keeps head against the freshets, Sick and wan
The brothers faces in the ford did seem,
Lorenzo's flush with love. They passed the water
Into a forest quiet for the slaughter.
(Stz. XXVII. ll. 209-16)

The slaughter takes place besides a gurgling river in a silent forest. Water is symbolic of the life-principle and the green forest is symbolic of regeneration. However, the brothers crazed with anger disrupt the natural sequence of events. Autumn sets in and the 'breath of winter' kills all vegetation as it wrecks havoc with 'a roundelay of death'. Deceit and betrayal raise their heads again as Isabella is informed that Lorenzo has left for distant lands to make his fortune. Lorenzo communicates with his 'widow' in a dream and describes his green grave to her:

Saying moreover, Isabel my sweet;
Red whortle-berries drop above my head
And a large flint-stone weighs upon my feet;
Around my beeches and high chestnuts shed
Their leaves and prickly nuts; a sheep-fold bleat
Comes from beyond the river to my bed:
(Stz. XXXVIII. ll. 297-302)

The scene incorporates Gothic elements. The horror grows as Isabella escorted by "an aged nurse" proceeds to the "dismal forest-hearse":

Upon the murderous spot she seemed to grow,
Like to a native lily of the dell
Then with her knife, all sudden, she began
The dig more fervently Then misers can
(Stz. XLVI. ll. 365-68)

The ominous and mysterious mood is combined with the desperation of Isabella. The women "labour" for three hours at "this travail sore". In a grotesque move, Isabella beheads the body and claims the head:

In anxious secrecy they took it home,
And then the prize was all for Isabel.
She calmed its wild hair with a golden comb,
And all around each eye's Sculptural cell
Pointed each fringed lash.
(Stz. LI. ll. 401-5)

Isabella hides the head in a garden pot of 'sweet basil, which her tears kept over wet'. In a disquieting subversion, the lovers are united and Lorenzo can 'drink her tears' as he had desired. The basil flourishes 'as by magic touch'. Isabella's brothers curious about her obsession with the pot, decide to steal it. The mummified face of Lorenzo exposes the wild and gruesome aspect of love before them. This transcendence of death terrifies them:

And so left Florence in a moment's space,
Never to turn again, away they went,
With blood upon their heads,
To banishment.
(Stz. LX. ll. 478-80)

Ruined by the malevolence of her perverse brothers, Isabella lapses into delirium:

And so she pined, and so she died forlorn
Imploring for her basil to the last
(Stz. LXIII, ll. 497-98)

Isabella and Lorenzo suffer because of the callousness of the materialistic brothers. The losses however are shared by them as they lose their wealth and are forced to flee into the desert. The deviant conclusion is a caustic comment on social and psychological constraints suffered by the lovers.

Lamia is the love story of a scholar and a partially evolved snake. When the poet commenced on this task, he was conscious that he had to," unweave a rainbow". Lamia, in her reptilian form develops an obsession for a handsome youth committed to scholarship. She slithers around the forest, "midst grasses and full lowering weeds" lamenting:

"When from this wreathed tomb shall I awake!
"When move in a sweet body fit for life,
"And love, and pleasure, and the ruddy strife
"Of hearts and lips! Ah, miserable me!"
(Bk1, ll 38-41)

Keats encountered the story of Lamia in Robert Burton's *The Anatomy of Melancholy* (Part 3, sec. 2, Memb. 1st, sub. 1st). Lycius, a young philosophy student of Corinth, met a 'phantasm' in the guise of a beautiful, young woman:

The young man, a philosopher, otherwise staid and discreet, able to moderate his passions, though not this of love, tarried

> with her a while to his great content, and at last married her, to whose wedding amongst other guests came Apollonius, who by some probable conjectures, found her out to be a serpent, a lamia; and that all her furniture was like Tantalus' gold, described by Homer, no substance but mere illusion. When she saw herself thus described, she wept, and desired Apollonius to be silent, but he would not be moved, and thereupon she, plate, house and all that was in it vanished in an instant. (Allott 614)

The poem is located on the island of Crete. Hermes, smitten by a wood nymph stumbles upon an enchanting serpent:

> She was a Gordian shape of dazzling due,
> Vermilion-spotted, golden, green and blue;
> Striped like a zebra, freckled like a pard,
> Eyed like a peacock, and all crimson barred ...
> (Bk. I. ll. 47-50)

Her 'Circean head' culminates in a "woman's mouth" that communicates. The snake is the most bestial of all living organisms. When fused with a woman's form, it combines attraction with fear. Hermes is warned that Lamia has rendered the nymph invisible and she would be released only if Hermes would change her into a woman by touching her with his caducean wand, Hermes's wand is made up of two snakes coiled together Hermes yields and a hideous and painful transformation takes place:

> Her mouth foamed, and the grass, therewith besprent,
> Withered at dew so sweet and virulent;
> Her eyes in torture fixed, and anguish drear,
> Hot, glazed, and wide, with lid-lashes all sear,
> Flashed phosphor and sharp sparks,
> The colours all inflamed throughout her train,
> She writhed about, convulsed with scarlet pain.
> (Bk.I. ll 148-54)

Lamia's willingness to undergo trauma and agony for the sake of presenting herself in an acceptable form to Lycius highlights her determination. The evolution is painful because she has to rise from the lowest level to the highest. She burgeons into a 'virgin purest lipp'd'. She now gains the dual authority of gender and culture to approach Lycius.

Though Lycius is in control of his scholarship, he has imprecise knowledge about women. He succumbs to Lamia's effervescent display of love. His rational purity disintegrates before this incomprehensible and flamboyant temptation. Lamia weaves around him a lethal web of tender passions and delicate sentiments:

His fantasy was lost, where reason fades,
In the calmed twilight of Platonic shades.
(Bk. I. ll. 235-36)

Lamia confesses that she was charmed with him on the night of "the Adonian feast" in the temple of Venus. The primary communication between the lovers highlights a dynamic. Lycius appears naïve, weak and manipulated. Overwhelmed, he slips into unconsciousness and thus creates an impasse. 'The Cruel Lady' resolves this by inducting him into the world of sensual pleasure. She:

Put her new lips to his, and gave afresh
The life she had so tangled in her mesh;
And he from one trance was wakening
Into another.
(Bk.I. ll. 295-97)

The realms of fantasy expand as she leads him to her 'Purple-lined palace of sweet sin' in Corinth. The cultural irrelevance and irreverence does not prey upon his conscience because of the "swoon". As they walk ahead, they pass his teacher Apollonius:

With curl'd gray beard, sharp eyes, smooth bald crown,
Slow stepp'd, and robed in philosophic gown
(Bk .I. ll. 364-65)

Lycius shudders at the sight of him and averts his eyes. This reaction is tragic and inevitable. It indicates the intellectual bankruptcy of

Lycius and the stubborn efficiency of Lamia. Lycius absolves himself of all responsibility and anxiety regarding commitment to social, cultural and educational values by surrendering totally to Lamia and delinking from 'all the congregated world'. The indulgence in effusive, perverse and ruinous pleasures destroys his ambition and rationality.

Lamia confines Lycius within the illusory palace. The dream home cannot gain the permanence of reality. It remains, at best, an imitation of reality as Lamia remains an imitation of womanhood. Lamia's anxiety is to nurture the illusion as long as possible. Trouble begins when Lycius rouses himself out of his stupor and asks her if she," Hast any mortal name? Fit appellation to this dazzling frame?"(Bk II 88-89). He now desires to marry her and introduce her to his family and friends as is the requirement of "catalogue of common things." He is unable to realize that she is a figament of the imagination and her existence is essentially illusory. Like his knowledge of women, his knowledge of philosophy is also imprecise.

Overwhelmed by the sense of doom, Lamia prepares for the nuptial feast. Magically, the banquet hall is converted into a leafy glade. The spherical tables are adorned with legs like leopard's paws and laid with goblets and dishes made of pure gold. Rumours spread like wildfire. The crowds of Corinth throng to the wonderous palace to see the reversed fortunes of young Lycius:

So in they hurried all, maz'd, curious and keen:
Save one, who look'd thereon with eye severe,
And with calm-planted steps walk'd in austere;
'Twas Apollonius:
(Bk II, ll157-59)

Lempriere described Apollonius as,"A Pythagorean philosopher, well skilled in magic, and thoroughly acquainted with those arts which can captivate and astonish the vulgar ... he aspired to the name of the reformer of mankind". (Allott 632-33) To Lycius, he appears evil and malignant, "Look upon that gray-beard wretch!/ Mark how, possess'd his lashless eyelids stretch/Around his demon eyes!" (II,287-9). Lycius is gripped with horror as precludes the tragedy about to take place. The patriarch of rational and masculine orthodoxy assumes the aspect of a treacherous destroyer. He claims

"from every ill
Of life have I preserv'd thee to this day,
And shall I see thee made a serpent's prey?"
(Bk II, ll 296-98)

The restrictive nature of the education imparted by the old philosopher becomes clear to Lycius and he desires him to leave. The patriarch however is determined to settle scores. He refuses the offer of intoxicants that Lamia had served to the 'gossip rout' to prevent them from recognizing the "elfin' character of the feast:

When the wine has done its rosy deed.
And every soul from human trammels freed ...
(Bk.II. ll 209-10)

In the masculine scheme of things, the love of learning had to be prioritized. Apollonius had spent his life gaining and imparting scholarship. Persisting in his mission to preserve the control of knowledge on the world:

The bald-head philosopher
Had fixed his eye, without a twinkle or stir
Full on the alarm'd beauty of the bride.
(Bk.II. ll 245-47)

Lamia shrivels and shrinks, and screams in agony. Ignoring Lycius's pleas, Apollonius declares 'shall I see thee made a serpent's prey?' The 'Spear of his gaze' is 'keen, cruel piercant, stinging' and Lamia vanishes before the entire congregation –

And Lycius' arms were empty of delight
As were his limbs of life, from that same night.
On the high couch he lay; his friends came round —
Supported him – no pulse, or breath they found,
And in his marriage robe, the heavy body wound.
(Bk II, ll. 307-11)

Apollonius's cold philosophy is not regenerative or reviving. It does not have the power to establish a new order. It does not acknowledge the powers of imagination. It turns the wedding into a funeral and the marriage robe into a shroud. The lovers are separated forever. Apollonius,who in his final action precipitates a tragedy, is comparable to Isabella's brothers. The conclusion has a stifling quality about it.

'La Belle Dame Sans Merci' is a ballad that deals with chivalry. A love-lorn knight "sojourns" on "a cold hillside" waiting for an elfin damsel who enthralls and then deserts him. True to the chivalric tradition, he binds himself to the woman he professes to love. He loiters around in search of his beloved despite the seasons having changed and nature preparing for hibernation with the onset of the winter. The full "granary" of the squirrel contrasts with the emptiness of the knight's existence. The all-consuming desire has drained him of manly faculties and he is disoriented and distraught. The anonymous narrator questions the knight about his degeneration and listens to his pathetic tale.

The poem is primarily a portrait of the anguished knight. Unlike the other three lyrics, it is not a coherent narration. The Belle Dame is dealt with in absentia. The slighted knight endows her with dangerous potential. She appeared to him as a vision during day-time and as a dream at night. This mode was popular during the Romantic period. The reawakened interest in the conventional English and Scottish folk-ballads in the second half of the eighteenth century is considered to be an important milestone in the reaction against rationality which led to the Romantic Movement. A number of Romantic writers published collections of ballads. Sir Walter Scott published a collection in 1802.

Keats' title 'La Belle Dame Sans Merci' may be simply translated as 'The beautiful woman without mercy'. Leigh Hunt claims Keats used the title of Alain Chartier's poem 'La Belle Dame Sans Merci' (1424). Keats probably read the English translation included in *The Poetical works of Geoffrey Chaucer (1782)*. In the Eve of St Agnes, Porphyro wants to awaken Madeline, and:

He played an ancient ditty, long since mute,
In Provence called 'La Belle Dame sans mercy'
(Stz.XXXIII, ll. 291-2)

The Belle Dame shares some of the characteristics of Lamia. She, too, is shrouded in mystery and suspicion. She is, thus, connected to cultural history. The old song serves to document evidence that the concept of *femme fatale* was present in the cultural imagination long before it was used in modern narratives. Her succubus nature inspires fear as well as deadly attraction:

Full beautiful, a fairy's child
Her hair was long, her foot was light
And her eyes were wild.
(Stz. IV. ll. 14-16)

The physical beauty of Belle Dame is virulent. Not only the knight but the sedge also "withered from the lake" She has a paradoxical sexuality, combining innocence of a child with demonic experience. The poet draws upon excesses to portray her. The magical length of her hair, the hypnotic quality of her eyes and the incredible gliding gait incarcerate the knight. The food, too, is excessively sweet:

She found me roots of relish sweet
And honey wild and manna dew
And sure in language strange she said,
"I love thee true".
(Stz.VII. ll. 25-28)

Manna and dew, the perfect heavenly food, drizzled with honey and combined with sweeter roots creates a dizzying effect. The sensuousness is heightened in the "elfin grot" where submerged in the heavy perfume of flowers, the lovers consummate their love. The enchantress speaks a mesmerizing language and lulls her lover into a deep sleep. The knight dreams of powerful men ruined by this perverse damsel. They are doomed to remain enthralled and wait with "starv'd lips" for her kisses. The congregation collectively condemns her as a daemon.

The knight's narration shocks the anonymous questioner and enthralls the reader. The absence of the fatal enchantress suggests a distortion under the male gaze and enhances the possibility of the narrative being reworked into a feminine, subjective experience. Allure and powers of seduction of the *femme fatale* exist because she is unattainable. The questioner turns into a voyeur. Voyeurism is not connected with ordinary, attainable women who are associated with unpaid labour like cleaning, cooking, looking after children, maimed or elderly relatives. The absent Belle Dame cannot appear in the scheme of the poem because in order to define true female beauty, the poet has to evolve out of the patriarchal mode.

In a letter to Bailey, Keats described a 'Gordian complication':

> I am certain I have not the right feeling towards women … when among Men I have no evil thoughts, no malice, no spleen. When I am among women I have evil thoughts, malice, spleen … you must be charitable and put all this perversity to my being disappointed since Boyhood – Yet with such feelings I am happier alone among Crowds of men, by myself or with a friend or two … I must absolutely get over this – but how? The only way is to find the root of evil and so cure it "with backward mutters of disserving Power". That is a difficult thing; for an obstinate Prejudice can seldom be produced but from a gordian complication of feelings, which must take time to unravel and care to keep unraveled. (Rollins 341-42)

These romances represent the 'backward mutters of disserving power' on this gordian complication. Keats's heroines are much more than mere objects of lust. The poet, at this point in his career, was looking forward to a maturity that would relieve him from the trammels of patriarchal controls.

WORKS CITED

Allott, Miriam (ed), *The Poems of John Keats* London: Longman Group, 1970. Print.

Gilbriath, Maria "The Etymology of Porphyro's Name in Keats's Eve *of St Agnes in Keats-Shelley Journal vol. XXXVII* 1988. P.25. Print.

Finney, Claude Lee, *The Evolution of Keats's Poetry*, New York: Harvard UP, 1963. Print.

Ford, Newell *The Prefigurative Imagination of John Keats,* Stanford: Stanford UP, 1951. Print.

Hunt, Leigh, *Indicator*, 10 May, 1820. Print.

Kristeva, Julia. *Powers of Horror: An Essay on Abjection*, Columbia: Columbia UP, 1982 Print.

Rollins, Hyder E. (ed) *The Letters of John Keats*, Cambridge: Cambridge UP. 1958. Print.

5

Exploring *Terra Incognita*: Johnson's and Boswell's Journey to Scotland

Shehla Ghauri

The English people's dislike of the Scotch is very well-known and many stories about it have been in circulation. The following note by James Boswell in the *London Journal* very engagingly reveals not only this English prejudice but Boswell's own Scotch reaction to the slight:

> ... At night I went to Covent Garden and saw 'Love in a village', Just before the overture began to be played, two Highland officers came in. The mob in the upper gallery roared out, 'No Scots! No Scots! Out with them!' hissed and pelted them with apples. My heart warmed to my countrymen, my Scotch blood boiled with indignation. I jumped up on the benches, roared out, "Damn you, you rascals!" hissed and was in the greatest rage. I hated the English; I wished from my soul that the Union was broke and that we might give them another battle of Bannockburn... (71-72)

Boswell's first meeting with Dr. Johnson would always remind one of what ensued between the two with regard to Johnson's prejudice against the Scots. Boswell greatly desired the acquaintance of Dr. Johnson, but he felt very hesitant and diffident in approaching him as Johnson's strong antipathy to the Scotch was well known. When Mr. Davies first introduced Boswell to Johnson, he deliberately added: 'From Scotland' on which Boswell summoned some courage to say 'Mr. Johnson, I indeed come from Scotland but I cannot help it.' And Johnson replied, '... that, I find, is what a great many of your countrymen cannot help.' Boswell was, however, not deterred by Johnson's criticism and this meeting paved way for an everlasting friendship.

Given his age, ailments and purported opinion of the Scots, Johnson may have seemed a highly unlikely traveller to the distant region of Scottish Highlands, but in the opening pages of his *A Journey to the Western Islands of Scotland*, he confessed to a longstanding desire to make the trip and the inducement of having Boswell as his companion. Johnson was propelled by a curiosity to see strange places and study modes of life unfamiliar to him. In 1773 Boswell enticed Johnson to accompany him on a tour through the Highlands and Western Islands of Scotland. Johnson was then in his mid-sixties and well known for his literary works and his Dictionary. The two travellers set out from Edinburg and skirted the eastern and north-eastern coasts of Scotland passing through St. Andrews, Aberdeen and Inverness. They then passed into the Highlands and spent several weeks on various islands in the Hebrides including Skye, Col, Mull etc. After a visit to Boswell's estate at Auchinleck the travellers returned to Edinburg.

Both Johnson and Boswell kept detailed notes of their impressions and later published separate accounts of their journey. These works contain some of the finest pieces of travel writing ever produced; they are also magnificent historical documents as well as portraits of two extraordinary men of letters. Together they paint a vivid picture of a society which was still almost unknown to the Europe of the Enlightenment. Entertaining, profound and marvellously readable, they are a valuable chronicle of a lost age and a fascinating people.

Johnson's *Journey* is written in a recognizable and the then popular genre of travel book and time and again he has expressed his opinion and also of some of his contemporaries about what such a book should contain. Johnson had heard Dr. Edward Browne's book of travels commended as 'written with scrupulous and exact veracity, such as is scarcely to be found in any other book of the same kind'. Not agreeing with the viewpoint, he says: 'But whatever it may contribute to the instruction of a naturalist, I cannot recommend it as likely to give much pleasure to common readers; for whether it be that the world is very uniform, and therefore he who resolves to adhere to the truth will have few novelties to relate'. In his essay in *Idler 97*, Johnson states that most travel books prove disappointing. He also states that one of the chief reasons for their failure is that 'nothing is found but general accounts as leave no distinct idea behind them, or such minute enumerations as few can read with either profit or delight'. In the same essay, Johnson goes on to say, 'every writer of travels should consider, that, like all other authors, he undertakes either to instruct or to please, or to mingle pleasure with instruction.' He further says that the traveller must 'remember that the great object of remark is human life' and that he 'must offer to the mind something to be imitated, or something to be avoided; as he that pleases must offer new images to his reader, and enable him to form a tacit comparison of his own state with that of others'.

Arthur Murphy in his appreciation of Dr. Johnson writes: 'The account of his journey ... is a model for such as shall hereafter relate their travels. The author did not visit that part of the world in the character of an Antiquary, to amuse us, with wonders taken from the dark and fabulous ages; nor as a Mathematician, to measure a degree, and settle the longitude and latitude of the several islands. Those, who expected such information, expected what was never intended.... Johnson went to see men and manners, modes of life, and the progress of civilization'. Sir John Hawkins, in his recognition of Johnson's accomplishment in the *Journey*, writes: 'If any particular subject may be said to have engaged his attention, it must have been the manners of a people of whom he knew little but by report, the knowledge whereof might furnish him with new topics for reflection and disquisition, an exercise for his mental powers which, of all others, he most delighted in'.

Many journeys have since then been undertaken to Scotland to retrace the course of Johnson and Boswell. Frank Delaney in the author's note to *A Walk to the Western Isles: After Boswell and Johnson*, writes:

Of journeys that might reward re-tracing this one promised most. The Johnson and Boswell presence in English letters, and the relationship that led to Boswell's great Life of Johnson has yielded so much to biographers and scholars that it seems a bottomless well. Their journey to Scotland, however, had an intriguing dimension; Johnson went there because he wanted, he said, to see what the past looked like, what it might feel like to live in a previous historical period (His belief that Scotland had not changed since the Middle Ages proved un-endearing to the Scots). By following them, I hoped to find such footprints as they lift – and I did, abundantly, unexpectedly and delightedly.

A twenty-first century literary pilgrimage was undertaken by William W. Starr to retrace the famous eighteenth century Scottish journey of Boswell and Johnson. In his memoir, *Whisky, Kilts and the Loch Ness Monster: Travelling through Scotland with Boswell and Johnson*, Starr recounts the experiences of the famous duo.

Johnson published his *A Journey to the Western Islands of Scotland* on 18th January 1775. It was widely read, discussed and even criticized. The image of Scotland given by Johnson presents it as a place still enveloped in wilderness. Marauding privateers and slave-ships worked the coasts; the destruction of Scottish forests was in full swing; the Scottish clan system had been dismantled by act of Parliament; Scotch whisky was distilled illegally and profusely. But this part of Scotland was also a romantic place due to large chunks of Highland Clearances. It was relatively empty of people and nearly unspoiled by commerce, roads and other trappings of modern life.

Johnson in his *Journey* finds Scotland devoid of culture and destitute of learning. He assumes the role of 'Enlightenment empiricist', challenging Scottish credulity. He was convinced that whatever feeble vestige of culture there was, or even had been, relied solely on oral tradition passed on by bards and sennachies and that this weak and unsatisfactory mode of transmission had collapsed with the suppression of the clans after the failure of the last Jacobite

Rebellion in 1746. Johnson's observations of the customs, food and dress etc. of the Highlands of Scotland provide a cultural perspective to the journey. He goes to compare and contrast the Scottish culture with his own English culture: ' In Scotland, the necessaries of life are easily procured, but superfluities and elegancies are of the same price at least as in England, and therefore may be considered as much dearer'(*Journey* 10).

Johnson's description of the solitude and barrenness of the Highland terrain evokes an uneasy calm. He talks of the 'uniformity' of this barrenness and reflects on the amount of amusement it could provide to a traveller, referring to such journeys as 'useless labours, which neither impregnate the imagination, nor enlarge the understanding'. But, he further asserts that until we come to experience such things our ideas about them will always be incomplete: ' ... at least, till we have compared them with realities, we do not know them to be just' (35). The deforestation drive in the Highlands is aptly taken note of by Johnson. The larger implications of felling of trees can be better understood in the present scenario of global warming: 'The country is totally denuded of its wood, but the stumps both of oaks and firs, which are still found, shew that it has been once a forest of large timber.' Describing Armidel as well shaded by tall ash trees, Johnson observes that 'the present nakedness of the *Hebrides* is not wholly the fault of Nature' (44).

Jeffery Hart's essay 'Johnson's A Journey to the Western Islands: History as Art', in *Essays in Criticism*, views the Journey as having a 'tragic vision' with Johnson repeatedly lamenting certain losses. Hart's views have been challenged by Arthur Sherbo who is of the opinion that instead of tragic vision there is light-hearted humour which 'has too often been either overlooked or completely misunderstood'. The examples he gives in support of his viewpoint, however, are just a few stray incidences during the journey: 'The country is still naked, the hedges are of stone' (11), of which, to adopt a Johnsonian phrase, every reader is free to make what he will. Boswell thought Johnson was trying to be funny for he writes, 'Dr. Johnson has said ludicrously in his Journey that the hedges were of stone'. Sherbo further cites an example when Boswell tells of how Johnson 'laughed enormously' upon Glavel Nairne's saying that a fine old plane tree in his garden was one of only two large trees in the country. Arthur Sherbo's outright rejection of Hart's opinion is, however, unsatisfactory. Johnson does show his concern over the plight of the inhabitants and their loss of the old character. Even the index of Chapman's publication lists pages devoted to 'Barrenness and solitude' and to 'Trees, or lack of trees', which definitely are not always treated in a light-hearted manner or intend to be funny. Johnson has invariably described the flora and fauna of the places he visited. The rocky terrain is not so much conducive to farming but can provide rich fodder for animals. The rivers of the region, having surplus fish, help in fish export:

At the tables where a stranger is received, neither plenty nor delicacy is wanting. A tract of land so thinly inhabited, must have much wild-fowl; and I scarcely remember to have seen a dinner without them. The moorgame is every where to be had. That the sea abounds with fish, needs not be told, for it supplies a great part of Europe. The Isle of *Sky* has stags and roebucks, but no hares. They sell very numerous droves of oxen yearly to England, and therefore cannot be supposed to want beef at home. Sheep and goats are in great numbers, and they have the common domestick fowl.

But as here is nothing to be bought, every family must kill its own meat, and roast part of it somewhat sooner than Apicius would prescribe. Every kind of flesh is undoubtedly excelled by the variety and emulation of English markets; but that which is not best may be yet very far from bad, and he that shall complain of his fare in the Hebrides, has improved his delicacy more than his manhood (49).

In generalising the customs of the inhabitants of the mountains Johnson talks of rivalry amongst clans, justice, subordination, superstitions etc. His rational outlook provides reasons in support of his assessments: 'Mountaineers are thievish, because they are poor, and having neither manufactures nor commerce, can grow richer only by robbery. They regularly plunder their neighbours, for their neighbours are commonly their enemies'. (40)

In the Highlands it was a law, that if a robber was sheltered from justice, any man of the same clan might be taken in his place. This was a kind of irregular justice, which, though necessary in savage times, could hardly fail to end in a feud, and a feud once kindled among an idle people with no variety of pursuits to divert their thoughts, burnt on for ages either sullenly glowing in secret mischief, or openly blazing into public violence (39).

Almost all aspects of the Scottish Highlands and life of the Highlanders are sketched by Johnson in his *Journey*. He, however, does not forget to include the southern inhabitants of Scotland who are as unfamiliar with this part of Scotland as the English:

> To the southern inhabitants of Scotland, the state of the mountains and the islands is equally unknown with that of Borneo or Sumatra: Of both they have only heard a little, and guess the rest. They are strangers to the language and the manners, to the advantages and wants of the people, whose life they would model, and whose evils they would remedy. (79)

After Johnson's death in 1784, Boswell published his travel accounts in *The Journal of a Tour to the Hebrides*. This work was based on a diary Boswell had kept during the tour and included detailed descriptions of where he and Johnson had gone and what Johnson had said. Best remembered today as friend and biographer of Samuel Johnson, Boswell was an extraordinary figure of the eighteenth century society. For years Boswell moved in the same circles as Sheridan, Goldsmith, Rousseau, Voltaire and Walpole. And he was an inveterate note-taker. A perceptive observer blessed with a retentive memory, Boswell's narrative has dramatic power. These gifts and his industry have given us an incomparable picture of his times. Boswell assiduously wrote his daily Journal, but whether he had at that time any thought of publication is not known. He himself records Johnson's suggestion that it might be 'printed', but no comments are made by Boswell:

> He came to my room this morning before breakfast, to read my Journal, which he has done all along. He often before said, 'I take great delight in reading it.' To-day he said, 'You improve: it grows better and better.'—I observed, there was a danger of my getting a habit of writing in a slovenly manner.—'Sir, said he, it is not written in a slovenly manner. It might be printed, were the subject fit for printing'. (311)

When *Dr. Johnson's A Journey to the Western Islands of Scotland* got published Boswell wanted to bring out a supplement to it. Johnson, however, was not desirous of Boswell publishing his supplement. On 10 May 1775, he wrote to Temple: 'I have not written out another line of my *Remarks* on the Hebrides. I found it impossible to do it in London. Besides, Dr. Johnson does not seem very desirous that I should publish any supplement. Between ourselves, he is not apt to encourage one to *share* reputation with himself '.(Introduction, R. W. Chapman,) Whatever the exact meaning of Boswell's suggestions that Johnson discouraged the publication of *The Journal of a Tour to the Hebrides* in his lifetime, it may be inferred that Johnson did not regard his work as in need of amplification from Boswell.

Boswell considered himself very fortunate in getting a real friend in Dr. Johnson. He got *The Journal of a Tour to the Hebrides* published in 1785 after Johnson's death. Boswell's *Journal* and Johnson's *Journey* make an interesting study in contrast. Johnson considers things philosophically and maintains a high level of generality. Boswell's approach, on the other hand, is more anecdotal, sometimes even gossipy and succeeds in large part because of Boswell's keen eye and ear for detail. Johnson's extraordinary knowledge, strength of expression, great humour and kind-heartedness made him very agreeable to Boswell who regarded his friend a supreme authority on everything connected with human nature. Boswell extremely appreciated and valued Dr. Johnson's conversations. It was also from these conversations that Boswell could realise the full stature of Johnson's genius.

But Boswell's *The Journal of a Tour to the Hebrides* is not just his observations of Dr. Johnson's personality and his 'golden words', it fulfils all the requirements of a travel book perfectly. It 'instructs to please' and 'pleases to instruct'. Boswell proudly records: 'He (Johnson) said today, while reading my Journal, "This will be a great treasure to us some years hence" '(345). Johnson intrigues, but Boswell is downright enthralling. His awe and reverence for Dr. Johnson is obvious from the opening pages of his *Journal* when he writes to Dr. Beattie to write a letter appropriate enough to persuade Johnson to visit Scotland: '... I wish that every power of attraction may be employed to secure our having so valuable an acquisition ... that I may read it to the mighty sage, with proper emphasis before I leave London' (169).

Boswell's account of Dr. Johnson in the Journal offers an intimate picture of the 'literary giant'. He could see and appreciate that the ugly and dreadful looking Johnson possessed beauty of the mind. He takes care in his description of his friend, not to miss out on any aspect of his personality, be it within or without:

> *While therefore Doctor Johnson's sayings are read, let his manners be taken along with them.* Let it however be observed, that the sayings themselves are generally great ....His person was large, robust, I may say approaching to the gigantick, and grown unwieldy from corpulency. His countenance was naturally of the cast of an ancient statue, but somewhat disfigured by the scars of that *evil*, which it was formerly imagined, the *royal touch* could cure.... His sight had always been somewhat weak; yet, so much does mind govern, and even supply the deficiency of organs, that his perceptions were uncommonly quick and accurate. His head, and sometimes also his body, shook with a kind of motion like the effect of a palsy: he appeared to be frequently disturbed by cramps, or convulsive contractions, of the nature of that distemper called *St. Vitus's dance*. (p.171)

The *Journal* served as a 'teaser' for the longer biography Boswell was preparing for publication which would exhibit the same qualities. In *The Life of Samuel Johnson*, Boswell describes Johnson in the same terms. Boswell often said that he wanted to write *Life* like a 'Flemish picture' meaning rich in painstaking detail. He was a superb reporter, adept at ferreting titbits from Johnson's acquaintances, and of course he had 'shrewdly teased many vivid nuggets' out of the man himself during their journey to Scotland, keeping an especially sharp eye for 'tics and odd behaviour' such as his personal appearance, his 'convulsive starts and odd gesticulations' and his appalling manners at dinner table: Having taken the liberty, this evening, to remark to Dr. Johnson, that he very often sat quite silent for a long time, even when in company with only a single friend,... he smiled and said, 'It is true, sir.... Tom Tyers described me the best. He once said to me, "Sir, you are like a ghost: you never speak 'till you are spoken to" (205).

Unlike Johnson's *Journey* which records the names of the places both Johnson and Boswell visited together, as chapters; Boswell's *Journal* keeps record of the journey through dates as entered in a diary. Although chronology is followed with regard to dates, his entry of Friday, 8th October reads: 'I shall here insert, without regard to chronology, some of his conversation at different times' (358). At another place he writes: 'Let us now gather some gold dust, --- some more fragments of Dr. Johnson's conversation, without regard to order of time' (273). Besides breaking the monotony of reading a diary, such occasional intrusions confirms Boswell's admiration for the literary genius. He however, at times shows his regret and helplessness at not being able to take down 'his (Johnson's) full strain of eloquence.'

Boswell's description of the places he visited has no lesser charm than what we find in his description of Johnson. In a graphic description of the little isles of Flada and Rona in Rasay, he overwhelms the reader's imagination. Painting a vivid picture of rocks and the caves he comes across, he goes on to write: 'I find a great difficulty in describing visible objects' (272).

Some important letters included in the *Journal* have become a crucial pattern in the fabric of the text. The same pattern can be discerned in Boswell's biography of Johnson. In one of these letters written by William Forbes to James Boswell, the praise of some of the pages sent to Forbes for approval is stamped thus:

> They contain a curious picture of society, and form a journal on the most instructive plan that can possibly be thought of; for I am not sure that an ordinary observer would become so well acquainted either with Dr. Johnson or with the manners of the Hebrides, by a personal intercourse, as by a perusal of your Journal. (441)

Both Johnson's *Journey* and Boswell's *Journal* have generated diverse criticism, time and again, with critics trying to emphasize the superiority of one text over the other. From the first contemporary reviews, criticism of Johnson's Journey has been dominated by a debate over essentially one question, namely the degree to which Johnson unjustly blames the Scots themselves for the conditions into which their society, by 1773 has degenerated. John N. Morris's statement regarding Boswell's unique artistry bespeaks volumes about the true appreciation of his work: 'Boswell's is a book of moments – millions of them. It is impossible to speak intelligibly of the form of such a work. It has no form, yet again almost paradoxically this deficiency itself has one of the effects that we have been taught to admire in the willed order of the shapeliest productions of art.' However, a negative review against Boswell's *Tour* was that it included much private conversation and much trivia. A true appreciation of the 'great travel' undertaken by the two friends can be achieved in studying both the texts as complementing each other. Such a reading would enhance our understanding of the culture and society of the Highland and Western Islands of Scotland, as unknown to us, as to Johnson and to quite an extent, even to Boswell when the two set out on their memorable journey. Johnson had the time of his life during his tour of the Hebrides; his account of that tour reflects the pleasure he experienced. Boswell's account of the same Journey prepared him in advance for the forthcoming stupendous task he was to undertake in the form of his biography.

WORKS CITED

1. Boswell, James. *London Journal* ed. Frederick A. Pottle, Yale University Press, 1950. Print.
2. Delany, Frank. *A Walk to the Western Isles: After Boswell and Johnson*. Harper Collins, 1993. Print.
3. Johnson and Boswell, *A Journey to the Western Islands of Scotland and The Journal of a Tour to the Hebrides*, Ed. by R.W. Chapman. London: Oxford University Press, 1970. Print.
4. Murphy, Arthur. Essays in the life and Genius of Samuel Johnson, *Johnsonian Miscellanies*, ed. G.B. Hill, 1897. Print.
5. Starr, W. Williams. *Whisky, Kilts and the Loch Ness Monster: Travelling through Scotland with Boswell and Johnson*. University of South Carolina Press, 2010. Print.

6

Lady Mary Montagu's Rhetoric(s) in *The Turkish Embassy Letters*

Farha Hiba Parvez

Lady Mary Wortley Montagu (1689-1762) had become an accomplished socialite in London by the time she was an adolescent. Her family background involved her in Whig politics. Later, she represented her country as an Ambassadress and the first ever English woman traveler to Turkey. It was chiefly on account of this travel that she could pen down her popular letters for which she is remembered today and has earned various critics' accolades. For instance, Billie Melman brands her work as "the very first example of a secular work by a woman about the Muslim Orient". (Melman 1992) She also championed the feminist cause of her day and introduced smallpox inoculation in England. Of late, it is opined that she also nurtured a scientific bent of mind. Truly, she left her imprint in almost every phase inspiring contemporary English women, especially those cherishing the might of the pen.

Lady Mary was a prolific letter-writer ever since her adolescence. She regularly corresponded with her grandmother Denbigh, Uncle William, and others, right from her teenage years. All these letters are compiled in Halsband's, *The Complete Letters of Lady Mary Wortley Montagu* in 3 volumes. *The Turkish Embassy Letters (TEL)* is a distinct collection of her letters written during her travel to Constantinople and back in the company of her husband Edward Wortley, an Ambassador Extraordinary. As the Letters were clearly intended for print, she revised them extensively and entrusted the manuscript of these letters to the Reverend Benjamin Sowden in

Holland in 1761 while returning from her journey to the Orient, but her daughter and son-in-law, Lady and Lord Bute, tried to prevent their publication. Finally, the letters somehow found their way to the press almost one year after Lady Mary's death and the 'London Chronicle' reviewed them in 1763. Dr. Johnson and Gibbon also reviewed them. In fact, the Letters were an immediate success and were reprinted several times, which added to her literary reputation.

The outcome of Lady Mary's travel to the Orient has been largely taken as an addition to travel literature. In fact, this is also an exercise in exploring Oriental veracities. Her depiction of the Orient, which contrasts with earlier Orientalist repertoires on a number of issues, must be given credit for rectifying some misconceptions inherent in them. Isobel Grundy has described the expanse of Lady Mary's Oriental project:

> She firmly sets the record straight from the perversions of 'voyage' writers who traduce the Mohammedans: who 'never fail giving you an Account of the Women, which, 'tis certain they never saw, and talking very wisely of the Genius of the Men, into whose Company they are never admitted…(200)

She delights in exploding received ideas. Lady Mary's account of the Orient was not meant to promote or propagate Islam or project a Muslim image but 'an Enlightenment travel treatise' meant to present factual data before well-meaning and rational audience. Another purpose of her Oriental writing was to slacken the East/West divide and foster religious understanding in order to create an atmosphere congenial to 'speaking for the other' and 'listening to the other'. Lady Mary's Orientalist project challenges the trend to consider Islam as irrational, derelict or to spread hostility against Islam and Muslims. She censors the hegemony of the West and refutes Europe's claim to be the birthplace of reason. No doubt her efforts correct the popular concept of the Orient and generously support universal amity and goodwill.

Lady Mary is acknowledged as one of the most important of women writers. Some critics rank her in the category of Aphra Behn and Jane Austen. Her prose, in general, is provocative and entertaining. Her narratives in *Romance Writings* appeal to both sexes equally. She is fond of experimentation in fiction and autobiography writing. She seems more influenced by the French than by the English. Like her poetry, her prose also reflects her engagement with literary issues, cross-cultural relations, gender ideologies, and other social, political and literary debates.

Halsband recalls Lady Mary Wortley Montagu as 'the first distinguished woman of letters that England had seen' (94). In Isobel Grundy's opinion, 'Even if she had allowed nothing to survive, or if she had not written, Lady Mary would be an object of interest today…she saw herself as a writer, she has made the world accept her as a writer, too' (XXII), referring to her many accomplishments as an intellectual, a literary personage, a passive player in domestic and international politics, an adventurer, a pilgrim of antiquity and the first English woman to travel to a non-Christian and non-European country, to experience and evaluate political and social life there and to report these developments back home.

The main sources of Lady Mary's letters written during Wortley's embassy days are, first, the letters she wrote to her friends and relatives back home and, second, her journal which she maintained during the journey; though very little matter, only two passages, according to Halsband, has been taken from the latter. Various compilers/editors have given slightly varying versions of the text which mainly differs in addressee or address or annotation details.

TEL is meant to be a travelogue, but basically these were letters embodying the representations of Lady Mary's own self and her soliloquy, with the added advantage that this representation could be planned and scheduled. Lady Mary has dexterously exploited this potential of her letters in projecting her pleasant personality and conveying her personal point of view.

When Voltaire declared her letters superior to those of Madame de Sevigne, Lady Mary's opinion in this regard was more ambitious: 'very pretty they are, but I assert, without the least vanity, that mine will be full as entertaining forty years hence. I advise you, therefore to put none of them to the use of waste paper (Desai XXIX). We can, therefore conclude that posterity included Lady Mary's audience and she was not much off the mark on this count.

The significance of ascertaining the audience lies in the fact that Lady Mary was very selective in her choice of the addressee. She always considered the level of discourse, tastes and abilities of the addressee and the time available with him/her before sending the letter. She had a discerning mind and thoughtfully considered what to write to whom, and weighed the details, documentation and background information of the letter. This helped make an intelligent correlation between the addressee and the content. While drawing a correspondent, she actually intended to ensure that her recipient will pay attention to what she wants to emphasize and shall grasp the seriousness of purpose expressed between the lines. This is the reason that her letters sensitize its readers. They find a new cultural discourse in it and come to conclude that *TEL* is not a run-of-the-mill travelogue.

Expressing his reaction over the newly-published volume of *TEL*, the renowned historian Gibbon had remarked in exclamation: 'What fire, what ease, what knowledge of Europe and Asia (5)!' These sentiments are further corroborated by Halsband's judgment on *TEL*: 'These letters are her public testament, the brilliantly polished record of the observations and thoughts of an enlightened, emancipated woman whose view goes beyond insular England to embrace all of Europe and the realm of Islam. The letters are Lady Mary's credentials as simultaneously a benign spirit and (by precept and example) a feminist champion. Through being a great letter writer she achieved her ambition of being a woman-of-letters' (6). Both these excerpts encompass the coverage and brilliance of Lady Mary's Orientalism.

Indeed, Lady Mary set many precedents through her travel and travelogue. Fanny Parks, a woman traveler to Turkey, admitted in 1850, 'The perusal of Lady Mary Wortley Montagu's work has rendered me anxious to visit a zenana, and to become acquainted with lives of the East'(XXXI). It is just one, though thoroughly unconventional and tempting aspect of Lady Mary's vision of the Orient presented in *TEL*.

European technological developments had been conducive to foreign travels and in turn, these travels opened diverse vistas to expedite the flowering of scholarship on Eastern literature, history, philosophy, and religion. George Sale had already completed his translation of the *Koran*, and scholars like William Jones, who translated Oriental literature from Arabic, Persian, Hebrew, and Sanskrit, had acquainted Western readers with classical texts like the *Mahabharata* and the *Arabian Nights*. Besides, the developing environment had established the importance of military as well as the cultural reconnaissance of the Orient, especially after the threats of war. This was enough of a background motivation for travel to the Orient but what was more congenial for Lady Mary, is the latent fact that she was born and brought up in the 'Enlightened society of eighteenth century that boasted of the Age of Reason. While the 'enlightened society' was characterized by knowledge, self-control and open-mindedness, the 'age of reason' added 'tolerance' as a litmus test of being a true European. These values translated in Lady Mary's quest for truth and veracity as, in what Anita Desai calls, an "extraordinary" attitude to an alien culture, the two key features of her brand of Orientalism.

In *TEL*, Lady Mary has amassed almost everything Turkish and of interest for an Orientalist. It is not devoid of the art of creating imaginary geography; ancient is much resurrected there as is the Holy Land, as are references to Arabian tales and Turkish passion for violence, but Lady Mary does not distort the real world she witnesses all around her. She engages in detailed Orientalist discourses, but as a nonjudgmental observer and concerned informer she leaves the judgment up to the reader. These approaches gave her the moral authority to point out the errors of previous voyage writers and indicate that this contentious knowledge could be the source of hegemony and disunity in the name of Orientalist discourse.

A seminal question at this juncture is: what was the reference point of Lady Mary in writing these letters? No single point can be pin-pointed as her writings display a range of reference points. Culturally and politically, English nationalism is her reference point to which she reverts very frequently. In her March 10, 1718, letter to her sister, she refers to Holland as a parental and ideal nation:

> Her house was magnificently furnished and very well fancied, her winter rooms being furnished with figured velvet on gold ground, and those for summer with fine Indian quilting embroidered with gold. The houses of the great Turkish lades are kept clean with as much nicety as those in Holland. (TEL 120)

She keenly observes dissimilarities in habits of the two countries and promptly reports to Lady Bristol:

> The difference of the dress here and at London is so great, the same sort of things are not proper for caftans and manteaus. However, I will not give over my search. (TEL 65)

In a similar vein, she addressed Abbe Conti, a cosmopolitan Catholic:

> Mohammedism is divided into as many sects as Christianity, and the first institution as much neglected and obscured by interpretations. I cannot here forbear reflecting on the natural inclination of mankind, to make mysteries and novelties, The Zeidi, Kudi, Jabari etc. put me in mind of the Catholic, Lutheran, Calvinist, etc., and are equally zealous against one another. (TEL 62)

II

A deeper study of *TEL*, shows that Lady Mary employed ten distinct strands of rhetoric: rhetoric of difference, rhetoric of identification or likeness, rhetoric of tolerance, rhetoric of compassion, rhetoric of semiotics (of natural scenes, Turk architecture and), rhetoric of otherness, rhetoric of reason, rhetoric of savagery, rhetoric of erotica and rhetoric on Islam. It is not very difficult to discern that like Lady Mary's personality, some of these strands are contrary to others.

Seen this way, it becomes easy to relate Lady Mary's reference points with her strands of rhetoric. Clearly, savagery, semiotics, differences and otherness is narrated with reference to her English nationalism, her views on identification, tolerance, reason and Islam reflect Enlightenment values, compassion speaks for Christian values and erotica is a Greco-Roman heritage. Thus the whole scheme of Lady Mary's rhetoric shows that the overwhelming focus of *TEL* has been on issues of immediate consequence.

Rhetoric of Identification

Lady Mary utilizes the rhetoric of identification in a positivistic and progressive way. She performs best in her pursuit where she encourages 'partial identification' with aristocratic classes of England and Turkey. Her most forceful argument for identification is 'as it is with us'. This allows her to project the possibility of 'inclusion'. But Meyda Yegenoglu, has put forward a novel argument while justifying her feminist credentials, "Lady Mary assumes a masculine role (a role unavailable to her in the 'masculine' West), 'attaches a penis to herself,' and penetrates a 'feminized' East, thus complementing rather than challenging the work of the male colonist (45-50). Ostensibly, she implies that Lady Mary had been working for expansion of imperialist colonization. Whatever the case maybe, *TEL* does not seem to support this conjecture.

With the dexterity of a master artist, she paints the following picture of Turkish grandeur, in her description of the Grand Vizier's Lady. She highlights the Oriental set up and characteristic features and practices of the East but maintains comparable decorum:

> I was surprised to observe so little magnificence in her house, the furniture being all very moderate and, except the habits and number of her slaves, nothing about her that appeared expensive. She guessed at my thoughts and told me that she was no longer of an age to spend either her time or money in superfluities; that her whole expense was in charity, and her employment praying to God. There was

> no affectation in this speech; both she and her husband are entirely given up to devotion. He never looks upon any other woman and, what is much more extraordinary, touches no bribes, notwithstanding the example of all his predecessors. He is so scrupulous on this point, he would not accept Mr Wortley's present till he had been assured over and over that 'twas a settled perquisite of his place, at the entrance of every ambassador. (TEL 87)

However, this information leaves one perplexed regarding the efficiency of Turkish administration. Alternatively, one feels compelled to think if correct data were accessible to her or she was prognosticating the impending decline of Turkey:

> The Greek lady with me earnestly solicited me to visit the Kabya's lady, saying he was the second officer in the empire and ought indeed to be looked upon as the first, the Grand Vizier, having only the name, while he exercised the authority. I had found so little diversion in this harem that I had no mind to go into another. (TEL 88)

At places where Lady Mary does not want to concur or is in partial agreement or wants to downplay the subject, she avoids direct confrontation by resorting to the rhetoric of 'otherness'. This helps her disown the details without causing any annoyance or precipitating any bias. Such discourse usually pertains to 'their religion', 'their law', or 'that nation/country', 'that religion' or 'that people'. Even Catholic religion is 'that religion' for her. If the context supports dissociation, she may replace 'that' with 'this'. Otherness of 'their' is present markedly in her Islamic discourse:

Her lack of Islamic knowledge is quite evident. Actually her view of Islamic law is sharply coloured by her class perception, according to which Turks of rank and distinction are always upright while vulgar Turks are disregarded:

> 'Tis a degree of generosity to tell the truth and 'tis very rare that any Turk will assert a solemn falsehood. I don't speak of the lowest sort, for as there is a great deal of ignorance,

> there is very little virtue amongst them, and false witnesses are much cheaper than in Christendom, those wretches not being punished (even when they are publicly detected) with the rigour they ought to be. (TEL 137)

Lady Mary has also furnished details of certain social customs of Turkey using the same rhetoric some of which are positive to the extent of being unconventional while parts of these are contestable:

> ‘Tis true; their law permits them four wives, but there is no instance of a man of quality that makes use of this liberty, or of a woman of rank that would suffer it. When a husband happens to be inconstant, as those things will happen, he keeps his mistress in a house apart and visits her as privately as he can, just as 'tis with you. Amongst all the great men here, I only know the tefterdar (i.e. treasurer) that keeps a number of she-slaves for his own (that is, on his own side of the house, for a slave once given to serve a lady is entirely at her disposal) and he is spoke of as a libertine, or what we should call a rake, and his wife won't see him, though she continues to live in his house. (TEL 72)

Rhetoric of Tolerance

Lady Mary makes use of the rhetoric of tolerance in convincing her audience that contrary to the opinion of most voyage writers, the Orient is not very different from the West. Most of her narrations of Turkish customs and the religion of Islam are penned in this vein. She demonstrates that ‘the manners of mankind do not differ so widely’. Her force of persuasion comes from her favourite argument: as 'tis with you (Letter 72), or she pleads: “Which divinity is most rational I leave you to deter¬mine. (Letter 100) or I know not what your thought may be concerning this”. (Letter 110) The spirit of humanism finds full expression in such letters. Rather, she appreciates Turkish practices in these letters, a trend that had been unconventional and non-traditional till her day. Here are some examples:

Lady Mary's trend-setting views on Muslim women have earned her both exceptional acclaim and harsh criticism. She has, nevertheless, raised a number of misconceptions in vogue in the West, especially England, under the influence of previous writers. In writing these letters she was inspired by two strong motives: one, searching for the truth and two, extending the horizons of feminism, and, therefore, coming 'out of a true female spirit of contradiction', which imbued her with a missionary zeal, as the following topics suggest:

> Our vulgar notion that they do not own women to have any souls is a mistake. 'Tis true they say they are not of so elevated a kind and therefore must not hope to be admitted into the paradise appointed for the men, who are to be entertained by celestial beauties, but there is a place of happiness destined for souls of the inferior order where all good women are to be in eternal bliss. (TEL 100)

Though her refutation with existing misconception is justified and her conclusion is also valid, her argumentation is unsound and seems to be founded on opinions held by lowly masses of the Turkish community. However, the following argument is framed in better words:

> As to your next enquiry, I assure you 'tis certainly false, though commonly believed in our parts of the world, that Mohammed excludes women from any share in a future happy state— On the contrary he promises a very fine paradise to the Turkish women. He says indeed that this paradise will be a separate place from that of their hus¬bands. But I fancy the most part of them won't like it the worse for that, and that the regret of this separation will not render their paradise the less agreeable. (TEL 109-10)

After studying the condition of Turkish women in the harem as well as in markets and bagnios, she explodes another Western myth regarding them:

> I am more inclined, out of a true female spirit of contradiction, to tell you the falsehood of a great part of what you find in authors; as, for example, the admirable Mr. Hill — 'Tis also very pleasant to observe how tenderly he and all his brethren voyage-writers lament on the miserable confinement of the Turkish ladies, who are, perhaps, freer than any ladies in the universe, and are the only women in the world that lead a life of uninterrupted pleasure, exempt from cares, their whole time being spent in visiting, bathing or the agreeable amusement of spending money and inventing new fashions. A husband would be thought mad that exacted any degree of economy from his wife, whose expenses are no way limited but by her own fancy. 'Tis his business to get money and hers to spend it, and this noble prerogative extends itself to the very meanest of the sex. Here is a fellow that carries embroidered handkerchiefs upon his back to sell, as miserable a figure as you may suppose such a mean dealer, yet I'll assure you his wife scorns to wear anything less than cloth of gold, has her ermine furs, and a very handsome set of jewels for her head. They go abroad when and where they please. 'Tis true they have no public places but the bagnios, and there can only be seen by their own sex. However, that is a diversion they take great pleasure in. (TEL 134)

Rhetoric of Difference

Truly speaking, Lady Mary has not used this rhetoric much, so its instances are few in *TEL*. This rhetoric characterizes travelogues written by male travellers who were bent upon highlighting differences between Western and Oriental cultures, even by exaggerating or fabricating facts. By suppressing this rhetoric Lady Mary also attempted to augment the traditional feminist rhetoric. Instead of this rhetoric she positively promoted the rhetoric of identification and the rhetoric of tolerance.

A brilliant example of this rhetoric found in *TEL*, when she speaks of Tunisian peasants is:

> They are not quite black, but all mulattoes, and the most frightful crea¬tures that can appear in a human figure. They are almost naked, only wearing a piece of coarse serge wrapped about them, but the women have their arms to their very shoulders and their necks and faces adorned with flowers, stars and various sort of figures impressed by gunpowder; a considerable addition to their natural deformity, which is, however, esteemed very ornamental amongst them, and I believe they suffer a good deal of pain by it. (TEL 129)

Rhetoric of Reason

Lady Mary stood for modernity and as a product of the Age of Reason, she was enamoured of reason but she did not encourage producing another divide; the East/West divide in the name of modernity. Therefore, she always preferred to resort to reason. For instance, she seems to be sharing with Achmet Bey the ridicule of Whiston's philosophy of Transubstantiation. In another letter, she suggested to Samuel Clark preaching in the Orient as he was known for his rational theology. Here are a few excerpts from *TEL* representing Lady Mary's rhetoric of reason:

> The yasmak, or Turkish veil; is become not only very easy but agreeable to me, and if it was not, I would be content to endure some inconvenience to content a passion so powerful with me as curiosity. (TEL 126-27)

At other places she claimed that the veil serves the purpose of hiding the persona so that illicit overtures do not become known. One may call it utilitarian ethics, an attitude she frankly demonstrates with respect to money-matters:

> You know how, to divide the idea of pleasure from that of vice, and they are only mingled in the heads of fools but I allow you to laugh at me for the sensual declaration that

> I had rather be a rich effendi with all his ignorance than Sir Isaac Newton with all his knowledge. (TEL 122)

Rhetoric of Semiotics

It has been suggested that as a woman and a traveler, Lady Mary not only extended the horizons of geographical knowledge about the Orient but also produced considerable imaginative geography. In her rhetoric of semiotics, she uses narrations of natural scenes to evoke the memory of pastoral England and her architectural data conjures the ancient:

> The description may serve for all the mosques in Constantinople; the model is exactly the same; and they only differ in largeness and richness of materials. That of the Valide is the largest of all, built entirely of marble, the most prodigious and, I think, the most beautiful structure I ever saw, be it spoke to the honour of our sex, for it was founded by the mother of Mohammed IV. Between friends, St Paul's Church would make a pitiful figure near it, as any of our squares would do near the Atmeydan, or Place of Horses, 'at' signifying horse in Turkish.
>
> This was the Hippodrome in the reign of the Greek emperors. (TEL 129)
>
> ...Mr. Wortley resolving to pursue his journey the next morning early I was in haste to see the ruins of Justinian's church, which did not afford me so agreeable a prospect as I had left, being little more than a heap of stones. (TEL 60)

Rhetoric of Compassion

Whereas Lady Mary's emphasis on compassion and concern for the distressed peasants reaffirms the eighteenth-century feminist discourse and extends a 'philanthropic' role to the women of the Victorian era, it also represents the value of humanism, instant concern for man. Nevertheless, she skillfully uses this rhetoric to communicate other messages between the lines as this excerpt shows:

> I saw here a new occasion for my compassion. The wretches that had provided twenty wagons for our luggage from Belgrade hither for a certain hire, being all sent back without payment, some of their horses lamed and others killed, without any satisfaction made for them. The poor fellows came round the house weeping and tearing their hair and beards in the most pitiful manner, without getting anything but drubs from the insolent soldiers. I cannot express to your Royal Highness how much I was moved at this scene. I would have paid them the money out of my own pocket, with all my heart, but it would only have been giving so much to the aga who would have taken it from them without remorse. (TEL 56)

Rhetoric of Savagery

To place emphasis on their barbarity, Lady Mary paints a disgusting scenario, in which she deploys her rhetoric of savagery:

> I am threatened at the same time with being froze to death, buried in the snow and taken by the Tartars, who ravage that part of Hungary I am to pass. 'Tis true we shall have a considerable escort so that possibly I may be diverted with a new scene by finding myself in the midst of a battle. How my adventures will conclude I leave entirely to Providence; if comically, you shall hear of them. (TEL 44)

> The Greeks are subjects and not slaves. Those who are to be bought in that manner are either such as are taken in war or stole by the Tartars from Russia, Circassia or Georgia, and are such miserable, awkward, poor wretches you would not think any of them worthy to be your housemaid. (TEL 104)

Rhetoric of Erotica

The Turkish Bath has been highly debated as the site of homoeroticism between women since 1610 when George Sandys viewed the hamams, or public baths during his travels in the Ottoman Empire. Lady Mary not only entered but countered imaginative male accounts of lesbian sex there, although her description of these baths challenges this notoriety. A look at the text is necessary for vouchsafing these commentaries:

> —without any beauty or defect concealed. Yet there was not the least wanton smile or immodest gesture amongst them. They walked and moved with the same majestic grace which, Milton describes of our general mother. There were many amongst them as exactly proportioned as ever any goddess was drawn by the pencil of Guidor or Titian, and most of their skins shiningly white, only adorned by their beautiful hair divided, into many tresses, hanging on their shoulders, braided either with pearl or ribbon, perfectly representing the figures of the Graces....
>
> I perceived that the ladies with finest skins and most delicate shapes had the greatest share of my admiration, though their faces were sometimes less beautiful than those of their companions. To tell you the truth, I had wickedness enough to wish secretly that Mr Gervase could have been there invisible. I fancy it would have very much improved his art to see so many fine women naked, in different postures, some in conversation, some working, others drinking coffee or sherbet, and many negligently lying on their cushions while their slaves .....
>
> They generally take this diversion once a week, and stay there at least four or five hours, without getting cold by immediate coming out of the hot bath into the cool room, which was very surprising to me. The lady that seemed the most considerable amongst them entreated me to sit by her

> and would fain have undressed me for the bath. I excused myself with some difficulty, they being however all so earnest in persuading me, I was a last forced to open my shirt, and show them my stays, which satisfied them very well, for I saw they believed I was so locked up in that machine, that it was not in my own power to open it, which contrivance they attributed to my husband. (TEL 59-60)

Judy Mabro further elaborates: "When Lady Mary Montague was pressed by the women in a Turkish bath to take off her clothes and join them, she undid her blouse to show them her corset. This led them to believe, she said, that she was imprisoned in a machine which could only be opened by her husband. Both groups of women could see each other as prisoners---and of course they were both right." (TEL 123)

Rhetoric on Islam

In her rhetoric on Islam, she seems intent on representing Islam with the maximum possible accuracy but frequently shows lack of information as perusal of the following excerpts shall clarify:

Islam

Lady Mary has nowhere mentioned Islam, but 'their law', 'their religion' or 'the law of Mohammed', which she often calls 'Mohammedism'.

> Mohammedism is divided into as many sects as Christianity, and the first institution as much neglected and obscured by interpretations. I cannot here forbear reflecting on the natural inclination of mankind, to make mysteries and novelties. (TEL 62)
>
> She further says about Muslims:
>
> In effect there's nothing so like as the fables of the Greeks and of the Mahommedans and the last have multitudes of saints at whose tombs miracles are by them said to be daily performed, nor are the accounts of the lives of those blessed

> musulmans much less stuffed with extravagancies than the spiritual romances of the Greek papas.[36]

However, her account of what Achmet Bey told her about Al-Qur'an is much better:

> He assured me that if I understood Arabic I should be very well pleased with reading the Alcoran, which is so far from the nonsense we charge it with that it is the purest morality deli¬vered in the very best language. I have since heard impartial Christians speak of it in the same manner, and I don't doubt but that all our translations are from copies got from the Greek priests who would not fail to falsify it with the extremity of malice. No body of men ever were more ignorant or more corrupt. (TEL 63)

3. TEL's Influence on Later Writers

Lady Mary's Travelogue, *TEL*, embodying her Orientalism has cast wide-ranging influence on the later Orientalist writers, especially on Byron and Thomas Moore. A brief sketch of this influence is briefly given in this section:

Byron is an established Oriental poet. Even Edward Said who is otherwise critical of the entire Orientalist representations acknowledges Byron's creative skill in this arena:

> —William Beckford, Byron, Goethe and Hugo restructured the Orient by their art and made its colors, lights and people visible through their images, rhythms and motifs. At most, the "real" Orient provoked a writer to his vision; it very rarely guided it. (TEL 22)

Jeoffery W. Vail has identified two phases of Byron's Oriental writings, first, their 'Early Lyrics', ranging from 1801 till the winter of 1811-12, when both of them became acquainted as 'Whig poets'. Byron was very much under the influence of Thomas Moore during this period. Besides mutual respect, Byron, as a young poet, was deeply influenced by their shared convictions that often Lady Mary's influence is another significant factor in Byron's Orientalism. Byron discovered Lady Mary in Europe where he came across a copy of *Turkish Embassy Letters*. Byron read it with avidity and admired its contents. Later, he recommended its fresh publication and advised many others to consult it. Emphasizing the over-all effect of *TEL* on Byron, Kidwai remarks:

> Lady Montagu's *Letters*, in a sense, anticipate Byron's Orientalism in that both writers make a clean break from the conventionally prejudiced view of the Islam, show a fine understanding of Islam helped partly by their eyewitness accounts, rich in genuine local topographical and cultural description, and use the Oriental setting for examining a wide range of issues by comparing the Islamic code of life with the traditional Christian/British one, without claiming the latter's moral superiority. (Kidwai 28-9)

Just like Lady Mary was the first woman to travel to the Orient, Lord Byron was the only Englishman among his contemporaries who actually travelled to the Orient. Both of them experienced it intimately, by absorbing it into their daily routine, not for political and/or religious propaganda but for grasping the real feel of the culture. Byron also adopted the Oriental habit.

Search for truth was another common factor between Byron and Lady Mary. Lady Mary's influence on Byron is also visible on a literary plane. Byron has number of terms used by Lady Mary in her travelogue.

It is worth mentioning here, that Lady Mary's indirect influence may also be traced in Scott and the Orientalist Blunts (Lady Anabella and Wilfrid Scawen Blunt) via Byron. Regarding Scott's 'The Talisman', the book is praised for its insight into Islam by no less an authority than H.A.R. Gibb. Edward Said conjectures: 'Scott's knowledge probably came from Byron and Bedrock' (101).

Lady Mary's Orientalism was both infectious and effective. It seems she had at the back of her mind the idea of generating a new plan for Oriental studies and setting an agenda of change for the acceptance of new ideas while she embarked on writing these letters. Her travel to the Orient made Lady Mary aware of previous voyage writers' unscrupulous statements: "Now that I am a little acquainted with their ways I cannot forbear admiring either the exemplary discretion or extreme stupidity of all the writers that have given accounts of them" (TEL 71). She has pointed out a number of lapses in male writings in several letters included in *TEL*:

> Your whole letter is full of mistakes from one end to the other. I see you have taken your ideas of Turkey from that worthy author Dumont, who has writ with equal ignorance and confidence. 'Tis a particular pleasure to me here to read the voyages to the Levant, which are generally so far removed from truth and so full of absurdities I am very well diverted with them. They never fail to give you an account of the women, which 'tis certain they never saw, and talking very wisely of the genius of men, into whose company they are never admitted, and very often describe mosques which they dare not peep into. (TEL 104)

But she also traces the path through which written mistakes have crept into otherwise reputed records:

> ....but I cannot forbear taking notice to you of a mistake of Gemelli (though I honour him in a much higher degree than any other voyage-writer). He says that there is no remain of Calcedon. This is certainly a mistake. I was there yesterday and went cross the canal in my galley, the sea being very narrow between that city and Constantinople, 'tis still a large town and has several mosques in it. The Christians, still call it Calcedonia, and the Turks give it a name I forgot, but which is only a corruption of the same word. I suppose, this an error of his guide, which his short stay hindered him from rectifying, for I have, in other matters, a very just esteem for his veracity. (TEL 140)

At one place she describes the dilemma confronting voyage writers as a potential source of misleading narrations:

> We travelers are in very hard circumstances. If we say nothing but what has been said before us we are dull and we have observed nothing. If we tell anything new, we are laughed at as fabulous and romantic, not allowing for the difference of ranks, which afford difference of company more curiosity, or the changes of customs that happen every twenty year in every country. But people judge of travelers exactly with the same candour, good nature and impartiality they judge of their neighbours upon all occasions. For my part, if I live to return amongst you I am so well acquainted with the morals of all my dear friends and acquaintances that I am resolved to tell them nothing at all, to avoid the imputation, which their charity would certainly incline them to, of my telling too much. But I depend upon your knowing me enough to believe whatever I seriously assert for truth, though I give you leave to be surprised at an account so new to you. (TEL 118)

For her own travelogue, she writes:

> You will perhaps by surprised at an account so different from what you have been entertained with by the common voyage writers, who are very fond of speaking of what they don't know. (TEL 85)

Contrary to the male travelers, female travelers were late comers, though they had been working in the Orient as ethnologists, missionaries, and reformists for a long period. It was a primary advantage with them that they had easy access to the private and personal spaces of Eastern women, and were able to observe their inner workings to the satisfaction of the search for the 'truth' of the 'Other' and thus they were equally capable of strengthening the West's position as the knowing subject, notwithstanding the rigors of a female's travel those days. Nevertheless, their writings are substantially different and better disposed towards the Orient.

It is often claimed that Lady Mary is one of the most important, most provocative and most entertaining women writers between

Aphra Behn and Jane Austen. Concluding their assessment of Lady Mary, Ehrenpreis and Halsband write:

> Her career, with its span over mid-century, bridges the gap between, on the one side, women writers as tawdry Sappho's or stately ladies, and, on the other side, women writers as professional and respectable members of the republic of letters. (50-51)

By disrupting the monolithic narrative of Orientalism, Montagu could highlight the good breeding of the Turks, high culture of the Ottoman court, parity of the Turkish elite class with those back home, and freedom and financial self-reliance of Turkish women. She honestly states her identification with Turkish women and raises no objection against 'four wives' or gender relations. As a matter of fact, she praises the Turkish women's veil, their Harem and demolishes myths of promiscuity. She also highlights Turkish women's superior beauty, though some critics term it as 'fetishization of white skin'. Some readers may feel some lapses in her description of Islam and its emblems but one should realise that her responsibilities did not require her to interpret or represent Islam. In fact, what she set out to achieve was to present a faithful portrayal of Turkish Muslims. If they erred in their practice of Islam, this was not her fault as a foreigner.

Nevertheless, she addresses and dismisses Islam-bashing and builds a strong argument for bridging the gap between feminism and Islam. She condemns the polemic against Islam----depiction of the Prophet of Islam as an impostor, or 'the Anti-Christ', charges of iconoclasm, Islamic lore as the locus of a wanton sensuality and inherent violence besides shunning the polemics of the 'Middle Ages'. She frankly appreciates the Turkish elites' steadfastness and their good behaviour towards their slaves.

As a child of the Age of Reason and a member of the enlightened society characterized by knowledge, self-control and open-mindedness, Lady Mary vastly demystified the Orient as a dark, obscure, unintelligible, and unpredictable territory and presented it on a pleasing aesthetic level. She delved into the heterogeneity of Turkish society and came to conclude that as stolid as earlier male travelers have painted them, their grasp of reality is not staled by 'previous Oriental knowledge' rather, the West needs to further open up within its polemical spaces.

While Lady Mary's Orientalism maintains positive ideals, her travelogue, the second aspect of *TEL* supports progressive and inclusive philosophy downplaying cultural, racial, and economic differences besides producing a kind of geography that does not sustain the conquering voice of a European representative but promotes the emotional response of a gendered discourse that is both authentic and socially secure. Here she does not seem interested in 'seizing' or 'owning' the Turkish woman as seen in the colonialist narratives, but in cooperating with them and assisting them. She has tried in her travelogue, to sensitize her readers to visualize and think in terms of co-existence instead of vilification. In her travelogue, she appears to be distinctly inaugurating a new discourse which is both cross-cultural and empathetic. Indeed, she is not a run-on-the-mill type of ordinary travel-writer.

Lady Mary's critics have been somewhat irrational in ridiculing her, thereby underscoring her other qualities as a writer, an opinion-maker and a human being of forbearance, tenacity and persistence. She was censured at the Court for writing a pamphlet not suiting their decorum. When she tended to neglect Wortley, he called her 'friend of an immoral lady,' and when her beauty was ruined by smallpox, Wortley bore it, but her literary opponents, Pope and Hervey used the disaster to call her 'pox'd Sappho' and 'Moll Worthless'. Even today, she is vilified. With reference to Lady Mary's description of Turkish baths, Briony Llewellyn and Charles Newton write, "We do not know if Lady Mary Wortley Montagu's famous account of the vocabulary of this romantic practice among the Turks still held good for Cairo in the 1840s, but the Lady is supposed to be the consort of a Turkish Bey (Starky 46)." One thing her adversaries cannot negate is her being an accomplished woman writer, and a lady of extraordinary talents.

Such were the personal and professional characteristics of Lady Mary; born in aristocracy, but found herself in the bondage of class customs and fought against it in both her personal and social life. She promoted a literary circle in London and magnanimously faced its ire. She ventured to bridge the East-West cultural divide and augment the spirit of Enlightenment and Reason. She suffered agonies of her time as a lone philosopher and passed away from this world with the solace of an enduring author.

It seems appropriate here to conclude with what Joseph Spence wrote to his mother in a communication, "Lady Mary is one of the most extraordinary shining characters in the world, but she shines like a comet; she is all irregular and always wandering. She is the most wise, most imprudent; loveliest disagreeablest; best natured, cruelest woman in the world." (Desai XXXIV)

WORKS CITED

Desai, Anita, 'Introduction' in Malcolm Jack (ed.), "*Lady Mary Wortley Montagu: Turkish Embassy Letters*," William Pickering, London, 1993, p. xxix. Print.

Grundy, Isobel. *Lady Mary Wortley Montagu*, Oxford University Press, Oxford, 2001. Print.

Halsband, Robert "*Lady Mary Wortley Montagu and Her Place in the Eighteenth Century*," History Today 16 no. 2 (1966). Print.

I.E. and R. Halsband, *Lady of Letters: the Eighteenth Century: Papers*, William Andrews Clark Memorial Library, Los Angeles, 1969. Print.

Jack, Malcolm (ed.), "*Lady Mary Wortley Montagu: Turkish Embassy Letters*" William Pickering, London, 1993. Print.

Kidwai, Abdur Rahim, *Image of the Orient in English Literature upto 1832*, AMU, Aligarh, 1997. Print.

Kronenberger, Louis, 'Kings and Desperate Men': Life in Eighteenth Century England, Transaction Publisher, 1952. Print.

Mabro, Judy. *Veiled Half- Truths: Western Travellers' Perception of Middle Eastern Women*, L. B. Tauris & Co. Ltd. London, 1991. Print.

Said, Edward W. Orientalism, Penguin Books, U.K., 1977. Print.

Starkey, Paul and Janet, *Interpreting the Orient: Travellers in Egypt and the Near East*, Garnet Publishing Limited, U.K., 2001. Print.

Vail, Jeoffery W., 'The Literary Relationship of Lord Byron and Thomas Moore' Baltimore and London: John Hopkins University Press, 2001. Print.

Yegenoglu, Meyda. "Supplementing the Orientalist Lack: European Ladies in the Harem". Inscriptions 6 (1992), 45-50. Print.

7

'Agony and Glory' of Clym in *The Return of the Native*: A Study in Humanistic-Existential Model of Behaviour

Nikhat Taj

> "For this is the journey the men make: to find themselves. If they fail in this, it doesn't matter much what else they find."- Michner
>
> (*qtd. in Coleman 692*).

Clym Yeobright in Thomas Hardy's *The Return of the Native*, is a passionate victim of an abstraction. He is a man whose entire will is set to returning to Egdon Heath, a journey back to his native land in order to find his true self and having found it, in trying to realize/ fulfil it. Hardy locates Clym's tragedy in this vision:

> Unlike Jane Austen, George Eliot or Henry James there is no gradual revelation of character, all is declared at the outset, sometimes even before a sentence is spoken-caught in physical appearance, a way of dressing, of walking. What does attract his imagination is not individual character but a kind of individual being. And it is failure to give recognition to this that weakens the approach to Hardy as elegist for a rural community. (Gregor 292)

Ian Gregor made this comment in a different context, yet his perception that Hardy's imagination is attracted to a kind of an "individual being" is very much to the purpose of this study. It brings the novelist into the role of a philosopher, a psychologist, a creator of character in an effective relationship:

> The nineteenth century was an age of growing self-consciousness. People were investigating psychology and analyzing motive as never before. The novelists led by George Eliot, were doing it too. Hardy was aware of this tendency. He even said it was not to be resisted: novels must be more analytical. (Cecil 419)

David Cecil observes that Hardy tried to create some typical complex figures of his time – Knight, a modern thinker; Fitzpiers, a modern sceptic, Sue an advanced woman (419) in this new style. He gave his conscientious best to make these characters psychologically convincing and true to life by painstakingly detailing their opinions, doubts, sensitivities and feelings, strengths and weaknesses. In *The Return of the Native*, Clym Yeobright's personality may be defined in light of humanistic-existential1 perspective and be judged as psychologically true, in his quest to give meaning to his existence through the realization of his personal choice.

The interdisciplinary approach of contemporary literary criticism has increasingly moved towards psychology in its analysis and understanding of character. Literature complements psychology and yields valuable insight/information of personality dynamics and inner experiences of the individual. It captures the motives, factors, and causes underlying various types of human behaviour. Coleman, observes that literary classics in their description of human behaviour deal with infinite subtleties of degree and variety which often achieve a lifelike vividness and an emotional force that science cannot achieve. Masters of fiction and drama have given brilliant character studies based on their keen observation of human behaviour: Sophocles (Oedipus Rex and Electra) gave us the first intimation of incest motives; Aeschylus (Oresteia Trilogy) dealt with severe feelings of remorse and guilt; the many characters of Shakespeare – Macbeth, Lady Macbeth, Othello, Jacques, Hamlet are manifestations of ambition, guilt, jealousy, melancholy, indecisiveness, respectively; Don Quixote is an example of a noble but deluded idealist (8). Rene Wellek and Austin Warren in their book Theory of Literature have emphasized upon psychology as one important "cognitive value in the drama and novels" (33) and have referred to Horney's recommendation of Dostoevsky, Shakespeare, Ibsen and Balzac as its inexhaustible sources. Furthermore they write:

> There remains the question of 'psychology' in the works themselves. Characters in plays and novels are judged by us to be psychologically true. Situations are praised and plots accepted because of this same quality. Sometimes a psychological theory, held either consciously or dimly by an author, seems to fit a figure or situation. (91)

Considered in this light to quote Carl Jung: "art, like any other human activity deriving from psychic motives is a proper subject for psychology" (Campbell 301). The intangible qualities as evoked in literary and artistic creations provide valuable insight into human nature. The psycho-social perspective of a good personality theory provides a meaningful context within which human behaviour can be consistently described and interpreted. The personality theory interrogates what it means to be a human being, taking into cognizance a host of important features that constitute the "fabric of modern psychology" (Hjelle 8).

II

Hjelle and Ziegler observe that in the 1960s, humanistic psychology came as a "viable theoretical alternative" (364) to the most influential intellectual currents in psychology- psychoanalysis and behaviorism. Humanistic psychology is not a single organized theory/system but a converging point of a number of lines of schools of thought – called the "third force" psychology. Some of the fundamental concepts shared by the proponents of this group have deep roots in the history of western philosophical thinking. More specifically, humanistic psychology is heavily steeped in European existential philosophy and psychology as developed by Kierkegaard, Sartre, Camus, Binswanger, Boss and Frankl. The humanistic model2 is oriented toward human beings and their potentialities; it is not only concerned with characteristics we share in common with human beings but with the uniqueness of each individual; it posits strong emphasis on man's inherent capacity for responsible self-direction and personal growth, a natural inclination, an inner propensity towards self-actualization. At this point the humanistic model closes upon the existential model; in fact many humanistic psychologists are also referred as existentialists writes Coleman. Both models of psycho-social behaviour are unified by a central concern with the ultimate challenge of human existence: "to find sound values, to grow as a person and to build a meaningful and a socially constructive life" (Coleman 70). The existential and humanistic models of human behaviour (third force) take into account either the existential problems or the full potentialities of contemporary men and women. Their perspective is based on the assumption that the individual has the freedom to control his/her own behaviour and can reflect upon the problems, make choices and take positive action. The basic theme being to "find themselves." However, the existential model takes a less optimistic view of human beings and places more emphasis on the irrational tendencies in human nature and the difficulties inherent in self-fulfillment. It posits more faith in the inner experience of the individual rather than in modern science.

A basic theme of existentialism is that our *existence* is given, but what we make of it – our *essence* is upto us i.e. to live a meaningful and constructive life. This, however, engenders inner confusion, deep emotional and spiritual strain concerning the kind of person we should *be* and *become* and the way of life we should try to build for ourselves. Our essence is created by our choices, for our choices reflect the values on which we base our lives. As Sarte puts it "I am my choices" (Hjelle 365).

Clym Yeobright in *The Return of the Native*, is one such human being who is striving for increased self-definition in the reality of his own existence. His character/personality makes a fascinating read in context of the humanistic-existential perspective. Many of his personal traits and tendencies are a manifest of humanistic-existential subtleties of behaviour. They provide an understanding of his psyche as well as demand a more profound investigation and understanding of his personality – a study of will, inner strength, intellectual response and imaginative intensity. In light of this psychological perspective, he is seen as an individual striving to know how to live and to live the life he knows. He is as one who is at once in strife and harmony with existence. Clym's subjectivity affirms the relevance of the inwardness and the spatial interiority of the individual. As an individual/person he is involved in the business of life and trying to find his bearings in the darkness of human condition; striving to assure both himself and others of the worth of relationship and his own worth as a person. His dramatic persona serves as a window into the state of his psyche/self/being:

> Hardy's sharp sense of 'story' is as exploratory as Lawrence's probing of psychic conflict. Because both Hardy and Lawrence have an unusually heightened sense of life flow... (Gregor 293-94)

III

Critical opinion and attitude to Hardy's fiction has been mostly with regard to his tragic vision of life: a recognition of the hopeless plight of the characters as sensitive and emotionally vulnerable beings in an unconscious, indifferent and seemingly malignant universe. According to Miller Hardy's feelings about the indifferent force/ Immanent Will, at work in the lives of his people, are so intense that he seems to be "urging things to happen, weaving the web of circumstances, shaping things in patterns determined by its irresistible energy" (15). Thus the lasting impression is that man is not born free and is ushered into the world in a certain spot in space and time; that no man's situation is of his making or satisfies his desire (Miller 2). Against the malignity of universe, Hardy makes the "injured spirit" of man attempt vain efforts to escape. He measures his characters for their endurance, courage, honesty with which they suffer the capricious circumstances of their life and try to metamorphose their personal life/fate, observes Dusseau. But how little free is their free will. Each man in Hardy's view enjoys a paradoxical freedom: "His own power of willing is, as in Schopenhauer's System, only his embodiment of a tiny part of the vast energy of the Immanent Will," (Miller 21) which remains inimical to his efforts and desires.

The prevailing critical readings of Clym Yeobright's character and person present him as an "over spiritualized modern man", who has chosen the different way of self-denial and devotion to the good of others in opposition to his wife's "pagan self-assertion and passion." The two are almost figures in an "allegory of flesh and spirit", comments Leonard W. Deen (71). Clym with his superior mind and sensibility, ravaged by thought, "has strong suggestions of the prophet – who retires from a luxurious and self indulgent society in order to criticize and reform it" (Deem 61). He becomes the inevitable victim of a world whose worldliness he does not comprehend. John Paterson speaks of his theoretical and pious intelligence, his denial of life in light of Christian self-renunciation, whose allegedly advanced views are a thin disguise of the Christian Champion. His mother sees him as a visionary in disguise, to his wife's association of him with Apostle Paul (71). However, even then he is seen as eventually becoming an innocent victim of malignant fate:

> The real struggle or ironic discrepancy rather, is between hopes or dreams and immovable and incalculable circumstances which frustrate them. The discovery is usually the characters realization of the inevitability of frustration ... recognition of their hopeless plight at sensitive and emotionally vulnerable beings in ... seemingly malignant universe. (Deen 64)

Miller views Hardy's characters as "distinguished by the shallowness of their minds. They have no profound inner depths leading down to the 'buried self' or to God," (4) that even their coming to self-awareness does not lead them to a recognition of the intrinsic quality of the mind. However, Clym Yeobright's personality analysed in context of the humanistic and existential models is distinguished by his need and response to his inner space/interiority leading to his self/being. His mind is not only turned towards the outside world, asking as to why things are as they are but also reveals why his mind works in a particular fashion. Hardy describes Clym as a man to whom: "*My mind to me a Kingdom Is.*" His will is apparently under the control of his mind and that he can act freely rather than being pushed by external energies.

My concern in the course of this study is less to delineate the character of Clym in general terms than to present/identify him as a literary presentation and manifestation of the psycho-social view of the humanistic and existential models of behaviour positing a belief in the strength of rationality and freedom of choice in human behaviour. These particulars show that the cause of tragedy may lie very much within. Thus the freedom to shape our *essence* can be both - a blessing as well as a curse. Arnold Kettle speaks of Hardy's recognition of a very strong element of determinism in human existence: "that he gives his books too rigid a pattern and takes a certain perverse pleasure in turning the screws of coincidence or fatality to do down the aspirations of his characters" (461) yet he finds "his people are not wholly free: but they are free enough to make irreparable mistakes or to struggle to make their lives whole and united, at one with the external world; free enough in short to be human beings" (462).

IV

It is imperative to examine the characteristics of the humanistic-existential approach that identify with the person/behaviour of Clym. A central theme in the existential model, explains Coleman, is the will-to meaning i.e. primarily a matter of finding satisfying values and guiding one's life by them, learning to live constructively with themselves and others. It places a strong emphasis on our obligations to each other– what we can contribute to life; a commitment and fulfillment involving social constructive values and choices (Clym's educational programme for his native Egdon). Furthermore, the existential encounter with non-being (nothingness) i.e. death– the inescapable fate of human beings leads to existential anxiety; a deep concern for living a meaningful life. The individual is assumed to be capable of rational and responsible choices because existential philosophy believes each person to be responsible for his/her actions. It appeals to humanistic psychology that each individual is the chief determinant of his behaviour and experience- deciding and freely choosing his/her actions. As Sartre comments, "I am my choices" (Coleman 70-71).

In positing the concept of self as a unifying force, the humanistic model emphasizes the importance of individuality i.e. the individual's consistent self-perception and beliefs about himself. It consists of all the ideas and values of "what I am" and "what I can do." Self-actualization becomes a single force of life. Thus meta-motivated they are devoted to working for self-improvement and perfection; to enrich living by enlarging experiences and thus increase the joy of being alive. According to Abraham Maslow's hierarchical theory of motivation that when lower order (physiological and safety) needs are satisfied, the individual becomes motivated by higher needs *metaneeds/growth motives* (Hjelle 368-73).

The individual's knowledge of his/her self-worth, capability of mastering tasks and responsibilities is attended by feelings of confidence, competence, personal strength, freedom and achievement. As well as the need to win esteem from others - attention, acceptance, and appreciation. Maslow the noted personologist, explains that the "motivational life of self-actualizers is not only quantitatively different but also qualitatively different from non-self-actualizers"(Hjelle 376). Whereas ordinary people are motivated by basic need gratifications, self-actualizing people strive to grow to perfection and to develop more truly in their own style. They are "beyond determinism and homeostatis"(Hjelle 376).

The most important concept that the existential psychologists have extracted from existentialism is that of *becoming* – the need to become everything one is capable of becoming; the responsibility of realizing as many of his/her potentialities as possible; and by actualizing them to live a truly authentic life (Hjelle 365). In *The*

Return of the Native, what we perceive in the person of Clym is the quest for becoming. In the existentialist view the quest for an authentic existence.

Maslow believes that creative people have pursued the development of their life's goals despite serious hardships; that their values and ideals are so strong that they are willing to suffer rather than renounce them. Any perceived threat to the *self* is followed by the narrowing and rigidification of perception and behaviour as is the case of Clym Yeobright. There is a strong sense of values which guides his choices to achieve a fulfilling way of life. Involved in the business of living, he tries to find his bearings and give meaning to his existence, striving to live the life he knows – to become a real person, an authentic human-being. The significance he gives to his own life, is through the realization of personal freedom (choice), through passionate commitment, through responsibility and the integrity of recognizing that responsibility. "It must therefore be in every man's power to become what he is – an individual" said Kierkegaard (121). According to him it is this glorification and maximization of striving which gives meaning to life.

A reading of *The Return of the Native*, leaves us with a vivid impression of Clym – the man himself. We feel the direct impress of his personality as we go through the novel – his overwhelming personal urgency of aspirations, desires, conflict, dilemma, despair and anxiety.

Clym though prosperous in life, rejects the glamour and false attraction of Paris to return to his native heath in a "mood of Tolstoyan simplicity" (Gregor 297) to become "a school master to the poor and ignorant – to teach them what nobody else will" (177). Paterson views his theoretical and pious intelligence in contrast to the practical and instinctive intelligence (71) of the rustics: "in a few weeks he'll learn to see things otherwise… he had better mind his business" (173). However, Clym's business only drives him further into illusion. In Eustacia Vye, he sees a companion to further his educational schemes for improving the lot of his neighbours (unmindful of Eustacia's plans for herself). "Their marriage is rash from the start, as they see each other not so much as persons, but as opportunities for realizing their dreams" (Gregor 297). His temporary blindness/ weak eye-sight forces him to abandon his reading to take up furze-cutting; and eventually with eyesight restored albeit weak he revises his scholastic plans to become an itinerant preacher. Clym fails to see things as they are. The tragedy of his life lies in the incongruity of his desires – the vision of educational pioneering – a pursuit of illusions:

> Yeobright loved his kind. He had a conviction that the want of most men was knowledge of a sort which brings wisdom rather than affluence. He wished to raise the class at the expense of the individuals rather than individuals at the expense of the class. What was more he was ready to be the first unit sacrificed. (174)

Hardy writes that in "Clym Yeobright's face could be dimly seen the typical countenance of the future" (169). It arrested the interest of an observer "as a page, not by what it was, but by what it recorded." He had, been "a lad of whom something was expected" that "he would not stand still in the circumstances amid which he was born"; of whom the neigbhouring yeomen would ask, "Clym Yeobright: what is he doing now?" As Timothy Fairway expressed it on his (Clym) extended stay in Egdon "He's got some project in's head – depend upon that" (169-72). Clym, as a boy had been seen interwoven with the heath, that no one could look upon Egdon without thinking of him. He was the product of the heath, "permeated with its scenes, with its substance and with its odour"(175). His estimate of life was covered by it. His fame had spread before he left home – that he had the potential to do something. As he grew up, he was helped out in life by a neighbouring gentleman who had undertaken to give him a start. This had set him on the road to Paris where he remained till he returned home to make a new beginning. His conviction that the need of mankind was knowledge could have owed to his studious life in Paris – the "nerve centre of all the ethical systems" popular at the time (174).

Hardy has devoted two chapters (II & III/Book3) to interrogate the efficacy and possible success of Clym's plan for his native people the "Egdon eremites". He writes, "Successful propagandists have succeeded because the doctrine they bring into form is that which their listeners have for sometime felt without being able to shape" (174-75). He further describes Clym as John the Baptist (174) who took ennoblement for his text; a man ahead of his time, whose "vaward in aspirations is fatal to fame" (174). Thus, Hardy asks the question:

> Was Yeobright's mind well proportioned? No, A well proportioned mind is one which shows no particular bias; one of which we may safely say that it will never cause its owner to be confined as a madman, tortured as a heretic, or crucified as a blasphemer. Also on the other hand, that it will never cause him to be applauded as a prophet, revered as a priest or exalted as a king… It never would have allowed Yeobright to do such a ridiculous thing as throw up his business to benefit his fellow creatures. (175)

Clym came back to Egdon, to carve out his destiny; fashion his essence (what one is) from the fact of existence (that one is). When he had left Egdon, he thought of the place and its life as contemptible and very depressing only to realize later that he hated the "flashy business" of "selling trinkets to women and fops and pandering to the meanest vanities" (177), when he had health and strength to do anything. Revealing his plans for the future to the peasant community he speaks thus:

> I have come home because, all things considered I can be a trifle less useless here than anywhere else. But I have lately found this out … That my business was the silliest, flimsiest, most effeminate business that ever a man could be put up to. That decided me: I would give it up and try to follow some rational occupation among the people I know best, and to whom could be of most use. I have come home; and this is how I mean to carry out my plan. I shall keep a school as near

> as Egdon as possible, so as to be able to walk over here, have a night-school in my mother's house. But I must study a little at first, to get properly qualified. (172)

Thus the native returns home to give meaning to his existence, and to live a truly authentic life. His mother's pained exclamation that his new course of life was nothing but a dream and would be his "ruin", he explains with philosophic calm:

> "But I shall not do better in the way you mean. I suppose it will be called doing worse. But... I want to do some worthy thing before I die. As a school master I think to do it. A school master to the poor and ignorant, to teach them what nobody else will." (176-77)

Despite his love and devotion to his mother, her opposition to his plans of teaching and marrying Eustacia, is perceived as a threat to his *self* and makes him more rigid: "at my age I am old enough to know what is best for me" that "I have never yet supported what is bad" and "I do not care only for her [Eustacia], I care for you and for myself, and for anything that is good" (205). Exercising his freedom to choose, Clym had made his choice in ways consistent with his self-concept and view of the world. His own *ideal-self* so overwhelms him that he fails to acknowledge the reality of the situation facing him. He is metaphorically blinded by the worthiness of his purpose in life. Conscious reality is pushed aside by his pride in his own thoughts and ideas. Thus, the freedom to shape his *essence* becomes "both a blessing as well as a curse" for Clym. For the "freedom to choose does not ensure that all the choices will be wise ones" (Hjelle 365).

Motivated by the nobility of his ideals, his vision for the happiness and growth of humanity is attended by feelings of *self-esteem* and *self-worth.* Maslow asserts that "the growth motive demands a constant willingness to take risks, to make mistakes, to break old habits furthermore the realization of one's full potential required an openness to novel ideas and experiences" (Hjelle 375). So strong is his commitment towards realizing them to make *actual* his potential (growth motives/metaneeds) and reach self-fulfillment that he becomes reckless to the needs of his mother (Mrs. Yeobright) and wife (Eustacia) – whom he loved so dearly. Mrs. Yeobright in her conversation with Thomasin speaks of his behaviour thus:

> "How can he bear to grieve me so, when I have lived only for him through all these years?"
>
> ...
>
> "It is not a passionate quarrel that would have broken my heart. It is the steady opposition and persistence in going wrong that he has shown. O Thomasin, he was so good when he was a little boy- so tender and kind." (214)

Thus this process of *self-actualization/becoming* is strewn with difficulties and obstacles especially hampered by the expectations of both his mother and wife. It eventually leads their lives to a tragic end. The bitterness that seeps in the relationship with his mother and wife is countered by Clym's perception of the worthiness of his purpose and acts as a refuge for him.

Confronted by the bitterness of her position and unpleasant circumstances of life, Eustacia implores Clym to improve it. She questions him on her right as a wife, "a sharer of his doom" to have a voice in the matter. "Yes, take me to Paris, and go on with your old occupation Clym. I don't mind how humbly we live there at first, if it can only be Paris and not Egdon Heath" (249). This unexpected mine of hope in Eustacia, disconcerts Clym but his intention remains unshaken though he loved her. Sure, that he had never led her to such an expectation, he dismisses her remark and resolves to "chain himself more closely than ever to his books" so as to enable "substantial results from another course in arguing against her whim" (249). He was ready to sacrifice every "unit" that came in the way of reaching his ideal - scholastic plans. The severe strain on his eyes results in a semi-state of blindness, affording him sight enough to walk about without straining upon any definite object.

Though grave at the intelligence of his affliction, he does not allow it to master his spirit- that he was not blind was blessing enough. Thus with quiet firmness he prepares himself to face his adverse circumstances. An "absolute stoic in the face of mishaps" he looked for satisfaction in the humblest walk of life that "could be made to work in with some form of his culture scheme" (252). To keep a cottage night-school was one such possibility. And till that could be done he was ready to get a living by becoming a furze-cutter. His daily life was reduced to a "microscopic sort" – "his whole world being limited to a circuit of a few feet from his person" (253). But in the wake of his adverse circumstances, the spirit of perseverance, endurance and goodliness of temperament comes to the forefront to help him face his troubles with equanimity. Though cheerfully disposed to his lot, he is depressed by thoughts of his mother's estrangement and Eustacia's unhappiness.

The occupation of furze-cutting appears to Clym as an honest and honourable mode of living till the time he could resume his earlier scholastic plans. Unambitious in the worldly sense, his conscience does not permit him to remain idle and unoccupied. It becomes bitterly plain to Eustacia that loss of social standing and the low class work of furze-cutting did not matter to him. This mood and condition of her husband has a "blasting effect" upon the proud and fair Eustacia; her future blighted and chances in life mired by the adamancy of her husband (in following his ideas) she cries out in despair:

> " Well you follow your own ideas and won't give in to mine when I wish you to leave of this shameful labour. Is there anything you dislike in me that you act so contrarily to my wishes? I am your wife, and will you not listen?"
>
> ...
>
> "I deserve pity as much as you... I think I deserve more ... Even had you felt careless about your affliction you might have refrained from singing out of sheer pity for mine. God, if I were a man in such a position I would curse rather than sing." (255-257)

This angry outburst of Eustacia elicits a response from Clym that captures the very soul of his nature and personality:

> "Now don't you suppose, my inexperienced girl that I cannot rebel in high Promethean fashion against the gods and fate as well as you? I have felt more steam and smoke of that sort than you have ever heard of. But the more I see of life the more do I perceive that there is nothing particularly great in its greatest walks, and therefore nothing particularly small in mine of furze-cutting. If I feel that the greatest blessings vouchsafed to us are not very valuable, how can I feel it to be any great hardship when they are taken away?..." (257)

Clym's measure of life is guided by his simplistic norms, which come in conflict with his mother's hope for him and his wife's romantic desire for "music, poetry and passion" (285) from life. His pleasure principle is to be found in simple living- "for him Egdon was a place where he could live and die in a hermitage, with proper work to do" (200). The rustics realize him to be a "real perusing man, with the strangest notions about things"(106). Despite her unhappiness and disenchantment with Clym, Eustacia too realized his gift for contentment. She tries to explain his nature to Wildeve thus:

> "That's because you don't know him. He's an enthusiast about ideas and careless about outward things. He often reminds me of the apostle Paul."
>
> . . .
>
> "but the worst of it is that though Paul was excellent as a man in the Bible he would hardly have done in real life." (284)

Mrs. Yeobright who had hoped to see her son rise and succeed like other men into something higher in life, is pained by his notion of "doing well" by being a "poor man's school master." Clym realized that "from every provident point of view his mother was undoubtedly right," yet he is unable to reconcile his idea "of comparative poverty" with her hope of an "essentially the higher course for him" (190). Aware of his *self-worth/self-concept* he tries to convince her that he was different from other men/people thus:

> "Why can't you do it as well as others?"
>
> "I don't know-except that there are many things other people care for which I don't. And that's partly why I think I ought to do this. For one thing, my body does not require much of me – I cannot enjoy delicacies; good things are wasted upon me. Well, I ought to turn that defect to advantage, and by being able to do without what other people require, I can spend what such things cost upon anybody else." (177-178)

In the process of his *self-actualization*, Clym is challenged with the task of healing the breach between him and his mother as well as take care of Eustacia's happiness. Hopeful of revoking his mother's trust in him by reconciling her to his new scheme, he is confronted with the news of her death. At that moment the breach between them is forgotten by him "the present joined continuously with that friendly past" (295). Johnny Nunsuch's disclosure of the bitter last words uttered by Mrs. Yeobright of being "a broken hearted woman and cast off by her son" (306) drives him to a pitch of maddening grief. Unable to come to terms with his sense of guilt, which was no less than a sin for him, he expends his grief in words of self loathing and condemnation. What a return he had made for all her sacrifices, he thought. "I cannot help feeling that I did my best to kill her" that "I never went to her. When I set out to visit her it was too late (312-13)". With passage of time his grief gets mitigated by wearing itself out and he devotes himself to preserve all things that belonged to his mother. However, the later revelation that his mother just before her death had visited his home but the door was not opened by his wife drives him into a murderous rage. He speaks cruel words to Eustacia which drives her to leave his house and eventually to meet a tragic end. Fevered by thoughts of guilt, Clym writhes in remorse, "She is the second woman I have killed this year. I was a great cause of my mother's death; and I am the chief cause of hers" (381).

He frequently walked the heath to mitigate his sorrow. That he had been ill used by fortune he did not maintain for long; neither did he invent excuses to defend himself as is usually the case with human beings. A man with meager wants and austere habits, the house and the hundred and twenty pounds he had inherited from his mother were enough for his worldly needs. He found relief in a direction of his own choosing. He had but three activities alive in him: to visit daily his mother's grave and the distant enclosure where Eustacia was buried, the third was the self-preparation for a vocation of an itinerant preacher (398) which seemed to satisfy his *self- worth and ideal* in context of the altered circumstances of his life. His eyesight having improved considerably, he weighed and tested his earlier convictions and saw no reason to change them but to lessen his educational plans – to open a night school and become a preacher, in keeping with his capabilities: "Yet he did not repine: there was still more than enough of a unambitious sort to tax all his energies, and occupy all his hours" (407-08). Though his "bodily features were marked with decay" and his face "pensive and lined", but the tones of his voice were "rich, musical and stirring" (411). Hardy concludes that, "Yeobright had, in fact, found his vocation in the career of an open- air preacher and lecturer on morally unimpeachable subjects" (412).

Hardy's delineation of Clym's personality gives the reader a minutiae of his temperament. The fixity of his motives comes in conflict with the expectations and hopes of both his mother and wife. Clym's decision to remain at Egdon, to become a school master, a furze-cutter, and finally an itinerant preacher to the end of his days is conterminous with his *self-image*. But the novelist's presentation of his character is such that Eustacia's reaction to it as boorishness and self-absorption (Gregor 299) or of Mrs. Yeobright as defiance and obstinacy becomes understandable as well. At the end of the novel we find him able to alleviate and reach an understanding with his *self*. Thus, fostering a clear cut sense of self-identity and opening pathways to a more meaningful existence. We come to realize that "the locus of valuing" is to be found within each individual as emphasized by Coleman (70). The problems of choice and responsibility often become an agonizing burden – a lonely and difficult matter which can engender inner confusion, deep emotional and spiritual strain concerning the kind of person one *is* and should *become* and the way of life one should try to build for oneself. Thus, the freedom to shape our *essence* is "both our agony and our glory" (71).

NOTES

1. This paper is based on the humanistic and existential model/ theory of behaviour. See Coleman and Hjelle. For this purpose their explanation/discussion has become a point of reference throughout this study.
2. The term model is a conceptual tool that can help to organize and interpret data. The psychosocial models e.g. humanistic and existential models represent more of a perspective or a point of view. Although these models are commonly referred to as theories, the concept of models seems more appropriate in view of the need for maintaining flexibility in our thinking about human behaviour. See Coleman.

WORKS CITED

Cecil, David. "Hardy the Novelist: A Reconsideration." Clarke, 454-62.

Clarke, Graham, ed. *Thomas Hardy: Critical Assessments*. Vol. IV. Cornwall: Helm Information, 1993. Print.

Coleman, James C., *Abnormal Psychology and Modern Life*: 5th ed. Glenview: Scott, Foresman, 1976. Print.

Deen, Leonard W., "Heroism and Pathos in The Return of the Native." Clarke, 56-65.

Dusseau, John L., "Three Hardy Flowers." *Thomas Hardy: A Critical Study*. Eds. Robert Hudson and Edwin Arnold. New Delhi: Anmol, 2005. 168-84. Print.

Gregor, Ian, "What kind of Fiction did Hardy Write?" *Essays in Criticism*. XVI. 2 (2008): 290-308. Print.

Hardy, Thomas. *The Return of the Native.* New Delhi: Peacock, 1994. Print.

Hjelle, Larry A., and Daniel J. Ziegler. *Personality Theories: Basic Assumptions, Research and Applications.* 2nd ed. Auckland: Mc Graw Hill, 1987. Print.

Kettle, Arnold. "Hardy the Novelist: A Reconsideration." Clarke, 454-62.

Kierkegaard, S. *The Point of View.* Trans. Walter Lowrice. London: Oxford UP, 1939. Print.

Miller, J Hillis. *Thomas Hardy: Distance and Desire.* Cambridge: Belknap-Harvard UP, 1970. Print.

Paterson, John. "Introduction to The Return of the Native." Clarke, 66-72.

Welleck, Rene and Austin Warren. *Theory of Literature.* Harmondsworth: Penguin, 1973. Print.

8

Nathaniel Hawthorne's *The House of Seven Gables*: A Discourse of History and Culture

Rubina Iqbal

The House of Seven Gables [1851] is a historical document of a transitional phase in the middle of the 19thcentury America. It captures the social and political upheaval in New England after the revolution. Apparently, it seems to be a tale of a glorious past and an inherited curse of an aristocratic Pyncheon family of New England and as the author writes, "the wrong- doing of one generation lives into the successive ones, and, divesting itself of every temporary advantage" (preface to *The House of Seven Gables*). But the tale originates in the history of the Puritans of Massachusetts Bay Colony in the 17th century and it has an influential bearing on the 19th century democratic America.

This novel is an important social and political discourse, which registers its cultural presence among other discourses of the 19thcentury. It seems attuned to contemporary America of Hawthorne's time, and makes significant use of gender conflict, decline of nobility and emergence of democratic ideology, mesmerism, and the growing power of individualism. It also provides the author with an opportunity to salvage his political commitments as well. Hawthorne's personal commitments and democratic credo has shaped this text and helps to disseminate the same ideology through this discourse.

The House of Seven Gables attempts to juxtapose the 17th century feudal culture with the19th century classless society in America. Hawthorne has deliberately etched a contrast between aristocratic

Pyncheon family of New England and the principles of the rising democracy in the text. The democratic principles are projected through the characters of Holgrave, uncle Veneer, and Phoebe. They reflect the tension and acceptance of the altered ideologies. Andrew Jackson's election as the president of America shifted the focus from the nobility to a decentralized governance and equality of opportunity based on individual merit. All these issues have been reemphasized through fictional projection of the characters and their destiny in *The House of Seven Gables.*

> As the people of the colonies became more numerous and more prosperous, they began to acquire a new outlook. Belief in the need for hereditary class distinctions and for authoritarian government became weaker, and men began to acquire faith in the capacity of the average man and in his right to freedom and economic opportunity. This growth of democratic sentiments was strongest in the newly settled regions of the back country. Along the eastern seaboard, on the other hand, traditional European attitudes were more deeply rooted, and wealthy families continued to defend aristocratic principles. The resultant conflict between the new spirit of democracy and the traditional belief in aristocracy was one of the main factors in American political development both before and after the revolution. (Parkes 58)

In 19th century America, issues of common men were gaining momentum while the aggrandizement of Plebeian classes had swept away the societal paradigm of hierarchy. Hawthorne did not fail to notice the torrent of change in the new democratic regime with political processions and public manoeuvring to entice the commoner in the wake of the upcoming election of governorship. Hawthorne called the country "republican" and pointed out at the transitional phase of time by referring to the "fluctuating waves of our social life". The American Revolution was decisive both for American political development and its social evolution. Nelson

Manfred Blake wrote about this time:

> . . . Socially the revolution weakened the old aristocracy and laid the basis for readjustment of classes. Thousands of the gentry fled the country; those who remained were forced to share prestige with new men, thrust up in the social upheaval. Landholding was disrupted by confiscations and new laws of inherit
>
> -tance . . . New opportunities were opened for the merchants and speculators.
>
> Artisan and journeymen became discontented with their traditional status. Old institutions and modes of thoughts were widely challenged. (124)

The central character of the novel Hepzibah Pyncheon belongs to an aristocratic lineage. She is a symbol of hollowed and fallen gentility whose character is grounded in the pre -revolutionary ideals of English aristocracy. Her life is circumscribed by a code of decorum, a sense of decency and propriety which is governed by an aristocratic ideology. She lives alone in an ancient but grand mansion, the house of the seven gables which represents past values and traditions which are facing serious threat in the new social infrastructure. The proper maintenance of this house is beyond her impoverished means still she looks after the house as she sees her role as the guardian of this house, and a repository of Pyncheon family's lore and tradition. Her preoccupation with the past forces her to live at the margins of Salem's social life.

Hepzibah is a convincing portrait of a genteel poor, who is too aristocratic to go into trade and too proud to accept the acts of charity. In spite of her isolation and poverty, she is rigidly conscious of her pedigree and avoids confrontation with modern world. The displacement of the feudal civilization has led to compulsive readjustment in the community; hence, it becomes obligatory for Hebzibah to face reality. With the arrival of her only brother Clifford from the prison, she is forced to earn her bread. In an unprecedented move to support herself and her brother, she opens a cent shop in the family mansion. It is a turning point in the history of the nobility when a patrician lady is transformed into a plebeian woman to meet the challenges of the new times. This move is hailed by her tenant, the new man Holgrave:

> I look upon this as one of the fortunate days of your life. It ends an epoch, and begins one. Hitherto, the life-blood has been gradually chilling in your veins, as you sat aloof, within your circle of gentility, while the rest of the world was fighting out its battle with one kind of necessity or another. Henceforth, you will at least have the sense of healthy and natural effort for a purpose, and of lending your strength-be it great or small-to the united struggle of mankind. This is success –all the success that anybody meets with! (HSG 43-44)

Hepzibah's neighbour Uncle Veneer's character is also governed by a realistic ideology of that time who encapsulates the social transformation from monarchy to republicanism in these words, "those old gentlemen that grew up before the Revolution used to put on grand airs. . . . Now –a-days, a man would not dare to be called king, if he feels himself a little above common folks, he only stoops so much the lower to them" (HSG 57). Hepzibah's business transaction furnishes her with an opportunity to surrender her condescending approach to commonalty. But the raging battle in her heart and soul at this new move and her nervousness at the shop counter communicates her failure to grasp the lessons of the egalitarian community. She longs desperately to die and to be buried in the family tomb with her ancestors as she finds the world, "too chill and hard,-"(43).

She retains her old stateliness and craves for the special treatment like a "lady". She recoils from expressions of sympathy and says wistfully, "I was born a lady, and have always lived one –no matter in what narrowness of means, always a lady!"(HSG 44) There are various instances of her so called generosity or rather social snobbery scattered all over the novel. She sells biscuits to her tenant Holgrave but refuses to take money. Her aristocratic upbringing does not allow her to accept money from a friend for providing him with food. She desperately desires to clutch on to her old status, "Let me be a lady little longer" (HSG 44).

She refuses to take money from a child who buys "Jim crow" [ginger bread] from her shop. Her consciousness of her superior lineage is a hurdle in a successful business transaction. Like a selfish individual, she zealously safeguards the interest of her family and denies new trends and mores. Her old gentility is, "contumaciously squeamish at sight of the copper coin..." (HSG 48). Her lady-like sensibilities are seriously infringed upon by the familiar tone of people who address her as their equal or even inferior. She repudiates the sentiments of democracy through her inward dislike of those people by whose penny she hopes to sustain herself. She unconsciously flatters herself with the idea - that there would be a gleam or a halo of some kind about her person - which will insure an obeisance to her sterling gentility.

She feels miserable that her commercial transaction, which is such a breathless episode in the history of Pyncheon nobility, is merely another insignificant episode in the life of a common man in New England. The comments of the two men from the labor class, Dixey and his friend represent the attitude of the community towards her fall. They find her "sour tempered" hence, incapable of succeeding in that "overdone" business. They find nothing remarkably singular in her fate amid the clarion call for an alternative regime, ". . . we might point to several little shops of a similar description; some of them in houses as ancient as that of the seven gables; and one or two, it may be, where a decayed gentlewoman stands behind the counter, as grim an image of family pride as Miss Hepzibah Pyncheon herself" (HSG 40).

Hawthorne displays his sympathies for Hepzibah's predicament by exploringherconcept of gentility, "A lady who had fed herself from childhood with the shadowy food of aristocratic reminiscences and whose religion it was that a lady's hand soils itself irremediably by doing aught for its bread-this born lady,... "(HSG 38). She desires to keep her hand "white and delicate" amid Laissez-faire economic philosophy. This philosophy envisioned an egalitarian society and focused upon the general well-being of every individual. The novel suggests the recognition of economical and historical progress as democratic principles advanced and aristocratic lineage declined. Common man was no longer under the influence of hereditary name and wealth.

> The revolution in short, had given the American people an independent place in the family of nations. It had given them a changed social order, in which hereditary wealth and privilege counted for less, and human equality for more; in which the standards of culture and manners were temporarily lowered, but those of equality were raised. (Nevins, Commager 111)

Hepzibah is clueless with regard to the "new notions" and nor does she wish to comprehend them. Many 19th century genteel practices reflected an aspiration towards a life of leisure and luxury which were enjoyed by the English aristocracy. These fallen aristocratic families in America had a tendency to copy, "the beliefs and way of life of English gentry" (Parkes 61). In New England, where family name and history had strongly influenced one's place in the social fabric and one's sense of pride, it was difficult for Hepzibah to abandon those ideals.She belongs to the upper class whose superior position was fixed by law and custom in the colonial time. "Early colonial laws forbade any but upper class men to wear silver buttons and any but upper class women and daughters to wear silk dresses"(Bragdon 23).

She still wears a black silk gown. She is full of pride for being the proprietor of old and invaluable china cups which are as ancient as the custom of tea-drinking itself. They belonged to her great, great, great grandmother, who was a Davenport of a good family. She flaunts her old silver crested tea-spoons, and antique china tea –set to drink tea when her cousin Phoebe arrives at her place. By these possessions, she is flattering herself with ideas of gentility and tells Phoebe with pride, "they were almost the first tea-cups ever seen in the colony" (HSG 68).

Even after starting her trade, she still cherishes an idea that some trick of fortune will intervene in her favour as a rich uncle will suddenly declare her as his heiress or the great claim to the heritage of Waldo County may finally be decided in favour of Pyncheon. These fantasies of miraculous rescue from her fallen fate mark the unreality of her existence. "The Eastern Land Claim, occupying central importance in the plot of Seven Gables, translates the Hawthornes' never realized right to nine thousand acres in Maine deeded to their ancestor, in 1666, by an Indian Sagamore" (Warren 89).Young reformer Holgrave confronts her with the unreality of her fabricated existence, "These names of gentleman and lady had a meaning, in the past history of the world, and conferred privileges, . . . In the present –and still more in the future condition of society-they imply, not privilege, but restriction!"(HSG 44).

Her aristocratic arrogance is a sin against new paradigms of political thoughts and new form of government. In this transitional phase, plain people had started taking more active interest in politics and insisted, " that leadership and office holding should no longer be restricted to the wealthier and well educated classes"(Parkes 237). The forces of egalitarian society had worked incessantly which gave rise to trading, manufacturing, and a host of other opportunities for the middle class to rise in the world. Hawthorne retained a working class perspective through various means, "He ignored the more aristocratic society of Salem in favor of limited companionship with the less literate but perhaps wiser citizens, especially one William pike, a carpenter"(Cowie 330). He was not politically but by conviction a democrat.

Andrew Jackson's victory as the president of the United States in 1828 was instrumental in bringing change in the community. He was a natural –born leader and a self-made man. He was orphaned at the age of thirteen and was without the advantage of wealth and education enjoyed by the earlier presidents. Since his presidency roughly coincided with the various democratic reforms such as manhood suffrage; his election became a symbol of the growing power of the common men in politics. Jackson favoured egalitarian principles and declared that everyman was a king in theory. It was the time when the common men took in their own hands the nomination of the state-officials and election of the judges. It was a privilege which was earlier exercised by the members of the legislature and governors respectively. It revealed an aggressive and self- assertive spirit of common men who had suddenly awaken to a consciousness of their rights and their strength for mobilizing political and social infrastructure. At the time of revolution, American political leaders held the democratic contact theory of the government. According to this theory, all political authority or sovereignty belonged to the ordinary men. It emphasized that the Commonalty had the right to elect government of their choice, to select their officers, to carry on the government, and to determine what power their officers should exercise. Hawthorne was a Jacksonian democrat and a lifelong admirer of Andrew Jackson. His experience in England made him realize the values of egalitarian ideology more forcefully. His friends Horatio Bridge, Jonathan Cilley and, Franklin Pierce were all Democrats. The father of American constitution, Thomas Jefferson stated the theory of equality and freedom in his "Declaration of Independence" on 4th July 1776. He said:

> We hold these truths to be self-evident. That all men are created equal; that they are endowed by their creator with certain unalienable rights;. . . That, to secure these rights, governments are instituted among men, deriving their just powers from the consent of the governed; that, whenever any form of the government becomes destructive of these ends, it is the right of the people to alter or to abolish it, and to institute a new government, ...(Baker, Commager 975)

Thomas Jefferson like Adams believed that ". . .that there is a natural aristocracy among men .The grounds of this are virtue and talents . . . There is also an artificial aristocracy founded on wealth and birth, without either virtue or talents; . . .The natural aristocracy I consider as the most precious gift of nature for the instruction, the trusts, and government of society . . . The artificial aristocracy is a mischievous ingredient in government, and provision should be made to prevent its ascendancy alone" (bigeye.com).In Jacksonian era hereditary title and class distinction commanded no respect but individual merits were considered greatest asset in the eye of people. The concept of Bourgeoisie society was emerging. It was a clear sign of the growth of democracy and the end of feudalism that almost everyone belonged to the middle class.

Like Thoreau and Emerson, Hawthorne believed that it was the moral necessity for all human beings to establish an original relation to the universe. Thomas Jefferson and Thomas Paine reiterated that every generation should be allowed to set up its own laws and contracts, "Paine thought that to escape the infelicitous prejudices of the past it was necessary for men to think as though they were the first man who thought"(Hall 166).

Hawthorne juxtaposed Hephzibah's genteel helplessness against the demurely charming self- reliance of her niece Phoebe who is a native of rural New England. In chapter IV, "A Day behind the Counter", she emerges as a foil to her aristocratic legacy. She has come to live under Hepzibah's guardianship after her mother's second marriage. She appears to be spirited, active, and dynamic within her chosen domestic sphere. She is fresh and unconventional yet orderly and "obedient to common rules" (HSG 61). She knows how to earn her bread because she has "not been brought up a Pyncheon"(HSG66) but as ordinary girl. The antithesis between aristocracy and democracy comes to the surface when Hepzibah laments that Phoebe is an excellent shop keeper but not a lady. Hepzibah's initial responses to Phoebe are governed by the standards according to which she has lived in the past- establishing a formal distance between them.

Phoebe possesses plebeian capabilities and easily adjusts in the new circumstances. She can manage kitchen, run school and shop with equal dexterity. She is not conscious of her superior ancestry and believes in individual talent and worth. She proves herself a better shopkeeper and housekeeper than her elderly cousin. Even Hepzibah gradually acknowledges her ability as a shopkeeper and starts acknowledging her advice and suggestions to increase the influx of trade and gain profit, "without hazardous outlay of capital" (HSG 70).

Apart from bridging the gap between the labor class and gentility, Phoebe is a model of conformity without any discordant element in her personality. She can shock no canon of taste and is admirably in keeping with the ideals of conformist society, "it would be preferable to regard phoebe as the example of feminine grace and availability combined in a state of society, if there were any such, where ladies didn't exist"(HSG 71). Phoebe is a reservoir of cultural values and victim of adulation. She has internalized stereotypical forms of female behaviour and conducts herself as she is expected to. Amy Schrager Lang opines the same, and says that Phoebe exhibits, "all the virtues of middle class feminity" (37-38). Minrose Gwin observes, "since white women were victims of adulation rather than violence, they often internalized stereotypical forms and attempted in great earnestness to become what they were expected to be"(405). Phoebe's inner strength makes her fit for the type of role she has to play in the life of her lover Holgrave. She is governed by a set of values where woman's sense of self and her concepts of success are shaped in accordance with her ability to conform to societal expectations.

Young and energetic Holgrave is a citizen of New America without any hereditary possessions but lively intelligence to his credit, a protean in his capabilities. He is only twenty two year old but has already worked as country school master, salesman, editor, peddler, dentist, mesmerist, and daguerreotypist, not restricted him to a single craft. He is comfortable in a society that rewards men and value them for their professional skill and marketable strategies. After the revolution, the idea of self-sufficient and the self-made man of American mythology was born. It was known as an era of "American boundlessness". Ethos of manly striving was taking form in the culture at large which had been exemplified through the character of Holgrave who is willing to try his luck in any profession that promises reward. He is quite modern in his outlook and does not hesitate to make himself presentable as a commodity in the growing materialistic and competitive world. As a transcendentalist and reformer, he has spent some time in the community of Fourierists and his prophetic vision is full of promises for a better future.

Holgrave is inspired by the radical doctrine of individualism which is directed against the established order in the government, economics, and religion. His character projects the young New England liberal of 1850. Individual rights were foremost in constitutional thinking at that time. Holgrave internalizes and acts out the conflict men felt in the 19th century America between the aggressive, domineering ideology of Jacksonian democracy and heroism and comparatively selfless- ideal of Christian gentility. He desires to slough off the second hand arrangements of the defunct past and to work out a new relation to the world. It was a prime individual responsibility according to the best theories of democratic individualism and enlightenment, "Jefferson repeatedly declared himself a rebel against the past. He believed that each generation should be allowed to make laws to suit itself and should be free of the public debts incurred by its predecessors. If any act shall be hereafter passed to repeal the present or to narrow its operation, such act will be an infringement of natural rights" (Peterson 112-124). The failure to fulfil this responsibility was sinister to the intellect and the heart. It was the result of democracy which generated self-reliance.

Holgrave's works as political and social reformer are closely scrutinized by Hawthorne. The author was critical of any organized philanthropy as it narrowed down one's perception at the expense of broader human sympathies. Holgrave is radical in his outlook and asserts on the need to reform capitols, state-houses, court–houses, city- halls, and churches but is not allowed to use his energy for any philanthropic scheme. His energy is diverted within the periphery of conjugal bliss through his marriage with Phoebe.

Holgrave is an expert in mesmeric art. His temptation to overpower his lover Phoebe through mesmerism enabled the author to discuss mesmerism, the popular 19th century practice in psychology. Hawthorne was particularly interested to study it in the context of male-female relationship. Mesmerism trod closely on the heels of phrenology. Monsieur Poyen, a French Creole from one of the west India Islands had come to America [Boston] and introduced this new science to the American public. His lectures were succeeded by experiments and the publication of his successful cases. Mesmerism came to America in two waves. The first subsided almost before Hawthorne was born and left without making any noticeable influence. The second wave had begun in the mid-1830s, and reached in an ultra scientific phase with its merger in phrenology and phrenomagnetism in the early 1840s.

In both his novels *The Blithedale Romance* and *The House of Seven Gables*, Hawthorne borrowed heavily from mesmerism. Holgrave narrates the story of Alice to Phoebe which is linked to magnetic art and definitely in the negative light owing to Hawthorne's dislike for this nefarious art. Alice's father Gervayse Pyncheon was a greedy man like his ancestor Colonel Pyncheon. He sold his daughter to a carpenter in exchange of a document which was essential to establish his claim to a large territory at the eastward. The carpenter belonged to the Maule's ancestry. He was looking forward for an opportunity to take his revenge upon Pyncheon family. He came to know that the property on which the house of seven gables was erected was illegally snatched from his ancestors by Colonel Pyncheon through the abuse of his power. The carpenter put a proposal before Gervayse Pyncheon. He asked for the house of seven gables in exchange of the information about the territory. He insisted a meeting with his daughter Alice Pyncheon as that the information regarding the document can be obtained only " through the clear, crystal medium of a pure virgin intelligence, like that of fair Alice"(HSG 160). In his greed, Gervayse Pyncheon entered into this bargain which led to a mesmeric control of the carpenter over Alice.

The most common means of subjugating the will of the somnambulist was through the eyes of the mesmerist. When these mesmerists fastened on their eyes on their victims, they engaged them in a test of mental and spiritual power, the outcome of which was usually beyond the control of a helpless female. The carpenter asked Alice, ". . . to fix your [her] eyes on mine!"(HSG162). Alice complied with his command without any estimate of the power pitted against her. The carpenter converted her mind into a kind of telescopic medium through which he could obtain a glimpse into the spiritual world. "The mesmerist's power over the will of his somnambulist shocked and intrigued the public more than any of the mysterious feats of clairvoyance, telepathy, and psycho kinesis" (Taylor 54). When the carpenter waved his hand, she awoke from that trance and forgot all her visionary experiences as well as her real self. Thus afterwards, till the time of her death, she remained a bonded slave of the carpenter. It was not a fanciful idea which Hawthorne was entertaining here but it was based on his first-hand experience of this spiritual science as "Reports of insanity induced by magnetic and spiritualist experiments were common, especially after 1850 " (Taylor 59). The power of Maule was implicitly sexual because Alice lost her dignity and could never marry afterwards. Commager and Nevins wrote:

> Mesmerism vulgarly culminated in an exhibition of what was called, absurdly enough 'psychology' or 'biology' a process of hallucination by which a number of susceptible persons selected by a lecturer from his audience were made to believe and to do the most ridiculous things–to fancy they were swimming, or flying or drinking, at the will of the operator, and to dance, sing, declaim, and do many things they never thought of doing in their normal condition. (417)

The heyday of animal magnetism was 1840s, just before the publication of Hawthorne's *The House Seven Gables* and *The Blithedale Romance*. Matthew Maule mesmerized Alice Pyncheon to learn the location of a lost document and Westerwelt in *The Blithedale Romance* overpowered Priscilla to enhance his theatrical reputation. Dr. Robert H. Collyer was a well-known mesmerist in the 1840s. Collyer was busy in public lectures on phrenology, mesmerism, phrenomagnetism, and psychography throughout New England from 1839 to 1843. He was successfully engaged in Boston from May through July 1841 and moved to Salem in August. At that time, Hawthorne was at Brook farm, and might have seen Collyer on one of his visits to the city.

Hawthorne's great distrust for this radical branch of science is reflected in his letter to his fiancée Sophia Peabody who was interested in animal magnetism. In a letter to him, she expressed her desire to meet Mrs. Park who practiced it to get cure of her headache which had paralyzed her normal life. Hawthorne did not relish that idea and replied on 18, October, 1841:

> I am unwilling that a power should be exercised on thee, of which we know neither the origin nor consequence, and the phenomena of which seem rather calculated to bewilder us, than to teach us any truths about the present or future state of being . . . Supposing that this power arises from the transfusion of one spirit into another, it seems to me that the sacredness of an individual is violated by it; there would be an intrusion into thy holy of holiest – and the intruder would not be thy husband ! . . . And, sweetest, I really do not like the idea of being brought, through thy medium, into such an intimate relation with Mrs. Park! (Taylor 42-43)

He was highly critical of mesmerism and all its related branches in which a power was exercised over man to penetrate his deepest being. He was aware about the interest of Sophia's sister Elizabeth in mesmerism so he wrote to Sophia, "Thy sister Elizabeth would like nothing so much as to proclaim thy spiritual experiences, by sound of trumpet" (Taylor 44). Hawthorne equated it with unpardonable sin. He believed that the unpardonable sin might consist in a want of love and reverence for human soul; in consequence of which, the investigator pried into its dark depths, not with a hope or purpose of making it better, but from cold philosophical curiosity.

Hawthorne found in mesmerism the 19thcentury version of witchcraft. There were accusations of sexual immorality against the mesmerists. His uneasy fascination with the sexual implications of magnetic power was noticeable in *The Blithedale Romance*, "At the bidding of one of these wizards, the maiden, with her lover's kiss still burning on her lips, would turn from him with icy indifference; the newly made widow would dig up her buried heart out of her young husband's grave, before the sods had taken root upon it. . ." (556).

Hawthorne's mesmerists were men of strong intellect and ambition and his female characters like vaguely Alice suffered heavily in their bondage -especially in reputation, since a sexual threat was pervasively if vaguey attendant on this subjugation. Hawthorne stressed upon the seductive power of the mesmerist over his young female subjects and cited instances of the miraculous power of one human being over the will and passions of another; in so much that "settled grief was but a shadow beneath the influence of a man possessing this potency, and the strong love of years melted away like vapor" (B R 555-556).

This power of an individual to get control over other through mesmeric art was exercised more frequently during 1830s and 1840s. Hawthorne discovered a pervasive desire for the power behind the use of this science in the overwhelmingly materialistic society, "Modern psychology, it may wall endeavor to reduce these alleged necromancies within a system instead of rejecting them as altogether fabulous," writes Hawthorne of the theory that in the dream world the Maules ruled the Pyncheons. (Warren 95)

Holgrave's initial temptation was strong to seduce Phoebe through his mesmeric art but he resisted that because of his respect for women and their individuality. His integrity never allowed him to violate the inner most of a man and he carried his conscience in all circumstances. His love for Phoebe was his greatest strength and redeeming power.

Holgraveis, a successor of Maule ancestry, was involved in the witchcraft trial of 1691. Through this connection, Hawthorne found an opportunity to discuss about the social, religious, and political motives behind the persecution of the so called witches in the 17th century Boston. Holgrave's ancestor Matthew Maule is shown a victim of witchcraft delusion in which Phoebe's ancestor Colonel Pyncheon acted as a judge. Matthew Maule's name had historical association with the name of an important member of early Salem, Thomas Maule who left an indelible mark through his freeways on the history of the 17th century New England.

Maule was an outspoken Quaker who lived in Salem, Massachusetts during the trials of witchery. Through his writings, historical Maule vehemently attacked self –styled church and state elite for their intolerance and fanaticism in the execution of witches. He questioned the reliability of alleged confession of people, who were accused of being witches and doubted the validity of "Spectral evidence".

Maule brought forth his view regarding witchcraft trials in "Truth Maintained and Set Forth in 1695". He was tried for seditious libel because he accused the ministers of Salem for preaching lies and instructing in the doctrine of the devils. He was whipped for creating national upheaval at the time when even minute disregard for the authoritative opinion was regarded a sin. He was arrested but acquitted because evidence against him was insufficient. His acquittal was seen as the triumph of common man against coercive mandate of theocracy. He used his common sense against repressionists to prove him innocent. He objected against the arrogance of a theocracy that imposed its interpretation of God's will on everyone, within its reach (James Edward Maule).

More than a century later, Hawthorne used his name for his novel *The House of Seven Gables.* It was not so important whether the house of seven gables was actually the house of Thomas Maule or not; what mattered that the historical Maule of the 17th century was a commoner who became the conscience of the community during the witchcraft delusion. He was a severe critic of religious persecution and fought for the freedom of expression like fictional Maule's successor Holgraveis in the 19th century. Holgrave's ancestor Matthew Maule was hanged on the charges of witchery. It highlighted the underlying relation between the two figures -one fictional the other real. Hawthorne's forefather, John Hathorne was one of those magistrates who had presided over the trial. The novel gave Hawthorne a platform to indulge in speculation regarding the truth of his great grandfather who added a significant chapter to American history.

The land on which grand and antique mansion seven gables is constructed, belongs to Holgrave's ancestor Matthew Maule. This property was desirable in the eyes of a prominent man Colonel Pyncheon. He asserted a plausible claim to the ownership of this piece of land and a large tract of land adjacent to it on the strength of a grant from the legislature. Matthew Maule, though a commoner, was not ready to leave what he considered his right to hold. He refused to sell it. Colonel Pyncheon was a greedy man and he was not ready to give up easily what he desired to obtain. In the late 17th century, the sense of community was beginning to disappear and a well-off person's influence had greater hereditary weight in Salem than any other New England town in that time. The wealthy and powerful Colonel Pyncheon ruthlessly contrived to implicate Maule in a sin of religious heresy out of selfish motive and hanged him on charges of witchery. The historian Croce wrote, . . . history consists essentially in seeing the past through the eyes of the present and in the light of its problems, and the main work of the historian is not to record but to evaluate for if he does not evaluate how can he know what is worth recording? (Carr 21-22).

Like a historian, Hawthorne studied the event of the past from present perspective and found that the execution of Matthew Maule for the sin of witchcraft brought us a lesson from history that: "The influential classes, and those who take upon themselves to be people, are fully liable to all the passionate error that has ever characterized the maddest mob" (HSG 15).

After the death of Maule, Colonel followed his original design and built his house over that piece of land which originally belonged to the executed Maule. In the mid-17th century, theocratic rulers became merciless in the persecution of Quakes. The possession of too great power intoxicated their brain. Once the Puritan establishment was convinced that their rules of polity and conduct were according to biblical guideline; they rigorously followed their course in enforcing the law of conduct as they liked. In the process, "many very human motives played an important part in interpreting the law of God and personal likes and dislikes, hypocrisy, prejudice, and passion got badly mixed with the higher and more spiritual impulses that were actively at work purging the church of its error" (Andrews 430-431).

Colonel Pynchon did not act as a man of conscience and integrity in the trial of Maule. Even Matthew Maule could detect his selfish motive and cursed Colonel from the gallows that "God will give him blood to drink" (HSG 16). Hawthorne had read widely in the 17th century history and took information of that period from Cotton Mather's *Wonders of the Invisible World*. In this book, Mather recorded his eloquent belief in this phenomenon. In *Robert Calef's* More *Wonders of the Invisible World* [1700], which was published in reply to Cotton Mather's book, a record of the trial of Sarah Good had been given which was held on 30 June 1692. She was convicted for conversing with the devil. In her trial, one of the magistrates Noyes, urged her to confess her witchery:

"You are a witch, and you know you are!" to this the dying woman replied:

"You are a liar,-I am no more a witch than you are a wizard, and if you take away my life, God will give you blood to drink!" (Calef 209)

It is significant to relate the curse of Matthew Maule from the gallows to a curse inflicted upon Hawthorne's ancestor John Hathorne. He apparently found this idea in his own family annals. According to some historical documents, his witch hunting ancestor incurred a malediction from one of the victims a result the prosperity of the race faded away. John Erskine wrote about John Hathorne: "As a judge he presided at several witchcraft trials, and a curse was laid on him and his blood by one he condemned to die. During his life the family lost the title deed to the land in Maine where afterwards the town of Raymond grew up, and papers were recovered only when the claim had become valueless" (183). Hawthorne used both these incidents - inherited curse and a lost deed of land in the present tale.

II

In the 19th century, one of the successors of Colonel Pyncheon is Jaffrey Pyncheon who appears to be an atavism of his ancestor in his brutality, avariciousness, and lack of compunction for the weaker section. He is a politician who uses common men as tools to realize his ambition in the equilateral society. His contemporaneity provides Hawthorne with a context to indulge in speculation regarding professional politicians in the 19th century America. A discourse of history is constituted by multiple consciousnesses hence; it can mean different things to different readers. This novel provides a plurality of perspectives through different characters and different time periods. Apart from past associations, present becomes vocal in the delineation of a shrewd- political figure of the 19th century America.

Jaffrey Pyncheon is a cousin of Hepzibah and Clifford Pyncheon. Hawthorne's dislike for the professional politician after his unfortunate experience at Salem custom house underlines Jaffrey's character in negative light. In sketching out the hypocritical character of judge with his calculated smile and purposeful charities; his gradual rise to public eminence, his political ambition of becoming the governor of Massachusetts; Hawthorne was taking revenge upon his political opponents: Daniel Webster, Charles Wentworth Upham, and Horace Conolly; and borrowed heavily from their characters. Jaffrey appears to be a composite creature, having grey shades of all these political personages.

Judge Pyncheon is model civil servant whose zeal for public services is a façade. He is a man of eminent respectability and is acknowledged by church and the state. Except for daguerreotypist, Hepzibah, and his few political opponents, nobody doubts his sincerity in doing public good. He is consciously working out on his public image to project himself as an ideal candidate in public eye for the upcoming election for governorship. In this election, he depends on popular opinion for his success. The purity of his character as judge, his faithful public services, his zeal as the president of Bible society, his unquestionable integrity as treasurer of a widows and orphans fund are result of an admirable arrangement of his life. It is a portrait displayed meticulously before the world. His smile of broad benevolence is his weapon to win favorable opinion of the commoners in the newly emerging democratic set up.

He has real estate in town and country; numerous bank accounts; insurance share, United States stock, yet he covets more. His ambition is a more powerful talisman than the witchcraft. Judge Pyncheon is a portrait of dissonance and discordance. Hawthorne's contempt for professional politicians is reflected in this comment in the novel:

> . . . practiced politicians, every man of them, and skilled to adjust those preliminary measures which steal from the people, without its knowledge the power of choosing its own rulers. The popular voice, at the next gubernatorial election, though loud as thunder, will be really but an echo of what these gentlemen shall speak, under their breath, at your friend's festive board. (HSG 215)

Hawthorne was embittered by the loss of his post of Surveyor in the Salem custom House when Zachary Taylor was elected as the president of America. His appointment was cancelled on political grounds as the new president belonged to Whigs who were dominating every sphere at that time. In spite of all the assurance of the new government that qualified people would not be removed from their office position, he was ousted from office on 8thjune, 1849 for his association with members of democratic republic. Hawthorne defended his appointment by saying that his selection was not politically motivated and he never acted as politician since his appointment. He even wrote a letter to clarify that he made local democrats angry by not helping them from his post. He pleaded in vain that his fate should not be left in the hands of the politicians whom he considered "thick skulled" and "no- hearted ruffians" (Mellow 293).

It had been affirmed in other sources that Mr. Charles Wentworth Upham served as a model for Jeffery Pyncheon. This was done by

Hawthorne to take revenge upon him for his inimical influence in removing him from the Salem custom House. Upham was an influential Whig and a member of Congress who through his intrigue helped in Hawthorne's removal from the office. In view of high local support for Hawthorne, Upham and other Whigs intensified their assault on him. Charles Wentworth Upham, the former-minister turned politician was the chief villain in the whole episode, "who has proved himself a liar and a most consummate hypocrite for he always professed himself the warmest friend" (Mellow 294).

After knowing Upham's role in the whole episode, Hawthorne wrote to Horace Mann, his wife's brother–in–law about Mr. Upham that "I shall do my best to kill and scalp him in the public prints; and I think I shall succeed" (Mellow 302). Hawthorne gave only surprisingly oblique remark regarding Upham who was also a priest. He wrote, "that stubborn fidelity with which a man's friends-and especially a clergyman's –will sometimes uphold his character; when proofs, clear as mid –day sun shines, on the scarlet letter, establish him a false and sin stained creature of the dust" (Mellow 307).

Notwithstanding some external differences between the character of Upham and Judge Pyncheon, Hawthorne found their moral basis identical. Hawthorne's view regarding the matter was brought before the wide audience through his introduction to *The Scarlet Letter*, entitled as "The Custom House". Hawthorne wrote about his political enemies as "slang whangers" and "Vole distributors" (Mellow 293).

Hawthorne had come to know about the betrayal of his friend Horace Conolly who joined hands with his political enemies. He was very close to Hawthorne but started to attend Whigs political causes after eyeing political opportunity on the other side. This episode further embittered his perception of professional politicians. Hawthorne confessed:

> . . . it stirs up a little of the devil within me to find myself hunted by these political bloodhounds. If they succeed in getting me out of office, I will surely immolate one or two of them. Not that poor monster of a Conolly, whom I desire

> only to bury in oblivion... But, if there be among them (as there must be, if they succeed) some men who claim a higher position and ought to know better. I may perhaps select a victim, and let fall one little drop of venom on his heart, that shall make him writhe before the grin of the multitude for a considerable time to come. (Mellow 293-294).

As a shrewd politician Hawthorne anticipated his dismissal since Zachary Taylor was elected the president of America. He even wrote a letter to his friend a prominent Whig and lawyer George Hillard to use his influence and forestall a move by Salem's Whigs against him. In spite of all his clarification against the charges leveled against him and all his attempts to generate favorable public opinion, he was removed from the office. He wrote:

> I do detest all offices; all, at least, that are held on a political tenure, and I want nothing to do with politicians. Their hearts wither away, and die out of their bodies. Their consciences are turned to India- rubber, or to some substance as black as that and which will stretch as much. One thing, if no more, I have gained by my Custom-house experience–to know a politician. It is a knowledge which no previous thought or power of sympathy could have taught me; because the animals or the machine, rather, is not in nature. (James 65-66)

The character of the judge in the present novel is an American materialist. We see the principles of aristocracy and democracy are in conflict in the American society of the 19th century in the fortunes and aspirations of Jaffrey Pyncheon. Jaffrey has attended splendid banquets and has poured out his eloquence as the guest of honor, "to ears yet echoing with Webster's mighty organ tones" (HSG 214). Reference to Daniel Webster in the novel cannot be ignored who was a senator from Massachusetts Bay Colony. Various critics found in the character of the judge a few traits suggesting Daniel Webster for whom money and respectability were everything. Like him, judge is also a public figure and greedy man. Webster was the greatest orator of his day who was well known for his eloquence. Hawthorne praised Webster for his charismatic personality who was a marvellously gifted statesman but he was wary of certain traits in his character and defined his life as "vague and empty" (Mellow 292). Hawthorne registered his dark suspicions regarding a flaw in Webster's character by writing, "that whatever he might choose to say, his auditors had no choice but to believe him; wrong looked right, and right like wrong"(Mellow 292).

Jaffrey Pyncheon has headed many magnificent banquets like Webster in the course of his eminent political career. He is a distinguished figure in both the branches of the state legislature. He is well publicized in the newspaper as, the Christian, the good citizen, and the gentleman yet his repeated offer of luxury to his cousins are refuted by Hepzibah because she suspects his motive.

Jaffrey implicates innocent Clifford Pyncheon in murder of his uncle who died because of apoplectic stroke. At the time of his uncle's death Clifford was present in the chamber. To serve his own selfish end, Jaffrey manipulated the situation and evidences in such a way that innocent Clifford was presumed guilty of a murder and suffered like Hawthorne in the hands of a professional politician.

This case of an innocent being implicated had also another historical association. Hawthorne would have been definitely familiar with "The White Murder Case" through his reading of Felt's *Annals of Salem*. In 1681, Nicholas Manning the brother of Hawthorne's great, great maternal uncle Thomas Manning was accused by his wife for incest with his two sisters- Anstis Manning and Margaret Manning Polfery. After the accusation Nicholas Manning fled into the forest, and returned after eight years. His sisters were convicted and fined on the testimony of two servants. Here are the excerpts from the Annals: "1681, March 29. Two females, for incest, are sentenced to be imprisoned a night, whipped, or pay 5£, and to stand or sit, during the services of the next lecture day, on a high stool, in the middle alley of Salem meeting-house, having a paper on their heads with their crime written in capital letters (Tuttleton).The sisters were unjustly punished for a crime in which they had no role.

Jaffrey was instrumental in proving Clifford a murderer and later on he used his political influence to release him from prison with a sinister motive. He was convinced that Clifford knew about some map or documents which would guide him to unexplored territory and a vast treasure of wealth, which belonged to his uncle.

His uncle was supposed to be immensely rich. According to his last testament, he bequeathed all his property to Jaffrey but later on changed his previous will and transferred the ownership to Clifford after observing vicious conduct of Jaffrey. After his uncle's death, Judge changed his uncle's second will and replaced it with the older testament. Still, he was not satisfied with the amount, he received. He was assured that a large amount was still unknown and Clifford knew about it. Judge Pyncheon threatened Clifford to send him to a public asylum by proving him insane, if he did not share the secret with him. Hepzibah confronts Jaffrey, and asks". . . why should you do this cruel, cruel thing? So mad a thing, that knows not whether to call it wicked! . . ." (HSG 188).

The mental illness of Clifford and a threat of confinement by Jaffrey Pyncheon brought to the surface, one of the cruellest abuses of the 19th century. It was the treatment of the mentally ill as criminals. This drew the attention of so many reformers, especially a school teacher from Massachusetts, Dorthea Dix. She visited a jail in 1841 and proceeded to visit nearly all the jails in her native state in a short period. In 1842, she wrote a report to present it to the legislature. It described the conditions of those who were mentally ill and were imprisoned in jail. She persuaded the state legislature to provide more humane treatment for the feeble minded. Their miserable condition improved after her effort. She wrote, "I proceed, gentlemen, briefly to call your attention to the present state of the insane persons confided within this common wealth in cages, closets, cellars, stalls, pens! Chained, naked, beaten with rods, and clashed into obedience ..." (Commager and Nevins 420).

Just before Jaffrey was going to attend a dinner with some political friends, he died due to hammohreage owing to a familial trait. After his death, Holgrave showed the document was essential for

Pyncheon to claim the right over the whole eastern territory and for which Jaffrey contrived Clifford's imprisonment. While constructing the seven gables, the son of executed Maule carved a recess in the wall and concealed the Indian deed, a folded sheet of parchment signed by several Indian saga mores. This document was discovered only after it lost its significance. It was what, "Pyncheon sought in vain, while it was valuable; and now that they find the treasure, it has long been worthless" (HSG 247). It was a fate similar to the fate of Hathornes who lost the title deed to the land in Maine during Judge Hathorne's life, "where afterwards the town of Raymond grew up, and the papers were recovered only when the claim had become valueless" (Erskine 183).

The critical crux of the novel opens for the readers at the end when Hepzibah, Clifford, and Phoebe decide to leave the old mansion which stands for spurious values. They go to the country seat which, "suggested comfort, refinement, and hospitality..." (Leopold and Link 558). Aftermath of the revolution was a turbulent phase in American history. There was decisive changes for American political development and social evolution, "Old institutions and modes of thought were widely challenged" (Blake 124). It weakened the foundation of old social order and, "laid the basis for readjustment of classes. Thousands of the gentry fled to the country" (Blake 124) like the characters of the present novel. Hence, their migration to country from town is not unusual. It was an expected move in that turbulent time, yet it focused on the escapist nature of Hepzibah who after all did not learn the lessons of republicanism. Those who stayed in the city were forced to share prestige with new men, thrust up in the social upheaval. Instead of confronting the wave of change and adjusting in new social order, Hepzibah preferred to snug in a country seat. The focal point of the novelist in the concluding chapter is the inner transformation of the character of Holgrave. The proclamation of Emerson regarding the reformers becomes significant here:

> They mix the fire of the moral sentiment with personal and party heats, with measureless exaggerations, and the

> blindness that prefers some darling measure to justice and truth. Those, who are urging with most ardor, what are called the greatest benefits of mankind, are narrow, self-pleasing, conceited men, and affect us as the insane do.(Leopold and Link 325-326)

These public pronouncements of Emerson, who was the leading figure of the transcendental movement, concurred with Hawthorne's apprehension regarding reformers. Hawthorne ridiculed the reformer's lack of conscience at the cost of conscientiousness. He believed that as long as a man's heart was corrupt, little could be accomplished by a change of beliefs or institutions. In spite of Hawthorne's avowed dislike for the reformers, he saved Holgrave from his bitter virulence. His ambivalence towards the character of Holgrave was the result of his respect for Holgrave's faith in democratic ideology and individual dignity; his egalitarian principles; and his faith in the worth of common man. Hawthorne's underlying desire to change his radicalism and reformist outlook was displayed through Holgrave's association with the conformist Phoebe.

This change in Holgrave is unexpected and shocking even for Phoebe who was earlier appalled by his lawless energy. Holgrave sacrifices his radical ideas in favor of conventional relation under the mesmeric power of love. He tells Phoebe. "You are my only possibility of happiness!" (HSG 240) and tells her, "You will make me strive to follow you, where it is pathless" (HSG 240). The alteration in his radical outlook is visible in these words of Holgrave:

> The happy man inevitably confines himself within ancient limits. I have a presentiment that, hereafter, it will be my lot to set out trees to make fences,-perhaps, even, in due time, to build a house for another generation,-in a word, to conform myself to laws, and the peaceful practice of society. Your poise will be more powerful than any oscillating tendency of mine. (HSG 240)

The same man, who earlier desires to overthrow the entire establishment of the society, now wants to conform to the laws of society. It refers to an internal transformation pre-requisite for any kind of change in the society rather than any coercive mandate of external law. Holgrave looks forward to Phoebe's assistance and guidance. "You must be both strong and wise! For I am all astray, and need your counsel. It may be, you can suggest the one right thing to do" (HSG 236). Hawthorne redefines Holgrave and depicts an inner transformation of his heart by showing him non-vengeful towards Pyncheon unlike his ancestors. It reveals Hawthorne's longing for an internal change in man and repudiation of radical principles that inspire any reform movement, as revolutionary temper jeopardizes peaceful existence in society. Holgrave proves himself a good human being by resisting his erotic power which can give him mastery over Phoebe's free spirit.

His union with the conventional Phoebe serves two ends. Apart from the aforesaid goal, it also resolves the possibility of any enmity in the future between Pyncheons and Maules through their marriage. The ending of the tale has a close association with the author's ancestral history, "but it was not until 1838 that Nathaniel Hawthorne was told the story of Philip English. The daughter of Philip English was supposed to have married one of John Hathorne's sons. If this were true, then the blood of curser and accursed had mingled in the second generation" (Turner 21), the same has been projected at the end of tale *The House of Seven Gables* through the union of Holgrave and Phoebe.

WORKS CITED

Andrews, Charles. M. *The Colonial Period of American History.* Vol.1.New Haven: Yale U.P., 1934.Print.

Barker, Eugene C, and Henry Steele Commager. *Our Nation.* New York: Row, Peterson and Company, 1952.Print.

Blake, Nelson Manfred. *A Short History of American Life.* New York: MC Hill Book Company, 1952. Print.

Bragdon, Henry W, and Samuel P. McCutchen. *History of a Free*

People. New York: Macmillan Publishing Company, 1981. Print.

Brennan, Robert Edward. *The Image of His Maker*. Milwaukee: The Bruce Publishing Company, 1948. Print.

Calef, Robert. *More Wonders of invisible World*. Salem Reprint, 1823.USA: Kessinger Publishing, March 2010. Print.

Carr, E.H.*What is History*? Ed. R W Davies. 2nd ed. London: Penguin Books: 1961. Print.

Commager, Henry Steele, and Allan Nevins, eds. *The Heritage of America*. Boston: Little Brown and Company, 1949. Print.

Cowie, Alexender. *The Rise of American Novel*. New York: American Book Company, 1948. Print.

Erskine, John. *Leading American Novelists*. New York: Books for Libraries Press, 1966. Print.

Fick, Leonard, J. *The Light Beyond*. Westminster: The Newman Press, 1955. Print.

Fiske, John. *New France and New England*. Boston: Houghton, Miffin, and Company, 1902. Print.

Gwin, Minrose C. *Black and White Women of the Old South: The Peculiar Sisterhood in American Literature*. Knoxville: University of Tennessee Press, 1985. Print.

Hall, Lawrence sergeant. *Critic of the Society*. New Haven: Yale U. P., 1944. Print.

Hawthorne, Nathaniel. *The House of Seven Gables*. New York: The World Popular Classics, Books, Inc, 1951. Print.

—*The Scarlet Letter*. London: Penguin Books, 1994. Print.

James, Henry. *Hawthorne*. London: Macmillan & co., Ltd., 1879. Print.

Lang, Amy Schrager. *The Syntax of Class: Writing Inequality in Nineteenth - Century America*. Princeton: Princeton University Press, 2003. Print.

Leopold, Richard W, and Arthur S. Link, eds. *Problems in American History*. New York: Prentice Hall, 1954. Print.

Maule, James Edward. *Better than Hundred Witches Should Live*. Published by James Edward Maule. Web. 17 Oct..2008. www.jembook.com,Rev.ed.

Mellow, James R. *Nathaniel Hawthorne in His Times*. Boston: Houghton Mifflin Company, 1980. Print.

Nevins, Allan, and Henry Steele Commager, eds. *A Short History of United States*.5th ed. Newyork: Alfred. A. Knopf, 1968. Print.

Parkes, Henry Bamford. *The United States of America –A History*. Rev.2nd ed. Calcutta: Scientific Book Agency, 1967. Print.

Pearson, Norman Holmes. *The Blithedale Romance inThe Complete Novels and Selected tales of Nathaniel Hawthorne*. New York: The Modern Library, 1937. Print.

Peterson, Merrill D."Jefferson and Religious Freedom." The Atlantic Monthly. 274.6 (Dec 1994): 112-124.Print.

Stewart, Randall. *Nathaniel Hawthorne-A Biography*. New Haven: Yale U. P., 1948. Print.

Taylor, Stoehr. *Hawthorne's Mad Scientist*. Hamden: Archon Books, 1978. Print.

Turner, Arlin. *Nathaniel Hawthorne: A Biography*. New York: Oxford U. P., 1980. Print.

Tuttleton, James. "Hawthorne's "Secret." [Jan 1985] Web. 2nd Apr. 2011. www.newcriterion.com.

Warren, Austin. Rage for Order. Chicago: The University of Chicago Press, 1948. Print.

All references to Thomas Maule from Maule Family Newsletter, vol.8.2, (Mar 1988) Web.17th Oct 2008. maulefamily.com.

All reference to Thomas Jefferson are from "Thomas Jefferson on Aristocracy`, letter to John Adams"bigeye.com. Web. 31st Dec 2010.

9

The Self and the Environment: Tom Canty's Struggle with Authentic Identity in Mark Twain's *The Prince and the Pauper*

Madihur Rehman Suhaib

The Prince and the Pauper, "a grave and stately" work in the opinion of Mark Twain himself, has had a chequered career. It was well received by Twain's contemporaries: William Dean Howells in his review commended it highly for its moralistic point of view, and it drew a quite a favorable and enthusiastic response from Twain's wife and daughters. But twentieth century response to the novel, at least from critics, has been far from enthusiastic. It is ironical that this most positive of Twain's novels is generally believed to be the least significant of his major works. Frank Baldanza is of the view that "Above all else it is a children's tale (and) the simplicity of mind that pervades the story is ideally suited to the blunt moral perceptions of children. One is reminded of the landlady in a short story of James Joyce, who is said to attack moral problems with a meat cleaver (71)." Tom H. Towers holds that "*The Prince and the Pauper* remains a children's book not because it indulges Tom Canty's childish fantasies of omnipotence, but because it encourages the nostalgic denial of history, a dream which, even less than Tom's, admits of the sad truths of history(202)." Critics who have not specially dealt with the novel as a children's book have, nevertheless, read a simple and straightforward meaning in this "happy" tale of a prince who becomes a more humane king after witnessing how the lives of the common people are made miserable by harsh laws, and a pauper whose dreams are turned into reality when he accidentally becomes king. It is not hard to come across such verdicts as: the novel is "a curious romaunt, indeed, and quite a happy one considering Twain's usual political disposition, since it seems to suggest that, with sufficient role-play exchange between king and subject, monarchy might become a bearable state of society (Schleiner 340-41)," and, "*In The Prince and the Pauper*, Twain illustrates both in Edward VI and Tom Canty how poverty fosters mercy and justice (Rogers 117)." It is significant that Bruce Michelson, whose analysis is the most penetrating and who believes that the novel deals with quite a complex theme, reads a negative meaning in it. According to him, the novel is "about limbo, about how easily the self can slip away, or be obliterated precisely because it will not slip, about the perils of being incompletely made, and of being made too solidly and well (Michelson 151)."

If one cares to look beyond the plot and the speeches, numerous as they are, proclaiming the need for humane social systems, and how kings should go to school in their own laws, the novel is about the problem of identity ___ the relationship between the self and the environment. *The Prince and the Pauper*, like other major novels of Mark Twain, explores the possibilities of acquiring a genuine, authentic identity in a corrupt and pretentious society. The fact that the novel comes up with answers that are radically different from the vision of the other novels should not blind us to the complexities of *The Prince and the Pauper*; nor should we feel compelled to read a negative meaning in the novel to suggest that its theme is as complex as that of any other of Twain's works. *The Prince and the Pauper* is significant not merely because its author happens to be a major writer, but because it deals with problems that are central to Mark Twain's work, and because it serves as a link in the chain that extends from *Tom Sawyer to No. 44, The Mysterious Stranger*.

The Prince and the Pauper revolves around the theme of movement from given identity, that is, identity created by social environment, to genuine identity that the protagonists must acquire through an understanding of the self in a new social environment, one which they are not equipped to deal with properly. The journey from one identity to the other is not a smooth one. It is full of obstacles that prove almost too great to surmount. The young protagonists have to contend both with the corrupt social environment and with their own weaknesses. Society tries to break their will and to make them accept the identities it has created for them. It creates identities for its members in order to make the system work; and since it is a corrupt and dehumanized system that has to be sustained, the identities that are created for this purpose are against the instincts of a pure and innocent heart. The protagonists have to find ways of dealing with the temptations and the threats that they encounter. This is not an easy task. If Tom and Edward are to survive their respective ordeals and emerge unscathed, they must understand both the self as well as external reality; then only can they deal with the twin perils of temptation and fear. And if the two heroes succeed without rejecting society itself, it is because they are guided by the instincts of their pure hearts.

Both Tom Canty and Prince Edward start out with identities that they inherit with their birth, for in a stratified society like the one in *The Prince and the Pauper* identity is not a matter of choice. It is the accident of birth that decides whether one will grow up to be a pauper ---- unwanted, despised, superfluous, or the king ---- dreaded, obeyed, the object of reverence of the mighty and the powerless alike. The accidental aspect of identity is emphasized at the very beginning of the novel:

> In the ancient city of London, on a certain autumn day in the second quarter of the sixteenth century, a boy was born to a poor family of the name of Canty, who did not want him. On the same day another English child was born to a rich family of the name of Tudor, who did want him. All England wanted him too.... There was no talk in all England but of the new baby, Edward Tudor, Prince of Wales, who lay lapped in silks and satins, unconscious of all this fuss, and not knowing that great lords and ladies were tending him and watching over

> him ---- and not caring either. But there was no talk about the other baby, Tom Canty, lapped in his poor rags, except among the family of paupers whom he had just come to trouble with his presence.(Twain 1-2)

Since identity is a given fact, immovable and unwavering, that precedes the consciousness of identity, the consciousness of both Tom and Edward develops in accordance with the identity that each has inherited, and they accept their respective positions without question or protest.

In this paper, however, I will confine myself to Tom's struggle with reclaiming his true self.

Tom, as a pauper in Tudor England, is born into a hard lot. He grows up in a dirty, over-crowded, decayed hovel amidst surroundings that are equally abominable. Inhuman conditions have robbed the people of the last vestiges of humanity. "Drunkenness, riot, and brawling was the order there, every night and nearly all night long. Broken heads were as common as hunger in that place" (Twain 4-5). Tom's father and grandmother, the two persons who control his immediate environment, are typical products of the general social environment. They are "a couple of fiends. They got drunk whenever they could; then they fought each other or anybody else who came in the way; they cursed and swore always, drunk or sober; John Canty was a thief, and his mother a beggar" (Twain 4). Tom becomes a victim of the environment, like everybody else. He is forced to beg in order to escape severe physical punishment. Whenever he comes home empty-handed, he is beaten black and blue by his father and grandmother who take sadistic pleasure in torturing him.

His early experiences produce in Tom a confusion of identity. Three factors contribute to this confusion. One is Tom's natural self. Despite all his mental training and social conditioning, he is different from others around him. Though his father and grandmother succeed in making a beggar out of him, it is certain that Tom is a reluctant beggar. He begs "just enough to save himself", and often prefers hunger and physical pain to begging, for he comes home empty-handed quite often. His good heart, which has found few opportunities for expression so far, prompts him to seek the company of Father Andrew, the only good person apart from Tom's mother and sisters, whom he has come across. Tom has the ability to rise above his circumstances and act against his fears. So he learns "a little Latin, and how to read and write" from Father Andrew, while his sisters resist the efforts of the good priest to teach them as much because "they were afraid of the jeers of their friends, who could not have endured such queer accomplishments in them" (Twain 4). The second factor that contributes to Tom's sense of identity is his social experience. Since there is nothing in his experience with which he can contrast his own situation, he accepts it without misgivings. Not only does he bear the squalor, hunger, misery and physical and emotional abuse without protest, he "was not unhappy. He had a hard time of it, but did not know it. It was the correct and comfortable thing" (Twain 5). So Tom's acceptance of his inherited identity comes from ignorance. He has no way of knowing that life can be different from what it is because the evil that characterizes society is all pervasive.

The third factor that is responsible for the confusion is Tom's dreams and fantasies. Father Andrew tells him "charming old tales and legends about giants and fairies, dwarfs and genii, and enchanted castles, and gorgeous kings and princes" (Twain 50). It is through these tales and through Father Andrew's old books that Tom reads avidly that he gets a glimpse of an alternative life, a dreamland that is pleasant and beautiful instead of being cruel and ugly, like the reality. Dreams become a means of escape from the harsh reality in which Tom finds himself trapped: "His head grew to be full of these wonderful things, and many a night as he lay in the dark on his scant and offensive straw, tired, hungry, and smarting from a thrashing, he unleashed his imagination and so forgot his aches and pains in delicious picturing to himself of the charmed life of petted prince in a regal palace" (Twain 5). Under the influence of his "dreamings and readings", Tom's perception of his surroundings and his own condition undergoes a change, and he starts making tentative efforts to improve them:

> His dreamings and readings worked certain changes in him by and by. His dream people were so fine that he grew to lament his shabby clothing and his dirt, and to wish to be clean and better clad. He went on playing in the mud just the same, and enjoying it, too; but instead of splashing around in the Thames solely for the fun of it, he began to find an added value in it because of the washing and cleaning it afforded. (Twain 6)

Since the change in Tom's perception of reality and the self cannot be expressed in any significant action because the resources at his disposal are meager, it is expressed in symbolic action. Like Tom Sawyer, he starts incorporating into his games what he has read in the books. He organizes a mock royal court where he can be the prince and give orders and be obeyed. As in the case of Tom Sawyer, this play-acting is both a means of escape from a reality that is perceived to be hateful, as well as an expression of the unconscious desire for power and control.

To a limited extent, Tom's desires are fulfilled because of the changes that take place in his personality under the influence of his readings and dreamings. As he starts acting differently from others, as his manner, behavior and speech change and become "curiously ceremonious and courtly," he earns the respect and admiration of the other boys of his circle. Even older people start acknowledging his superiority and begin "to regard him as a most gifted and extraordinary creature." He becomes a sort of a leader. "Full-grown people brought their perplexities to Tom for solution, and were often astonished at the wit and wisdom of his decisions"(Twain 7). But dream cannot replace reality. Moreover, Tom's dreams of grandeur and beauty only highlight for him the squalor and ugliness of his environment:

> And when he awoke in the morning and looked upon the wretchedness about him, his dream had its usual effect ---- it had intensified the sordidness of his surroundings a thousand fold. Then came bitterness, and heartbreak, and tears. (Twain 9)

And Tom is aware of his weak position. Though his dreams of grandeur and glory are persistent, the most powerful desire for him remains "to look just once upon a real prince, in the flesh," and not to become one. He knows that he can never break through the barriers of class erected by society. He may go on playing his games that symbolically empower him,

> After which he would go forth in his rags and beg a few farthings, eat his poor crust, take customary cuffs and abuse, and then stretch himself upon his handful of foul straw, and resume his empty grandeur in his dreams. (Twain 7)

Even the desire to just look upon a real prince may be impractical for a person of his class. When he talks of his desire to his Offal Court colleagues, "they jeered him and scoffed so unmercifully that he was glad to keep his dream to himself after that" (Twain 6).

So Tom embarks upon his journey of self-discovery with a confused sense of identity. His inherited identity negates the impulses of his good heart and his circumstances make it impossible for him to realize his potential. The identity that he creates for himself in his dreams and fantasies and which he tries to achieve through symbolic action cannot be made actual because it cannot be reconciled with reality. It is a hopeless situation and Tom is left with no option but to accept the identity that has been created for him by society. So Tom never tries to put up a fight and accepts the situation meekly. He tries to find temporary escape from harsh reality in his dreams, but they only intensify his perception of the sordidness of reality many fold for the simple reason that they are so beautiful.

It is an accident that delivers Tom from his impossible predicament and gives him the opportunity to see his dreams turned into reality. When he exchanges his clothes with Prince Edward and the prince is kicked out of the palace for a pauper, Tom acquires a new identity and his dream of being a prince is turned into reality. But assuming new roles is not as easy as it may appear. Standing before the mirror after exchanging their clothes, Tom and Edward may marvel at their physical similarity and may feel that no change has taken place, but the fact remains that identity is more than a matter of clothes or other outward signs. Social conditioning creates the sense of identity. So while everyone at the palace is deceived by his resemblance with Edward, mere change of clothes and circumstances cannot alter Tom's sense of identity. Though he might not have found it difficult to "play the prince" at Offal Court, he now realizes that acquiring a new identity in real life is no child's play. He finds that he is not equal to the challenge and reacts to the unimaginable situation with fear. When Edward does not return for a long time and Tom is left alone in the princely chamber wearing the prince's clothes, he starts feeling lonely and uneasy,

> then restless, then distressed. Suppose some one should come, and catch him in the prince's clothes, and the prince not there to explain. Might they not hang him at once, and inquire into his case afterward? He had heard that the great were prompt about small maters. (Twain 25)

This is a new fear for Tom. In his former surroundings he has known the fear of retribution and punishment, of pain and hunger, but the situation he faces now may lead to annihilation of the self. As his fear mounts, it takes on the dimensions of an existential crisis and it appears that his dreams have turned into a nightmare. When the servants pay him respects, mistaking him for the prince, Tom concludes that they know him for who he is and are simply making fun of him: "Oh, they mock at me! They will go and tell. Oh! Why came I here to cast away my life?" (Twain 25). Out of fear for his very existence, he proclaims his former identity whenever he is addressed as the prince. Lady Jane Grey, distressed at his agitation, asks with genuine concern. "Oh, what aileth thee, my lord?" Tom stammers out in response, "Ah, be merciful, thou! In sooth I am no lord, but only poor Tom Canty of Offal Court in the city. Prithee let me see the prince, and he will of his grace restore to me my rags, and let me hence unhurt. Oh, be thou merciful, and save me!" (Twain 25). The situation is ironical. Tom is on tenterhooks to get back the very identity that has till so recently been a burden to him and from which he sought escape in dreams and fantasies. Now that his dreams have come true, the identity that he has all along been pining for becomes a source of terror and he wants to disclaim it. The situation has gone from bad to worse; the confusion of identity has developed into a crisis of identity.

The crisis is real: Tom's very existence is threatened. If his worst fears do not come true, it is only because he is presumed to have lost control over the self, that is, to have gone mad. This presumed madness earns for Tom not only safety, but also love and compassion, that too from the king himself ---- the power behind the system that had earlier victimized him.

> Tom was assisted to his feet, and approached the Majesty of England, humble and trembling. The king took the frightened face between his hands, and gazed earnestly and lovingly into it awhile, as if seeking some grateful sign of returning reason there, then pressed the curly head against his breast, and patted it tenderly. (Twain 28)

Sane, Tom is the lowliest of subjects, tortured, threatened, persecuted; presumed mad, he is the prince, powerful, loved, respected. But still a slave. Earlier, his actions were controlled by the circumstances and his dreams, now they are controlled by the new circumstances and his fears. At Offal Court, trapped in the identity thrust upon him by the accident of his birth, he had imagined freedom in the fiction of the identity created by his dreams; in the palace he finds himself trapped by the reality of the fiction thrust upon him by another accident, and now he imagines release in a return to his origins ---- another fiction. He dreams of "the meadows and the fresh air" when the present reality becomes too much for him not because the charms of his former life have been revealed to him, but because the perils of the present one are too frightening to face. He tells the king, "Peradventure I mistook; but I did think me free, and so was I moved to seek again the kennel where I was born and bred to misery… whereas these pomps and splendors where unto I am not used ---- oh, please you, sir, to let me go!" (Twain

29). Just as he had earlier mistakenly believed that dreams could provide freedom, so now he believes that going back to his origins will mean freedom. The irony of the situation is highlighted when the king says to Tom, "Thou art better now; thy ill dream passeth is't not so? And thou knowest thyself now also ---- is't not so? Thou wilt not miscall thyself again, as they say thou didst a little while agone?" (Twain 28). While the king is of course hinting at Tom's insistence upon his former identity of a pauper, it may also be taken to mean the opposite. It Tom could go back now to his former life, his "ill dream", the dream of being prince, would indeed pass. He "knows" himself now, at least in the negative sense of knowing what he is not, what he cannot be. He would not "miscall" himself again, he would give up his dream of an alternative identity and his acceptance of his inherited identity would be reinforced because he has come face to face with the perils that any exchange of identity entails. But going back would mean returning to the slavery of a false identity. None of the two identities can deliver him from bonds of servitude, since both are fictions created by the social system. If Tom is to be free, he must discover his true, authentic identity. This cannot happen unless he knows himself positively ---- what he is, and what he can be. Tom has to learn that freedom cannot be had by replacing one illusion with another. And mere negative knowledge of the self cannot free him of his illusions. So his ordeal must continue, he must "tarry yet a little", he still has no place to go to, as the king points out to him (Twain 29).

At the present stage in his development, however, Tom does not realize that the identity he created for himself in his dreams is an illusion. Fear cannot free him of his illusions, because fear leads to loss of the self; whereas what Tom needs in order to discover his authentic identity is contact with the self. So if he disclaims the identity that circumstances have thrust upon him, it is to escape the threat that the new identity seems to entail, and not because he has become disenchanted with "populous and institutionalized society (Spengemann 53-54)." Had this been the case, Tom would not want to go back to "the kennel where he was born and bred to misery," for pauperhood is as much an institution as is monarchy. True, he often expresses aversion to the duties associated with his new position, but it is simply because he fears that he may not be up to the task and may commit mistakes, thereby exposing himself to be an imposter and invite disaster. It is for this reason that as he surmounts each hurdle, as all his mistakes are attributed to his "madness" and nobody seems to doubt that he is the prince, Tom starts feeling better and the desire to escape from his present reality wanes. "Snags and sand-bars grew less and less frequent, and Tom grew more and more at his ease, seeing that all were so lovingly bent upon helping him out and overlooking his mistakes" (Twain 39). True, even after realizing that he is safe and there is no danger to him he is often bored by courtly decorum and feels hampered and restricted by the elaborate rituals that must be followed in performing even normal every- day tasks, it is but a passing phase. He soon realizes that "being a king is not all dreariness ---- it hath its compensations and conveniences" (Twain 114).

So, after his initial fears and discomfort concerning his new identity, what Tom is worried about is not "to regain his identity, which is initially the identity conferred upon him by being his... father's son (Stahl 74)," but to disentangle himself from the influences of this "conferred" identity that make it difficult for him to assume his new identity. As soon as he becomes fully conscious of the safety granted him by his supposed madness, he tries everything possible to adjust with his new environment and to fulfill the requirements of his new identity. He reads the books on court etiquette and princely behavior that he finds in the chamber of Prince Edward; he tries to gathers as much information from the whipping-boy as possible by taking advantage of his gullibility; he follows the advice of the Lord Protector as best he can. Gradually, as his new identity becomes less cumbersome and terrifying to Tom, the distinction between his former dreams and his present reality seems to fade. He gives orders, and when they are immediately followed,

> Tom experienced a glow of pride and a renewed sense of the compensating advantages of the kingly office. He said to

> himself, "Truly it is like what I used to feel when I read the old priest's tales, and did imagine mine own self a prince, giving law and command to all, saying, 'Do this, do that', while none durst offer let or hindrance to my will." (Twain 115)

The experience of exercising the power vested in him by "the kingly office" fills Tom with excitement, and his new position starts having a bright side for him.

> This bright side went on brightening more and more every day; in a very little while it was become almost all sunshine. He lost his fears; his misgivings faded out and died; his embarrassments departed, and gave place to an easy and confident bearing. (Twain 233)

Since Tom plays an active part in his acclimatization, and since he finds his new situation enjoyable and gratifying, it is clear that he has taken a decision in favor of his new role. The intensity with which Tom comes to identity himself with his new position can be judged from the sentiment he expresses while going for his coronation in a grand procession, surrounded by the symbols of his new-found power, that "the one thing worth living for in this world was to be a king, and a nation's idol" (Twain 239).

Because of this growing sense of identification, certain changes take place in his personality. The very things that had initially seemed cumbersome and tedious now appear pleasant and enjoyable.

> He came to enjoy being conducted to bed in state at night, and dressed with intricate and solemn ceremony in the morning.... He even learned to enjoy sitting in council, and seeming to be something more than the Lord Protector's mouthpiece.... He enjoyed his splendid clothes, and ordered more; he found his four hundred servants too few for his proper grandeur, and trebled them. (Twain 233-34)

Tom's perception of reality and his approach to it get heavily influenced by his new environment and he adopts the ways and behavior associated with his new identity so much so that "upon occasion, being offended, he could turn upon an earl, or even a duke, and give him a look that would make him tremble" (Twain 234). The change in Tom's personality is so basic that even his good heart seems to be in danger of being obliterated under the influence of corrupting power. Though he remains kind and gentle, and keeps on waging "tireless war upon unjust laws," he grows more selfish and self-centered. The fear of losing his newfound power and glory makes him forget his benefactor, Edward, the rightful heir to the throne. Not only this,

> Tom's poor mother and sisters traveled the same road out of his mind. At first he pined for them, sorrowed for them, longed to see them; but later the thought of their coming some day in their rags and dirt, and betraying him with their kisses, and pulling him down from his lofty place, and dragging him back to penury and degradation and the slums, made him shudder. At last they ceased to trouble his thoughts almost wholly. (Twain 235)

What the degradation of Offal Court could not accomplish, the glory of Westminster palace seems to have achieved. It is a measure of the corrupting influence of his new environment that Tom finally disclaims his mother, the very person who had upon many occasions endangered herself in order to save him from abuse and torture, telling her, "I do not know you, woman" (Twain 242). When he denies knowing his mother, Tom is not only negating his finer feelings, he is also disclaiming his past and everything associated with it; he is trying to disown his origins and to reject the identity he inherited at the time of his birth in order to protect the identity he has acquired through an accident.

But there is something in Tom that resists change and which he cannot disown. He may exchange his rags with the gaudy dress of Edward; he may change his manners, his behavior, his language; he may disown his past and his origins, but he cannot banish his self, the real self that lies hidden deep down, beyond the reach of environmental influences and social conditioning. "I do not know you, woman"---- as Tom utters these words, as he negates his history, a psychological void is created. The act of negating the past also exposes the reality of the present, and on the instant Tom realizes that the identity for which he is rejecting his inherited identity is an illusion, and the happiness he seemed to derive from it was not real, for real happiness cannot be derived from illusions. As his mother "turned for a last glimpse of him, whilst the crowd was swallowing her from his sight, she seemed so wounded, so broken-hearted, that a shame fell upon him which consumed his pride to ashes, and withered his stolen royalty. His grandeurs were stricken valueless; they seemed to fall away from him like rotten rags" (Twain 242). Tom has already cast away the rags that symbolized his Offal Court identity. Now, as the rags of his palace identity also fall away from him, his raw, naked self is exposed to his view. The symbols of power and authority, the pomp and show of the royal procession, the cheers of the crowd that had made him feel elated cannot reach him any more, for he has rejected the identity associated with them. He exclaims, "Would God I were free of my captivity!" (Twain 242), seeking release from the trap of a false identity because unless this happens he cannot build an authentic identity based upon the real self with which he has come in contact.

It is again an accident that releases Tom from the trap of false identity. He was entrapped when Edward disappeared; he finds release when Edward as suddenly reappears. But, unlike the earlier occasion, Tom plays a significant role in the process of release. It is he who makes it possible for Edward to prove his claim of being the real king. Had Tom but remained silent, he could have usurped Edward's rightful place. Edward himself acknowledges Tom's role in securing for him his crown: "But for him I had not got my crown again..." (Twain 259).

But it is not an act of sacrifice on the part of Tom. Rather than sacrificing his position of power, he is working towards gaining his authentic identity. If he helps Edward in reclaiming his rightful place, it is not simply because of any sense of justice or feelings of guilt, though these emotions are there and play a role. The panic that Tom feels and the urgency with which he acts when nobody believes Edward and when Edward himself seems to be giving up the struggle, go beyond the call of justice or the promptings of guilty conscience:

> "O folly, O madness, my king!" cried Tom Canty in panic, "wait! ---- Think! Do not give up! ---- the cause is not lost! Nor shall be, neither! List to what I say ---- follow every word ---- I am going to bring that morning back again ---- every hap just as it happened…." (Twain 257)

The panic and the sense of urgency with which Tom reacts to the situation underline the fact that he clearly understands the significance that the moment has for him personally. This is his last chance to secure his freedom. If Edward fails to prove his case, Tom will forever remain a prisoner of a false identity. And Tom cannot accept this situation ---- he has too much at stake. He has finally come to realize that neither accepting the given, inherited identity passively, nor seeking refuge in the identity created by illusions and dreams can guarantee true happiness. Now that he has come in contact with his self, he cannot let the chance of gaining the freedom to live with his true identity pass by. And to gain such freedom, he must work for it; he must undertake positive action in the light of his understanding of external reality and his knowledge of the self. So Tom acts in time and is saved from being the imposter king.

WORKS CITED

Baldanza, Frank. *Mark Twain: An Introduction and Interpretation.* New York: Barnes and Noble, 1961. Print.

Michelson, Bruce. *Mark Twain on the Loose: A Comic Writer and the American Self.* Amherst: University of Massachusetts Press, 1995. Print.

Rogers, Franklin R. *Mark Twain's Burlesque Patterns.* Dallas: Southern Methodist University Press, 1960. Print.

Schleiner, Louise. "Romance Motifs in Three Novels of Mark Twain". *Comparative Literature Studies*, 13:4. Print.

Spengemann, William C. *Mark Twain and the Backwoods Angel: The Matter of Innocence in the Works of Samuel L. Clemens*. Kent: The Kent University Press, 1966. Print.

Stahl, J.D. *Mark Twain, Culture and Gender: Envisioning America Through Europe*. Athens: The University of Georgia Press, 1994. Print.

Towers, Tom H. "The Prince and the Pauper: Mark Twain's Once and Future King". *Studies in American Literature*, 6:2. Print.

Twain, Mark. *The Prince and the Pauper*. New York: Harper and Brothers, 1909. Print.

10

The Glass Menagerie: An Interdisciplinary Approach

Sami Rafiq

The focus of interdisciplinary studies in essence is to attempt to break down walls between different subjects and disciplines. This results in the emergence of challenging new areas of study. In this context the plays of Tennessee Williams provide a rich and diverse experience in which the juxtaposition of painting, Arts and drama work together to bring out the intensity of life. In fact 'Plastic Theatre' is the name that Tennessee Williams himself gave to his unique drama which was a combination of theatre and other Arts. This paper will attempt to study the use of painting in Williams' play *The Glass Menagerie*.

Music and colours in *The Glass Menagerie* have been used repetitively according to the Impressionistic pattern of colouring. Williams himself admitted to being under the influence of Impressionists around 1939 which implies that he used those influences consciously, and sub-consciously in the years that followed in several of his plays:

> I suppose that summer (of 1939) was the happiest and healthiest and most radiant time of my life. I know that I kept a journal then, and in this journal I referred to that season as Nave Nave Mahana, which is the title of my favourite (Tahitian) painting by Gaugin and which means 'The Careless Days'. (Williams, *Memoirs* 6)

Tennessee Williams's popular play *The Glass Menagerie* was a revised version of an earlier play titled *The Gentleman Caller*. It was written in 1943 and has received much critical attention for the use of expressionistic devices. However, the unusual patterns of repetitive colours and images in this play which require in-depth analysis have not received much critical attention.

The origins of *The Glass Menagerie* can be traced to a story in Williams's early writings "Portrait of a Girl in Glass". As the title indicates the intention behind the story was to create a picture of a girl (his sister) but the picture that evolved in the form of *The Glass Menagerie* is a much more complicated and carefully constructed large painting constituted of seven smaller paintings. All the seven scenes or miniature paintings, through the medium of repetitive colours and colour analogues taken from other Arts, create a portrait of the world of the girl, which is the Wingfield family. *The Glass Menagerie* is an impressionistic portrait of a family built through flashes of memory in Tom Wingfield's mind. The Impressionists, too, captured life on canvas in sudden momentary flashes.

The moments of memory are painted in colour and as analogic equivalents to colour such as images, legends, setting and music, all of which symbolize specific emotions. The opening lines of Scene I hint at the major thematic concern of the play which is dream versus reality:

> The Wingfield apartment is in the rear of the building, one of those vast hive-like conglomerations of cellular living-units that flower as warty growths in over-crowded urban burning with centers.... The apartment faces an alley and is entered by a fire escape, a structure whose name is a touch of accidental poetic truth, for all these huge buildings are always the slow and implacable fires of human desperation....(*The Glass Menagerie* 3)

The gross reality of an over-crowded urban center is confronted with unreal escape in the form of the fire escape, "whose name is a touch of accidental poetic truth." All the three characters, Amanda, Laura and Tom, framed in the portrait of memory in Tom's mind, are figures seen struggling with reality and trying of find refuge in illusion. Their struggle is static and they remain where they are from the beginning to the end – this is characteristic of a typical impressionistic painting.

The constant refrain of the legend, 'where are the snows', and Amanda's repeatedly recalling (her past) the Blue Mountain are once again a focus on illusion symbolized by the fire escape. The screen legends and screen images have special significance in relation to the Impressionistic or undefined structure of the play. According to Esther Merle Jackson:

..., the basic structure of narrative line may be obscured from the audience; the effect may seem fragmentary rather than architectural.... The legend or image upon the screen will strengthen the effect of what is merely allusion in the writing....(91)

The following lines reveal a soft, dreamlike atmosphere where the legend, the gestures and the soft light are muted background tones (of impressionistic painting), creating the Wingfield world of hopes and illusion:

> Legend on Screen: "Ou sont Les Neiges, (Where are the snows)
> .....AMANDA and LAURA are seated at a drop leaf table.
> Eating is indicated by gestures without food or utensils...
> The interior has lit up softly...(*GM* 4)

Against the soft-toned world picturised above, there is the intrusion of reality followed by the Glass Menagerie Music.

This is Amanda's sudden collision with reality when Laura points out that there is not going to be any gentleman caller:

> Amanda: You must be joking!... (A shaft of clear light is thrown on her face against the faded tapestry of the curtains.) (Music: "THE GLASS MENAGERIE" UNDER FAINTLY. (*GM* 6)

The intrusion of reality against the lighted figure of Amanda in a softly-coloured background of fading colours and music is presented impressionistically.

Scene II is a picture of the inner worlds of each member of the Wingfield family. Colours individualistically represent the disparate world of each of the three characters and their relationship to reality. The following lines are highly significant for understanding, through colours and images, the differences between the psyche of Laura and that of Amanda:

> On the dark stage the screen is lighted with the image of blue roses... Laura is seated in the delicate ivory chair at the small claw foot table. She wears a dress of soft violet material... She is washing and polishing her collection of glass. Amanda appears on the fire escape steps... (She has) a look that is grim and hopeless and a little absurd. She has on one of those cheap or imitation velvet-looking cloth coats with imitation fur collar... she is clasping an enormous black patent-leather pocket book with nickel clasps and initials. (*GM* 6)

While Laura is symbolized by the blue roses which mean a lack of vitality; (blue is an anti-natural colour for a rose), she is rooted in her world of glass through the images of 'the delicate ivory chair' and the dress of 'soft violet material'. She has no wish to escape her delicate dream world. Amanda, seen standing on the fire escape steps, is trying to escape the reality of her daughter's fragile personality. Her imitation-jewellery and clothes give a clue to her desperate evasion of reality.

The colours used as such and their analogic equivalents reveal the inner worlds of the three characters and also give momentary flashes of their daily lives:

Image: A Swarm Of Typewriters

> But I stopped off at Rubicam's business college to speak to your teachers about your having a cold and ask them what progress they thought you were making down there. (*GM* 7)

The swarm of typewriters is suggestive of dark overpowering shades of reality and the words 'down there' indicate a (dark) world opposed to the one of the (soft-toned) Blue Mountain. Laura's walking out in the (white coloured) snow to avoid the typewriting class (dark swarm) shows us how dream and reality are presented in soft and dark tones:

> LAURA: It was the lesser of the two evils mother, (IMAGE: WINTER SCENE IN PARK).(*GM* 7)

After the image of the winter scene we have the far removed 'LEGEND: THE CRUST OF HUMILITY', which is supposed to represent the appearance of Amanda's face which Laura likens to the picture of Jesus's mother in the museum. Such a comparison shows that the characters in the play are static, immobile figures of an Impressionistic painting rather than full-blooded beings. The sad, suffering face of Amanda is contrasted with youth and liveliness in the following image:

(SCREEN IMAGE: JIM AS HIGH – SCHOOL HERO BEARING A SILVER CUP.) (*GM* 8)

This image of youth and vitality is followed by the image of blue roses which stands for a lack of vitality. Thus we find that Scene II is one picture out of Tom's memory that reveals the Wingfields, their hopes, illusions and memories through contrasting colours..

In Scene III the legend on screen, 'After the Fiasco', implies a struggle which ends in a fiasco. Amanda, Laura and Tom are all part of the struggle to escape from reality into dream, and Tom and Laura are seeking desperately to fulfill their desires. The following lines supply us with an image that symbolizes this struggle:

> It became an obsession. Like some archetype of the universal unconscious, the image of gentleman caller haunted our small apartment……

(IMAGE: YOUNG MAN AT DOOR WITH FLOWERS.)(*GM* 9)

Other images are used to express Amanda's craving for youth and beauty as in the following lines, which collectively create the image of the Glamour Magazine Cover:

> ...the type journal that features the serialized sublimations of ladies of letters who think in terms of delicate cup-like breasts, slim, tapering waists, rich, creamy thighs, eyes like wood-smoke in autumn, fingers that soothe and caress like strains of music, bodies as powerful as Etruscan sculpture. (*GM* 9)

While the image of the gentleman caller represents Amanda's desire for love, the image of the glamour magazine cover represents her yearning for youth and beauty.

Just after this sojourn into Amanda's inner world the legend on screen is seen as- ("YOU THINK I'M IN LOVE WITH CONTINENTAL SHOEMAKERS") – revealing Tom's desire for freedom: Before the stage is lighted, the violent voices of Tom and Amanda are heard. (*GM* 9)

The soft tones of the images that represent Amanda's yearnings are suddenly juxtaposed by loud tones in the over-powering reality of the image of the Continental Shoemakers. In addition, the sounds have grown loud and violent just as the Impressionist enjoyed using loud and sharply contrasting tones. There is a quarrel between Amanda and Tom. Amanda tries to control Tom while he goes on a wild spree.The following lines suggestively indicate the passionate intensity in Tom which she tries to suppress.

> Amanda, I took that horrible novel back to the library – yes! That hideous book by that insane Mr. Lawrence. (GM 9)

The mental state of Amanda is presented through a number of images and the conflict between Amanda and Tom is represented by the smoky glow:

> Tom: I don't want to hear anymore! (He tears the portieres open. The upstage area is lit with a turgid smoky red glow). (AMANDA'S hair is in metal curlers and she wears a very old bathrobe, much too large for her slight figure....)(*GM* 9)

Donald Spoto has commented on the picture-like quality of the Gentleman Caller, a seminal version of *the Glass Menagerie*. "With its indication of dissolves and image-overlays, its insertion of musical motifs and it's plastic, dreamlike construction, it was conceived as a film of memory.(97)" The term 'film' here is very important as the Impressionists were trying to film reality on canvas more through the vision than the intellect.

It can be observed in Scene III as in the whole play that in each miniature portrait of the family we are presented with succession of colours and their analogic equivalents not merely telling a story but creating an Impressionistic portrait of a doomed family.Scene III which began with the legend "After the Fiasco' develops into the images of the Gentleman Caller and the associated images of the Glamour Magazine Cover. It eventually leads to a catastrophic collision of soft and loud tones in the turgid smoky glow. Finally Tom makes a bold attempt to break free from the pinioning reality of The Glass Menagerie:

> His arm catches in the sleeve of the coat as he struggles to pull it on. For a moment he is pinioned by the bulky garment. With an outraged groan he tears the coat off again, splitting the shoulder of it and hurls it across the room. It strikes against the shelf of LAURA'S glass collection, there is a tinkle of shattering glass. LAURA cries out as if wounded. (*MUSIC, LEGEND. THE GLASS MENAGERIE.*) (*GM* 11)

The 'tinkle of shattering glass' is an analogic equivalent of loud colour that contains all the other analogic colours in the scene. It is followed by a cry from Laura and the Glass Menagerie music. Laura's cry is indicative of the catastrophic reality of the Glass Menagerie to which the Wingfield family members are pinioned and the Glass Menagerie music is used as an analogic equivalent to a repetitive 'colour' in the play- signifying the fragility of the Glass Menagerie built on illusion.

Scene IV is once again a painting of the Wingfield family with a dark and faintly-lighted background and a series of images in the background that represent their individual problems. The opening concentrates on the dark background of the painting in which there is dim light:

> The interior is dark. Faint light in the alley. A deep voiced bell in a church is tolling the hour of five as the scene commences. (*GM* 11)

The tolling of the bell and the faint light impart a dream-like softness to the scene. A disagreement between Amanda and Tom is like a loud tone which impinges on the soft background. The description of Amanda with the subtle interplay of light and darkness on her face has Impressionistic overtones.

> (As Tom enters listlessly for his coffee, she turns her back to him and stands rigidly facing the window on the gloomy fray vault of the areaway. Its light on her face with its aged but childish features is cruelly sharp, satirical as a Daumier print. (GM 13)

This description of Amanda is followed by the Music, 'Ave Maria', which is equivalent to soft tones that enhance her motherliness which is implied repetitively by her arguments with her son. Motherliness is also emphasized by the music 'Ave Maria' when Amanda is discussing Laura, her daughter, who is characterized by the screen legend 'Laura' and the Glass Menagerie Music.

Tom's adventurous spirit is highlighted by the following image:

> (*IMAGE ON SCREEN: SAILING VESSEL WITH JOLLY ROGER.*) (*GM* 14)

Towards the end of Scene IV the focus on Amanda's suffering becomes highly significant: "You're a Christian martyr, yes honey, that's what you are. A Christian martyr (*GM* 15)." This statement suggests that Amanda lives in a world of illusion which is the Glass Menagerie and is the victim of reality.

In Scene V we find a picture in which the accent is on hope. This is done through colours and their analogic equivalents such as images and legends. The legend on screen is 'Annunciation' which refers to the announcement of the incarnation by Angel Gabriel. The legend therefore sets the tone of hope and expectancy with a mock religiosity.

> It is early dusk of a spring evening. Supper has just been finished in the Wingfield apartment. AMANDA and LAURA in light coloured dresses are removing dishes from the table, in the upstage area, which is shadowy, their movements formalized almost as a dance or ritual, their moving forms as pale and silent as moths. Tom, in white shirt and trousers, rises...(GM 16)

The colour white and other light tones give the scene a dream-like etherealness which is a flash of memory of different time periods in Tom's mind. This however is the construction of time present which is contrasted to time past in Amanda's mind through rich and intense colours.

> On evenings in spring the windows and doors were open and the music came outdoors. Sometimes the lights were turned out except for a large glass sphere that hung from the ceiling. It would turn slowly about and filter the dusk with delicate rainbow colours. Then the orchestra played a waltz or a tango, something that had a slow and sensuous rhythm. (*GM* 16)

The slow and sensuous rhythm is an equivalent to richer and fuller colour and so are the rainbow colours. Contrasted to the lightly coloured present the picture of the past seems richer and filled with vitality.The following lines by Amanda give us an idea of the arrest of time in sudden moments in the play:

> Amanda: You are the only young man that know who ignores the fact that the future becomes the present, the present the past...(*GM* 18)

Amanda reveals the impressionistic pattern of reality vs dream alternating as light and dark tones in *The Glass Menagerie*.Tharpe comments:

> The underlying structure of The Glass Menagerie is formed by a tension between the illusion of the moving forward and the reality of the moving backward, between dream and

> destiny, the two so perfectly balanced that the effect is the arrest of time (Tharpe 685)

In Scene IV, too, the alternating pattern of dark and light tones can be seen. The following lines that show a changed appearance of the Wingfield apartment hint at Amanda's attempt to conceal the darker tones of reality with the lighter tones of the dream world:

> (AMANDA has worked like a Turk in preparation for the gentleman caller. The results are astonishing. The new floor lamp with its rose-silk shade is in place, a colored paper lantern conceals the broken light fixture in the ceiling, new billowing white curtains at the window, chintz covers are on chairs and sofa…) (*GM* 21)

A similar pattern of alternating light and dark tones can be seen as Amanda reminisces over her past:

> Evening, dances!- Afternoons, long rides! Picnics-lovely!- So lovely, that country in May – All lacy with dogwood, literally flooded with jonquils! That was the spring I had the craze jonquils. (GM 22)

These bright tones are flooded by ominous music that hints at the darker shades of reality. Similarly, the first legend expresses Terror i.e. the nervous state of Laura and the next legend reads as 'The Opening of a door". The first legend expresses fear as contrasted to the second which expresses the softness of expectancy. The earlier images are used repetitively such as the image of Jolly Roger and Amanda as a young girl.A third image of the Executive at desk represents Jim the gentleman caller. These three opposing images remind us of the Impressionists' use of disparate colours. Towards the end we are presented with a comingling of loud and soft tones,

> (LEGEND: "TERROR!")
>
> (Outside a summer storm is coming abruptly. The white curtains billow inward at the windows and there is a sorrowful murmur and deep blue dusk.) (*GM* 26)

The emotion, of 'terror' is an analogic equivalent to a loud tone, the sorrowful murmur to a soft tone. The deep blue is yet another colour here. The white colour too is prominent. The impact of the scene which shows the overpowering darkness of reality is in the gentle relief brought by the deep blue which symbolizes hope.It is worth noting here that 'blue' has a symbolic significance in this play as in Williams'other plays. The blue in *The Glass Menagerie* is native to Laura's inner self. It represents not only her fragile world of dreams and hopes, but also represents the entire world of the Wingfield family ensconced in its memories and dreams.Thus in Scene VIII we are given a wider use of the colour blue:

> As the curtain rises LAURA is still huddled upon the sofa, her feet drawn under her, her head resting on a pale blue pillow, her eyes wide and mysteriously watchful. The new floor lamp with its shade of rose-coloured silk gives a soft, becoming light to her face, bringing out the fragile, unearthly prettiness which usually escapes attention. There is a steady murmur of rain, it is slackening and stops soon after the scene begins: the air outside becomes pale and luminous as the moon breaks out.
>
> A moment after the curtain rises, the lights.... flicker and go out. (*GM* 26)

The blue of her pillow, the pink of her lamp, the murmur of rain in the background and the pale moonlight, are tones that highlight Laura's fragility. Laura's gradual movement out of her cloister is conveyed through the medium of colours. During her interaction and communication with Jim, her feelings intensify when she reminisces about being called 'Blue Roses' by Jim in the past. There is an intimate exchange between them:

> This one is one of the oldest. Its nearly thirteen.
> (Music: ("THE GLASS MENAGERIE")
>
> (He stretches out his hand.)
> Oh, be careful- if you breathe. It breaks! (GM 32)

The music of the Glass Menagerie intensifies the growing bond between Laura and Jim. They discover mutual attraction between each other and both have a need for each other. As they begin to dance, the Image on Screen is Blue Roses and as he tries to kiss her the music swells tumultuously. After this sudden intensity and depth of colour, Jim acknowledges his love for someone else:

> (The holy candles in the altar of LAURA'S face have been snuffed out. There is a look of almost infinite desolation). (GM 35)

The legend on screen, 'Things have a way of turning out so badly!' and the image of the Gentleman Caller waving good bye- gaily,' all signify a change of colour, mood and tone. Towards the close of the play Tom's summing up of the pictures of his memory presents to us the whole play which is a family portrait created of moments and pieces of colour. It is a still, lifeless picture to which Tom returns often symbolically:

> Perhaps I am walking along a street at night, in some strange city, before I have found companions. I pass the lighted window a shop...... The window is filled with pieces of coloured glass, tiny transparent bottles in delicate colours, like bits of shattered rainbow. (GM 38)

The play is the portrait of a family which embodies Williams' vision of life. Williams communicates in this play, as in his other plays, two worlds-the world of illusion and the world of reality which are perpetually in conflict with each other. It can be said that through the Impressionistic portrait of the Wingfield family William presents a slice of life animated with colours.

WORKS CITED

Jackson, Esther Merle. *The Broken World of Tennessee Williams.* London: The University of Wisconsin Press, 1966. Print

Spoto, Donald. *The Kindness of Strangers: the Life of Tennessee Williams* .Boston: Little Brown, 1941. Print.

Williams, Tennesse. *Memoirs.* New York : Doubleday & Company, Inc,.1975. Print

Williams, Tennessee. *The Glass Menagerie in Best Plays of Modern American Theatre,* Second Series, ed. John Gassner. New York: Crown Publishers lnc.,1957. Print. All subsequent references to the text are from this edition.

11

Buckling Under Feminist Charges: Women in Ayn Rand's Lesser Known Works

Akbar J. A. Syed

Ayn Rand's work has been devoured by generations of readers. A cult figure, her popularity has given birth to die-hard fan clubs which have shown devotion to her of the kind seen in devotees towards their gods and goddesses. This has often resulted in her work not being properly evaluated. In our time of critical theory which adopts a questioning attitude towards most received ideas, Ayn Rand's work may appear in a different light. Marxist-feminist approach to her work reveals her female characters in a very negative light. A critical analysis of Ayn Rand's fiction indicates that far from presenting assertive, successful and sexually emancipated heroines with a revolutionary and novel theme, her fictional works are no less guilty of usual feminist charges. Her heroines and plot, in fact, do more harm than good to feminist cause. Despite being a woman novelist she reinforces stereotypical images of women in her fiction, making her works all the more distressing to a gender-conscious reader.

Marxist-feminists are of the view that women are a 'class' in themselves just as the working class and are a subject of the ruling class, which happens to be bourgeois and male. This ruling patriarchal capitalist class subjugates women two-fold – gender wise and economically. In most cases there also exists the race and caste angle. In fact, the intersectionality of race, class, caste and gender defines the oppression of women in most social formations.

Ayn Rand's fiction is her foremost achievement and all of Ayn Rand's major literary works follow similar plot patterns, protagonist profiles and thematic content. In her major fictional works, some ideas, plots and themes are repeated. In this brief paper the focus is on two of her relatively lesser known works in which she almost unashamedly celebrates the institution of patriarchy.

Nights of January 16th (1936) is Ayn Rand's first professional writing. She originally titled it as the 'Penthouse Legend', but its Broadway presentation was titled *Night of January 16th* and the name has remained. It is a gripping drama about the mysterious death or disappearance of Bjorn Faulkner and the trial of Karen Andre, the protagonist, who is his secretary and mistress and is accused of his murder.

For Ayn Rand, this was to be a 'sense of life' play. Bjorn Faulkner is presented as a free-wheeling, world-class entrepreneur whose financial kingdom was in dire straits at the time of his death. Two versions of his mysterious death are presented in court. The prosecution blames Karen Andre and her lover 'Guts' Regan to have black mailed and murdered Faulkner when he refused to give them the money they were asking for. The defense contends that Faulkner's marriage to Nancy Whitfield was a sham as he never liked or loved her and he used himself as collateral so that John Graham Whitfield, Nancy's father, would extend a ten million dollar loan to him.

At the end of Act II, in a dramatic reversal, 'Guts' Regan, the gangster and alleged lover of Karen Andre, shows up to announce that Bjorn is really dead. He explains that he, Bjorn and Karen had planned a fake suicide so that Bjorn and Karen could disappear with Whitfield's money. Regan contends but Faulkner's bookkeeper verifies that fact that Whitfield found out about the money being embezzled. Regan accuses Whitfield of murdering Faulkner. The jury is left to decide whether a respected banker and his socialite daughter or a secretary- mistress and her gangster lover are telling the truth.

Karen Andre, the female protagonist is a typical Ayn Rand heroine, for whom Bjorn Faulkner is a 'God like hero' to be served with her mind, soul and body. For Ayn Rand, the play was a presentation of the 'sense of life' which she defined as a person's 'emotional, subconsciously integrated appraisal of man's relationship to existence' (Baker39) and in *Night of January 16th*, this 'sense of life' is Karen Andre's feelings for her ideal man.

We may note that the 'sense of life' presented in this play is consistent with those presented in her novels. Karen Andre like all of Ayn Rand's heroines is active, independent, sure of herself and her ideas, clear with the direction she wants her life to take and sexually emancipated. However, a close analysis of Karen Andre's character and personality reinforces the feminist argument that Ayn Rand demeans and diminishes women and femininity morally and intellectually through the offensive images of women. This celebration of patriarchy by Ayn Rand demeans and dehumanizes women at large. In scene 1 of Act 1, Karen's character profile is thus described: "One's first impression of her is that to handle her would require the services of an animal trainer, not an attorney..." (NJ16th 22).

During her questioning in Act II, Karen's masochistic perverseness is evident when she narrates her 'rape' at the hands of B'jorn Faulkner: "he seemed tc take a delight in giving me orders. He acted as if he were cracking a whip over an animal... I liked it... then he asked me suddenly if I had ever belonged to a man. I said, no, I hadn't... (NJ16th 82-83). When Karen refused his offer of a thousand Kroners to have sex with him, he threatens forcing himself on her, "he said if I didn't, he' d take me ....he did" (NJ16th 83).

This continual reference to Karen as if she is an animal and not a human being, tantamounts to refusing to attribute to women any spiritual and intellectual profundity. She is an 'object' at the hands of man's mercy, to be used, consumed and exploited. Since man in an androcentric patriarchal dispensation is the 'meaning and signifier' women's feelings are inconsequential and Ayn Rand celebrates this patriarchal subversion. For Karen Andre, B'jorn Faulkner is 'an ideal man' whom she served as a secretary, mistress and confidant.

The character of Nancy Lee Faulkner, the other female character in the novel, brings back what the feminists should call the 'neurotic, manipulated' stereotypical image of women into focus. She is presented as a cold, man- manipulating nymphomaniac, determined to get Bjorn Faulkner at any cost. She offers herself, her sexuality to be precise, for his agreeing to marry her and in return he would get the extension of a certain ten million dollar loan…(NJ16th 85).

Nancy Lee Faulkner's commodification may be understood better with reference to the 'use, consumption and circulation' theory where her body is used as a bartering object between Bjorn Faulkner and her father John Graham Whitfield. Nancy Lee Faulkner demeans herself by asking Bjorn to marry her and thus provide their marriage as collateral to her father for extending the loan. This incident may be understood in terms of women's conditioning and socialization' in a patriarchal set-up. In the patriarchal scheme of things a woman's primary function is to facilitate and make the conditions of a social and cultural life possible. Patriarchal societies function on the basis of 'systems of exchange', where according to Luce lrigaray, "women's bodies- through their use, consumption and conditions- provide for the conditions making social life and culture possible' (Oliver 212). In the process they become an unknown 'infrastructure' and thus are instrumental in stimulating wealth among men. We observe Karen Andre's use of and traffic between her husband and father in a similar vein. The exploitation of Nancy Lee by Bjorn Faulkner is more in economic terms for as a commodity she is two things at once: a utilitarian object and a bearer of values (economic exchange value).

We thus see in *Night of January 16th*, how Karen Andre and Nancy Lee Faulkner, through their 'sense of life', contribute in lending support to the forces of patriarchy. We may add that the 'sense of life' presented in this play is consistent with those of the novels. The novels, in fact, deal with more than 'sense of life', they involve a 'conscious philosophy' i.e. a conceptually defined view of man and existence.

We the Living (1936) is Ayn Rand's first novel written between 1931 and 1933 and published in 1936. The plot of *We the Living* concerns a young woman's struggle to fulfill her desires under the stultifying structures of the Soviet System. The central figure of Kira Argounova in this novel was to become the arch model for her later fictional works. Andrei Taganov and Leo Kovalensky, the two male protagonists, can be viewed as the prototypes of Howard Roark and John Galt.

The story of *We the Living* revolves around Kira Argounova, and her family's exile and return to Petrograd after the revolution. The small industries run by her family are confiscated by the government under a nationalizing scheme and this gives Aya Rand a chance to introduce her 'state versus the individual', pattern here. As soon as she enters the technological institute she meets a young communist leader named Andrei Taganov. She spends the college hours with him while her nights are spent with an unregenerate aristocrat named Leo Kovalensky.

Andrei likes and loves Kira while her amorous feelings are heavily titled towards Leo Kovalensky. Kira's relationships with Andrei is platonic, but when Leo contracts consumption and must go away to the Crimea, if he is to live, Kira is determined to save him. She pretends to love Andrei to secure money from him and thereby forces Leo to go to a sanatorium in the south. This was to become a familiar theme in Ayn Rand's later fiction, where a woman gives herself sexually to one man to save another and as pointed out earlier James T. Baker terms this peculiarity of the Ayn Rand theme as the 'Tosca theme'. The second half of *We the Living* deals with corruption of Leo and the heroism of Andrei. Leo's return from the Crimea shows his spiritual and intellectual graph falling while Andre's faith in the Soviet system is seen shaking. Oddly enough, Kira is attracted to Leo in his 'fallen' state even more than she was earlier. Glimpses of Ayn Rand's feminine masochism are evident here. Andrei sets out to expose the corruption in the Soviet system and during his investigations he discovers that Kira is living with Leo and she only pretended to love him (Andrei), rather she used him to help another man. Andrei far from feeling bitter promises to save Leo from the net he (Andrei) has cast to apprehend the bourgeois saboteurs and their patrons in government. At a communist party gathering he delivers a speech that sounds more like Howard Roark's in *the Fountainhead*. In the later novels Howard Roark and John Galt were to represent his idealism.

Kira Argounova is Ayn Rand's first fully developed heroine and she was to be the model for later Ayn Rand heroines: active, assertive, fiercely independent, career conscious and sexually emancipated. Unmindful of her material surroundings, she wants only to be allowed to fulfill the best that is in her. Such focus and determination was to be the attribute of all of Ayn Rand's heroines. However, despite creating such a positive image of heroine Ayn Rand taints this image with Kira's hero-worshiping of Leo and forcing her (like all her other heroines) to bow to masochistic impulses.

Superficial readings of Ayn Rand's works may not reveal her 'celebration of patriarchy' but a closer reading exposes just that. In the novel *We the Living* violence accompanies sex, "…but he tore her off the ground, and then she arched limply in space… her breast at his mouth" (WTL113). For Leo Kira is nothing more than 'an object'. She deifies him and is always ready to please him: "Leo threw his coat in a corner… it was torture. Waiting. Three days- and three nights" (WL121). For Leo Kira is a product, which he 'consumes and uses', and when he gets a better proposition, he leaves her. Leo shifts into Tonia's apartment after Citizen Morozov leaves town. Morozov has left Tonia a nice little sum of money and she is going for a rest and vacation in the Caucasus's. Tonia asks Leo to go with her to which he agrees:

> He's left Tonia… he's left her a nice little sum of money… she's going for a rest and vacation in the Caucasus. She has asked me to go with her. I have accepted the job… the great gigolo of the U. S. S. R.!... She's an old bitch… she has the money and she wants me ….. (WTL423-424)

Kira worshipped Leo and for him she became a mistress to Andrei. When Leo had to be sent to the Crimea for recuperation and there was no money with them, Kira went to Andrei. She saved the money he gave her, because "she thought of someone at home who needed it. She took the money" (WTL179). For all her worshipping and sacrifice when Leo gets to know about her liaison with Andrei and wants to go away with Tonia he arrogantly and contemptuously calls her, 'you little bitch!' (WTL422). We observe here how Kira's body is nothing more than a commodity, which is two things at once, a 'utilitarian object' for Leo and Andrei to use, consume and circulate between them and a 'bearer of value', for as mistress to Andrei, she receives money in return. In fact, she gives herself sexually to Andrei only for the money she will get.

We further observe that Kira and Leo's relationship is akin to that of a slave and his master: "he approached her and his hand closed over here throat and he jerked her head back to hold her lips to his. There was a contemptuous tenderness in his movement, and a command, and hunger; he was not a lover, but a slave owner..." (WTL312). With Andrei too her relationship has similar refrain, "you won't miss me ... I've made you happy, haven't I?" (WTL237) and when she tells Andrei, "Andrei when you told me you loved me, for the first time, you were hungry. I wanted to satisfy that hunger" (WTL265).

Kira Argounova's worshiping of Leo and becoming a mistress to Andrei and sexually bowing to both of them is a fine example of 'celebration of patriarchy' in the novel. Kira's sexuality is exploited by the two male heroes and Kira's compliance just like the other heroines in Ayn Rand's fiction, is founded on the notion "that whether premarital or extramarital: the man's inner life is a privilege to share..." (EIlman119).

Anthem (1938) was Ayn Rand's second novel of only seventy seven pages. It was published in England in 1938 and it was only in 1946 that an American edition was published when Pamphleteers, a right wing publishing house, brought out an abridged paperback edition. Originally conceived of as a play while Ayn Rand was at university in Petrograd, *Anthem* has retained a theatrical quality unto itself. We observe in this novel the economic and political ideology of capitalism for which she would become famous later through *The Fountainhead* and *Atlas Shrugged*.

While all of Ayn Rand's works are famous today, one may agree with Mimi R. Gladstein writing in the *The Ayn Rand Companion* when she says that "if any of Ayn Rand's works becomes a staple on high school reading lists, it will be this book" (34). *Anthem* is a brief novel about a dystopia, a collectivist state where conformity and drudgery are the norm. Ayn Rand's utopia was to be a place where men will hunt and women admire them, where men will be the life force and women its worshippers. *Anthem* was the beginning for the opera to come, composed of *The Fountainhead* and *Atlas Shrugged*.

The story is written in the form of a journal kept by a man of the future, living in a collectivist state, a state where people do not have names but numbers. His is equality 7-2521 and is viewed suspiciously by the elders of his society. Much of the pleasure of the story is derived from the reader's use of their imagination as they fill in the gaps in the hero's knowledge of the 'unmentionable times' before the ascendance of the collectivist state. Equality 7-2521 wants to be a scholar and this desire of his brings him on a collision course with the Council of Vocations. For his impudence he is punished to become a street sweeper.

However, Equality 7-2521 manages to hoodwink the elders and quench his thirst for knowledge when he discovers a tunnel, a remnant of structures from unmentionable times. He goes there to study manuscripts stolen from the clerks in his bid to tinker with the chemicals and dissect animals.

Committing another 'sin of preference', he falls in love with Liberty 5-300 whom he sees in the fields. He is twenty one and she only seventeen and before this he has known women only during the 'Time of Mating'. She returns his love like any Ayn Rand heroine and she knows her 'hero-man' when she sees him. Out of his passionate love for her comes a desire to say the Unspeakable Word 'I' for which the punishment is burning at the stakes.

When Equality 7-2521 escapes from the city she follows him into the Unchartered Forest. Liberty 5-3000, who is now called the Golden One, says: "we have followed you... Do as you please with us, but do not send us away from you. Then they knelt, and bowed their golden head before us" (A82-83). For Ayn Rand servility and submissiveness of her female protagonists was actually 'woman trying to find meaning' for after all 'woman is defined by her relationship to man'. Equality 7-2521 learns to hunt like a man, while Liberty

5-3000 learns the pleasures of looking into a mirror presumably like a woman, bringing to the fore the stereotype of women being vain and dependant on the man for protection and support. When they find a place and Equality 7-2521 tells her that this is their place, she says to her Lord and master: 'your will be done' (A 19).

From a manuscript he has found in the house he takes the name Prometheus and gives to Golden One the name Gaea, for he is to be the source of light, while she is to be the Mother Earth: "her name was Gaea… for you are to be the mother of a new kind of gods" (A 99). Luce Irigaray, the eminent feminist critic, writes that in a patriarchal social order which is founded on the exchange of women 'as mother', woman's value is in the reproduction of children (and of the labor force). Her reproductive value underwrites her exchange value in the social order. As mothers their responsibility is to maintain the social order by 'reproducing children and thus 'the labor force'.

In *Anthem*, 'the compliant stereotype' is also once again visible, where the man's inner life is a privilege to share. As a servant to her lord and mother to his children, Liberty 5-3000 fulfills two sub -divisions of this stereotype.

WORKS CITED

Baker, James T. *Ayn Rand.* Boston: West Kentucky University, 1987. Print.

Gladstein, Mimi R. *Ayn Rand and Feminism: An Unlikely Alliance. London*, 1978. Print.

Oliver, Kelly. (ed) *French Feminism Reader*. Oxford, 2000. Print.

Rand, Ayn. *Anthem.* New York: New American Library, 1979. Print.

—*We the Living*. New York: New American Library, 1959. Print.

— *Night of January 16th*. New York: New American Library, 1968. Print.

12

Home in Exile, Exile at Home: The Case of Asian Diasporic Writing

Ameena Kazi Ansari

The twentieth century witnessed the demise of imperialism and colonialism as well as the concomitant history of decolonisation. It was marked by a spurt of mass migration by peoples from Asia to the West, especially to Britain and the US. Waves of immigrants, formerly under colonial rule, chose to make their way to the metropolitan centres of the West. This transition from their homelands into unfamiliar places/spaces gave rise to huge immigrant or diasporic populations that came to be referred to as 'melting pots,' 'mosaics,' or as 'salad bowls' over a period of time. These nomenclatures were symbolic of what the white West expected of their immigrant populations, as well as what the immigrants themselves perceived their position to be. The first generation immigrants were expected to melt into their new environment, pushing the baggage of memory into the remotest corners of consciousness. The descendants of this first generation grew more assertive after being perceived as figurative pieces in a demographic mosaic. They saw themselves as a mosaic of cultures where each piece/diasporic segment had equal significance. With time, the nomenclature evolved as the seeds of immigrant assertion germinated and gave rise to the perception that each cultural segment was a vital, distinct entity in the salad bowl of a nation's demographic makeup.

In the literary world, immigration and diasporic realities resulted in the emergence of new literary configurations and expression. This was grounded in the transculturation of experience and outlook. The diasporic writing that surfaced, gave voice to assorted memories, varied experiences and diverse idioms which define diasporic existence. These writings embodied the diaspora's consciousness, negotiating between memory of old nation, culture and history and the new dimensions of immigrant existence. Writers had to engage, disengage, and re-engage with the realities of identity, culture and politics in their new social milieu. Their creative effort involved imaginative re-configurations of place and space that defined these experiences and realities. In order to engage with the shifting trends and perspectives of diasporic writing, it becomes essential to examine the conditions that contributed to its evolution.

I

Asian migration to North America and Britain started way back in the early nineteenth century. The first wave of immigrants from the Indian subcontinent comprised workers/labourers, mostly Sikhs, who first reached the west coast of North America in 1830. The number had reached thirty thousand by 1910. Most of them had settled in the region between Vancouver and San Francisco. In 1913, many of them had come together to form the Hindustan *Ghadar* Party prompted by the ghadar or rebellion against the British in India in 1857. They drew their inspiration from a rebellion which may have ended in failure, but its spirit lived on as a desire to overthrow colonial rule as also a vision to struggle against slavery and oppression, wherever it existed in the world. The duality of desire and vision can be seen, firstly, as a reaction to a 1910 US immigration commission report which stated that Indians were 'regarded as the least desirable race of immigrants thus far admitted to the United States;' secondly, it was 'part of a well organised diasporic attempt to combat imperialism in India' (Kumar xii).

Subsequent waves of Asian migrants were driven to North America by the compulsion of politics and poverty. Circumstances made them hapless and helpless collaborators with colonial powers who pushed ahead with their imperialistic designs, consolidation of territory and access to cheap labour. It resulted in many being transported to unknown continents as indentured labour, as soldiers enlisted for a war being fought beyond the pale of their existence, as political exiles waiting to assume the reins of power whenever an inconvenient regime was made to fall, and as moral police whenever popular revolts threatened to dislodge deeply entrenched colonial rule. In whatever circumstances these immigrants found themselves, they were torn between effacing themselves and joining the mainstream, or struggling to maintain their cultural identity even as they grappled with the dynamics of wages, labour and standards of living. For them, life was marked by the contraries of assertion and reconciliation, minority and mainstream, inclusion and exclusion. Caught in the cleft of these dichotomies, the migrant's most powerful and effective tool was the word, the ability to be vocal and articulate so as to make oneself heard. With time, the immigrant's voice has indeed made itself heard. On the political front, this voice has registered its presence as Senator Bobby Jindal, The Honourable Ujjal Dosanjh, or Lord Swaraj Paul; in the literary arena, it is the writings of Michael Ondaatje, Hanif Kureishi or Jhumpa Lahiri that have reiterated diasporic presence. The fact of the matter is that language has become the diaspora's tool for relating to, and negotiating with, his/her world. With variations of idiom and attitude, the diasporic writers have announced their arrival.

Language has long been a symbol of empowerment. The choice and usage of a word defines the self as also the environment in which that self has been engendered. In addition to this, the Asian diasporic writer's world and word is coloured by the shifting contours of postcoloniality and the simultaneity of difference and belonging which symbolise the immigrant's environment. This harks back to the lived reality of each immigrant, that is, having to juggle with the acknowledgement of difference while forging a sense of belonging in the new space of arrival. The immigrant is constantly aware that he/she is an alien, a foreigner placed in the daunting situation of having to come to terms with a dominant foreign culture and language. In the case of Asian immigrants in Britain and North America, there has to be a negotiation with the formidable world of English language, its many linguistic cultures and ideologies. The creative impulse in diasporic writers operates on two levels—the thematic and the idiomatic. The former has to do with choice of subject, the latter involves the choice of words that give life and vibrancy to the subject. Diasporic writing often becomes a subtle tool for self-discovery as the writer goes about making a foreign language his/her own, striving to incorporate rather than be incorporated. In this literary endeavour, marked divergences can be observed as perspectives shift between longing and belonging, servility and rebellion, homage and hatred.

In the postcolonial world, literature has become the arena for negotiation and contestation, for self-fashioning and refashioning. Invariably, such writing gets back at the erstwhile hegemonic centres. The many strategies of narration emanate from, and have their roots in, the writers' story-telling traditions from the space and place left behind in the homeland. Diasporic writers see themselves in an unfamiliar environment where things have to be understood in shades of grey so as to better comprehend the subtleties of difference and bi-culturality. In *Imaginary Homelands*, Rushdie refers to this as 'hybridity,' a condition marked by the intersection of multi-layered compositions and diverse cultural trajectories. This, then, is the space which engenders the diasporic writers' counter discourse. This discourse foregrounds immigrant experience which fictionalises 'otherness' and 'difference' in the context of self and environment.

Asian diasporic writing in the West is characterised by three basic facets: the panoramic, the interpretative, and the prophetic. The panoramic facet has to do with the immigrant's considerably rich emotional and cultural baggage comprising the subtle warp and weft of life in the spaces/places of homeland and settlement/resettlement. The texture and weave of this writing fuse the contrarieties of immigrant experience—memory and forgetting, the plural and the personal, the self and the 'other.' The interpretative facet involves describing and defining experiences born out of straddling two cultures. As a consequence, new angles of experiential reality, encompassing both distance and geography, can be identified in these writings. The facet of the prophetic becomes apparent as intellectual logic and imagination converge to envision realities and paradigms of diasporic representations of the future. A new 'literary nation' thus seems to emerge and it is rooted in the re/interpretations of a space and identity that is the patent of each writer (Smith 6-7).

The construct of this literary nation owes much to the socio-political concept of the nation/nationalism. Each diasporic writer creates his/her own rubric of a community which has its own history, character, culture, and ideology. There thus emerge myriad imaginary homelands which underline the variety and power of diasporic writing. The scattered 'nations' of immigrants create much of their literature from the phenomenon of cultural transplantation. This transplantation gives rise to two distinct strains that are prominent in their writings. One is the reflection of their own racial history; the other is a cultural and political history born out of the writers' experience of migration and displacement. Though immigrants are a minority group in the places of their settlement, their literature endeavours to creatively majoritise their realities. Consequently, there emerges a dual perspective in their writings—they are both insiders and outsiders in the new space they occupy and have chosen to depict. As insider-outsiders they have to face the dilemma of being hedged in and yet wanting to break out; there is a strong sense of feeling ghettoised but an equally strong tendency to transcend that ghettoisation through their words and address a world beyond their community. The insider-outsider perspective of the creative writer has evoked critical response and evaluation.

The study of the poetics and politics of diasporic writing engages with what Amitava Kumar terms 'immigritude' (x). Immigritude is a term that points to the immigrant's culture, identity and environment, all of which blend to give diasporic writing its own special flavour and identity. Diasporic writing is the product of a multicultural environment; immigritude forms its content. This writing fictionalises the realities of immigrant life and psyche by foregrounding identity, culture and history of individuals or groups, by evaluating complex situations of social interaction, by problematising issues of racialism and self-esteem, and by openly voicing contentious political and ideological contexts of diasporic existence. These texts embody 'a new re-creative sensibility' as they engage with the realities of survival and adaptation in the immigrant's world (Sofield). They very consciously and stridently counter the derogatory stereotypical references, the 'essentialisms'—like 'the filth of Asia'—that the white West has for its Asian immigrants (Adams).

Diasporic writing in the last decades of the twentieth century has broken the earlier template in which it was cast. It has been in a constant state of flux that marks the diasporic world. Each text seems to be creating its own definitions and paradigms of culture, history and identity as the descendants of original immigrants find themselves in—

> a sort of theatre where various political and ideological causes engage one another. Far from being a placid realm of Apollonian gentility, culture ... [comes] to be a battleground in which causes expose themselves to the light of the day and contend with one another. (Said xiii)

As new trajectories of self and identity open up for the immigrants from Asia, there can be perceived a very assertive streak in their writings. Diasporic writing has the unique capacity of juxtaposing places/spaces—Lahore and London or Delhi and Denver. In every conceivable way, these writings symbolise 'a writing back' to the white West with all its various subtle discriminations. They underline difference and heterogeneity, selfhood and otherness, angst and anger, all of which are embodied in the diasporic writer's experience. In their own ways, these texts ensure that their 'words become a defence against invisibility' as they go about asserting the voice of the diaspora (Kumar 14).

II

To make visible the hitherto invisible facets of immigrant existence, diasporic writing resorts to cultural resistance as well as reconciliation. This entails simultaneous negotiation with the realities of isolation and chauvinism which not only co-exist within diasporic experience and imagination but also find space in its narratives. Very often, such writings emerge as reactions to the predominant brand of white Western popular culture. An example of this is apparent in the corrosive lyrics of a song sung by the group Guns N' Roses:

> Immigrants
> and faggots
> They make no sense to me.
> They come to our country—
> And think they'll do as they please
> Like start some mini-Iran
> Or spread some fuckin' disease.

Migrant discourse, especially its literature, comes to terms with such rhetoric by redefining, reconfiguring, and reinventing idiom, identity and ideology. This happens because of the stark contrast between life in the West and its counterpart in Asia. Initially, diasporic imagination and writing looked inwards in terms of portraying the impact of the World Wars and the aftermath of postcolonialism. An example is Kazuo Ishiguro's novel, *An Artist of The Floating World*, which is a reflection on how art can succumb to the militaristic designs of a crumbling imperial power. It portrays an aesthetics which, rather than conforming to the principle of art-for-art's-sake, bows to art-for-establishment's-sake and results in an insipid artistic expression that is only commercial and leaves much to be desired. This bizarre reality is shown springing out of imperialistic designs that went awry and resulted in the humiliating defeat of Japan.

A short story, like Anjana Appachana's 'Her Mother,' is an example of how the diaspora re-creates or recasts Western mythologies. The Rapunzel syndrome of the long-haired beauty in the fairy tale is given a new twist. A young girl in India, who has shared intimacy with her brother-in-law and then been cast aside, chooses to flee to the US in the hope that the world of academia there can restore her sanity. The gesture that symbolises the snipping away of her ties with her home/homeland is the cutting off of her beautiful locks which her mother had so lovingly nurtured. It is a rebellious act to discard the mother who failed to perceive and empathise with a daughter's trauma. The story becomes an expression of breaking free from the shackles of both male chauvinism and female indifference at 'home' to enter the free world of another home-away-from-home.

Vassanji's novel, *Amrika*, is also woven round the diasporic issues of displacement, exile, longing, and eventually acceptance of fate. The 1960s world of war and conflict, protest, sexual freedom, proliferation of religious cults, and peace marches in the US, are the novel's backdrop. Ramji inherits this turbulent world and has to adapt to it, making it his own. In many ways, the work is prophetic as the shadows of 9/11 loom large in the background.

Hanif Kureishi is a writer of zeitgeist, capturing Britain's diasporic dynamics in terms of place/space and trajectories of thought. His works dramatize the evolution of a multiracial, multicultural Britain. *My Beautiful Laundrette* is a depiction of racism, gang violence, drug peddling, and gay sex through the eyes of Asian entrepreneurs. *My Son the Fanatic* is a story born out of the insidious ostracisation of second and third generation immigrants in the West. In an interview with Geoff Gardner, Kureishi talks of interacting with Asian youngsters who

> feel repudiated by the west. They felt they had been dumped in the West by their parents, who were immigrants, in a place where they weren't really wanted. You could see that fundamentalism was a good way for them of finding an identity, finding a place and sealing themselves off from the rest of society. … they didn't like women, they didn't like gay people … they didn't like anything much. It was kind of terrifying and moving. … it seemed as if in life … they were hemming themselves in with this terrible ideology. (<senses of cinema>)

My Son the Fanatic grew out of this interaction, and points to the unattended reasons that go into the racial, ethnic and ideological confrontations between immigrants and the establishment that governs their lives.

More recent immigrant narratives and fictions seethe with angst and anger, power and powerlessness, assertion and retaliation as they voice 'the existential dilemmas' and realities of diasporic existence (Kumar 162). Diasporic voices foreground the contestation and protestation of immigritude by being centred in East-West problematics that reflect shades of the political, social, cultural and historical. Polemical writings like Amitava Kumar's *Passport Photos* underline this reality even further. His analysis is that an immigrant has 'to negotiate between two poles, one of them anthropological and the other autobiographical. The former is distancing, the latter is enabling and self-transformative' (Kumar 55). In the immigrant's balancing act between the two poles lies the space of his new realities in which, Janus-like, the immigrant writer looks in two directions. He/she has to re-write self and identity, and also bridge the binaries.

Amitava Kumar's poems resonate with facets of immigrant reality and experience in the US. One of his poems, 'Lord Macaulay's Tail,' foregrounds the politics and history of language and colonialism. It recalls the past when 'TheEnglishlanguage' was the middle name of Macaulay's pet dog and 'we,' the colonised, 'became its tail.' This impression gave way to another when, in the postcolonial scenario, 'we' saw themselves mastering Macaulay's idiom and 'wagging the dog.' The bitter irony of the situation is highlighted by the poet's reference to 'the teeth of the dog' which devour places and people afresh while 'we keep wagging the tail vigorously,' happy to live cocooned lives far away from immigrant spaces/places.

The space of the non-migrant after the departure of the migrant is another focus of the diasporic writer. One such piece is Amitava Kumar's 'A Mother Writes in Her Letter from India.' This piece is a poetic postcard from the homeland, underlining the isolation, the distance and the separation that mark the lives of the dying generation whose offspring have sought the greener pastures of immigrant life in the West. The mother sums up her lonely existence by saying

> I can only speak
> of waiting and loneliness:
> these choices, somehow, were never mine.

Perhaps Kumar's most powerful composition on immigrant realities is entitled 'Poems for The I. N. S.' It is set in the US embassy in New Delhi and depicts a prospective migrant being interviewed by the visa officer. It is a poem dedicated to the Immigration and Naturalisation Service of the US, which is a dreaded stumbling block for immigrants headed to that country. The poem catches the entire suspense of the occasion when an aggressive visa officer holds the future of the submissive visa applicant in hand. Anyone who has gone through US visa application procedures can rarely forget the experience.

Distrust, arrogance and fear mark both the officer's attitude as well as that of the visa applicant, but the specific shades of these feelings differ. The officer sees the applicant as one given to deception, one who will vanish into the US and stay on as an illegal immigrant. So Kumar has him asking—

And how do I know
you are going to come back
—that you aren't going to stay there in the States?

The fear of the US establishment is also brought out through one of the absurd queries listed on the visa form—

Do you intend to overthrow
The Government of the United States
by force or by fraud?

In both cases, the immigrant is regarded with suspicion more than anything else. The applicant, on the other hand, fears the rejection of his application for not giving the 'right answers' but is also enraged by the officer's questions to determine the certainty of return to the homeland—

Do you have property in India?
Land? Relatives? Anything?

The applicant takes both the high moral ground through poetic imagery 'to establish his return', and arrogantly retorts—

'Write down, officer:
The yellow of mustard blossoms…
My grandmother's tears …
the music of my sister's laughter…
Four friends …
The bend in the river …
Women's voices from across the waters …
The smell of hot pepper being roasted over a naked fire.

In the end, the poet asserts his own selfhood and status as an immigrant by caustically responding to the US dispensation:

'Do you understand
that every time a doctor, teacher, engineer, or scholar
comes to the United States from India
you save more on bills …
that your saying we can't be trusted
is like the owner shouting his worker's lazy
after he has stripped his skin and taken his soul.'

Ironically, what was once 'the least desirable of the race of migrants' is depicted as 'the model minority' in the US. This nomenclature not only reinforces the difference that lies carved within the hearts of the diaspora, but it also reflects a justified pride in the niche that diasporic individuals have carved out for themselves as the elite in American society.

Another facet of diasporic experience is conveyed in a poem like 'Changes'. This is rooted in the social fragmentation that marks the worlds of India and the US. It begins on a strident note—

In a letter from Los Angeles
written by an upper-caste chemist,
the untouchable poet in india
learns that Indians in the United States
are treated like dogs.

The poet back in India gloats over the knowledge that, elsewhere in the world, the upper-caste is getting his just desserts. The upper-caste chemist's son, on the other hand, is caught in a cleft. He finds himself an immigrant as also a coloured in a predominantly white world. As the second generation immigrant, he has to contend with a greater identity crisis as he is culturally and racially 'neither here nor there.' The young man is shown to solve his dilemma by instinctively opting for survival by railing

> against affirmative action
> for Blacks, Asians, and Latinos
> whom he calls by other names.

Despite being victim of the racially tilted slurs of the Whites, he uses them against the very segment of society to which he belongs—the diaspora.

Kumar's 'Mistaken Identity' also portrays a double perspective that juxtaposes the coloured, Eastern pitted against the white, Western. The poem is about the terrible price that racism extracts from those who are unaware that they have been drawn into its vortex. A gullible Asian immigrant feels comfortable in the home of a White American because of its Indian décor and ambience. He is unable to grasp the insidious racialism that colours the monologue of his host holding forth on examples of mistaken identity—how Indians call all Nepalis 'bahadurs,' how Indians and Pakistanis pay exorbitantly to indulge in sexual voyeurism and watch lesbian acts, how an American boyfriend asks his Indian girlfriend to get over her 'difference' so as to help him forget 'the halal-style butchering of a prostitute in Southall.' Each example brings out the white world's racialism by naming and categorising the diaspora as the 'other,' the 'shadow' that has no substance.

'Arithmetic' is a poem that juxtaposes postcolonial India and the imperialistic US by resorting to the flashback/flashforward technique. It is set in India and ostensibly revolves round the slow police response to rioting after the rape of a Dalit woman. The poem's larger canvas, however, is both historical and political as it telescopes time, flashing back to the two decades it took independent India took to acknowledge its rural reality, and the century it took the British took to realise that India was 'not their property.' Then it flashes forward to demonic contemporary reality when hegemonic designs and technology combine, and it

> takes less than three seconds
> for President Bush to sign an order
> for the bombing of towns and villages
> in any given country.

It is a poem that underlines the immigrants' helpless wrath in the face national interest and political expediency which often targets their original homelands.

Another powerful immigrant voice is that of Ved Prakash Vatuk. His poems evoke different dimensions of diasporic realities. 'Jab Kabhi' is in memory of the Ghadar Party martyrs who strove to break free from the shackles of British rule by choosing to leave their homeland not only as a mark of protest but also as a quest for true freedom. To Vatuk, they appear as symbolic Lord 'Rams in exile,' going away to a foreign land, sacrificing everything they had, so that their descendants, the second generation immigrants—

> all of us
> could live like free people,
> become human. And live.

By juxtaposing myth and reality, Vatuk draws attention to the sacrifices and hurdles that marked the life of first generation immigrants who toiled hard to give their children a secure future and freedom.

'Poem' is an intensely personal piece in which Vatuk speaks of his home as 'a prison of time' which embodies 'the world of my exile.' Far away from his homeland, which was 'a security' that he had spurned, Vatuk perceives the adopted homeland as 'a prison … a scattering … a straying away from one's roots.' He reconciles to the pathos and the lonely reality of his situation by asserting 'my home is in exile/and I'm in exile at home.'

In 'Clinton ke Naam,' Vatuk addresses President Clinton from the vantage point of a foreigner/outsider in America. On behalf of the world, he poses questions on the equations of truth and power. Clinton is questioned as to why he, as president, declared a one-hundred-and-eighty second silence for those killed in the Oklahoma bombing by Timothy McVeigh while no one recalled, let alone observed silence, for the thousands who were dying as a result of 'terrorism' unleashed by the strategic interests of the US abroad. Vatuk recalls Palestine, Vietnam, Cuba, Congo, and Iraq to ask:

> Those weapons
> whose were they?
> Is there a continent
> where your bloody claws
> have not reached,
> where has not been established
> your official terrorism.

The poet emerges as a politically conscious immigrant who understands and reacts to the hidden agenda behind US interventions abroad. Their objective has little to do with democratisation but everything to do with neo-colonialism and its concomitant aggression, violence and terror. No bones are made about this reality in this hard-hitting poem.

Krisantha Sri Bhaggiyadatta is another forceful diasporic voice, this time emanating from Canada. His poetry has a satirical edge and revolves round the experience of ethnic minority in a foreign land, with all the nuances of racism, class difference, neocolonialism, and the West's assertiveness of its superiority. Perhaps his most evocative poem about immigrant sensitivities is 'Aay Wha' Kinda Indian Arr U?' While its title is a manifestation of the mocking racial slurs of the white West, the content is aggressively assertive about the immigrant's special identity and culture. Adopting a rhetorical style, Bhaggiyadatta problematises significant issues of immigrant existence like asserting markers of cultural identity, contending with the contentiousness of assimilation, and facing the humiliations engineered by immigration authorities, especially highlighting some of the demeaning measures that women immigrants are subjected to—

Am I the Indian wearing salwar or sari, a turban or a pottu
... the baby who puts off being born, awaiting a Jullunder Spring
... the Indian who must submit to virginity tests from immigration's con/sultants
... who is kept oceans apart from her lover?'

Other diasporic poets in Canada like Lakdasa Wickramasinha come across as voices of postcolonial assertion, wanting to hold up a mirror to the colonial project of domination that wiped out the culture and history of colonised spaces. Lakdasa Wickramasinha's Matisse poem evaluates art from an angle that is Asian and postcolonial. In 'Don't Talk to Me about Matisse,' Gauguin, van Gogh and Matisse are seen as hunters intruding into the pristine, aboriginal world of the South Sea Islands. In the guise of art, these men, rages the poet, traded in violence, sex, and cultural decimation. Negating their aesthetics, the poet asserts—

Talk to me instead of the culture generally—
how the murderers were sustained
by the beauty robbed of savages: to our remote
villages the painters came, and our white-washed
mud-huts were splattered with gunfire.

Works of Kumar, Bhaggiyadatta and Wickramasinha are a few examples of contemporary diasporic articulation. This writing adopts idioms and stances that are assertive and denunciatory. Contemporary diasporic writing continues to revolve round major thematic concerns like nostalgia for a homeland, history and culture left behind, of an acute consciousness of dislocation and loneliness, of having to straddle the dichotomies of assimilation on one hand and racism and generational conflict on the other. What sets it apart today is its tone that is aggressively assertive and critical. On one hand, it is concerned with the problems of assimilation, on the other, it exults in difference. Clarifying that blanket assimilation can never be the desirable objective for the diaspora, it seeks to alternatively posit that it is the West which should reconcile and learn to respect its immigrants' baggage of memory, history and culture. By foregrounding immigrant sensibilities and sensitivities, this vibrant genre of writing makes a case for the immigrant being seen as an equal shareholder in the social enterprise of Western society. As Himani Bannerji points out, an 'ahistoricity' has to evolve in the process of multiculturalism which, in turn, has to assure the immigrant population of an equality of citizenship, security, and lifestyle (71).

For the diasporic sensibility, it is the white West which is the 'other' and this 'other' has to reconcile to and accept the identity, culture, and transferred environment of the immigrant. Kip's outburst in Ondaatje's *English Patient*—'American, French, I don't care. When you start bombing the brown races of the world, you're an Englishman'—embodies a postcolonial reaction to the hegemony of all that is white, Western, and oppressive to the Asian immigrant. It is an example of how contemporary diasporic writing makes a clear, unapologetic case for representing the politics of the white Western 'other.' Immigrant rage was always there but it was concealed and implosive. Illusions and conventional respectability are now cast aside. Today, it is a modulated rage that makes the immigrant speak and write. Keenly felt scars of immigrant reality push him into doing this. The idea of resistance has been an alternative way of conceiving and drawing one's history. The tables, in a sense, have been turned as the diaspora challenges the long-held view of assimilation, and looks forward to a situation of reconciliation on an as-is-where-is basis.

NOTE

1. Vatuk is a Hindi poet settled in the US. English translations of some of his poems appear in *Passport Photos*.

WORKS CITED

Bannerji, Himani, ed. *The Dark Side of the Nation: Essays on Multiculturalism, Nationalism and Gender*. Toronto: Canadian Scholars Press, 2000. Print.

Brians, Paul. 'Postcolonial Literature: Problems with the Term.' 1998. <www.wsu.edu/~brians/anglophone/postcolonial.html>

Kumar, Amitava. *Passport Photos*. Penguin, 2000. Print.

Kureishi, Hanif. Interview by Geoff Gardner, 2000. <www.sensesofcinema.com/2000/10/kureishi>

Said, Edward. *Culture and Imperialism*. Vintage, 1994. Print.

Smith, Anthony D. *Nationalism*. Atlantic, 2001. Print.

Sofield, Heather. 'Postcolonial Identity, Postcolonial Literature.' 1999. <http://www.postcolonialweb.org/zimbabwe/sofield/6.html>

13

Reading Select Plays of Tagore in the Post-Colonial Perspective

Nazia Hasan

An artist of true vision can surprise in many ways, Rabindranath Tagore is astonishing in his literary works by the variety and nuances spread all around. So, the mystic poet of '*Gitanjali*' emerges in different garbs in varying phases of his writings – as a nature lover, a social activist, a nationalist, an internationalist, a landlord sans his misconceived power, a poet, a dramatist, a painter, a musician, a sculptor… and of course, as a humanist.

The present paper tries to evoke Tagore as a resisting figure- who did not just rejoice in the glories of the equally important and warm reception of his poetry in both East and West, but who kept his conscience clear with devotion towards his immediate society and its uplift. The chosen plays depict this honey-toned mystic poet in a startling new light, who could think of and act on the thorny paths of revolt and rebellion against every kind of inhuman restriction. Tagore had witnessed feudalism, colonialism, nationalism and finally industrialization as different forms of the 'protean imperalism' (Benita 37). A postcolonial reading of Tagore's writings comes alive with apparitions of blood, gore, exploitation, inhuman cruelty, bondage system and totalitarian practices under cover of his fragrant words and musical rhymings. The two plays chosen especially for the present theme's exploration are- *The Waterfall*, and *The Red Oleanders*, written in the years1922 and 1923 known in history for a period of intense revolt on the national and internal fronts which had unveiled the true face of British imperialism to all its colonies-India being one of the most alluring and bounteous of all.

The Waterfall/The Muktadhara (Tagore, TWF 163) is a dramatized version of Tagore's ideas and beliefs expressed about the onslaught of Westernization through industry, machines and technology. Tagore needs a careful study because he is progressive in many aspects of life, warns countrymen of 'the desert of dead habits' and simultaneously does not welcome novel ways of making life easier, with new techniques in use. *The Waterfall* helps in removing cobwebs of such ambivalence regarding Tagore's views for modernity in a very well-emphasized manner. The poet fears death of soul and stretching of the 'waste-land' in hearts when surrounded by machines all around. He fears the impending loss of humanity by the lure of 'god, gold and glory' perspectives of the colonizing rules. He fears drowning of the natural voices under the cacophonous noises created by new found heaps of coins and meshes of mechanical coils entrapping lives from all sides. Tagore could sense it strongly that the great new stream of civilization coming from the West was simply a heavy outpour of all uncivilized means and purposes, as he writes in his essay entitled *Nationalism*, "We have seen that with all its vaunted love of humanity ... and freedom, it has proved to be itself the greatest menace to man, ... has produced worse forms of slavery than ever were current,' ... with (unbreakable) chains; because they assume the names and appearance of freedom itself'(Tagore, Natn 22). Whereas, Tagore wished changes in the aspects of modern civilization which could 'infuse life in to the machine, substitute human heart for its cold expediency' and in which power and success help in maintaining a balanced, 'harmonious and living growth' (Natn 23). The mechanical power should not act as a 'soft- soaping (empire) power' (Meclintock 413) to destroy truth and beauty.

Thus, the play *Waterfall* begins on a high note with great hype and applause of the new machine of 'embankment' which has taken 'twenty five years' (*TWF*, 165) of strenuous labour to be completed. The adventurous and extra-ordinary engineer named Bibhuti is going to be felicitated by the king Ranajit for this grand success.

The town folks have been invoked about this construction in such high sounding way that they take it as a festival to be celebrated with feast and gaiety- as if this dam is going to end all their malaise and sorrows as a panacea. It reads very much like what Amitav Ghosh said about the 11th May, 1998 nuclear tests of India in *Countdown*, "The bomb is much more than a weapon…It is a great vessel filled with all the unfulfilled aspirations and thwarted dreams of the last fifty years" (Ghosh 18).

Amartya Sen also observed in *The Argumentative Indian* that "weapons of mass destruction have a peculiar fascination today" (Sen 251). The power generated by these weapons is sundered from the inhuman brutality and genocide which measures its potency. These changes stand as an allegory for the whole world which is 'vying over' the power of 'modern technology' after losing their individuality and self definitions. Rabindranath Tagore could sense the threats in a prophetic way. He could make out that violent aspect of science as a colonial imposition, received gullibly by the elites of the colonized Orients like India, Egypt and Africa – they all attributed mystical hopes and beliefs to these machines and later to the weapons of mass destruction. The Uttarakut people have also embarked on the same boat of a false dawn, pinning all hopes on Bibhuti's creation.

But as no ideology can sweep over the whole masses, there are one or two persons of the province who view it differently causing a rift in the hard-earned unanimity of general public. The crown prince Abijit, youngmen Vishwajit and Dhananjay form a pressure group, by opposing this engineered installation. They find the machine to be 'monstrous', with its sacrilegious height (*TWF* 165), working as a blasphemous barrier between God and man. Amba, the lonely widow mourns for his son Suman's loss and complains that the tall machine filches away her prayers on its way to God's heart (166), so no respite comes for her painful cravings to see her child. Her unfortunate case like that of Batu, is linked to those totalizing ideologies of modernity, scientific developments, instrumental rationality which were imposed gifts of colonization. It demanded innumerable people to be sacrificed in the name of development.

Whereas, Bibhuti's name is revered like a semi-god and he himself starts playing-god in words and action. He claims that by controlling the flow of the water, he has 'dethroned' God (167) and people sing in ecstasy the might of machine which could 'melt iron and crush rocks and whose claws could wrench bare the entrails of the earth'(169). So, god is dead as man can do everything now as per his wishes and whims.

The Uttarakut town people are drunk with pride in this 'celebration' (169) without paying heed to the fate of neighbouring Shiu Tarai people who would be deprived of water even by a drop. Bibhuti, the King and all authorities rejoice in this scientific-God-given power to bind water (167), to triumph over nature and to be freed of natural relations with the immediate Shiu Tarai. They do not need to bother about their drought (167), death and demise. This water deprivation was also a weapon to subjugate the Shiu Tarai people as they were not ready to pay undue taxes to the King. It became a device to force them into submission. Dhananjay dares to incite the Tarai people for an active rebellion which is further strengthened by the crown prince's spiritual involvement with the *Muktadhara*. Crown Prince came to discover a tightly wrapped secret about his origin linked to the water fall (178)- that he was not a pure blood child of the royal family. This information came as a turning point in his life as he took pledge of freeing the water stream by removing all shackles on it. As he says, "I must pay off the debt of my birthright. The current of the waterfall has been my first nurse and I must set her free" (196).

The waterfall could stand for the country Bharat as a synecdoche as freeing of the mother land occupied each of the thinking mind and throbbing heart in the period when the play was penned down. Tagore also could not resist thinking about the fettered mother India. Now, the country was already viewed in metaphoric way as Ashis Nandy, a celebrated Tagore critic notes: "...in the most peasant cultures, the dominant image of authority in the ... cosmology of Bengal had always been feminine. It was that of a mother goddess who was the original or basic power and the ultimate principle of nature and activity" (Nandy 8). Besides mother nation, other Shakti cult figures were Durga, Chandi , Kali etc with specific characteristics. In the context of Decolonization, the waterfall as a bounteous source of life, nourishment, satisfaction of thirst, essential need for earth bound (or mother earth) activities like agriculture, cultivation, plantation and cleanliness – all relate it to the totem of identity. It was gradually mounted on to the level of 'nation', no matter how much Tagore tried to defy its notion. Thus, the water source can easily be interpreted in terms of the country, its' freeing basically meant freedom of India itself.

Rajendra Verma, a Tagore critic analyses this '*mukti* of the *dhara*'/ freedom of the stream episode as the crux of the play in terms of psychological freedom. This freedom is spiritual as well which underlines 'an inescapable necessity of recognizing, controlling and changing those institutions that cripple man's freedom' (Verma 29). This makes an important point in the context of the period the play was written in. The pre-independence decades saw various problems. The need to rebel against social and financial exploitation was highly demanded but the foremost thing was to realize the chains in the colonized people's body and mind. To wake them up to the imposed deprivations was the most essential part of the independence movement.

King Ranajit is representative of all those changing hands on the wheel of power and fortune. He symbolizes all authoritarian and totalitarian rulers who tried to usurp and control the Indian wealth and its people. British rule was exceptionally aggressive and imperialist in character for its pursuit of material aggrandizement was insatiable. That's why Tagore interpreted it as unnatural, too impersonal and mechanical when he said "Europe is making the earth yield more fruit than seemed possible, coaxing and compelling the great forces of nature into man's service…", (*Natn*, 28) with the credo that spirit of man could defy all limitations. This is manifestation of power which has become too abstract – it is "a scientific product made in the political laboratory of the nation"(*Natn*, 52), through dissolution of personal humanity. He wanted India and the East to be saved of this monstrous nationalism which he showed afflicting the Uttarakut region in *The Watefall*. The people were subjugated at the very mental and spiritual levels itself.

Ranajit Guha, a subaltern historian states conclusively that there was no class comparable to European bourgeoisie in the whole South Asia which was able "to fabricate a hegemonic ideology that made its own interests look and feel like the interests of all" (Guha 6). Tagore confronts this ever present proclivity in the West to present European expansion, which it performed through different means, as Western philanthropy, as a good Samaritan for the East and the world. He rather worked hard for piercing this idealistic and falsely humanistic Western veil. The play populated with common village folks, labourers and farmers thus alludes to E. J. Hobsbawm's ready admission that "our (19th) century is the most revolutionary in history (because) the peasants acquired a political consciousness" of their own (Hobsbawm 2-3). Tagore focussed upon nourishing an ethos which was based upon 'co-operation and not economic exploitation' (*Natn*, 99) - it was a difficult ideal to pursue. But with prince Abhijit's sacrifice, roused conscience of Vishwajit, Batu, Sanjay, Dhananjay – all from peasant class, to free the *Muktadhara* and the final unison of the neighbouring people, point towards a possibility. That's a glimpse of Tagore's Utopia which is very achievable and eventual in this world and life only.

The Red Oleanders (abbr RO) looks at colonialism and all its different avatars in their greater details – the ruling king, his officers and collaborators, the visible and invisible means of controlling the colonized masses, the heedless hard work they are subjected to – appropriately given the name of 'gold-digging', uses and misuses of education, religion and the elusive-illusive idea called freedom personified in Nandini. They all present the great organization of colonization from different perspectives in the most dramatic way possible.

Nandini, adorned with red oleanders, flows like wind and water amidst people of different fates and fortunes. She mingles with peasant labourers, professors, officers and even the King. Nobody can resist her charms, fragrance and the sense of freedom she infuses in whoever she meets. She is compared by the professor as a "light that breaks through a cracked wall…startling…" (*RO*, 212). Rest of the humanity in this gold bedecked town is impoverished spiritually and physically as well like 'cracked' beings – torn, melancholic and distressed. But she is unachievable unless one sacrifices all like Ranjan - he found Nandini by dying, smeared in red like her oleanders and she runs after him as well for an immortal union.

The present play has layers of symbolism which might have been the safest way to write in Tagore's days- 1923, the tumultuous era soaked in national fervour. A post colonial reading of the text finds echoes of decolonizing motives in every word and character of the play. The general public is represented as gold-diggers which hits one with resonances of 'grave-diggers'. They were doomed to hunt and "grope for gold" (212) treasure in the towns' dead soil (*RO*, 211), which Tagore terms as "the dead wealth buried for ages" in bowels (212) of the earth. They were the tunnel diggers working in 'dark holes' like 'worms' (211), in search of shining nuggets which were hoarded in the King's mechanized palace. It is a modern palace with a 'ghostly royalty', where the king is hidden, invisible behind walls of netting. He is unlike all previous emperors who did not even bestow a royal *darshan*/visit to his subjects ever. All that the public could view of the King were his heavy, strong hands only (217), symbolic of his commanding stature, which knew only to dominate people, snatch from them and possess them. As the envious King is helpless to Nandini's magic charms, he says "Why can't I strain out the tint of your oleanders? ...I want to grasp you within my closed fists and … break you to pieces" (216).

This reflects the masculine, crushing and destructive side of the power, but at the same time the King's longing to touch and possess her replicates another fact. He says, "I can extract gold from the fearsome depths of secrecy, but to wrest that magic from the near at hand I fail" (216), "How small you are compared to me, yet I envy you" (217). This could refer to the failure of this so called supreme power to usurp all that it desired, the subjects' mind and heart it could not possess by force or any other wily means. Ashis Nandy names it as the "uncolonized mind" which was the final victory of the colonized beings. It was the "untamed consciousness" (Nandy, *The Intimate Enemy* 100) of a portion of India which the mighty British rule could not overpower. It was a way of fashioning out 'a new meaning for suffering' and 'a new model of defiance'. In spite of their victimization, they tried to and succeeded in protecting their 'humanity and moral sanity', by viewing themselves as more than mere 'objects'(Nandy, 87) as colonizers made them out. This is decolonization itself when the objectified subjects resist and fight against becoming objects, they weather and refrain from being completely 'thingified' as Aime Casaire put it.

The invisible King could refer to the distant hand of Queen Elizabeth/Victoria having the reins of all colonies but rarely working with or amidst the people who hoarded her treasure boxes with the impoverished peasants' fruits of sweat and blood. The name of the king/Queen was enough to terrify people from the distance of thousand miles. This was a different kind of ruling which verged on plunder and loot of the remote and faraway lands. As Tagore writes- "... this time we had to deal, not with kings, not with human races, but with a nation, ... a political and economic union of a people organized for a mechanical purpose..." (*Natn*, 86). The simple folks especially the woman find the king and his governors to be 'nice' (*RO*, 222) but those who could knew his tricks and maneuvers called him a 'crocodile' (222) with unlocking 'jaws' and 'polished teeth' ready to bite and pounce on every possible chance. The polished teeth could refer to the civilizing mission of the Whites, their burdensome philanthropy towards the self- perceived uncivilized Easterners. Because this was a sham for sapping out the wealth, strength and beauty of 'other' lands, other cultures which they projected as a God-given right to them. The wrestler in the play thus says in pain that they only feel safe when "they rob the whole world of strength... these demons know the magic art of sucking away ... hope also" (RO, *239*).

But Tagore's inner eye could penetrate the King's dilemma also. It is self evident that a single person cannot rule or control one whole country, rather it is a well-formed organization of hierarchies and strata. But they share one common thing- their zeal to regulate and curb the commoners and workers, to subjugate and exploit them. They are all loyal and obedient to the king but at times they surpass the king in cruelty by imposing inhuman barriers, without concern for their effect and the caused plight. This was a well-crafted illusive network which employed every rule as a necessity, but in fact which was implied with some hidden deception. Tagore tried to explain these facts softly in his articles and letters too. As he writes in a letter to *The Manchester Guardian* about the Western power shaping and guiding human destiny –"the spirit of (this) organization is not social, but utilitarian… a phenomenon produced by her science… a titanic power… an endless curiosity but without sympathy, … with numberless arms to coerce and acquire, but no serenity of soul to realize and enjoy …" (Rajendra Verma, 36).

But the play was written with a decolonizing instinct is evident through the end. The King undergoes a sea change in his views- it is miraculous yet very much possible. The King realizes that he is an unwitting prisoner of what he built up with his own involvement – the network of power and corruption. He is fenced off from all sides, but simultaneously he is also ensnared and trapped in it. His governors and officers are so embedded in the power game that even the King's changed orders are not audible or comprehensive to them. They are dead habitual of their high-handed ways. Finally, the King also gets trapped in the self-created maze of illusion and deception. He moans to Nandidni, "These traitors have deceived me…my own machine refuses my sway. .. I have killed youth all these years… (kill me). That will be my emancipation" (RO, 250). The supreme power wielding King's end is metaphoric of colonization's end itself. It required precious lives' sacrifices but the coup de grace was that much awaited light at the end of the tunnel, as result of continuous strivings of the suffering people. Tagore dreamt of decolonization with the King's nightmare worded in the following way:

> "One day, Nandini, in a far off land, I saw a mountain as weary as myself. I could not guess that all its stones were

> aching inwardly. One night I heard a noise, as if some giant's evil dream had moaned and moaned and suddenly snapped asunder. Next morning I found the mountain had disappeared in the chasm of a yawning earthquake. That made me understand how overgrown power crushes itself inwardly by its own weight. I see in you something quite opposite" (RO, 217).

Ranjan, Nandini's beloved was a die-hard rebel like prince Abhijit of *The Waterfall*, both get killed by their daring acts. Ranjan challenged the high authority as he could not bear the insensitive and cheerless materialism prevalent all around. Tagore could thus visualize the colonial emphasis on capitalism as a contemporary form of Hell itself. Ranjan decides his fate differently along with the other few. These are the unbent and undeterred beings, preferring to live in glory though for short, instead of toiling in drudgery of slavish long lives. They are the heroes, mostly unsung and uncelebrated whom Tagore pays a homage.

The Red Oleanders is significant for its criticism of the society and the colonial methodology. It attacks their coercive plantations as the British compelled Indian and African colonized peasants to plant cash crops like cotton, sugar-cane, indigo, tea and poppy without heeding to their own needs and choices. This made villagers a sort of landed slaves, they could not get any profit of their labour and became poorer day by day. Their lives revolved around debts and toilings only, reducing them to *Girmitya mazdoors* at times. They were used like commodities, sent from one place to another with no say at all. The play has an instance in which Bishu and Chandra, the diggers complain that the roads to their villages were blocked and they had to work away from their families for years. Bishu says in a weary tone:

> "...we forget that we are chaind to our limits...A thousand times over have I told you that in these parts there are high roads to the market, to the burning grounds...everywhere except to the homeland" (*RO*, 222).

Besides these big issues, Tagore also reflects upon some superstructure formats of control like religion and education. The governor, Gosain and the Professor in *Red Oleanders*, the schoolmaster in *The Waterfall* are evident examples of the same. The Gosain's presence is a reminder of the fact that British flag was accompanied by zealous Christians on every journey of exploration. He is assigned the duty of pacifying the rebellious consciences of the general people so that they never forget the path of submission through religion. He terms the diggers as 'incarnations of the sacred tortoise…meekly suppressing themselves under their burden…' (223), always bowed down. Thus, his job is to guard their 'weak mind' from any sort of 'disturbance', give them 'moral talks…with texts of peace' (223). Tagore further emphasizes the fact that religion has always been misused for political purposes and this is pervasive even today in the technocratic times. The dramatist proves in another play *Malini* that it is debatable whether religion can be found by seeking or it is free for all like the sunlight? (Tagore, Malini 73) One of the characters named Supriya claimed that 'wandering in doctrines' and scriptures could not help him 'to find God or peace'; because, scriptures have been 'shaped to fit the narrow hearts' (*Mal*, 75) of those in power. Tagore speaks through these characters reinforcing that truth does not depend on force for existence. This is a personal journey for seeking peace, salvation or glory which could meander through sacrifices to that of peeping into human hearts only. It is a destiny in itself. Thus, Gosain is a representative of the spiritual policemen of the colonizers as missionary who brought the Bible. He was appointed like a soldier to maintain central authority or a merchant bringing money to their treasures. Om P. Juneja believes that all of them being together, "they plundered the natives of their ancient religion, traditional value system, communal living and land".

The educational system in practice was also a force-feeding activity where the very syllabus was upsetting for the appetite. Here education was used to malign one or the other race, with an attempt to uphold one region, one language or one kind of physical features to be greater and superior than others. It was never supported by any reason, rather it was indulged in making another set of myths, turning over the previous ones. Thus, the professors and teachers are also just instruments of justifying the Kleptocracy rampant in the Yaksha town. They help in spreading the centralized manufacturing of opinions, so that nobody can think ahead or out of the usual; otherwise, he/she is declared mad, insane and are thrown out of the system. The beautiful people like Nandini, Ranajit and Abhijit are victims of the same policies.

Thus, the schoolmaster in *The Waterfall* appears like a shadow of Lord Macaulay, comparing people and their characteristics of neighbouring towns and villages, calling themselves superior while insulting others. He makes the boys cram and repeat absurd and strangely nonsensible things, like the drinking water of the Shiu Tarai has been shut up to 'give them a lesson', because "they are terribly bad...with a rotten religion, don't have high bridged noses ...denoting greatness of race, as conquerors of the world!" (*TWF*, 174-75). In this way, the White, Eurocentic, mainstream race made every effort "to kill life with their arms and destroy minds with their books" (186) as Tagore observed in the same play.

In the same manner, the professor in *The Red Oleanders* does nothing more than lusting after the free spirit Nandini or 'invoking the gold jinn to enslave the world' (RO, 212). He speaks his mind but works as an agent of power for the King only. He seems to be a part of the "process of ideological and discursive incorporation effected through vast agglomeration of texts, discourses, and ... institutional rules" (Arnold 149), as explains David Arnold the new penology of the nineteenth century. They aimed at punishing the heart, 'the thoughts, the will and the inclinations' (Arnold, 140), using the body as 'a site for the construction of colonial authority and for the interrogation of indigenous society and culture' (Arnold, 149). The Yaksha town in The *Red Oleanders* appears like a dystopian town without soul, sunlight or space for humanity. The past life in villages is remembered as a lost paradise by the compelled gold diggers, as all ways going home have been blocked. It is rather a chronotope of Hell inheriting all its temporal and spatial characteristics.

Tagore in his plays appears as one of the very few and first visionaries to perceive the scientific and technologic advancements as infernal along with being enlightening. His plays and prose pieces present a critical forecast of what India and the world might become if it yields to the hyper capitalism and industrialistion approaching like a tidal wave from the West. The environmental dangers, failure of Fukushima, the oil wars, terrorism and regional-racial genocide prevalent in the twenty first century are realizations of Tagore minded rarities. Today our situation is worse than our primitive forefathers where the rule is to define or be defined like the animal kingdom's rule of 'eat or be eaten' (Szasz 20).

In the light of the present plays, it can be concluded that the enigmatic Rabindranath Tagore was inscribing a different history to the conflict of East and West. He wished the old to be examined in a new light. He preferred a more sensitive position of India and East's cultural pasts, preserving the cultural, intellectual and emotional resources of its own people, instead of getting drowned in the above mentioned tidal wave. Tagore in many ways, appears as a born post-modernist, just a little misplaced by chronological birth. He shows to be an inveterate dissenter who resisted being swept off the false dawn of Western imperialism. His critiques of prejudiced modernity were at par with the traditional rituals of gender, caste and economy. He was simply against the notion of colonialism being a moral statement on the ascendancy of some cultures and mediocrity of others. Its aim should, as the Indian bard himself said, lie in imparting life-breath to the complete man, who is intellectual as well as economic, bound by social bonds, but aspiring towards spiritual freedom and final perfection.

WORKS CITED

David, Arnold. "The colonial prison: Power, knowledge and Penology in Nineteenth century India", *The Subaltern Studies Reader*- 1986 to 1995, (ed.) Ranajit Guha, Delhi: Oxf. U. Press, 1998, pp. 140 -149. Print.

Ghosh, Amitav, *Countdown*. New Delhi: Ravi Dayal Publisher, 1999. Print.

Guha, Ranajit. Elementary Aspects of Peasant Insurgency in Colonial India, Delhi: Oxford University Press, 1983. Print.

Hobsbawm, E.J. *Primitive Rebels: Studies in Archaic Forms of Social Movement in the Nineteenth and Twentieth Centuries*. Manchester: Manchester U. Press, 1978. Print.

Juneja, Om. P. *The Post-colonial Novel: Narratives of Colonial Consciousness*, New Delhi: Creative Books, 1995. Print.

McClintock, Anne. "Soft soaping Empire", *The Post-colonial Studies Reader*. (eds.) Bill Ashcroft, Griffiths and Tiffin, London: Routledge, 2006. Print.

Nandy, Ashis. "Sati: A nineteenth century tale of women, violence and protest", *At The Edge of Psychology*. Delhi: Oxford University Press, 1998. Print.

Nandy, Ashis. "The uncolonized mind: A post colonial view of India and the West", *The Intimate Enemy*, Delhi: Oxford University Press, 1998. Print.

Parry, Benita. "Problems in current theories of Colonial discourse", *Oxford Literary Review* 9, 1987.

Sen, Amartya, "India and the Bomb", *The Argumentative Indian: Writings on Indian Culture, History and Identity*. London: Penguin Book, 2005. Print.

Szasz, Thomas S. *The Second Sin*. London: Routledge and Kegan Paul, 1974. Print.

Tagore, Rabindranath. *Nationalism* (1917), London: Papermac Macmillan, 1991. Print.

Tagore, Rabindranath. "Malini", *The English Writings of Rabindranath Tagore*, Vol. II, (ed.) Sisir Kumar Das, New Delhi: Sahitya Akademi, 2008. Print.

Tagore, Rabindranath. "The Red Oleanders", in *The English Writings of Rabindranath Tagore* ... Print.

Tagore, Rabindranath. "The Waterfall", *The English Writings of Rabindranath Tagore*. Vol. II, (ed.) Sisir Kumar Das, New Delhi: Sahitya Akademi, 2008. Print.

Verma, Rajendra. "The two plays", *Rabindranath Tagore: Prophet Against Totalitarianism*. London: Asia Pub. House, 1964. Print.

14

Spiritual Odyssey of Sindi Oberoi in Arun Joshi's *The Foreigner*

Rashmi Attri

The twentieth century especially the post-war period has been an age of great spiritual crisis. It is characterised by the state of frustration, disintegration, disillusionment and meaninglessness. There is loss of faith and absence of values. Modern man no longer possesses the ancient wisdom which served as strong foundation for values and purpose in life. There is wide gap between the aspiration of modern man and the hard realities of life. Man is hollow from within, with no support system to fall back on in the critical moments of life. He is fragmented from within and alienated from himself and his fellow beings. Man is shocked to find that he is no longer the master of his destiny, and that there are forces which threaten to wither his life and all its joys. As a result Modern man suffers from a deep sense of powerlessness and aimlessness in life. Though Man is free to make choices, his freedom is not absolute. It is limited in many ways. Death is one such inevitable and restricting factor in life. All this predicament of Modern man finds expression in the literature of the twentieth century which depicts the complexities and subtleties of modern man and life.

According to Stephen Spender "the 19th century novel is 'the' novel whose interest is to watch people, whom we recognise as possible neighbours moving through a world of influence ,judgement ... while the 20th century novel is an 'I' novel where each character sees his environment differently. Each is highly sensitive and unaware of his separate world". (Spender 74-77)

Arun Joshi's novels seem to belong to the latter category focussing primarily on man's effort to find his place in the tumultuous sea of life. Like Kamala Markandya, Anita Desai, Joshi peeps into human psyche, into the inner domain of man. Being influenced by Existentialism Joshi portrays life as an enigmatic riddle beyond rational comprehension. He admits having read and influenced by Camus and Sartre. *The outsider* appealed to him in special way. In the words of Meenakshi Mukherjee the foreigner is the first Indian novel to deal with the predicament of loneliness 'without compromise and without cliches' (Mukerjee 103)

Arun Joshi, who has six novels and a collection of short stories to his credit has depicted this existential angst of Modern man in his novel entitled *The Foreigner* written in 1968. Sindi Oberoi, the protagonist of this novel is an epitome of Modern man, who like all other protagonists of Arun Jhoshi's novels, suffer from a growing sense of meaninglessness, from the awareness that 'life runs out of one's hands like sand...that one dies without having lived" (Fromm 136). He fits in Erich Fromm's definition of angst as a feeling of 'alienation oneself, from one's fellowmen and from nature" (Fromm 86). 'Whatever the fiction may be said to deal with it is surely safe to say that it deals either manifestly or covertly, with our emotional problems' (Simmon 61). Joshi in his fiction depicts the poignant picture of angst, picture of a sinking man desperately trying to seek, organise and affirm. Once asked what message he wanted to convey in his novels Joshi remarked "One can't afford to continue with irresponsible existence but has to commit oneself at some point in time" (Cited in Bannerji).

Sindi is rootless, restless and luckless in a mad, bad, absurd world. For him life has been a long journey where he has wasted 25 yrs. searching for wrong things in wrong places. He calls himself dull school boy who always gets stuck with the same unanswerable questions'. The sudden fall of the spider from the ceiling, while aimlessly walking upside down from one corner to another "exploring his inverted universe" (Joshi, *the Foreigner* 90) is symbolic of man's precarious, painful situation in this world.

Sindi Oberoi feels that there is no centre in terms of strong traditions or religion which can hold his life together. "I have no roots. I have no system of morality. I have no reason to be one thing rather than another. I don't even have reason to live" (*Foreigner* 118). The novel seems to affirm Paul Tillich's views that "man's estrangement from his essential being is a universal character of existence" (74).

He feels small as he can't control his destiny. He suffers from a deep sense of powerlessness and experiences severe limitations in today's set up. So he sets out on a journey to find meaning in life. The author has chartered this journey of Sindi Oberoi. It is the realization of the meaninglessness in life which also serves as prelude to its diagnosis and cure. As Becker feels that various states of alienation including meaninglessness tend to become in proper hands quests for value, significance, meaning and transcendence (Becker, ch. 3 and 8). This is true in the case of Sindi Oberoi who moves from the state of detachment to the state of involvement only as a result of his initial realization of meaninglessness of life. The novel is in confessional mode from the beginning to the end. The narrator-hero, Sindi Oberoi is a man of mixed parentage. An Indian by origin, brought up in Kenya, who got his early education in London and went to America for an engineering degree. His parents die in an air-crash, when he was child and their only reality for him was a "couple of wrinkled and cracked photographs" (*Foreigner* 98). His rootlessness is borne of this bitter reality of his life. He never got the love of his parents. This deficiency in his life develops a deep sense of insecurity in him. He also believes that nothing is permanent in this world except for birth and death. He feels lonely, finds it difficult to relate himself with anybody and regards himself as "an uprooted man living in the latter half of the twentieth century" (195). He was brought up by his uncle, who also died. So the loneliness had crept in his life quite early, which affected him so deeply that he even contemplated suicide when he was a child. Thereafter his uncle sent him to London for education. But this feeling of alienation and insecurity became part of his personality. He passed his courses successfully in London but like a typical Sartrean character feels disappointed as the classroom teacher do not tell him "how to live" (153). This desire to know how to live makes him take up evening job as a dishwasher to have some experiences of life as he "wanted a different kind of experience to sort out his ideas" (166). He finds nothing satisfactory, but continues his journey. In London he also experiences two love affairs with Anna, a divorce and minor artist and then Kathy, a sensual married woman. Both these affairs end in pain. Perhaps it is from this point that he starts harbouring the concept of detachment as a shield to his emotions. Then the chance meeting with a Catholic priest in a village of Scotland gives birth to the idea that one can love without attachment, without desire.

Then he goes to America to pursue his Ph.D. course and meets June Blyth, a pretty American girl in foreign students' party. He soon develops strong feelings for her as "she had affected (him) in an unusual way" (23). He loves her passionately and even has physical relationship with her. But he also tries to detach himself. June feels this and says, "There is something strange about you, something distant" (29). He even rejects June's request for marriage because in his opinion love of any kind is an illusion which leads to pain and possession—possessing someone and being possessed by someone (91). So to avoid any kind of pain he thinks it wise to exercise detachment. He tells June that "Love is real only when you know that what you love must one day die" (145). This is so because he believes in the impermanence of everything except for birth and death; so "To love is to invite others to break your heart" (69).

June on the other hand is affectionate person who wants to be of use to people and for her love must blossom into marriage. So she gradually comes closer to Babu Rao Khemka and even decides to marry him. This is disturbing for Sindi Oberoi, he does not want to lose her. But the idea of marrying her in order to retain love, does not strike him. He thinks it to be hypocritical. Sindi's mistake was that he thought detachment lies in lack of action. It was only after the death of Babu Rao Khemka and June Blyth that he realises his mistake. It shakes his confidence. He feels drained and is full of guilt and says, "I had presumed I could make her (June Blythe) happy by simply standing still and letting her use me whichever way she wished. Nothing could have been farther from the idea of detachment. That was a fatal presumption" (165). He reflects on the randomness of life, feels utterly lost .June's memory lingered with him like an incurable ulcer .He realises that detachment consists in right action and not escape from it. " God had set a heavy price to teach [him] just that …June's death finally broke my attachment to myself. It was here that my hope lay" (162-62), muses Sindi.

He is overpowered by the sense of guilt, pain and despair. He wants to start his life anew, to leave behind his past, and wants to come to terms with life. It is just by flipping of a coin that he decides to come to India, the land of his forefathers. He feels like a river that hopes to leave its dead wood behind by taking an unexpected plunge over a steep precipice" (150).

In India he meets Mr. Khemka, father of Babu Rao Khemka, who offers him job in his firm, and Sheila, sister of Babu. He accepts the job but finds it hard to move in the world of Mr. Khemka which he finds sickening. Even Mr. Khemka finds him strange. He is disappointed to see that the social scene in India is as gloomy as he found it in America. He only finds it to be a change of theatre from America. The show remains the same. Here he notices the bronze figure of the dancing Shiva in Khema's drawing room and is struck by its intense beauty '…America, India, Egypt all mingled behind him in aeons of increasing rhythm. The dance went on unheeding and yet comprehending all .What did it matter if babu was dead, and I merely living to keep up appearances' (14). The deep layers of his unconscious unfold broadening his vision.

He is sad to see the exploitation of the poor people in the hands of people like Mr. Khemka. When Sindi comes to know of the corrupt practices of Mr. Khemka, that for ten years he had been evading income tax by maintaining two books he openly condemns Mr. Khemka. Sheila requests him to be a scapegoat and go to prison in place of her father, but he decides to leave this corrupt world of Mr. Khemka to take up another job. However, he gets involved in the affairs of the firm on the request of Muthu a worker in Mr. Khemka firm, who teaches him philosophy of real detachment when he says "sometimes detachment lies in actually getting involved" (188). How Muthu tries hard to feed his family with his meagre income reveals the true meaning of life i.e. having sympathetic understanding of the needs of other people. Sindi's meeting with Muthu brings about change in Sindi and he reflects saying "God alone knew what massive suffering lay behind those vacant eyes. It almost overwhelmed me" (189). Sindi feels compassion for these workers whose expressionless faces reflected neither love nor scepticism but only the accumulated despair of their weary lives. He comes to realize that fruit of action is not his concern. He decides to stay back, asks his servant to unpack his luggage with a new found sense of belongingness, and puts his heart and soul to save the crumbling empire of Mr. Khemka for the sake of its workers. He convinces himself for this responsibility though he 'felt as if (he) he had been dropped on a sinking ship and charged with the impossible task of taking it ashore' (239-40). In this deep sense of responsibility towards these workers, he finds true meaning in his life. Sindi is confident man now and instils confidence in the workers "I know you are afraid the business will never recover but things are not that bad ...there is no reason why we can't get this place on the right track again" (190). He now gives new interpretation to his name by calling himself Surrender Oberoi. Here Joshi seems to echo Abraham Maslow's views of self- enhancement which states that "human nature creates within itself the answers to the questions, how can I be good; how can I be happy; how can I be fruitful" (Maslow 102).

He painfully realizes the fallacy of his philosophy of detachment, which causes him acute pain and says "for twenty years I had moved whichever way life had led me. I had learnt to be detached from the world but not from myself" (*Foreigner* 165). He realises with the help of Muthu that "sometimes detachment lies in actually getting involved" (188). Thus we see Sindi Oberoi changing and growing. From distraught outsider he becomes a confident insider who is looking forward with hope and meaning. This is evident when he says at the end "... there would perhaps be useful tasks to be done;

perhaps if I were lucky, even a chance to redeem the past" (187). Earlier he thought that 'the past can not be redeemed', but now he wants to do 'something meaningful'. He is not ready to remain outsider for ever but cherishes the desire to make his life meaningful by being involved. He attains self-knowledge which "brings also a sense of identification with the world at large, so that by a seeming paradox, the more a man becomes himself, the more he realises his identity with the rest of nature" (May, 47).

Sindi Oberoi eventually learns to 'live' and realises that "life's meaning lies not in the glossy surface of our pretensions but in those dark mossy labyrinths of the soul that languish forever" (Joshi, *the Last labyrinth* 153). There are different "kinds of labyrinths that man passes through in his life, like an ant threading through a mass, knocking about against one wall than another" (*Labyrinth* 153). Sindi Oberoi also passes through this labyrinth, groping in the dark, only to find illumination at the end.

So we can say that the novel portrays the journey of Sindi Oberoi attached only with his own self towards the realization of humanity and responsibility which brings him very close to the concept of Karmyogi enunciated in Bhagavad-Gita (Cited in Dhavan 67).

Like Camus, Arun Joshi also suggests through his protagonist that it is only when we engage in the struggle to be true with ourselves, when we show solidarity to others that we can find true meaning of life.

Though Arun Joshi has depicted the existential crisis or rootlessness of modern man through Sindi Oberoi, the author also suggests a way out of this miserable, anguished state of existence for a man who is ready to undertake tedious journey in his life, like Sindi Oberoi. This is how Arun Joshi is different from other Western existential like Kierkegaard, Camus and Sartre, whom he had read and was influenced by. The novel ends not with the sense of eternal doom and darkness but with the feeling of hope and optimism.

The novel seems to say what Knoff says that "The process of creating meaninglessness itself becomes centrally meaningful" (Dhavan 67).

WORKS CITED

Bannerji, Purabi. *The Sunday Statesman*. 27th Feb. 1983. Print.

Becker, E. *The Birth and Death of Meaning*. Glencoe III: Free Press, 1962. Print.

Dhavan, R. K. ed., *The Novels of Arun Joshi*. New Delhi: Mehra Offset Press, 1992. Print.

Fromm, Erich. et al., *Zen Budhism and Psychoanalysis*. New York: Harper and Row, 1970. Print.

Joshi, Arun. *The Foreigner* (1968); rept. New Delhi: Hind pocket Books, 1972. Print.

Joshi, Arun. *The Last – Labyrinth*. New Delhi: Vision, 1981. Print.

May, Keith. *Out of Maelstrom: Psychology and the Novel in the Twentieth Century*. London: Paul Elek, 1977. Print.

Moslaw, Abraham. *Motivation and Personality*. New York: Harper and Row, 1954. Print.

Mukherjee, Meenakshi. "'Detachment': Rev. of *The Foreigner*". *Quest* 60 (1969). Print.

Simmon, Lasser O. *Fiction and the Unconscious*. London: Peter Owen, 1962. Print.

Spender, Stephen. *The Making of the Poem*. USA: Greenwood publishing group, 1973. Print.

15

Milan Kundera's *The Unbearable Lightness of Being*: An Existential Discourse

Mohammad Asif

In his Jerusalem Address, while receiving Israel's most important prize awarded to international literature, Milan Kundera (1929 -) observed that "the novel is the imaginary paradise of individuals" (*The Art of the Novel* 158). What Kundera holds to be true of the novel in particular is equally applicable to literature in general. Literature is a record of individual's consciousness about the world of existence. The question of existence has been the central enigma that literature has always tried to confront and respond in different forms. The Greeks discovered epic in order to explore the heroic side of man, his action, will, and free choice. In epic, individual seems to be in control of his destiny to some extent, in the sense that the condition he happens to be seems to be the result of his choice. When he faces his fall it is an affirmation that man cannot be in total control of things around him. Despite all metaphysical determinants the hero is relatively free in the world of epic and tragedy. Epic and tragedy are expressions of strong human action, passion and emotion. The Renaissance Europe, inspired by the Hellenic spirit, succeeded in revealing the heroic dimension of man, his freedom of action, individuality and nobility in its tragedy, as one finds in Shakespeare, for instance. It was this spirit of individuality inspired by the Greek poetry and philosophy that led to the birth of the spiritual identity of Europe. That spiritual identity was a passion to investigate and know the world. It is this obsession to know the world that gave birth to the modern science, which, as Sir Philip Sidney regards in his *An*

Apology for Poetry or *The Defence of poesy* (1595), is deeply indebted to poetry. This is not so difficult to understand, if one is guided by Vico's insight. Vico, the great Italian philosopher and historian of ideas, perceives, in his *New Science* (1744), that poetry deals with the senses of mankind and philosophy and science with his intellect. Poetry is based on senses while philosophy and science on reason. Therefore, the human mind can apprehend a phenomenon only after the senses have furnished an impression of it.

In the genesis of European science also lies the myth of rationality, enlightenment, individuality, freedom, progress and humanism, hence the dawn of the modern era, the era of Galileo (1564–1642) and Descartes (1596–1650). As science became obsessed with the external world of material reality, and philosophy with abstract truth, there emerged a new form of literature with the sole morality of not letting the world of man's being, his senses, feelings and emotions to fall into oblivion. That new literary form is the novel. Thus, science, philosophy and fiction sprang out like the three branches of knowledge during the seventeenth century dealing with different types of realities. The birth of the novel marks a great shift in the behaviour of the language of literature. Verse, an essence of poetry, gave place to prose. Hence the definition of the novel as an epic in prose. The change from verse to prose is not simply a question of aesthetics, but of existence. If poetry is an expression of strong feelings and emotions, and that the wisdom of all ancient civilisations has found expression in poetic form, prose is an expression of man's daily life, the prosaic side of life, which may not be of much interest because of its problems. If, in a symbolic sense, poetry is a reflection of human freedom, prose is a revelation of determinism and realism. The shift from poetry to prose reveals some bigger problem. It is perceived that in the eighteenth century language happened to be gradually purged of its symbolic nature to make room for precision and clarity, which was necessary for science and social science. As prose is regarded reason oriented, literary realism is indebted to prose. This led to a fissure, that T.S. Eliot calls in his essay *The Metaphysical Poets* (1921), a dissociation of sensibility. It is this discontinuity with which Michael Foucault and Claude-levi Strauss have tried to deal with in their own way.

Along with novel and prose one sees the emergence of an ironic sensibility. An ironic sensibility is one which renders ambiguous and relative everything it touches. It can unmask and expose what has been held to be an absolute and monolithic truth. One can perceive the power of irony in challenging absolutism in every form. In this respect the maverick and sceptical nature of irony contrasted starkly with rational, absolute, and binary nature of science and philosophy. The myth of freedom and progress which constitutes the very identity of science has always been challenged by the ironic sensibility of the novel as mere illusion. In fact, the novel has been very apprehensive and suspicious of human freedom, rationalism and heroism from its very beginning. Cervantes's *Don Quixote* (1615), considered to be the first novel in European literature, is a parody of chivalric romance. Written in the tradition of the Picaresque novel, saturated with ironic, humorous, and comic mood, it is a parody of human adventure, freedom and heroism, revealing the great ambiguity of the modern era, which contains the seed of both decline and development at the same time. Thus, the novel teaches us that things are not what they appear to be. Therefore, going beyond the appearance or "getting into the soul of things" is the sole responsibility of the novel (*The Curtain* 61). It is in this sense that literature makes us conscious of the problematics of our being. As man became preoccupied with science in an attempt to defend life against the forces of nature he unwittingly found himself caught in a crisis, that Kundera calls, in a magical phrase borrowed from Martin Heidegger, "the forgetting of being" (*The Art of the Novel* 4). That is, in order to attain control and mastery over the world of nature, man forgot the world of his concrete being, the world of his feelings and emotions, and gradually became victim of his own technology and inventions. It is in the twentieth century that the Europe has experienced the crumbling of the myth, which the modern era had created, idealised about human life and the world. Confronted with the incomprehensible power of technology, the unimaginable ascendancy of political power, which culminated in the aggresivity of the two world wars, the European writers, philosophers and thinkers were forced to rethink about man, rationality, individuality, heroism, freedom and dignity. The nightmarish experience of the wars turned the idealistic values of the Renaissance into what Umberto Eco calls "a theatre of illusions" (Eco 274). The advancement of science and technology, emergence of Nazism, Fascism, Communism and Totalitarianism, the uncontrollable behaviour of modern political power, the gradual reduction of the space for individual freedom, mark the death of the humanistic values of the Renaissance: a phenomenon which constituted what Kundera calls Europe's "terminal paradoxes of the Modern Era" (*The Art of the Novel* 12). It is this postwar monster of political power that the continental writers have tried to grasp, as one finds in Kafka (1883-1924), Hasek (1883-1923), Camus (1913-1960), Kundera, and others. As Gide notes with an air of despair and nostalgia "I believe we are witnessing the end of a world, of a culture, of a civilization" (Gide 192). The end of that spiritual and cultural unity of European civilisation of which Matthew Arnold and T.S. Eliot were among the great exponents.

Literature in general and the novel in particular have always been illuminating different dimensions of human existence. As one traces the genesis and development of the novel one perceives that the novel begins with adventure, which Cervantes parodies. Further examination shows that the novel of adventure was replaced by a very different kind of novel: the novel of character, or the psychological novel, which was discovered in the eighteenth century in England by Samuel Richardson (1689-1761). As the novel came to focus on man's feelings and emotion, and what happens inside his mind, the psychological novel marks the disappearance of the world of adventure and action. Natural landscape was replaced by the cerebral landscape. The nineteenth century realistic novel further reveals the shrinking space for human adventure in the industrial era, as one comes across in the novels of Balzac (1799-1850), and Dickens (1812-1870). And in the twentieth century, in the world of technology, and labrynthine bureaucracy, Kafka, Hasek, and their contemporaries suddenly exposed the illusion of human heroism, freedom and individuality. Faced with a ruthless omnipresent power, which abolishes the line between public and private, and offers no scope for escape, man seems to be isolated and alienated, realising the futility of his being. His world of adventure gone, his feelings, emotions and his inner self seem to have been sucked by the fear of the forces of politics and history. He seems to have been turned into the shell of his own person, a condition of life Kundera calls the unbearable lightness of being, a theme, which recurs in almost all his works especially in *the Joke* (1967), *the Book of Laughter and Forgetting* (1978) and The Unbearable Lightness of Being (1984).

It is interesting to note that this uncanny perception of human existence, encircled and entangled by the forces of history and politics, first appeared in fiction than in any other modes of writing such as, history, philosophy, and anthropology, where it was recognised much later. That is, literature, the novel in particular, came to grasp a possibility of human existence, the problem of power and politics, much before the postwar history and philosophy. The question is not of prescience only; it is deeply rooted in the essential difference between literature and other modes of writings. (This point is taken up again at the end of this paper).

The novel since its beginning has played an important role in protecting the concrete dimension of human existence from recession and regression. The aim of this essay, therefore, is to read Kundera's magnum opus *The Unbearable Lightness of Being* as an existential discourse in a historical context. In this respect one should not confuse existential philosophy and an existential projection of life in fiction. What one has in literature of the writer like Kundera is a projection of an existential outlook of life which probably has always been perceived in literature. On the other hand, there emerged an existential literary vogue in the twentieth century which uses literature to dramatise philosophy. Sartre and Camus are representative examples in this respect, who were philosophers as well as novelists. In fact, existential philosophy itself seems to be very much inspired by literature. Unlike philosophy, novel does not explore existence in abstract. The latter deploys some characters, incidents and events, a set of images, and words, in order to provide a concrete picture of life. These constituents are not only formalistic techniques essential to the composition of the novel, they also offer a possibility of understanding a problem. Therefore, technique or the Greek word "*techne*" does not simply signify a practical performance or a process of making something in the modern sense of the term, rather, as the great German phenomenologist Martin Heidegger remarks "the word *techne* denotes rather a mode of knowing" (Heidegger 180). That is, it is a way of apprehending and revealing the being of something. Hence, aesthetics seems to be inseparable from existence, as one can see in Kundera's *The Unbearable Lightness of Being* (1984). It is one of Kundera's greatest and most complex works both for the theme and the innovative narrative construction.

Kundera's *The Unbearable Lightness of Being* was written in the backdrop of the Soviet invasion and occupation of Czechoslovakia in August 1968, and the imposition of a totalitarianism regime. The novel is rooted in the Czech history whose echo resonates the whole narrative. It was a horrible event; its nightmare deeply affected and traumatised the consciousness of the writer. This event constitutes a concrete and recognisable historical context which finds its echo in almost all of his writings. Kundera grapples with the perplexing pathology of the totalitarian power and its impact on individual. The power which, equipped with technology, has encircled individual as the snake coils around its prey. It can humiliate and dehumanise individual, and can erase his existence in one click. Kundera explores what is the possibility for individual when the external conditions are so heavy and overwhelming that the internal impulses carry no weight. Kundera's cogent cogitation on the existential dilemma of individual in the contemporary world, where political power seems to have penetrated into the core of life, is very depressing. It shows the fortuity and futility of life. This is what he calls the unbearable lightness of being. He examines this central theme from different angles, by delineating a set of characters, situations, and by deploying a series of words, such as weight, lightness, soul, body, shit, kitsch, compassion, strength, weakness, vertigo, which constitute different leitmotifs, and reveal the existential enigma of his characters.

The novel, *The Unbearable Lightness of Being*, opens with Nietzsche's celebrated philosophical statement of the 'eternal return'. The idea of eternal return or eternal recurrence is one of the dominant ideas of Nietzsche's existential philosophy. It finds its echo in his *Thus Spoke Zarathustura (1883-85)* and *The Gay Science (1882)*. Though this complex idea has resulted into conflicting interpretations, it seems to suggest that everything which happens has happened before and will happen again. It signifies a cyclic process of time, which is a negation of the unilinear and progressive concept of time, a prominent western belief since the modern era, that is the seventeenth century, that with science and technology the human condition will improve. Nietzsche's concept of eternal return seems to negate the very idea of origin and end. If the universe and human existence have neither any definite origin nor end, then the idea of meaning becomes an illusion. Nietzsche seems to suggest that man given with reason can make anything possible, he can even make himself superman, an affirmation of human freedom, but his life will remain meaningless. No human effort can give his existence any purpose. Hence, the material progress should not be confused with existential progress.

The insertion of the myth of the eternal return in the narrative is important to understand the existential plight of the novel's one of the central characters Tomas. Kundera examines this myth by negation. The myth of the eternal return is indirectly related to the existential question of Tomas. It suggests the lightness and fortuitous nature of human existence in a world where there is no eternal return. If everything recurs as it once happened, it will alter our consciousness of the past and burden us with a heavy responsibility. And if a thing does not recur, it will disappear, it will be forgotten. What does not recur carries no significance, weight and meaning. It is quite ephemeral and light. If the idea of eternal return is the heaviest burden, as Nietzsche presumed, then, Kundera raises the question, is lightness the most splendid condition? In order to further unfathom the dichotomy between lightness and weight he alludes to pre-Socrates Greek philosopher Parmenides, who divided the world into binary oppositions designating lightness as positive and weight as negative. This demarcation seems unacceptable to Kundera's ironic disposition. He observes that the division of the world into lightness and weight is simplistic, and the choice of which one of them is positive is not free of ambiguity and problematic. He illuminates this ambiguity through the relationship between Tomas, a doctor, and Tereza, a waitress in a restaurant in Prague. In part one of the novel titled "lightness and weight" they are shown to meet in Prague by chance, embrace each other and then depart. Then one day she comes with a flu to stay with him. They live together and make love. The opening of the novel is so dramatic. The writer plunges his characters into the thick of the things. Unlike the nineteenth century realistic novel, Kundera does not give details of the background in his narrative. A few days after Tereza's departure, Tomas standing at the window of his flat looking across the courtyard at the opposite walls is unable to decide whether he should call her or not. Tomas, a compulsive womaniser, fears the burden of responsibility. He thinks that if he calls her back she will offer herself to him, if not, then, she will remain a miserable provincial waitress. He vascillates, while the memory of those erotic moments he had with her passes through his mind. By engaging his character in a baffling condition Kundera tries to grasp an insuperable dilemma: the utter inability of man to know and plan his life.

> We can never know what to want, because, living only one life, we can neither compare it with our previous lives nor perfect it in our lives to come. Was it better to remain with Tereza or to remain alone? There is no means of testing which decision is better, because there is no basis for comparison. We live everything as it comes, like an actor going on cold. And what can life be worth if the first rehearsal for life is life itself?... *Kinmal ist Keinmal*, says Tomas to himself. What happens but once, says the German adage, might as well not

> have happened at all. If we have only one life to live we might as well not have lived at all (*The Unbearable Lightness of Being* 7-8).

Life is important because what happens here happens only once. If it happens only once, it means that life is totally uncertain. It is a negation of human freedom. As critic Banerjee goes on to say that this unpredictability of life shows the author "experimenting with the tragic mode of feeling" (Banerjee 206). An action can have a series of consequence, which one might never have dreamed. Kundera explains it by invoking some biblical and literary allusions:

> If the Pharaoh's daughter hadn't snatched the basket carrying little Moses from the waves, there would have been no old testament, no civilization as we know it! How many ancient myths begin with the rescue of an abandoned child! If Polybus hadn't taken in the young Oedipus, Sophoeles wouldn't have written his most beautiful tragedy (*The Unbearable Lightness of Being* 10).

Tomas imagines Tereza as a child thrown to him in a basket. This image of Tereza constitutes a leitmotif which recurs throughout the novel. What Kundera seems to suggest is that how in a world without eternal return individual's choices, whose repercussions he never knows, determine his whole life, a condition of existential possibility which is both comic and tragic. A comedy devoid of laughter and a tragedy bereft of the heroic grandeur. The term comic here should not be confused with tragic-comic, as one can find, for instance, in Shakespeare. The comic here is not a counterpoint to the tragic to mitigate the psychological effect of the tragic. It is an ironic perception of human life which negates the very possibility of the tragic consolation. In the absence of tragic seriousness life looks so laughful, without weight and meaning. Such ironic representation of man is a dominant theme in the postwar European literature. The term anti-hero is just an objective correlative to explain this paradox. Aristotle, while enunciating his theory of drama, in his *Poetics*, had warned long ago that tragedy should not be confused with accident.

In an accident the individual has no role to play, it happens in its own way. It also symbolises ugliness. Tragedy, on the other hand, springs from the individual's choice and action, it shows his intention and will. Confronted with a monstrous political power which depersonalises man, which wills its own will, man is powerless. Consolidated by the power of technology, political power can unleash horror in which individual can be perished. History has turned Aristotle's observation into an existential truth: in the world of technology there cannot be any tragedy. Thus, man has been deprived of the consolation of tragedy. There would be terror, as Thomas Mann envisages in his *The Magic Mountain* (1924), not tragedy. Hence life would simply be accidental. As Blanchot, one of the greatest twentieth century French literary critics and theorists of literature, rightly remarks, while pondering over the threat technology poses to civilisation and humanity, that the truth and virtue of "the world of technology... is not to enrich us but to denude us. A barbarous world, without respect, without humanity. It empties us of everything we love and love to be" (Blanchot 82).

In the face of such vulnerability and uncertainty, can life be planned? Can man's inner being, the world of his soul, feeling and emotion have any weight when political power can disturb the whole fabric of life at any time? It is this paradox that Kundera's characters face in his novels. Tomas divorces his wife to remain a bachelor, and live a life of liberty with his mistresses. In his existential code love symbolises weight, a burden and responsibility. Suddenly Tereza enters his life with a heavy suitcase. Taken up with compassion for Tereza, he is unable to send her back. Having renounced his wife, son, and parents, he devises an erotic game with his mistresses in which no one is supposed to have claim upon any one's freedom. Tereza becomes jealous of his promiscuous life. Therefore, in order to satisfy her Tomas marries her. Thus, he acts against his own plan. He goes further, and has Sabina, a painter and mistress of both Tomas and Franz, find out a job at a weekly for Tereza. But he is unable to renounce his erotic adventure which increases Tereza's suspicion of his infidelity. All her dreams show her jealousy of Sabina and her weakness and helplessness before Tomas's infidelity.

Tomas is in a trap with no exit. As he arranges his personal life, he faces a monster that comes from the outside in the form of the Soviet invasion and occupation of Czechoslovakia. At this critical stage he is offered a job in a hospital in Zurich, but, he is unable to join it because of Tereza. He thinks she will not leave her country under occupation. And when they emigrate to Zurich, she is unable to live there. Though Tomas tries his best to keep her happy, he is incapable of dissociating himself from Sabina. Tereza, who feels herself weak in the face of Tomas's infidelity, identifies herself with the defeated people of her country. Hence, she returns to Prague. With the sudden departure of Tereza Tomas falls into melancholy and depression. The borders between his country and the rest of the world are closed, all modes of communication cut off, he is left only with the memory of the seven years with Tereza. The fortuitous relation seems to end the way it had begun. "Looking back on the years he had spent with her, he came to feel that their story would have had no better ending. If someone had invented the story, this is how he would have had to end it" (*The Unbearable Lightness of Being* 29). This is Kundera's concept of realism, that is, a story invented from some fortuitous events can be developed into life-like. It is from these fortuitous and fragmented series of situations that the self of the character emerges. What make Tomas a realistic character are certain situations. Kundera's innovation in constructing the plot of his narrative and developing his character is a strategy to challenge the nineteenth century tendency of psychological realism and progressive and unilinear mode of narration. Here one finds an element of metafiction. Metafiction is the contemplation of the art of fiction within fiction. Kundera in his novel often makes digressions to theorise his art of characterisation and construction of plot. Such digressions, which are common features of the contemporary continental fiction, as one finds in Andre Gide, Tomas Mann, are also strategies to counter traditional mode of constructing unilinear and realistic plot as expounded by Aristotle. So Tomas is born of the

German adage 'what happens happens only once'. As he returns to Prague under the compulsion of compassion for Tereza, he realises that if she had not fallen into his lot by chance there was an infinite realm of possibilities for her to fall in love with other men. It is because of this lightness of love that Kundera's characters indulge in excessive erotic exercises. He does not take any moral view of their extra-marital affairs. For him it gives an insight into an existential possibility in which man is reduced to his physical dimension. It reveals the plight and helplessness of life. As the critic Pichova notes that in Kundera the image of "the naked body can represent a frightening reduction of human existence to an indistinguishable uniformity. A naked body is one stripped of what makes a human being an individual. If existence is limited to the merely physical, the beauty of the soul can be too easily obliterated" (Pichova 101).

Kundera contemplates the lightness of being from different angles; by including a set of images, a chain of historical and fictional events, philosophical reflections, which bring an element of repetition to his narrative. By fusing history, fiction and philosophy, and by including digressions and leitmotifs in his narrative Kundera has discovered a new possibility of constructing the plot of the novel. In this way he has made a fundamental contribution to the development of the theory of the European novel. His narrative technique can pose great difficulty if one is not extremely alert. He uses the device of flashback with remarkable felicity. He often narrates an incident parsimoniously, and the details are postponed to some later stage. For example, the sudden meeting between Tomas and Tereza is reported at the very inception of part one of the novel, but the cause of their meeting is revealed at the end of part one. As the chief surgeon of the hospital was suffering from sciatica, Tomas was sent to attend to a neurological case in the town of Tereza. Tomas happened to stay at a hotel where Tereza was a waitress. This characteristic of narrative Shklovsky calls "displacement or transposition in "which the causes follow the consequences" (Shklovsky 32-33 in Hale). It is one of the recurrent features of Kundera's narrative.

The lightness of being suggests that existence is a mistake, an error, and a cruel joke. It is based on some chances and coincidences whose implications always elude our grasp. Part two, of the novel, titled "Soul and Body" is narrated from Tereza's point of view. It is an investigation into human weakness which constitutes her existential code. Kundera uses some key words and images such as, vertigo, her recurrent dreams of self-persecution, humiliation of Alexander Dubcek – the Czech President whom the Russian army abducted, took to Moscow, and forced to make compromise with the Soviet occupation – to examine her weakness, her problem of self and identity. Kundera, as already noted, has developed a very unique method of characterisation which goes beyond traditional realism. In the nineteenth century fiction, for instance, the reader is given maximum details about character's social background, physical appearance, his temperament, in order to fabricate an illusion of reality in the reader. Kundera perceives that a character created out of some essential situations is no less realistic. For Kundera a character is, what Andre Gide calls in his *The Counterfeiters* (1926) "artificially composed" or what Kundera calls 'experimental self'. A character emerges out of some basic situations. Therefore, there are certain words which constitute the existential code for a certain character, which might not have the same meaning for another character as Kundera explains in part three, of the novel, titled "words Misunderstood". So in order to apprehend a characrter's paradox, one has to penetrate into his or her existential code.

All Kundera's characters seem to be desperate entities. They seem to be caught in such a condition, in Doctorow's words, "in which all human choice swallows in irresolution" (Doctorow 30 in Petro). The weakness of her body is Tereza's great obsession. She regards her body as the continuation of her mother's. She gets rid of her mother and stays with Tomas. Before Tomas's infidelity she is quite hapless. She is gripped by vertigo: the insurmountable longing to fall. She is as hapless before Tomas as Dubcek before the forces of Brezhnev. She is often reminded of Dubcek's address to his nation on the radio, after his humiliating return from Moscow, in which he is unable to speak, the long pauses in his speech symbolise his weakness. Hence, she throws her destiny with the beaten people of her country.

The uncertainity of human existence is not a new discovery, this ontological reality has always been known to man. What makes life more uncertain in the contemporary world is political power. Kundera seems to be embarrassed that how the destiny of the people living far away and in remote parts of the world has become vulnerable and threatened. By abolishing distance technology has brought enemy to the door. Had the soviet forces not invaded the small country of the central Europe, the destiny of its people would have been rather different. Such control of political power in determining human life was probably never experienced. Thus Borges seems to be anguished at the gradual reduction of individual freedom, which has transformed man into an ineffective entity: "the most urgent problem of our time… is the gradual interference of the state in the acts of the individual", and he identifies this problem with "communism" and "fascism" (Borges 35). Kundera tries to expose in an ironic and comic mode the plight of his characters under communist totalitarianism. His characters seem to have been stripped of everything human. Reduced to their physical level and deprived of their self, they indulge desperately in physical pleasure. In Kundera sexual indulgence has not much to do with individual freedom and pleasure. It is the desperate search for freedom where freedom seems to be an illusion. Kundera rues that under repressive political regime "eroticism has become the only arena for freedom and self realization" (Finkielkraut 41 in Petro). His sceptical approach to his characters casts doubt on the very idea of free will, free choice, and individuality.

The relations between Kundera's characters seem to be incompatible. He highlights this incompatibility by deploying certain key words whose nuances differ for Franz and Sabina. Franz is a swiss University Professor in Geneva, and Sabina, a painter, a Czech émigré in Geneva. Sabina also serves as a link between Tomas and Tereza. Kundera's characters seem to be rootless entities, they live their life like fugitives. Wherever they go, they seem to carry the burden of their past. That is why in every conversation of Sabina about her country Franz hears words like: prison, persecution, enemy, tanks, emigration, banned books. Part three, of the novel, titled "words misunderstood" deals with some kernel words which have different existential meaning for Franz and Sabina. As in part one and part two, the writer examines the existential code for Tereza such as, body, soul, vertigo, weakness, and for Tomas such as lightness, weight. Similarly in part three the existential codes for Franz and Sabina are constituted by such words as woman, fidelity, betrayal, music, darkness, light, parade, country, cemetery. These existential codes are not investigated in abstract, rather, they reveal themselves in some actions and situations of these characters throughout the narrative. For example, the bowler hat, which Sabina has on her head during the coitus with Franz in her studio in Geneva, seems to Franz as a funny object. While it links Sabina to her lineage: it reminds her of her grandfather and father from whom 'she inherited it. Nothing is more endearing to an émigré than the things which connect her with her past. For Sabina the bowler hat symbolises some sentimental moments, but for Franz it has no significance. The writer seems to suggest that what a person takes to be true is deeply rooted in his personal experience of life. Similarly for Franz the word woman symbolises a value. And it is that value which he respects in a woman. He did not love his wife Marie-Claude but the woman in her. The platonic ideal of womanhood was aroused by his actual experience of his mother's suffering. On the other hand, Sabina is heading in an opposite direction. She is fascinated more by betrayal than by fidelity. The narrator relates her present behaviour with her past. She had experienced puritanical persecution both in her family and in her university life when she joined Academy of Fine Arts in Prague. Hence, her desperate attempts to betray, to break ranks and to go into the unknown. For her conformity, the essence of totalitarianism, is an antithesis of freedom; and the Grand March, in part six of the novel, which Sabina abhors, unlike Franz, is a strategy in a totalitarian state to induce conformity in the people. Sabina's whole life is a series of betrayals: she betrays her parents, country, husband, and at the end she betrays Franz.

Since Sabina wants to break rank, she does not like May Day Parade, an obligatory exercise in her communist country. While Franz is attracted by May Day Parade. The irony is that he regards his profession of teaching unreal and his public life real. Unlike Sabina, he has no sense of privacy. "For Franz, living in truth meant breaking down the barriers between the private and the public. He was fond of quoting Andre Breton on the desirability of living in a glass house, into which everyone can look and there are no secrets" (*The Unbearable Lightness of Being* 112). Kundera's characters seem to be disillusioned and alienated entities. Since they live under an extreme condition, there is a chasm between their actions and their implications. And in the absence of eternal return every action produces some unexpected results. In the reign of terror howsoever scrupulously one struggles to live one can be implicated in any way. As Herta Muller, the great Romanian novelist, observes, in her *The land of Green Plums* (1994), that it is a kind of repression which confounds all human reasoning. It is a condition in which silence makes individual unbearable, and speech makes him a fool.

As has already been noted that Kundera's obsession is with the investigation of human existence. That is, what is the possibility of human existence in a world which has become a trap, a world of which man is no longer a master, where irrational political power can erase man at any moment. In order to unfold this entrapment of existence Kundera uses a set of characters, historical and fictional events, philosophical meditations in a mode of narration which is episodic. As Kimball, commenting on Kundera's narrative technique, states:

> He tends to work with extremely short chapters and a shifting, episodic narrative that together create a montage of images, storylines, and characterizations. To this end, he has developed a terse, sinewy style, sharply ironical urgently engaged. The narrative is constantly interrupted as Kundera

> steps back to impart a bit of philosophy, autobiography as psychological conjecture (Kimball 200 in Petro).

That is, all the episodic events, images and words are linked and made subservient to the main theme: the entrapment of life in a world without eternal return. Since Kundera is concerned with existence, in his novel characters are subservient to the main theme with which the writer is primarily concerned. His interest in his characters seems to be secondary, but it does not mean that his characters have no real appeal. In fact, it is difficult to consider Tomas and Tereza, for instance, anymore less real, whose predicament and persecution the writer unravels in part four "Body and soul", part five 'Lightness and Weight' and part seven "Karenin's Smile". At the end of part three the reader is told about the death of Tomas and Tereza in a village where Tomas is conscripted as a truck driver and Tereza looks after a herd of cows.

Kundera exposes the behaviour of totalitarian power through the lamentable condition of his two leading protagonists Tomas and Tereza. Totalitarianism implies a denial of privacy and personal. After the Russian invasion Tomas and Tereza perceive the whole society narrowing down to a concentration camp. The state has erected a complicated network of spies and informers. They bug people's private conversations and broadcast them on radio and television. A man may talk about anything in privacy but when his intimate ideas are made public they assume a very different image. The photographed individual feels helpless before his own image. Camera, which modern state uses for the purposes of information, surveillance of its mobile population, provides not only evidence, but, as Sontag comments "in one version of its utility, the camera record incriminates" (Sontag 5). We can doubt what we hear but an image captured by camera becomes an incontrovertible proof that something has happened. Hence, it induces a sense of crime and guilt. Individual feels helpless in the face of his flashing image, because, the image deprives him of his intention. Being reductive by nature camera's rendering of reality hides more than it discloses. There was a time when words were suspected of fabricating a story which may have nothing to do with reality. Today that fear and suspicion of words have been replaced by photographic technology. Camera can create an image which may have nothing to do with reality. Kundera often shows in his novels how a totalitarian state uses photographic technology in order to chase, harass, persecute and punish those Foucault calls "dangerous individual". Individuality and privacy are great threat to a totalitarian dispensation, because, in the words of Camus a totalitarian state is one in which "Nothing beyond the state, above the state, against the state, everything to the state, for the state, in the state" (Camus 151). It is a highly bureaucratised and collectivised society closing all the possibilities to dissent and escape. Hence, individual has either to conform or to perish. In the face of such an incomprehensible situation Kundera's characters, finding their present ugly and future frosty, withdraw from the real world.

In the wake of the Soviet invasion Tomas is banned from practising his medical profession, and Tereza is expelled from the office of the weekly for photographing protesting people and the Russian tanks. From a prominent surgeon Tomas is reduced to a window washer, and Tereza, a photo-journalist is forced to work behind bar of a hotel. This is the image of the degradation and depersonalisation of individual. It is a reality so comic, yet it is ingenius enough to give one an insight into an unexplored possibility of human existence. After the publication of his Oedipus article Tomas finds himself into a trap. He has the apprehension of being watched. This is how Kundera reveals the psychological impact of power on individual. The fear of power works automatically and modifies the whole behaviour of individual. That is why Tereza suggests Tomas that they should leave for the countryside in order to scape the gaze of the power, to become light and insignificant. In Kundera individual confronted with a strong power withdraws himself like snail into its shell. This is how power induces fear, impotency, self-diminution and self-humiliation: a possibility of life characterised by unbearable lightness of being. Kundera's characters are trapped in a world where, Kundera's prominent critic Scarpetta writes, "there is no longer any logical link between an act's intentions and its effects" (Scarpetta 189 in Petro). It is this fissure between the self and a person's image that generates alienation and a sense of futility.

What leads Tomas to his existential extinction is the question which Sophocle's Oedipus poses, that is, is not knowing a proof of one's innocence? when the authorities fished out Tomas's Oedipus article they converted the ontological nature of the question into political one. Oedipus unknowingly killed his father and slept with his mother, yet he plucked out his eyes when he realised what he had done. Sophocle's tragedy poses an ontological question: man's inability to know the consequences of his action. How can he know when a fortuitous act can unravel a series of ungraspable implications. In the light of Tomas's article the authorities construe that the collaborators of the regime should pluck out their eyes. Tomas is baffled by this blatent misinterpretation. But what can he do when he has already been encircled by the police and spies. The chief surgeon of the hospital asks Tomas to retract his article or to write 'self criticism, at least. The whole situation is incomprehensible to Tomas. It forces the accused to seek his offence in a process of, what Kundera calls "Outoculpabilization", when Tomas does not know what wrong he has done (*The Art of the Novel* 103). In the face of the Kafkan, Tomas's life seems to be a joke, a mistake. The absurdity of the situation is quite unbearable. As he is punished by intensive police surveillance and interrogation, he loses his peace and privacy and becomes a window washer. Thus he becomes unbearably light.

Kundera focuses on the tyrannical and pugnacious tendency of totalitarian power in different ways. The Oedipus article symbolically reveals the ambiguity and relativity of human existence. Relativity or plurality is antithetical to totalitarian absolutism. Either one is with the angels or with the satan. The denial of ambiguity of human truth is a reflection of ignorance and arrogance. In order to illuminate the lightness of being in the face of ambiguity, Kundera includes the motif of shit in part six of the novel, titled "Grand March". Shit is something which blurs the line between serious and ludicrous, sublime and superficial. Man is ashamed of shit as if it were nonexistent, because, it brings him closer to his being. Kundera calls this aesthetic attitude "Kitsch". "Kitsch is the absolute denial of shit, in both the literal and the figurative senses of the word; Kitsch excludes everything from its purview which is essentially unacceptable in human existence" (*The Unbearable Lightness of Being* 246). The May Day Parade and the Grand March which fascinate Franz so much are communist Kitsch. Parade and grand march are exercises to impose conformity, which is a denial of plurality. The totalitarian Kitsch is a negation of scepticism, doubt, irony, question, individuality. Franz seems to be a symbol of totalitarian Kitsch. It shows how man in pursuit of certain ideals takes a one-sided view of thing and denies some fundamental realities.

In the name of truth, in the pursuit of some ideas, man crushes man without ever realising what else is being crushed in the same process. The question is inseparable from its corollary: what man can make of man, as Kundera shows through the plight of Tomas and Tereza, who recede into an inaccessible village, in order to avoid the gaze of power, where Tomas becomes driver of the pick-up truck and Tereza looks after the herds of cows. The narrator tells the story in such a way that reveals the marks of permanent defeat on their faces. Equipped with science and technology man can reduce man to nothingness. It seems to be a parody of Descartes's celebrated observation, which as a motif runs throughout the narrative, that by controlling the world of nature by science man will become the master and proprietor of the world. Kundera tries to show how man is threatened by the things of his own making. When God receded from the horizon of the western faith at the dawn of the modern era, it was man, the thinking ego, who was supposed to take the centre stage, now even that man is receding into the background. It is a lamentable condition which Kundera explores by mixing history, fiction and philosophy, contemplation of contemporary events, to explain his existential theme in a mode of narration designed on the polyphonic musical composition. Such a mode of narration demands 'condensation, or what the writer calls "ellipsis" or "radical divestment" (*The Art of the Novel* 71). One can find this technique of elliptic narrative, for instance, in T.S. Eliot's *The Waste Land* in which the poet uses a set of characters, historical and contemporary events, symbols and images, literary and mythical allusions, and only those details which are essential to explaining the theme of the spiritual predicament of the modern man. That is, it requires the inclusion of only those events, incidents, images, motifs, situations, which are directly relevant to the theme. It demands careful sense of selection and rejection on the part of the writer. By constructing his narrative in such a complex and innovative way Kundera has opened a new possibility for the writing of the novel. Moreover, it also shows the difference between craft and creation, which one can understand through comparison. Both these aspects constitute a work of art. Craft signifies techniques, a scrupulous process on the part of the artist to construct a work of art by combining the material resources at hand. Such a process of writing demands rigour and maturity of mind. On the other hand, there are works known for pure creativity. Creation is an spontaneous imaginative act. It even violates and ignores the established artistic norms in favour of the freedom of expression and creation. Such a work is known for the writer's imaginative fecundity as that of Kafka. It is purely symbolic. Kundera's work is a product of conscious and dexterous construction. Everything is premediated and deliberate. In Kundera one perceives craftsmanship, in Kafka free creativity. This analysis is not absolute, because, a great work is a fusion of both craft and creation. The idea is that, there are works known more for their technicalities, innovations, experimentation, constructive virtuousity, and less for free creativity as in Kundera. On the other hand, there are works known more for their freedom of creation, fertility of imagination, and less for artistry and technical sophistication as in Kafka. If Kundera writes in the light of his personal experience of history, Kafka transcends history. Kafka tries to go beyond the spatial and temporal limits. He tries to go beyond the appearance. That is why his works initially evoked religious and allegorical interpretations. Gradually the metaphysical in Kafka became historical in Kundera, a baffling change, which one can glimpse in Kundera's works.

Kundera's complex novel, *The Unbearable lightness of Being*, has received some of the critical opinions, which are different from the one taken in this paper. Some critics have interpreted *The Unbearable lightness of Being* in historical, political and psychological terms. For instance, Jungmann compares the predicament of the character Tomas with that of his creator (Jungmann in Petro). Tomas's merciless persecution by the authorities for the article is an extension of the persecution of its author by the totalitarian regime, which banned his book *The Joke* and derecognised his nationality. Apart from Jungmann's biographical approach, Scarpetta's approach is a mixture of history, biography and psychoanalysis. For him the plight of the character reveals the troubled life of the author under the post-invasion Czech society. In the light of psychoanalytical approach, he explains the problem of all the four major characters in *The Unbearable lightness of Being*. Scarpetta observes that Tomas's troubled relation with his son "barely escapes the classical oedipal conflict, which seeks radical separation between sexuality and tenderness" (Scarpetta 186 in Petro). Similarly, Franz is unable to separate himself from the maternal universe.

Though a work of art is open to various kind of interpretations, close examination of the novel shows that Kundera seems to be primarily preoccupied with the tyrannical behaviour of the totalitarian power and its negative impact on human existence. He explores the possibility of existence in the world that has become a trap in the technological era. He exposes the massacre of culture, persecution of individual, abolition of privacy and imposition of transparency in a totalitarian regime. A totalitarian power can exploit technology for surveillance of the people; and in this way it creates what Foucault calls "a panoptic society" (Foucault 70). That is a kind of society where the movement of individual is constantly watched. By erasing every vestige of privacy it creates hell. A totalitarian power induces fear and imposes conformity. It dehumanises and depersonalises individual. It shows the defenselessness of individual in the face of the horror of the political power.

By exploring the pathological dimension of power Kundera seems bemused that had man not acquired so much technology the existence of individual would probably not have become so frail and fragil. Man has always idealised knowledge as a means to defend life. Knowledge has always been associated with some positive values. But Nietzsche's ironic perception of human knowledge seems to be more convincing: "The entire apparatus of knowledge is an apparatus for abstraction and simplification – directed not at knowledge but at taking possession of things" (Nietzsche 274). In quest of becoming the master of the universe with science and technology, man has made his own existence something else of which he is no more a master. He has unwittingly created an apparatus for his own destruction: a possibility of life which no one ever dreamed.

By exposing the incomprehensible and arbitrary behaviour of totalitarian power Kundera reveals man's ambition to model his power on that of God. There are moments in human history when the line between divine power and man's power disappears. For Kundera the Soviet invasion of Czechoslovakia is a symbolic microcosm, which reflects the horror of a totalitarian power. It reveals the magnification of state power into divine power. He has consciously embedded in his narrative actual historical incidents in order to expose the dehumanisation and degradation of individual, who seems to be impotent and totally vulnerable and powerless before the power whose behaviour seems incomprehensible not only to those who are outside the circle of power, but even to those who run it. Equipped and intoxicated by technology the behaviour of contemporary political power has become as irrational as divine power. This irrationality and arbitrariness challenge the myth which has traditionally divided divine power and man's power. Given with technological power and ammunition the state power can behave in the same way. It induces fear and guilt, it can persecute individual, it demands obedience and conformity, and transparency, it can punish, humiliate and depersonalise. Individual has neither any chance of revolt nor of rebellion. In a world without exit he seems to have no possibility to escape from the world for fear of being traced any time. In the face of omnipresent and omnipotent power he can neither escape nor hide anywhere. It can liquidate and erase man. For instance, when the editor, of the newspaper which published Tomas's Oedipus article, meets Tomas along with the latter's son to get his signature on a petition for the release of political prisoners, he tells the story of political repression:

> The editor told the story of how his paper had been banned, what the artist who designed the poster was doing, and what had become of other Czech painters, philosophers and writers. After the Russian invasion they had been relieved of their positions and become window washers, parking attendants, night watchmen, boilermen in public buildings, or at best-and usually with pull-taxi, drivers (*The Unbearable Lightness of Being* 209).

This is how a totalitarian power humiliates and depersonalises individual by reducing them to a manual worker. This is how it deprives man of his self, which has always been considered as the source of all human authority. In a philosophical sense the authority which self bestows upon man, is, as Vico suggests, an essential property of human nature which not even God can take from man without destroying him. The authority with which self endows man lies in the 'free use of will'. By depicting an extreme situation Kundera envisions a possibility of existence in much man can even be deprived of his self and free will. It is this unfortunate possibility of life Kundera calls the unbearable lightness of being. It is a way of showing a regrettable human condition that what man was and what he has become.

A totalitarian power not only denies self, it massacres culture and erases people's memory. In this way it repudiates people from their past. In this way power makes people forget their past. Forgetting constitutes one of the dominant themes in Kundera whose expression and echo one finds in *the Book of Laughter and Forgetting* and in the *Unbearable Lightness of Being*, respectively. For example, "Terera suddenly recalled the first days of the invasion. People in every city and town had pulled down the street signs; signposts had disappeared, overnight the country had become nameless" (*the Unbearable Lightness of Being* 162). By erasing people's memory, a totalitarian power creates a sense of isolation and alienation. Because memory is the greatest threat to power as it encourages resistance. Eroson of memory is a way to make people incapable to identify with their past and to know their present and to blind them of their future. In this way power manages and controls man.

On the surface the frequent recurrence of actual historical and political events may lead someone to view Kundera's work as deeply political. Kundera is not much interested in history and politics per se. His interest is in the individual. But he contemplates about our contemporary age, when it has become impossible to grasp the entrapment of existence in any other way. Kundera seems to suggest that henceforth it is necessary to understand the behaviour of political power in order to understand the world in which we exist. Since existence means to be in the world, a world which seems to be dominated by political power. If the nature of power and its institutions changes man's existential possibility is bound to change. It is a denial of romantic and idealistic glorification of human freedom and autonomy of self. Kundera seems to envisage a new kind of determinism: the possibility of transcending the forces of history and politics has become the dream of the past.

Kundera is concerned with the unintelligible, arbitrary, mysterious, and irrational nature of totalitarian power at a particular point of history. But his observation transcends history and geography. Though he writes about his personal experience of his own country, his insight goes beyond it. What he perceives in totalitarianism is equally perceptible in the behaviour of the other modes of power: a bewildering reality of the contemporary world. There are moments in history when even a democratic power behaves like a totalitarian power. For Kundera the totalitarian is a tyrannical tendency of power which can manifest itself in other modes of power. The totalitarian is a possibility, which interests the wisdom of the novel, whether that possibility becomes a fact of history or not is a secondary question.

According to Barthes's pertinent remark that the novel "delineates an area of plausibility which reveals the possible in the very act of unmarking it as false" (Barthes 29). Literature hardly claims to know truth; it simply explores a possibility, which history discovers later. It does not solve any problem, it simply shows how a problem is being made. The birth of the modern era glorified human knowledge, encouraged science, created the myth of enlightenment, progress and development. After two hundred years of human history Nietzsche unmasks the whole myth of knowledge as simply a quest for material "possession". It is this horrible face of human knowledge, of science and technology, which European civilisation experienced in the First World War, a war, whose logic and consequences are still incomprehensible to European writers and philosophers as one finds in Hasek. It gives one a new perception of the irrationality of political power before which individual is defenseless. Empowered by technology modern political power can create a kind of horror whose marks are quite visible in the works of Kundera and his contemporaries. As about the entrapment of Tereza and Tomas the narrator says in a moving tone: "Now they were in a place that led no where. Where could they go from here? They would never be allowed abroad. They would never find a way back to Prague" (*The Unbearable Lightness of Being* 307).

This is not a denunciation of technology. In fact, denunciation looks so superficial. It is an investigation into how technology, in the hands of political power, has turned the world into a trap. It is a way of showing and enlightening the mind as to how a problem is being made. Kundera tries to grasp the existential possibility for individual in a world that has become a trap. It is a pathetic condition, which gives one a new conception of what man can make of man. At the very outset of the twentieth century Tomas Mann, in *The Magic Mountain*, also grapples with this apprehension. In a prophetic tone Naphta argues that if the medieval era was an era of repression the modern era would unleash a "terror of technology". In Kundera one sees that prophecy turning into reality. His work helps one realise that in the technological era the behaviour of power is bound to be totalitarian, intrusive and terroristic. The Soviet invasion of Czechoslovakia, for the writer, is an adumbration that what has happened here can happen anywhere else also. And even a democratic power in possession of technology can behave with the same irrational, willful, pernicious audacity and aggressivity as a totalitarian power. This uniformity is truly amazing. Erosion of privacy, persecution of individual, invasion and occupation, fabrication of alibi to wage war and destroy culture are not unknown to the people living under a democratic power. The novel has apprehended with profundity these horrific dimensions of power at the very beginning of the twentieth century in Kafka in a symbolic and transcendental sense, and in Hasek in a historical context. Kundera in *The Unbearable lightness of Being* seems to suggest that in the contemporary world individual confronted with power is condemned to die on the margin of life, or to live as a parenthetical entity. It is a condition of life which has permeated the post war European literature especially the one dealing with the communist reign of terror or emerging out of the experiences of the Iron Curtain.

Why is it so that fiction apprehended an enigma that history and philosophy discovered quite late. Unlike history and philosophy, literature is not bound by temporal facts. It tries to grasp a realm of possibility still unexplored. Moreover, unlike philosophy, it believes in the concretisation of life by creating characters and arranging incidents. Such concretisation and inclusiveness of life, as one finds in fiction, for instance, are conspicuous by their absence in other modes of writing. In this way the novel offers an alternative mode of life; it provides the reader with a glimpse of a new existential possibility. No other forms of literature, except the novel, can probably illuminate life in such breath and depth. Moreover, it indulges in the free use of language. Its capacity of incorporating heterogeneous knowledge is a strategy to counter the taxonomic tendency of science and philosophy. As Foucault thinks that after the seventeenth century it is literature where language survived in its unified form. These observations support the hypothesis which affirms the superiority of literature over other modes of writing. That is why after the publication of his *The Interpretations of Dream* (1900), Freud, in his lecture in Vienna, expresses his indebted to literature from which he gained an insight into psychoanalysis.

WORKS CITED

Banerjee, Maria Memcova. *Terminal Paradox: The Novels of Milan Kundera*. London, New York: Faber and Faber, 1991. Print.

Barthes, Roland. *Writing Degree Zero & Elements of Semiology*. Trans. Annett Lavers and Colin Smith. London: Jonathan Cape, 1984. Print.

Blanchot, Maurice. *Friendship* trans. Elizabeth Rottenberg. Stanford California: Stanford U. Press, 1997. Print.

Borges, Jeorg Luis. *Other Inquisitions* (1937-1952) trans. Ruth L.C. Simms. Austin: U. of Texas Press, 1975. Print.

Camus, Albert. *The Rebel*. trans. Anthony Bower. London: Penguin, 2000. Print.

Eco, Umberto. *On Literature*. trans. Martin McLaughlin. London: Vintage, 2006. Print.

Foucault, Michel. *Power: Essential works of Foucault (1954-1984) Ser; Vol. 3*. trans. Robert Hurley, et al. ed. James D. Faubion. London: Perguin Books, 2000. Print.

Gide, Andre. *Pretext: Reflections on literature and Morality*. ed. & intro. Justin O'Brien. London: Secker & Warburg, 1959. Print.

Hale, Dorothy J, ed. *The Novel An Anthology of Criticism and Theory (1900-2000)*. London: Blackwell, 2006. Print.

Heidegger, Martin. *Basic Writings: From Being and Time (1927) to The Task of Thinking (1964)*. ed & intro. David Farrell Karell. London and Henley: Routledge & Kegan Paul, 1978. Print.

Kundera, Milan. *The Unbearable Lightness of Being*. trans. Michael Henry Heim. India: Faber and Faber in Association with Penguin Books, 2003. Print.

_______, *The Art of the Novel.* India: Faber & Faber in Association with Penguin Books, 2004. Print.

_______, *The Curtain.* trans. Linda Asther. London: Faber and Faber, 2007. Print.

Nietzsche, Friedrich. *Will to Power.* trans. Walter Kaufmann. ed. R.J. Hollingdale, New York: Vintage Books, 1968. Print.

Petro, Peter, ed. *Critical Essays on Milan Kundera.* New York: G.K. Hall & Co, 1999. Print.

Pichova, Hana. *The Art of Memory in Exile: Vladmir Nabokov and Milan Kundera.* Southern Illinois University Press, 2002. Print.

Sontag, Susan. *On Photography.* London: Penguin Modern Classics, 2008. Print.

16

Through the Eyes of *the Aligarh Journal of English Studies*: Moments in the Narrative of Literary Criticism at Aligarh

Mohammad Asim Siddiqui

The role of literary criticism in defining, explaining, interpreting and shaping literature cannot be underestimated. The history of literary criticism at the Aligarh Muslim University is almost as old as the teaching of literature in the university. Ever since literature teaching started at the university academics at the university have produced a substantial body of criticism. These academics included the English faculty at the department like Sir Walter Raleigh (his book titled *Wordsworth*), Erid Hamer (*The Meters of English Poetry*), F.G.Fielden (*Three Essays of Sir Walter Temple*, edited with an introduction), as well as Indian faculty members like Itrat Husain (*Mystical Element of the Metaphysical Poets of the 17th Century*), Ghulam Sarwar (*17th Century Restoration Prose*), Amalendu Bose (his books on Browning, Tennyson and early Victorian poetry) and G. Singh (his book titled *Swinburne*).

Though members of the Department would keep writing articles and occasional books, literary criticism at the Department would get a firm foothold, or rather a habitation, as late as 1976 with the launch of the *The Aligarh Journal of English Studies* (henceforth *AJES*). The articles published in the journal--their variety, their focus on some specific areas, the gradual change in focus and, importantly enough, the standing of the writers contributing to the journal—have their own narrative. In the pages that follow an attempt is made to analyse some of the most memorable articles published in the journal so as to capture the threads of this interesting narrative. These articles can be considered important moments in the history of the journal.

The journal, started by noted Shakespeare and Blake critic Asloob Ahmad Ansari, was devoted to English Studies in its purest form. If Shakespeare was the toast of scholars, as the articles published in the journal bear out, major figures from the Romantic and Modern literature had their own avid takers among major critics. From the very beginning the journal has had an international identity and scholars and critics from different parts of the globe, particularly from the English speaking world, took pride in contributing to its pages. Critics of the stature of F.R.Leavis, Wilson Knight, Laurence Lerner, Kenneth Muir, Kathleen Raine (In fact, Raine contributed numerous articles to the journal) and E.M. Forster have been published in the journal. Some idea of the literary criticism published in the journal by these distinguished critics will help in giving a glimpse of the literary debates in the 70s and the 80s.

Kenneth Muir, a very prominent twentieth-century Shakespeare critic, the author of works like *Shakespeare as Collaborator, A New Companion to Shakespeare Studies, Shakespeare's Sonnets and Shakespeare's Tragic Sequence* contributed on almost a regular basis to the *AJES* in the eighties. In his articles published in the journal his distinct style can be glimpsed. His two short essays on *Hamlet* are not only very readable but they also throw rich light on the different lines of interpretations that the play encourages. In the article titled "Four Notes on *Hamlet*" (6:115-121), as the title suggests, he offers four interesting lines of inquiry on Hamlet in a very lucid manner. In the first section of his article he discusses the source of an extract from Dido play in the second act of *Hamlet*. Whether it came from Shakespeare's reading of Marlowe or from Virgil and what could have been the reasons for Shakespeare's taking some liberty in presenting his material is Muir's argument in this section. In the second section he turns to another aspect of textual criticism namely the difference between *Hamlet's* quarto 1 and 2. What is today called printer's devil(or typos) is to be seen in the many attempts to copy Q 1.Whether Shakespeare wrote 'his' or 'this' or "Corambis" or "Polonius" is discussed by Muir. Interestingly students today in Indian universities are usually not taught these aspects of textual research. In the third section Muir discusses how out of eight uses of the word "conscience" in *Hamlet*, at least one may not mean a sense of right and wrong. "But Shakespeare is a wily bird. As Hamlet says, he is not so easily played upon as a pipe. Although the primary meaning of conscience seems incontrovertible, it is quite possible that Shakespeare was aware of the other meaning; and the two meanings are implied in the lines in the last soliloquy in which for the first time Hamlet wonders why he has not yet killed his uncle... Here we have conscience related both to reflection and to moral scruples, and, as in the earlier soliloquy, conscience (in both senses) is the apparent cause of cowardice" (6:119). In the fourth section of the essay Muir takes the performance aspect of *Hamlet* and discusses how three different stage performances of *Hamlet* are essentially Bradleian, how they all "believed with Eliot that Shakespeare's theme was the effect of a mother's guilt on a son" (6:120), and how they all bear the influence of anti-war sentiment following World War II. After discussing the various influences on stage productions and film versions of a text as complex as *Hamlet*, Muir reflects his distaste for simplistic interpretations of the play and their pitfalls: "Such influences are inevitable; but one cannot help feeling that directors sometimes sacrifice the deeper significances of Shakespearian tragedies by pretending that he is our contemporary"(6:121).

Kenneth Muir's another article entitled "*Hamlet* among the Ideologues" (13:67-71) also talks about the "dangers involved in interpreting Shakespeare's plays in the light of our prepossessions, since our interpretations will be predictable and therefore suspect"(13:66).This short article appears a kind of journalistic piece without any footnotes, just to illustrate a point about the necessity of not being tied down to one particular approach in interpreting *Hamlet*, and by extension any text. In a very witty manner Muir talks about seven different positions on *Hamlet* that he took spanning a period of five decades. The seven positions result from his familiarity with Orestes complex, with Fabian society, his ethics springing from his belief in Christianity, his interest in French existentialism, his exposure to stage, his politics and finally his fascination for word-play. He makes four very interesting points about the dangers of what he calls ideological positions. (The word ideological, following Althusser, is probably the single most important concept in today's criticism. Muir's use of the term, though pre-Althusserian, contains a little bit of today's connotation in his discovering the anti-war nature of the performances of *Hamlet.*) Muir believes that all seven positions offer a partial picture and curiously they invite the opposite interpretation also. Shakespeare, he says, should not be used "as a means to an (our) end and there is also the danger that…we sacrifice our own complexities, as well as Shakespeare's when we plug a particular ideological line" (13:70).

AJES has also published some rare transcripts of discussions and interviews of celebrated names in English criticism. The special number of *AJES* on *Hamlet* published not only Muir's four notes on *Hamlet* but it also carried Brian Stone's interview of Wilson Knight on the characters of Hamlet and Claudius. In this interview Wilson Knight says some very revealing things about the character of Hamlet. He considers Hamlet's behaviour and attitudes very negative. In fact, his behaviour poses a kind of public danger. Claudius in Wilson Knight's account emerges in a very positive light and even his end is not considered "ignoble" by Knight. "Claudius is a man of reason, commonsense, normality, and a good governor. He is not a genius, but he is effective, and he sets about solving international problems by peace rather than by war" (6:140). Though Wilson Knight is what Stone calls "a practical theatre man", and he has something useful to say about how *Hamlet* should appear on the stage, his unwillingness to consider Claudius's marriage incestuous also has a ring of German reception theory: "…though the Ghost and Hamlet call Claudius' marriage incest, Claudius himself, and the court, show no signs of regarding as a sin. In sexual matters much may depend on convention, and conventions change. The marriage is, within the play's many transitional valuations, clearly a borderline case. Today it would not be considered incest at all" (6:142). Using insights of postcolonial criticism it can be added that if we took Knight's opinion outside the European world, the variety of views about incest and taboo would only confirm Knight's relative position on incest.

The distinguished names in English criticism mentioned above wrote on different authors and subjects and not only on Shakespeare. One of the most valuable pieces in the journal, entitled "Eliot's Permanent Place" was contributed by F.R.Leavis, one of those occasions when arguably the most influential critic of his time published outside *Scrutiny*. In retrospect the timing of this contribution, a footnote in the *AJES* announces it as the "text of an unpublished lecture delivered at the Catholic University of Milan", acquires significance. It was published a year before Leavis's death and four years after T.S.Eliot's. The piece calls to mind Matthew Arnold's essay on Wordsworth written thirty years after the great Romantic poet's death. Arnold, it may be recalled, had done the task of evaluating Wordsworth and placing him in the canon of not only English but world literature. Leavis, a successor of Arnold in many different ways—in his insistence on tradition, in his stressing the importance of English literature, his contempt of the marketplace and above all in his grand evaluation project—tries in this essay to achieve many things dear to him. Written in his inimitable style which includes analysis, evaluation, strong personal opinions and what Eliot once called innuendo in Dr Leavis's criticism, the essay also presents some contradictions in Eliot's personality. One such contradiction was Eliot's clever willingness to give himself over to Bloomsbury group. Leavis, who never made his dislike for the Bloomsbury group a secret, avers that Bloomsbury's appreciation of Eliot was not intelligent. And true to his style he adds the example of Lytton Strachey to stress his denunciation of Bloomsbury: Bloomsbury's "ethos is given you in the fact that it produced Lytton Strachey, and offered him to the world as a distinguished—even great—writer. What it found congenial in Eliot was the obvious and impudent daring of the technique, the showy sophistication, and the ironical 'disillusion' that it could feel, without suffering anything that disturbed the habitual Bloomsbury complacency, to be both profound and its own"(2:128). Leavis would score a point or two over the Bloomsbury by analysing Eliot's less talked about poem "Portrait of a Lady" which the "not intelligent" "advanced young"(Leavis's characteristic turn of phrase) missed. The qualities of this poem that Leavis stresses include its "living play of tone and inflexion", "its very poetic rhythms and metric" and above all a very "poetic use of the spoken language and the speaking voice "(2:129).Leavis takes delight in the fact that these qualities, perceptively discovered by him, were missed by the Bloomsbury.

Leavis praises *The Waste Land* but believes that "a higher kind of creative achievement than it actually was" (2:126) read into the poem and that is because of its being initially published by Hogarth Press, a Bloomsbury publication. Leavis is also critical of Eliot's tendency to seek the approval of wrong people. Eliot, according to Leavis, never really helped the disinterested critics (obviously Leavis is one of them) "who wanted to get real (that is, intelligent) recognition for his real distinction" (2:136). And Leavis, the disinterested critic that he considers himself to be (Arnoldian presence is unmistakable), establishes the superiority of *Four Quartet* over *The Waste Land*. Interestingly, contrary to all that talk about Eliot's use of *The Golden Bough* and the widespread view about the universality of meaning in the poem, Eliot's attitude to life and people and to men and women in *The Waste Land*, Leavis believes, is "morbidly personal one". Even *Four Quartet*, according to Leavis, is Eliot's personal statement.

In this piece Leavis also discusses Eliot as a religious poet, another major dimension of Eliot's poetry. Eliot's dependence on Dante is also explained by Leavis especially in *Ash Wednesday*. All through this piece Leavis's humanist—today we would call them liberal humanist—concerns and contempt of the marketplace view of the world are very prominent. He is critical of the fact that in his time in the collective educated view there is "no higher end to be considered than a rising material 'standard of living'" (2:132). Expressions like “our civilization”, “plight of humanity”, “human predicament”, “human condition”, “and bankruptcy of civilization” and “our world”, a staple of Leavisite criticism, are scattered on almost every page of the text of this lecture.

There appear a fair bit of Leavis’s prejudices as well in this lecture. He considers linguistic science a “menace”(2:140). His comment on Lytton Strachey, quoted above, is at best an example of a prejudice or what Terry Eagleton would describe as inane gossip. In fact, critics like S. Wiqar Husain have rightly disagreed with Leavis’s opinion about Stratchey. In a very balanced piece Husain discusses the form and content—its departure from usual biography and history writing—of Strachey’s major biographies. While taking into account the denunciation of the biographer-his use of clichés, his limitations as a psycho-analyst or his distortion of facts-- Husain praises, among other qualities, Strachey’s “ keenly felt and highly organized experience of history”(5:213), “his pervasive irony”(5:216), “his view of the human condition with an unmatched coherence, clarity and emphasis”(5:217), his presentation of “the complexity of human behaviour” and his “satirical wit”(5:219).

II

Since its very beginning *AJES* focused attention on British writers. Even among British writers Shakespeare received special attention as many of the faculty members at the Aligarh Muslim University were engaged in a serious study of Shakespeare. The write-ups by Muir and Wilson Knight are just suggestive of the interest of many other distinguished English critics who wrote on Shakespeare for *AJES*. The journal in its first thirty odd years has published approximately 75 scholarly articles on different aspects of Shakespeare’s art. The very first issue of *AJES* defined the character of the journal by including three articles on Shakespeares *Twelfth Night, Othello* and *Henry V*. The choice of the three plays is indicative of the wide-ranging focus on Shakespeare’s entire canon, his comedies, tragedies and history plays .In other words a statement to the effect that the journal would not confine itself to Shakespeare’s four tragedies or his major comedies but will take a researcher's approach to exploring all possible aspects of Shakespeare's art including the canon of Shakespearian criticism. In fact, from 1976 to 1995 there was no issue of the journal, except for some special numbers, which did not include an article on Shakespeare. Mention may be made of, apart from Asloob Ahmad Ansari, Z.A.Usmani and Maqbool Hasan Khan who regularly explored aspects of Shakespeare's genius in the pages of the journal.[1]

The quality and distinct identity of Shakespeare section in the journal owes a great deal to a series of articles and book reviews on Shakespearian criticism by Maqbool Hasan Khan. Shakespearian criticism appears to be not only his area of interest but a passion he has pursued since the beginning of his career. In his long career as academic-critic he has not only seen different trends in Shakespeare studies but has also acquired mastery of these trends. His deep study of the history of Shakespearian criticism together with his interest in philosophy has further equipped him to write knowledgeably and perceptively on different dimensions of Shakespeare's art. His critical and perceptive analysis of Dowdon's biographical approach, Bradley's philosophically coherent character studies, Walter Raleigh's 'humanizing' of Shakespeare, E.E.Stoll's historical perspective on Shakespeare's technique especially stage conventions, together with Khan's intelligent asides on the work of numerous other Shakespeare critics—among others, Coleridge, F.R.Leavis, Granville Barker, Wilson Knight, L.C.Knights, Derek Traversi, Kenneth Muir—make for very stimulating reading.

Reading Maqbool Hasan Khan's many pieces on Shakespearian criticism one gets the impression that just as in the work of some critics and schools a holistic approach to Shakespeare, considering all his works as a totality and not one individual work, is emphasized in the same way the entire corpus of Shakespearian criticism is a necessary reading for arriving at the proper understanding of one Shakespeare critic, minor or major. Probably with this view in mind, in his writing, even when he is writing on a single critic, it does not matter whether he be Dowden, Walter Raleigh or E.E.Stoll, Khan takes note of the work of almost all relevant Shakespeare critics belonging to different periods and schools. His characteristic method of reading a critic is to place him in a proper cultural perspective, linking his work to the work of other critics in terms of his technique and philosophical orientation and evaluating, in often comparative terms, the impact of different critics on his work. In the same way he traces the history of a concept or idea relating it to an older idea establishing linkages which an innocent reading would have missed. Thus when he credits Dowden for being one of the first critics to have embarked on "a systematic critical study of Shakespeare's plays in a chronological order"(2: 260), he also mentions scholars like Marlone, Furnivall and Fleay who may have helped Dowden. In tracing the history of personalist approach to literature, that Dowden adopted, he not only traces its roots to "disintegration of formalist classicism" and the "growth of a certain introspective self-consciousness" at the end of 18th century but also considers humanism to be the basis of both neo-classicism and romanticism: "It is possible, ironically enough, to trace the origin of this change (interest in experience and personality), one that dealt the death blow to the neo-classical conception of literary culture as sharing in the common fund of given experience, to the circumstances surrounding the birth of neo-classicism itself "(2:251).

In another remarkable and perceptive piece on Shakespearian criticism he touches on the thematic readings of poetic critics of 30s like L.C.Knights and Derek Traversi, and considers them to bear the influence of 'modernist poetic'. While acknowledging their departure and difference from what had so far been attempted in Shakespearian criticism Khan makes another interesting observation on their link with Romantic and Victorian conception of Shakespeare: "their reaction notwithstanding, the poetic critics of the thirties and forties were at one with their Romantic and Victorian predecessors in not only discovering schematized ethical patterns in Shakespeare but also in a neglect of his essentially dramatic communicative mode"(11:168). Khan also makes a fine distinction between historical approach commonly understood and the one adopted by E.E.Stoll which essentially focused on theatrical conventions of Elizabethan drama. While acknowledging Stoll's effort to restore an Elizabethan Shakespeare, Khan links Stoll not with Dryden, Johnson, Taine and Dowden, for whom the period of a work's production was very important, but with the modernists. He believes that "the anti-realism Shakespearian criticism of Stoll, artifice and convention oriented and opposed to simplistic notions of verisimilitude, may legitimately be approached as an anologue and ally of the modern, sophisticated, self-conscious, symbolic and poetic drama" (11:173-74). Never one to express his critical opinions tentatively, Khan's evaluation of Bradley is to be seen together with his approval to Stoll's accent on the traditional dimension of Shakespeare's plays: "...the fact is undeniable that in the process of philosophizing and psychologising of Shakespeare, the dramaturgy is not only ignored but inappropriately and unjustifiably transformed into vision "(11:181). His praise of scores of Shakespeare critics and his love of philosophy notwithstanding, his own position on the bard is very close to Stoll's. He expresses it in his essay on Walter Raleigh's criticism: "If Shakespeare is the greatest of the creative writers in English, it is not because he had some abstruse, esoteric philosophy, or philosophy not esoteric but philosophy still, that could be deciphered with the help of other philosophies; Shakespeare's kind of drama marks the apotheosis of improvisation that moves from imperfection to imperfection and yet achieves a comprehensiveness unparalleled anywhere else" (12:42).

Obviously the wider frame of reference of Maqbool Hasan Khan's work is the many trends in criticism and the orientation of different schools of criticism. And because he has so much to say about his subject of study, his writing, at times very dense but never lacking in clarity, is characteristically marked by allusions to the work of other critics and concepts. The intertextual connections in his writing impart it a distinctive flavour. Even one short sentence can serve as an example. While talking about Shakespeare's self-revelation in the context of his time he says that "in our age of objective correlatives and symbolic forms"(12:34) the idea may appear unpromising. While the reference to Eliot's theory of impersonality may be obvious in this, the allusion to Cassierer's view of man as a symbolic animal may go unattended because Cassierer, a rage in the period of archetypal and myth criticism, is little read today by literature students. Many other examples may be quoted from his writing where he writes very long sentences containing allusions to different works and authors. In his writing one frequently comes across a long sentence with many parentheses, each parenthesis packed with reference to some other work, often a very weighty idea which makes one think. That his writing is always interesting is almost a given. In fact, it goes to his credit that his writing arouses the interest of the reader into the subject; first it whets his appetite and then satisfies it to his delight.

The remarkable thing about Maqbool Hasan Khan's Shakespearian criticism is that he has also taken note of some very recent approaches to Shakespeare in his writing. The entire paradigm shift in literary studies following the onslaught of theory made many older academics/critics hostile to new trends because it meant a total disinvestment of what they had acquired in the major part of their career. It is not a question of unlearning what they learnt so diligently but rather of bracing oneself up to a newer and a stiffer challenge. Khan is equal to this challenge. He finds merit in new historicist approach also. He also takes note of the work of deconstructionist like Christopher Norris and Marxist-deconstructionist like Terry Eagleton in some of his recent pieces on Shakespearian criticism. The very vocabulary used in one recent article entitled "Interpretations Interpreted: Foregrounding of History in Shakespearian Criticism", its new historicist slant unmistakable, suggests his willingness to welcome the new in literary studies. One gets the impression that there is a logical link between his earlier distinction between two different notions of historicism and his ready acceptance of the more radical kind of historicism of the nineties in which power and ideology are the key concepts and the Elizabethan age, particularly the works of Shakespeare, is the focus of attention. There were shades of new historicist approach in his earlier criticism, certainly his earlier criticism is oriented towards welcoming the new historicist approach, though new historicism proper became a currency much later. In this piece his use of expressions like "decentered", "ideological construct", "social formations", "history-as-text" or "subversive force" bear out not only his keeping pace with the new but also his earlier belief that the history of Shakespearian criticism shows the rise and fall of many orthodoxies.

III

Even as Shakespeare, and for that matter Shakespearian criticism, was the focus of attention, *the Aligarh Journal of English Studies* never lost sight of literary criticism proper and prose fiction. For a period spanning two decades, Edward H. Strauch of the University of Maiduguri, would write a series of articles on literary criticism. His first article titled "Image, Metaphor and Symbol" which appeared in the second issue of *AJES* was a statement of sorts that the journal would not confine itself to the applied aspect of literary criticism alone. Later in different articles he would write on Freudian and Jungian approaches; discuss the roots of the science of literary criticism; explore various forms of genres of literature and analyse the nature and limits of New Criticism.

In talking about articles on criticism and prose fiction the names of G. Singh and S. Wiqar Husain can specially be mentioned. Both Singh and Husain write with clarity and conviction. An interesting feature of their style is their selection of interesting and relevant quotations to substantiate their point of view. From a reading of many of their write ups one also gets a very interesting idea of not only the subject under study but also of the literary politics of twentieth century Britain. Husain's criticism is further enlivened by his opinions, introduced unobstrusively in the text, on the nature of literature, art and reading in general. Thus in his essay on Lytton Strachey's biographies he supports the idea of reading for pleasure if it does not imply "a tacit rejection or undermining of the thematic aspect of the work in question" (5: 212). In the same way in his essay on Virginia Woolf's criticism he comments: "Perhaps no work of literature, worth the name, can help being somewhat allegorical or symbolic "(7:197). In fact, this essay together with the one on George Orwell displays not only the fine analytical ability of Husain but also his confidence and clarity of mind in expressing his disagreement with strong critical opinions of Virginia Woolf and George Orwell. At the same time that he explains the nature of Virginia Woolf's literary criticism, commenting intelligently on her subjective critical use of terms like life and soul and considering the mastery of perspective the "central principle of her criticism, he also finds her criticism of Walter Raleigh "rather unfair" , her views on E.M.Forster "unacceptable", her attitude to biography "a little condescending", her dismissal of *Eminent Victorians* not really an example of "sound judgement", her verdict on Joyce's *Ulysess* "not up to the mark" and her celebratory essay on Meredith "wasteful". Husain starts his article on Orwell with a very strong statement saying "...the essay, which can be traced back to Montaigne, was not his forte" (9:90). In this essay he considers Orwell essentially a sociological critic whose lifelong commitment was to truth, freedom and fight against totalitarianism of all sorts. Orwell's strong opinions on different subjects are critically analysed and the article is less about Orwell's style and more about his views expressed in his essays. In this piece also Husain does not shy away from disagreeing with Orwell's many opinions. Thus in the essay on "A Hanging", which reads like a narrative, Orwell's little comment is considered "a little sentimental", his preoccupation with an author's tendency is suggested "a weakness" and his distinction between prose and verse is "a flaw" in Orwell's art. Husain is convinced that Orwell lost "his multi-dimensionality" of early years.

G. Singh's approach is marked by his sympathetic handling of his subject and unlike Husain he generally approves of the opinions of critics he is writing on, rarely, if ever, venturing any critical remark. Singh's write-ups on the criticism of F.R.Leavis and Q.D. Leavis clearly bring out aspects of their credo, their strong opinions, *Scrutiny* approach to literature and their standing in relation to their other illustrious contemporaries. The article titled "F.R. Leavis: Later Writing" (3: 125-152) sums up the content of the tremendous output of Leavis after his retirement from Cambridge. Basically a survey of what Leavis wrote in his later phase, this piece also brings out the significance of Leavis's writings on subjects other than literature, topics as varied as education, university and civilization. Leavis's championing of Lawrence's originality is specially stressed in this article. In another article Singh discusses Q.D.Leavis's equally exciting criticism. Her anthropological approach to novel in which reading public has an active role in the writing of literature makes very interesting reading. On reading this article one can conjecture about Q.D.Leavis's relevance in the context of today's cultural criticism. The article published in the same year as Foucault's death quotes Q.D.Leavis thus: (The English novel) "is the art most influenced by national life in all its minute particulars. It has also been the art most influential upon English national life…" (9:187). In three other very interesting essays Singh's subject is Ezra Pound, the writer of crisp and meaningful letters and a promoter of the cause of modernism. In numerous letters that he wrote to his contemporaries like Eliot, Joyce and Yeats in his inimitable style marked by abbreviations, verbal economy and pithiness of presentation -discussed and quoted by Singh extensively- Pound talks about literature, the state of publishing, the nature of modernism and such subjects like only he could. All three essays give a peep into the literary politics of the day, the strains in the relationships of some of the iconic figures in modern literature, people like Joyce, Eliot and Pound. Above all presentation of literary gossip and politics, that too in a very interesting manner, supported by right quotations makes for breathless reading. Singh scores a perfect ten for being engaging and informative.

IV

In the literature courses both at the undergraduate and the postgraduate level the dominant tradition has been to teach English literature. In fact, English was synonymous with English literature. After America emerged as a super power following World War II, American policy makers would also invest in promoting American literature, and of course American English would also gain a foothold in the Indian academic system. American literature would make a definite headway in the sixties. In India a good start was provided with the establishment of American Studies Research Center at Hyderabad which not only stored a huge collection of books and periodicals on American literature under one roof but also liberally sponsored the visits of scholars and sanctioned easy grants for promoting research in American literature. Its impact on research on American literature, particularly in the southern part of India and in Orissa, has been phenomenal. However, it would take many years before American literature would achieve the kind of respectability reserved for the British literature. Though an occasional poem or story by American authors figured in literature syllabuses, systematic teaching of American literature at the Aligarh Muslim University started in the sixties in the form of an optional paper at the postgraduate level. In a few years time though American literature had firmly established itself in the university system, the articles published in *the Aligarh Journal of English Studies* on American literature were few and far between. In fact, American literature was rarely discussed in terms of its many divisions along genre, period, region and ethnicity lines like it is the norm today. The first article on American literature entitled "The Dimensions of Revolt in Emily Dickinson's Poetry" (2:90-100) was contributed by Salamatullah Khan, an expert of American studies and one of the most loved teacher-scholar that Aligarh has ever produced. M. Yaseen wrote the article titled "An Aspect of *The Ambassadors*" in the next issue of the Journal (2:221:30). Interestingly in the same issue S.Wiqar Husain reviewed Stephen Spender's book on British-American relations entitled *Love- Hate Relations*. Except for some occasional articles on Ezra Pound, Hemingway and Tennessee Williams, that too on their selected works, *AJES* appears to have shied away from accepting contributions on American literature liberally. It can also be seen that most of the American writers on whom articles were published in the journal appeared on the syllabus at some level. Here a special mention may be made of three different articles on Hemingway's *Old Man and the Sea* by Edward H.Strauch. The articles were titled "*The Old Man and the Sea*: A Numerological View" (6:89-100}), "*The Old*

Man and the Sea: An Anthropological View" (9:56-63) and "The Old Man and the Sea as Testament" (17:66-81).

American literature, though different in significant ways from British literature, is still discussed together with English literature in terms of its ethos, values and western world view. Articles published in the journal on American literature could slip in without raising an eyebrow. However, there appears some shift in the journal's focus from 18.1 (1996) onwards. This was the first issue of the journal since its inception when the journal went without an article on Shakespeare. Though *AJES* would occasionally include write-ups on Shakespeare in its future issues, Shakespeare henceforth would figure less and less in the pages of the journal.

The nature of change is suggested by the fact that the journal would start looking beyond Shakespeare, the Romantics and the modern British literature. Though there can be many reasons for the lack of interest in Shakespeare—non -availability of Shakespeare experts is one of them-one important reason was respectability acquired by some new areas which were not even discussed earlier in high-brow circles of literature departments. Indian Writing in English which drew a blank till about the mid-nineties made a gradual appearance. There is some irony in the fact that Shakespeare's loss is the gain of literature other than British. And perhaps to heighten this ironic effect it can be mentioned that Renate Sarma, a German scholar and a faculty member at the Aligarh Muslim University teaching German language who specialized in Indian fiction contributed a couple of articles on R.K.Narayan even before she wrote on classic German novels like *Buddenbrooks* and *The Tin Drum* and Harish Raizada, who is now considered one of the pioneers of criticism on Indian Writing in English with books like *R.K.Narayan* and *The Lotus and the Rose: Indian Fiction in English*, never published anything on Indian Writing in English in the pages of the journal, though he contributed quite a few articles on British fiction. G. Singh who otherwise had been writing regularly on English prose, fiction and criticism wrote an article titled "Gandhi as Prose Writer" (17:82-96). The first write-up on Indian literature in English was contributed by one Maya Shakar Pandey titled "Animal Imagery in the Poetry of A.K.Ramanujan" (19:73-83). More articles on Indian Writing in English have appeared in later issues.

The opening up of the journal to other areas of English studies is also noticeable at the turn of the century. Attia Abid's article on the content and context of Australian poetry was published in 1998(20). An article on Canadian writer Margaret Laurence, published in 1993 itself, had compared her fiction with that of Anita Desai's. English Language Teaching made its debut with Ismail Baroudy's long article titled "A Cumulative Approach to ESL/EFL Writing Pedagogy in 2002 (24:59-104). It will not be out of place here to recall that articles on stylistic analysis,--stylistics combines both literature and linguistics and as such is a borderline case--had already appeared in the journal. A special mention may be made of Syed Asim Ali's brilliant and fairly exhaustive stylistic analysis of Philip Larkin's poem "Afternoons"(13:207-223).

It is really debatable if all change is identical with progress. Taking its cue from the recent changes that have affected established notions about literature, English studies in India and at the Aligarh Muslim University is now a fairly inclusive phenomenon, including in its fold a variety of areas. Some literature departments in the country have been rechristened, some swallowed by the monster of cultural studies in which there is the danger of extreme catholicity, of 'anything goes' phenomenon. In this state of cultural anarchy there is also a sneaking feeling for some stability, for holding on to some centre, for not letting go the core of English studies and for retaining some of the basic character of the subject. There is also this feeling that *AJES* which has unwittingly reflected this change should retain its basic character. Unlike English studies a journal can afford to maintain its special character without being charged with parochialism. There are journals devoted to specific subjects. There would be still others which would concentrate on specific areas of English studies. *AJES* can ill afford to totally break free from its past, to discard its illustrious pedigree. In all fairness it should not.

NOTE

1. Asloob Ahmad Ansari's criticism is discussed in a separate article. And much as I would have liked to discuss Z.A.Usmani's penetrating articles on poetry and fiction, ranging from Dante to James Joyce, from Shakespeare to E.M.Forster and his equally critically alert book reviews especially on Shakespeare, space does not permit me to deal with his work in this piece. However, I must add that his brilliant critical work, though sparse yet marked by his unmistakably deep and focused scholarship, is an important chapter in this narrative of literary criticism at the Aligarh Muslim University.

WORKS CITED

Ali, Syed Asim. "Stylistic Analysis of Larkin's 'Afternoons.'" *Aligarh Journal of English Studies* 13 (1988):207-223. Print.

Husain,Wiqar S. "Lytton Strachey:Major Biographies." *Aligarh Journal of English Studies* 5 (1980):211-228. Print.

—"Virginia Woolf: The Critic." *Aligarh Journal of English Studies* 791982):192-206. Print.

—"The Essays of George Orwell." *Aligarh Journal of English Studies*.9 (1984):90-106. Print.

Khan, Maqbool Hasan. "Shakespeare's Self-Revelation: A Critical Theme in the Nineteenth Century." *Aligarh Journal of English Studies* 2(1977):247-266. Print.

—" E.E. Stoll and the Bradleian Tragedies." *Aligarh Journal of English Studies* 11(1986):167-187. Print.

—"Walter Raleigh's Shakespearian Criticism." *Aligarh Journal of English Studies* 12(1987):27-52. Print.

—"Interpretations Interpreted: Foregrounding of History in Shakespearian Criticism." *Point of View* 7 (2000) n 2: 8-14. Print.

Knight, Wilson. "Hamlet and Claudius." *Aligarh Journal of English Studies* 6(1981):139-47. Print.

Leavis, F.R. "Eliot's Permanent Place." *Aligarh Journal of English Studies* 2(1977):125-143. Print.

Muir, Kenneth. "Four Notes on *Hamlet*." *Aligarh Journal of English Studies* 6(1981):115-21. Print.

—"Hamlet Among the Ideologues." *Aligarh Journal of English Studies* 13(1988):67-71. Print.

Singh, G. "F.R. Leavis: Later Writings." *Aligarh Journal of English Studies*.3 (1978):125-152. Print.

—"The Achievement of Q.D. Leavis." *Aligarh Journal of English Studies*. 9(1984):185-214. Print.

17

Asloob Ahmad Ansari as a Literary Critic

Mohammad Asim Siddiqui

Literary criticism thrives on difference of opinion and a questioning attitude towards the work of others. Its corpus keeps growing with each passing year. However, there is often a tendency commonly observed in the work of critics to find faults with the work of the past generation of critics. In the zeal to accept the new and to prove its efficacy the old is not looked at with the kind of attention it deserves. In the hands of the less charitable critics the old is often reduced to clichés. The complexity and richness of criticism from Matthew Arnold to F.R. Leavis is often referred to by the pejorative epithet liberal humanism. New Criticism is today considered passé though the methodology of New Criticism is still widely practiced in the academia. F. R. Leavis is now believed to be the fall guy of the twentieth century criticism though his writings can still be read with pleasure and Leavisite Criticism has been a fact of life in literature departments. Sometimes the old sees a revival because many of the tendencies of the present cannot be understood without really coming to grips with the old. In fact, now there is a growing realization to stress the link between New Criticism and deconstruction. A parallel can be seen in language studies where the eighteenth-century grammarians who were attributed every conceivable fault are now being credited with contributing something useful too to language studies.

It is with some trepidation that I approach the English criticism produced by Asloob Ahmad Ansari. I take comfort in Paul de Man's view that there can be only misreadings of an earlier work, or Nietzsche's view, which was readily appropriated by deconstructive criticism, that there are no facts but only interpretations and that ultimately man finds in a text what he himself imports into it. I am aware that I have imported too much into what I have written in this piece.

Literary criticism at the Aligarh Muslim University achieved a real shot in the arm with the launching of *the Aligarh Journal of English Studies* (henceforth *AJES*) in 1976 by Asloob Ahmad Ansari. Since its inception Ansari, who remained the journal's editor till 1987, was very particular about giving a particular kind of voice to *AJES*. Soon *AJES* would develop an identity of its own specializing in British literature with special focus on Shakespeare studies. Ansari who wrote erudite pieces and insightful book reviews in every issue of *AJES*, contributed in no small measure to building what can be called the Aligarh sub-school of Shakespeare Criticism. In this endeavour he was ably supported by, among others, Maqbool Hasan Khan (who would later distinguish himself with a substantial body of work on Shakespeare), Z.A. Usmani and many of his other colleagues and students.

Besides the numerous articles in *AJES* (about twenty five or so) Ansari has authored several critically acclaimed books on Shakespeare and Blake, some of these books consisting of articles earlier published in *AJES*. What is remarkable is that Ansari has chosen to write on the entire Shakespeare canon. Never one to believe that Shakespeare's genius can be confined to his four great tragedies and some comedies, Ansari has written on all plays of Shakespeare as also on his sonnets. It goes without saying that his familiarity with Shakespearian criticism is equally impressive. His work has elicited praise from critics of the rank of Northrop Frye and Katherine Raine. However, it will not do justice to Ansari's vast body of criticism if he is considered merely a Shakespeare or, for that matter, a Blake critic. His scholarship on Langland, metaphysical poets like Donne and Marvell and romantic poets like Wordsworth is also very impressive. The insights gained from his Shakespeare and Blake scholarship are reflected in his fiction criticism too, a relatively neglected area of his writing.

Ansari's critical writings demonstrate his deep familiarity with various philosophical and intellectual traditions: Christian, Classical and Oriental. As Western literature owes a lot to the Christian and classical traditions, the familiarity with these traditions imparts depth and completeness to Ansari's writings. The reading of too many Indian students is hampered by their ignorance of these traditions. In essays after essays Ansari is able to explicate various Christian and classical motifs in Shakespeare and other writers. Thus he explicates classical and Christian motifs in his essay on *Measure for Measure* and dwells on the Biblical theme in *Much Ado About Nothing*. His thorough understanding of neo-Platonic tradition can be seen in his essay on Marvell. He has himself said that insights gained from his deep roots in Indo-Persian literary tradition sharpened his literary sensibility and made him "more responsive to the nuances of the English language than I (Ansari) could otherwise acquire"(15:113).

Implicit in Ansari's criticism is the celebration of the canon and the effort towards canon formation. In his entire career he chose to write on major writers. Apart from Shakespeare and Blake he also wrote on Wordsworth, T. S. Eliot and the metaphysical poets. It may be recalled that T. S. Eliot had already revived interest in the poetry of Donne and Marvell. In his Urdu criticism which undoubtedly bears the mark of his scholarship of English literary and critical tradition, Ansari wrote prolifically on Ghalib and Iqbal. As an editor of the famous Urdu journal *Naqdo Nazar* he saw to it that in every issue of this journal there was at least one piece on Iqbal. Right from his first article on Iqbal which he wrote while still in his teens to the more recent scholarly pieces, his devotion to Iqbal studies remains very passionate and steadfast.

It may be mentioned in passing that Ansari introduced an element of rigour in Urdu criticism. Qazi Afzal Husain is of the view that critics like "Abdur Rahman Bijnori had seen parallels in the poetry of Ghalib and some English poets but the links were of a thematic variety and their treatment of a very impressionistic kind. Ansari was the first Urdu critic who discovered parallels of art and craftsmanship between Ghalib and poets like Donne. His analysis of many rhetorical devices like synecdoche and conceit which characterizes Ghalib's poetry is a signal contribution to Urdu criticism (Personal interview)". Afzal Husain also notices the English connection of many other contemporary Urdu critics like Al-E-Ahmad Suroor, Majnu Gorakhpuri, Hasan Askari and Kalimuddin Ahmad. But unlike them Ansari maintains a fine balance between his English and Urdu criticism, not overawed by one and not defensive about the other (Husain).

The rigour and analytical skill is fully reflected in Ansari's use of language. Ansari's complete command of English language is an aspect of his painstaking scholarship and wide-ranging study of different areas of literature. His mastery of critical idiom and his confident use of it imparts a distinct flavour to his style. He can use words like "convincingness", "misplacedness" and "sustainment" to good effect. His mastery of the register of description, apparent at many places in his write-ups and book reviews, is no less impressive. The description of F. R. Leavis and especially of Q. D. Leavis demonstrates his command of this register: "In spite of her fitful cordiality and social accommodation she had in her a good deal of combative energy, a dogged refusal to forgive, a degree of nauseating aggressiveness and a firm conviction of her own infallibility..." (9:228).

In a paper as brief as this it is not possible to do justice to his vast body of criticism. Essays like this are bound to suffer from a reductive quality. I have not touched his Blake criticism at all and have rather concentrated on some of his essays on Shakespeare and English fiction, published in *the Aligarh Journal of English Studies*. My only endeavour in this piece is to arrive at Ansari's method of analysis, interpretation and evaluation, in other words, his way of reading a text.

II

The long history of literary criticism shows that there are different ways of reading a text. In his much talked about essay "Comment lire" Tzvetan Todorov mentions three popular methods of reading a text which he names as projection, commentary and poetics. Projection is the other word for what Rene Wellek categorizes as the extrinsic approaches to the study of literature in which some external entities are the focus and the text is used to talk about those entities (65-135). Traditional approaches like biographical, historical, psychological or even Marxist can well be described as projections. As against projection poetics "seeks the general principles that manifest themselves in particular works....Poetics...is open to the charge that it is a kind of projection, however privileged, which does not do justice to the individual work" (Scholes143-144).Some rigorous kind of archetypal criticism or for that matter structuralist criticism of the kind Barthes practiced in works like *S/Z* can qualify as poetics.

It is commentary which takes into account the different aspects of a text. In commentary the focus is firmly on the text. However, a good commentary does not degenerate into a mere paraphrase as it often does in less skillful hands. The New Critical close reading is the best example of Todorov's idea of commentary. Asloob Ahmad Ansari's criticism normally stays away from projection. We do not find examples in his critical practice where he dwells on the biography of the writer which we regularly come across in criticism by Indian critics. Not for Ansari the easy way out to seek a causal relationship between the work and the author either in his Urdu or English criticism. Though of necessity he would sometimes talk about some binaries like plebian and patrician (he takes up this opposition in his article titled "*Coriolanus*—the Roots of Alienation") he has not been inclined to use Marxist criticism either. In fact, projection is still a popular method practiced as it is in the form of a more sophisticated variety of Marxist criticism and its use in postcolonial theory. (It may be added here that in his perceptive essay--discussed a bit later in this paper– Abul Kalam Qasmi quotes many passages from Ansari's Urdu writings which show the influence of Marxist thought)Ansari's preferred mode of reading a text is paying close attention to the language of the text, the images, the symbols and how they interweave together to create meaning. That there is meaning is a given. It is up to the critic to discover that meaning through his reading of the images. The placing of the image in the text, its repetition or its echo in the text is also his concern. He is always alert to detect some dominant pattern in the text. All through, the text remains his focus and he rarely loses sight of it. The quotations from the texts are liberally cited in his essays.

Ansari's criticism bears the mark of his deep commitment to literature and his extensive reading of literature and different critical schools. He also makes a careful distinction between an ordinary reader and a critic, placing the critic a notch above the reader. In his critical endeavour one can see a conscious effort to break free from the expressive effusions of romantic tradition in criticism. The vulgar adoption of mimetic criticism also runs counter to Ansari's sophisticated approach. However, a closer scrutiny of his method does reveal, at the philosophical level, the hold of empiricist-rationalist tradition on his criticism. One can detect the methodology of Leavisite, New Criticism and, in some instances, aspects of archetypal criticism, though his close reading of the text may not incline him to adopt the basic principles of archetypal criticism. The recent advances in theory have established the inability of these schools to break free from the empiricist-rationalist thinking despite their professed goals to the contrary. At the philosophical level his sympathy for the existentialist philosophy is also very much evident in his criticism. In an important article on his Urdu criticism Abul Kalam Qasmi also sees in his criticism the influence of different critical schools. Taking up both his early and later criticism and giving evidence from Ansari's writing and seeing an evolution in his critical responses, Qasmi also notices an element of pluralism in Ansari's criticism. Qasmi touches on Ansari's questioning of moral and scientific criticism and believes that Ansari himself is not unaffected by scientific criticism. In the same way though Ansari was never swayed by the powerful current of Progressive Writers Movement, he was, argues Qasmi, not untouched by it either (150-172).

New Critical focus on the central importance of language of the text, especially its employment of image and symbols is clearly manifest in Ansari's work. This criticism was based on the principle of discovering unity in a text. Ansari's characteristic method of reading a text aims at discovering this notion of unity through unraveling various images and symbols in the text. Another important assumption in his criticism which he shares with New Criticism is to consider literature an entirely different kind of discourse which communicates at the symbolic plane. The writer has in his arsenal rich images and symbols. As such the critic should be alert to the use of such images and symbols in a work. Here the idea is that the meaning of the text lies not in the mind of the author but rather in the words on the page. The formalistic critics' disagreement with the expressive and mimetic tradition of criticism is present in Ansari's total shunning of the biographical method.

Thus Ansari picks out some key lines and words from *Antony and Cleopatra* and explicates them to arrive at some of the core concerns of the play in his essay titled "*Antony and Cleopatra*: An Image of Liquifaction". In fact, this essay is a classic of image and symbol method of close reading. In the line "Let Rome in Tiber melt" he offers a very incisive reading of the word "melt". He explicates other aspects of text also through his method of close reading: "Words like 'purple' and 'gold' become evocative of a resplendent visual image and the winds grow enamoured of the perfumed sails" (8:80-81). The images used by Shakespeare, wind images, kinetic images and others, are subjected to a rigorous analysis. In the same way in his reading of *The Tempest* Ansari is alert to the significance of some key words in the play: "Recurrent use of words like 'dream', 'wonder' and 'sleep' contributes to a pervasive atmosphere which is other than earthly or mundane"(1:228).

It is not only the images and individual symbols but also the symbolic patterns in the text which were stressed by the formalistic critics. Ansari shows this critical alertness to discover such patterns and motifs in the text. Thus in his highly philosophical essay on *Troilus and Cressida* he unearths two divergent orders of experiences namely the Trojans and the Greeks. He discusses the characters and circumstances in the play in terms of 'tonal ambiguities'. He reads

Trojans as passionate and idealistic and the Greeks as level-headed and restrained. The two different orders of experiences accumulate other similarly contrasting characteristics. The play's theme of honour and love is presented through these images which Shakespeare subjects "to a dispassionate, critical scrutiny" (3:199). Ansari also unravels many patterns of polarities in the poetry of Andrew Marvell (4:58-73). The dichotomy of body-soul, nature-nurture, art-artifice, harmony-alienation and intellect-emotion, believes Ansari, inform Marvell's poetry.

Particularly noticeable in his criticism is his love of existentialist thought. In a series of articles Ansari finds existentialist patterns in Shakespeare's plays. Maqbool Hasan Khan is of the view that in his reading of Shakespeare Ansari adopts "the strategy of allowing existentialist insights to serve as the underlying framework.... The implicit parallelism emerges into a sharp focus as the essay is brought to a close...However, even at the end the reader is not clearly told that what he was gradually being led into was a kind of analogical stud" (15:107). Ansari has himself admitted his interest in existentialist thought in his reading of Shakespeare. His comment is worth quoting:

> The existentialist approach to Shakespeare is a very valid and fruitful one and is relevant to some of the more important plays though not to all....I am rather cautious in my procedure so as not to give the impression of employing a critical strategy as a symptom of my 'allegiance to a contemporary fashion'. For me it is not a matter of imposing certain premises of existentialist thought on Shakespeare's plays but merely an attempt to discover analogies for this thought wherever they are traceable in his work. (15:108)

In an essay on *Measure for Measure* (2:231-246) he explores many existentialist ideas like the idea of loneliness, absence of communication and different attitudes to death in the play especially with reference to his reading of the character of Angelo. *The Merchant of Venice* is read by Ansari as an existentialist comedy. It "is charged with moments of deep anxiety" in which Antonio feels "wearied with life" (11:18) and his whole "existence shadowed with lonliness and a sense of being self-exiled" (11:18). Ansari dwells on his melancholy, and the feeling of boredom and ennui in the play. The ephemeral nature of the world and his loneliness despite his friendship with Bassanio is very much the focus of Ansari's study. "More or less like a protective shield for Bassanio he remains all along a care-worn person and suffers from a sense of alienation"(11:20). In his characteristic manner he identifies a particular pattern in this play too. This is the pattern of loneliness in both Antonio and Shylock, Antonio's loneliness a result of temperament and that of Shylock of social and racial factors. In the entire essay Ansari develops this idea invoking the existentialist vocabulary. One interesting feature of this article is Ansari's reading of consistency and solidity in the character of much-maligned Shylock, a point with which he concludes his essay.

Hamlet is perceptively analysed as an existentialist tragedy in which the meaning of the play derives from Hamlet's reaction to Dasein. He is ontologically forced to make a choice in all possible situations in the play. Ansari sees loathing and anxiety as the two most important attributes of Hamlet's self. His "sickness of the soul" and "nauseating sense of ennui against the body" (6:228) further define his situation. An interesting aspect of Hamlet's sense of void, as explicated by Ansari, is his loss of "faith in the efficacy of words" (6:235). Words no longer act as symbols of ideas and things, or to use a contemporary expression, the signifier-signified relationship is disturbed not in a poetic manner in the play but in a more absurdist manner. Ansari believes that "a disjunction has taken place between words and the heart of truth which is their ultimate referent" (6:236). Obviously words referring to truth immediately make Ansari's criticism sound pre-Saussurean but there is no mistaking Ansari's close and perceptive reading of Hamlet's problem.

Ansari's reading of *King Lear* also traces existentialist themes in the play. The view of man that Ansari discovers in the play is also put in existentialist terms. Man in this play is an isolated and tormented being and "his sense of estrangement and precariousness" define him (8:221). Ansari concludes this essay by offering an existentialist view of Lear's situation: "But the sense of living in a hostile and perilous world all alone and almost bereft of the sustainment offered by genuine and reciprocal love is what accounts for Lear's utter moral and spiritual collapse, and for the world being reduced to mere shambles for him" (8:222).

The use of the word "nothing" in the play, Ansari is of the view, is central to the play's meaning. Ansari's analysis of the foregrounding of meanings in this word is a staple of the explicative method of New Criticism. The word has its role in bringing about thematic unity in the play. Later deconstructive criticism would adopt the method of picking up on one word, not necessarily the key word, but putting it to a contradictionist use. But the vague similarity of the two methods can be discerned (even in this piece of Ansari) although their aims are very different.

Ansari uses the methodology of discovering these symbolic patterns, not necessarily the existentialist ones, in his fiction criticism too. The very first sentence of his essay on *Howards End* talks about a major antithesis round which the novel is built: "*Howards End* is built round a major antithesis—the contrast between the Wilcoxes and the Schelegels, and this contrast is sustained throughout the novel till the former are vanquished towards the very end" (5:67). Ansari's reading of this pattern is attempted through his commentary on the text which at times turns into a kind of paraphrase. A long summing up of the characteristics of Wilcoxes and the Schelegels follows. This kind of criticism can sometimes suffer from reductivism. It is in the later part of the essay that Ansari returns to his characteristic alertness to the use of images and symbols in the text. He argues that the "primary themes of the novel converge on and are mediated through the pattern of its symbolism "(5:77). Dwelling on the pattern of antinomies Ansari discovers the motifs of survival and continuity in this novel. A very important concern of Ansari in this essay is the analysis of house as a symbol in the novel. He talks about *Howards End* as a spatial symbol, Ruth Wilcox as the symbol of vitality and growth and rainbow bridge as symbolic of the 'need to connect'. True to his wont Ansari discovers a very important leitmotif in the novel, that of "the triumph which the imagination achieves over reason and the bodily passion"(5:79).

In his study of Virginia Woolf's *To the Lighthouse* (7:248-262) also Ansari unravels the symbolic world of the novel. while agreeing with the dominant view that Woolf tries to capture the 'moment' or what Milan Kundera says of Joyce the present moment, Ansari dwells at length on the internal action in the novel. However, this internal action in the novel develops through symbolic correspondences. With his focus on phallic symbols, Ansari talks about the symbol of "arid scimitar" and the counter symbol of "rosy flowered fruit tree" in the novel. He also talks about hieroglyphics in the novel and considers boar's skull as symbolic of a primitive and instinctive fear of death and dissolution. Ansari also discovers two important leitmotivs in the novel namely the expedition to the Lighthouse and Lily Brisoe's painting of the picture. Lily Brisoe's painting of the picture is interpreted as achieving integration and harmony for her. It is the feature of Ansari's criticism that he remains alert to the deeper import of the shape and structuring of the novel. His reading of the 'triangular shape' first constituted by Mr. and Mrs. Ramsay and James and later by Mrs. Ramsay, Lily Briscoe and Mr. Carmichael and his interpretation of 'Time Passes" in the tripartite structure of the novel further confirm his skill in discovering images and symbolic patterns in the text. The essay ends with Ansari foregrounding the central importance of the symbol of the Lighthouse. The ending of the essay with Ansari finding elements of unity and symmetry is every bit New Critical, something which has been naturalized by generations of critics: "Lily's drawing a line in the centre of the picture makes the 'hideously white space' disappear, and the picture and the Lighthouse—the two coordinates having a bearing on the relativity of things—merge into a final symmetry. And thus the novel, meant to demonstrate and symbolize a self-justifying achievement, ends on a note of serenity" (7: 261).

Ansari's reading of *Women in Love* is a commentary on the thematic patterns of the novel in the mode talked about by Todorov. At times the commentary appears to be degenerating into paraphrase in this piece. He slightly departs from his usual image and symbol method of analysis in this essay and focuses on characters and their relationships and does not select key words or images for rigorous analysis. Obviously the nature of the text greatly determines his criticism and symbol-hunting cannot be indulged in for the hack of it. The following quotation can give an idea of the type of criticism Ansari attempts in this piece:

> The two sisters—Ursula and Gudrun of the Brangwen family—products of the same cultural matrix—reflect distinct and divergent personality-types which are projected in their relationship with Birkin and Gerald, respectively. The novel opens with mutual discussion focused incisively on the nature and prospects of marriage and Ursula seems to be skeptical of the assumptions upon which it is conventionally based and thinks that it is validated only by the specific experience which it involves. The course of love in both cases is tumultuous and nerve wracking; it has moments of felicity and self abandon, indeed, but it never runs smooth and evenly. Contrasted with Gudrun---and the contrast is pronouncedly sharp—Ursula commands greater poise and stability of temper, is an inquiring intelligence, and has an inherent talent for accommodation and adjustment. (10:156)

A very important feature of Ansari's writing is his concern for the larger human context of literature. His interest in existential themes coupled with his mastery of New Critical and Leavisite concerns and archetypal paradigms makes him see the universal elements in the particularities of situations and characters. In his essentially humanist criticism Ansari often moves from individual and local to the universal. To him Hamlet's loathing would finally take in its fold not only Gertrude and Ophelia but the entire universe. The situation in the play is also read as "cosmic drama". True to his manner of criticism which universalizes the significance of an event or an experience Ansari also reads *King Lear* as an "attempt at probing the human condition" (8:205). When he talks about the Forest of Arden in Shakespeare's *As You Like It* he considers it "a microcosm within the larger design of the play: it is both a literary pastoral and a replica of the universe of ordered harmonies which glows with the halo of pristine purity and lack of self-consciousness" (7:59). Criticism now is averse to the idea of universality in any text and words like universal and cosmic to define a particular situation have gone out of favour in today's criticism. Instead there is the dominant view that in the context of British literature British values were often camouflaged as universal values. In the same way in his discussion of *Antony and Cleopatra* (8:79-93) Ansari equates Eastern world with pleasure principle, with oriental levitas while the Western world is identified with reality principle, with Roman gravitas. This kind of binarism, guilty of promoting stereotypical notions about the world and presenting a rabid Orientalist view is considered very problematic by postcolonial theory. The principles of New Critical and Levisite variety of humanist criticism were considered so natural, their view of the world naturalized by an entire generation of students and scholars that even critics from the non-Western world did not find anything amiss in the stereotypical East-West polarity. Another point to note is that even though structuralist criticism discovers patterns of comparison and contrast in literary works Ansari's analysis of these patterns differs from structuralists' because of his humanist concerns and his unquestioned belief in the centrality of human subject.

Today's criticism takes an amoral stance towards its subject matter. However, the entire critical tradition from Matthew Arnold to T. S. Eliot is marked by a moral stance. Indian readers of Western literature often find it difficult to relate to the candid depiction of sex in Western literature. Their upbringing in a particular moral set-up makes it difficult to identify with many situations in the Western literature. Their diffidence should be seen to be believed in the classroom with mixed groups. Ansari's criticism also reflects his moral vision. Thus in his essay on *Measure for Measure* he comments: "An unrestrained indulgence in sexual appetites leads not only to physical decay but ultimately to the death of the spirit" (2:234). Something of F. R. Leavis's moral fervour is visible in statements like this.

Contemporary critics make a very strong case for the intertextual nature of literature. Because of his extensive scholarship, Ansari is suitably placed to discovering intertextual patterns and motifs in his criticism. In his willingness to detect intertextual elements Ansari departs from the New Critical position and moves closer, perhaps unwittingly, to Northrop Frye's. However, his criticism gains quite a bit from his method of comparing and contrasting different representations of the same object/idea. Forster's London is compared by him to Blake's London and Eliot's "unreal city". Walter Raleigh's style is compared to Middleton Murray's. The theme of ingratitude in *King Lear* is compared to the treatment of filial ingratitude in Marcel Proust. In fact, in his Urdu criticism he uses the method of comparing texts much more frequently.

Ansari's criticism is characterized by his distinct confident style. The confident, categorical and almost authoritative tone is present from beginning to end in his articles. He starts his essays with an authoritative statement. In this kind of judgmental pronouncements he appears a Leavisite. This authoritative tone is matched by the evidence furnished by him in his essay to support his findings. Thus his essay on *The Tempest* begins by demolishing the popular opinion about the play: "To regard *The Tempest* as primarily a 'Romance' amounts to an exaggeration of a half-truth only" (1:228). He starts his study of *Measure for Measure* by loudly announcing his point of view:" "Though doubtless cast in a comic form and ultimately following the trail of reconciling and harmonizing process *Measure for Measure* is enwrapped in the shadow of death from beginning to end" (2:230). He comes to repeat the play's obsession with the existentialist theme of death at the end of this essay in equally emphatic terms. The confident and authoritative beginning also characterizes his essay on *Julius Caesar* : "The basic conflict in *Julius Caesar*, round which the entire pattern of play is structured, derives from and in a way is rooted in the opposed political passions and conceptions of the power-nexus"(10:17). More such examples of categorical beginnings can be given from his criticism.

The approach of many a critic today lacks this voice of authority especially in their comment on the nature and definition of literature because the concept and notion of literature has undergone a seismic change. The certainty of liberal-humanist criticism about the role and definition of literature is replaced by doubtful, dissenting and disruptive voices. Ansari could proclaim that "when we consider literature at the highest and deepest level art and metaphysics merge together into an indissoluble unity in our gesture of response" (15:112). In the same way he speaks about Shakespeare with a touch of finality. It can be said that every generation has had his/her own Shakespeare. Ansari's Shakespeare owes a lot to Ansari's clear notion of the nature of literature. It will be worthwhile to quote him on Shakespeare:

> (In Shakespeare) we come across insights into patterns of human behaviour and eternal and imperishable truths about life in general. Looking at the enigma of human life from the corner of his eye with steady gaze he never misses anything worthwhile to comment upon and his reactions are mediated through dramatic characters who are multi-faceted, engaging and alive to the very depths of their being. His grasp over the abundance and bewildering heterogeneity of life, his gift of synthesizing disparate experiences and presenting the synthesis in language that is highly creative, vibrant and marked with ambiguity: these things have never been attempted and with such tremendous success by any writer before or since.(15:105)

The key words in this passage which need to be looked at critically are "patterns of human behaviour", "eternal and imperishable truths about life", and "synthesis". These words together with many other passages quoted in this paper and still other common critical tendencies conspicuous by their absence in Ansari's criticism reflect Ansari's critical credo. Ansari stays clear of the certainties of expressive realism. No where in his work do we find the tendency to locate the source of meaning in the author's intention. The intentionalist stance, a throwback to romantic thought, about which Wimsatt and Beardsley have spoken so eloquently, is shunned by Ansari as a matter of principle. And though Maqbool Hasan Khan is right in denying the influence of Northrop Frye on Ansari's work (15:106), Frye's notion of human nature as constant and unchanging is an integral part of Ansari's critical vision. In the same way though he, much like the dominant critical positions of his time, tries to challenge the common sense view of literature, something which has been the staple of mimetic tradition, the pull of that tradition can be felt in the notion that literary works tell the truth, that they are about the world that they present human nature and that there is the human agency—elements which are very much present in Ansari's criticism. Certainly the credo of New Criticism together with the insights of T.S.Eliot, I.A.Richards, F.R.Leavis and William Empson has made a significant impact on Ansari's criticism. It is a measure of the influence of this formalistic credo that more than the values of spontaneity, which biographical/romantic criticism considers an important value, Ansari speaks about the value of integrity and unity. When he thinks about Shakespeare's plays or for that matter the work of others he looks for their skill at "synthesizing" "disparate" experiences. The New Critical orthodoxy about formal properties of the text (language that is highly creative, vibrant and marked with ambiguity) is very much the concern of Ansari's criticism. There is the faint resonance of Brooks's and Empson's views on language even in the passage just quoted.

It can be said that his criticism remains within the confines of empiricist-rationalist problematic, that despite his preference for formalistic method his work reconciles and unwittingly relies on various theories dominant in the twentieth century.

But the most problematic part of this criticism from today's perspective—Maqbool Hasan Khan feared that Ansari's Shakespeare criticism may appear dated--is its notion of truth and its tendency to validate a single meaning. The effort to discover "eternal and imperishable truth" brings a kind of orthodoxy, a kind of, to use Paul de Man's phrase, critical blindness. New Criticism has often been blamed for completely ignoring history. Catherine Belsey rightly says that "the problem is a more fundamental one, namely, the failure to recognize that meaning exists only within a specific culture, and that it cannot therefore inhere timelessly within the words on the page....New Criticism is compelled by its own logic to argue that the text simply 'means' in isolation, and means now what it has always meant, that the poem is a 'concrete universal', the individual instance of an eternally and universally intelligible verity" (Belsey 17-18). Ansari's Shakespeare is elevated to a position where he speaks universal truths, where the experience of the text has a transhistorical quality, where even the possibility of a female black critic pronouncing "black women are not Shakespeare's sisters" does not arise. In his other pieces also Ansari seems to celebrate the quality of unchanging experience. Historical dimension of self is not Ansari's concern because his sympathies are with New Criticism and Practical Criticism. It is rather the world rising above the flux, something which literature was supposed to present, the eternal and the unchanging which interests him. However, as the work in reception theory indicates, the meaning of a text is not fixed for all time and in different periods different notions of texts emerge. The idea of an authoritative, single meaning is an orthodoxy easily disproved by the history of criticism. As Hans Robert Jauss has so convincingly argued critics work with different paradigms in different periods; their "horizon of expectations" (Jauss's term) in each period is different. Ansari worked within his horizon of expectations in which (to borrow a phrase from Raman Selden's famous book) "New Criticism with its Practical Criticism basis" was the norm. Also in his celebration of canon, in his devotion to aesthetic-humanist credo and in his total concentration on text he is one with Anglo-American criticism—Practical criticism, New

Criticism and Leavisite criticism, in other words within empirical-rationalist problematic.

By way of concluding this paper we can again stress what was said at the beginning of this paper. Despite present criticism's quarrel with Ansari's kind of criticism, obviously because of the massive advantage given by hindsight, or because today's critic is working within his "horizon of expectations", the volume and depth, and the complexity and richness of Ansari's criticism cannot be captured by the use of some current terminology. Any easy evaluation of his work would be fallacious. One can agree with Ansari that the recent very exciting critical work on a writer like Shakespeare does not invalidate earlier work of critics.

Asloob Ahmad Ansari's criticism will certainly endure.

WORKS CITED

Ansari, Asloob Ahmad. "The Ambivalence of Caliban."*Aligarh Journal of English Studies* 1 (1976) : 228-243. Print.

—"*Measure for Measure* and the Masks of Death". *Aligarh Journal of English Studies* 2 (1977): 231-246. Print.

—"The Problem of Identity in *Troilus and Cressida*." *Aligarh Journal of English Studies* 3 (1978) :199-214. Print.

—"The Body-Soul Dialectic in Marvell." *Aligarh Journal of English Studies* 4 (1979): 58-73. Print.

—"*Howards End*:The Pattern of Antinomies." *Aligarh Journal of English Studies* 5(1980):66-82. Print.

—"*Coriolanus*–the Roots of Alienation." *Aligarh Journal of English Studies* 6 (1981) :14-34. Print.

—"Shakespeare's Existential Tragedy." *Aligarh Journal of English Studies* 6 (1981): 227-249. Print.

—"No Clock in the Forest of Arden." *Aligarh Journal English Studies* 7 (1982) :55-71. Print.

—"Structure of Correspondences in *To the Lighthouse*." *Aligarh Journal of English Studies* 7 (1982):248-262. Print.

—"*Antony and Cleopatra*: An Image of Liquifaction." *Aligarh Journal of English Studies* 8(1983):79-93. Print.

—"*King Lear*: The Vision of Horror." *Aligarh Journal of English Studies* 8(1983):205-222. Print.

—"Marcus Brutus:The Divided Self." *Aligarh Journal of English Studies* 10(1985):17-34. Print.

—"*Women in Love*: Search for Integrated Being." *Aligarh Journal of English Studies* 10(1985):156-177. Print.

—"*The Merchant of Venice*: An Existential Comedy." *Aligarh Journal of English Studies* 11(1986):18-32. Print.

—"A.A. Ansari Interviewed by M.H.Khan." *Aligarh Journal of English Studies* 15:105-15. Print.

—Rev. of The *Leavises: Impressions and Recollections*, ed. Denys Thompson. *Aligarh Journal of English Studies* 9(1984):227-234. Print.

Belsy, Catherine. *Critical Practice*.1980.London and New York: Routledge, 2009. Print.

Husain, Afzal Qazi. Personal interview. 20 May 2012.

Qasmi, Abul Kalam. "The Evolution of Asloob Ahmad Ansari's Critical Thoughts." *Asloob Ahmad Ansari: The Man, Criticism and Style of Writing*. Eds. Matin, Abdul, and Mohammad Yusuf Amin. Aligarh: Universal Book House, 2010. (my translation of the title). Print.

Scholes, Robert. *Structuralism in Literature*. New Haven and London: Yale University Press,1974. Print.

Selden, Raman, Peter Widdowson, Peter Brooker. *A Reader's Guide to Contemporary Literary Theory*. 5th ed. New Delhi: Pearson, 2005. Print.

Wellek, Rene. *Theory of Literature*. London: Jonathan Cape, 1949. Print.

18

Masoodul Hasan's Writings in English: A Bibliographic Essay

Mohammad Asim Siddiqui

It has been argued in this book that the Department of English of Aligarh Muslim University has contributed in no uncertain terms towards building what can be called the Aligarh sub-school of Shakespeare Criticism. Besides Shakespeare the Romantics have hogged a lot of critical attention. In fact, Shakespeare and the Romantic poets have engaged the attention of a disproportionately large number of scholars and laymen in India before and after independence.

The tradition of Shakespeare scholarship notwithstanding, there have been some notable efforts in the Department to focus attention on other areas of English studies. Masoodul Hasan, an untiring reader, a serious scholar and a public lecturer par excellence, has charted out an entirely different territory for himself in his engagement with literary studies spanning a period of more than sixty years. Though his literary interests have been varied—his insightful and frank opinions on subjects as different as literary criticism, ELT, contemporary Pakistani English fiction and even cultural studies including film studies bear testimony to this—his writings can be divided into three heads: seventeenth century English poetry, Sufism, and practical aspects of research activities in India. First is his interest in the seventeenth-century English poetry especially in the poetry of metaphysical poets such as John Donne. The interest in Donne's poetry was probably a literary trigger--though it would be a gross oversimplification to reduce it to only

Donne's poetry as Masoodul Hasan is deeply immersed in Persio-Urdu literary-philosophical-tradition— to awaken his interest in strains of Sufi thought in English literature. In any case his interest in Sufism has yielded a remarkably original book, his labour of love so to say. He followed his third interest with a lot of diligence all his life and it has also yielded three important books of bibliographic research immensely helpful for research students especially at the time of their first appearance.

His interest in the seventeenth century English poetry saw its first concrete realization in his book titled *Donne's Imagery* as early as 1958.His main argument in the book, illustrated through his almost exhaustive study of the poet's imagery, was to suggest that images were integral to Donne's cognitive universe and that they constitute "the texture of his thought". The book is neatly divided into sections, each section covering a few subjects which preoccupied Donne's imagination. The organization of his material not only enhances the readability of the book but is also an aid to memory as Hasan has carried out a subject-wise study of the images. In the first section Hasan discusses Donne's sex imagery and argues that sex and love were synonymous words for Donne. The viewing of sex in a mystic light and the tracing of the evolution of sex mysticism is an important aspect of this section. The second section of the book takes up images dealing with science and philosophy. Donne's belief in the hollowness of alchemy and the genuineness of chemistry, his use of astronomical images like galaxy, sphere and eclipse, geographical images like meridians, parallels and hemispheres, and sea images such as voyage are all detailed by Hasan. The section on theological images suggests Donne's interest in Christ rather than God. Sections five, six and seven are devoted by Hasan to law, war and death imagery in Donne's poetry respectively. Architectural, food and colour imagery are the subjects of Hasan's critical gaze in the remaining sections of this study. Hasan appropriately concludes his study by his argument introduced at the beginning of this short and very readable book: "The study of his imagery reveals the untold story of the man" (86).

Masoodul Hasan engagement with the seventeenth century English poetry resulted in a major study of a minor poet with the publication of his book on the relatively obscure seventeenth century English poet Francis Quarles. The book simply titled *Francis Quarles: A Study of His Life and Poetry* (1966) successfully carried out an appraisal of his poetry, to quote the author, "with special reference to the English heritage of the genres in which he worked and ...his likely influence on some later writers" (iii).The voluminous book (running into 335 pages) and consisting of eight chapters including Conclusion does not miss any aspect of Quarles's art. Hasan takes up both his divine and secular poems. In his study of his divine poems Hasan is alert to Quarles's use of rhetorical devices especially repetition of words and phrases, his debt to "the better pilots", and his many revisions of his poems. In his discussion of secular poems Hasan analyses Quarles's use of literary devices like suggestive symbolism, apostrophe, and his use of mythology. Hasan also discusses Quarles's poems of meditative character which are marked by his use of and departure from the genre of epigram which was popular in his time. In the same way Quarles used the form of emblem writing that was popular in his time.

It was probably the pressure of his time--the time of the celebration of very exclusive canon—that made Hasan unduly apologetic about his study of a minor poet like Francis Quarles. He reiterates the justification of his study in the Conclusion once again: "Certainly he is not a major poet; but perhaps for that very reason he deserves to be studied with some care, for sometimes even the relatively less important literary figures lead to a fuller understanding of their age by setting into focus some of its neglected, though otherwise significant aspects....he reveals his age...and fully represents its moralistic and partisan spirit.. "(288).

Time, however, has its own way of vindicating the past . Today the question of canon is fraught with literary politics. Terms like major and minor hide much more than they reveal. That Donne is more important than Quarles has less to do with the intrinsic quality of their poetry but because of many extra-literary considerations.

Seen in this perspective Hasan's study of the art and craft of Quarles's poetry appears much more significant than he himself might have anticipated it.

Hasan progresses from his study of individual poets like Donne and Quarles to his extremely broad-based, grand, ambitious and noble study of English literature in Sufic perspective. The book titled *Sufism and English Literature* traces Sufic influences, images and echoes in the works of literature written in English, particularly English literature from Chaucer to the present time. Though Masoodul Hasan's book shares a lot of ground with the subject called literary Orientalism—there are hundreds of books and articles on the subject—it will be a serious mistake to confuse his endeavour with that of scholars working under the broad umbrella of literary Orientalism. Hasan's originality lies in his sharp focus on Sufism, its various orders and concepts and the message of Sufis from different parts of the Muslim world. He maintains a very minute distinction between a mere Islamic/Muslim encounter with the West and an interaction which has Sufic significance. The subjects and authors covered in the study required not a nodding acquaintance but a deep engagement with their work. The book is the result of his life-long experience and living of two different traditions, Western and Persio-Arabic-Urdu, and his heart-felt commitment to the humanist role of literature. Coming at a time when the humanist basis of literary studies has been seriously questioned, the book makes a very fervent plea for the humanist values implicit in literature, the unifying role of literature, the commonality of experience, the universal mind, and the belief in a world in which God exists. The assumption in the worth of mimetic nature of literature is an important aspect of this project.

There are three very notable strands in the book: direct or indirect borrowings as a result of interaction between Western and Eastern culture, parallelisms, images, and echoes of Sufi thought in the works, and most importantly interpretation of literary texts in Sufic perspective Thus he talks about Marlowe's and Donne's possible awareness of the writings of Ibne Arabi.The possible influence of

Sa'di and Hafiz can be seen on the poetry of Thomas Herbert. The significance of the identity of Dervishes is explored in the works of writers like Nicholas Rowe, Joseph Addison, Lady Mary Wortley Montagu and Samuel Johnson. Obviously from the 18th century onwards tracing Sufi influences becomes more certain as details about works and writers are properly documented.The influence of Sufic concepts on the Romantic poets, definite though it is, may be a subject of interpretation but there is no mistaking the Sufic intent of Robert Graves, Sufic images in Ted Hughes and the pervasive and all important Sufic figures and allusions in the later twentieth century prose fiction especially that of Doris Lessing and Salman Rushdie. Hasan stretches the canvas of his study to include both canonical writers as well as the popular ones like Arthur Conan Doyle, English as well as the Australians, Indians and even Pakistanis.

The most remarkable and undoubtedly original contribution of Hasan is to build up a poetics of Sufic interpretation in his book. The voluminous book offers a score of Sufic readings of English texts. Shakespeare's Prospero in *the Tempest* is interpreted in Sufic light and so are W.B.Yeats's two plays. It is the positive and unmistakably humanist intent of Hasan that he reads supposedly Orientalist lines from Marlow's *Tamburlaine* in Sufic light invoking the concept of Insan E Kamil.Hasan's Sufic readings differ entirely from the highly ideological project of Islamization of Knowledge that has gained some adherents in recent years. Masoodul Hasan's Sufic readings are a result of his love of humanity, his awareness of living in a world marked by conflict, discord, suspicion and both misinformation and disinformation and his own sincerity to correct the wrong in his own way as a scholar of literature. The result is a rich and pregnant line of inquiry, a new and novel way of approaching the texts and a project with immense future possibilities. His work can be gainfully carried forward by students and researchers. There can be a debate about forcing a text to yield a particular kind of meaning but this charge was equally valid against many mimetic theories, Marxist in particular, but they continued to offer rich interpretations of literary texts. In the same way Masoodul Hasan's work generates thinking, provokes discussion and is good value for students and research scholars.

Students and research scholars have always been a major concern of Masoodul Hasan in his various roles as a teacher, administrator, educationist and a writer. The third important stream of his writing is entirely devoted to facilitate research in English literature. Perhaps in our time of information explosion it is difficult to visualize the difficulties researchers of earlier generations faced in collecting information about the availability of relevant material for their research. In fact, half of the time of the researchers was spent on the 'collection of material', running around different libraries in the hope of getting the required book or writing to different libraries about the possible source of a book. Painfully aware of the problems of the researchers, Hasan came out with three useful books on the rare books available in different libraries of India. The first of these books titled *Rare English Books in India: A Select Bibliography* compiled a list of books published, in most cases, before 1800 that were available in about forty-five different libraries of India. Obviously his own interest in the Elizabethan and the seventeenth-century literature and the problems of locating materials motivated him to take up this work. The book also has useful information about periodicals including their back issues available in India .This book was followed by another useful book titled *19th Century English Literary Works: A Bibliography of Rare Books Available in India*. In the first book he had included entries from different disciplines but in this book ,as the title indicates, he concentrated on literary works published or reprinted between 1800 and 1899.While research today focuses on contemporary writers/areas, in the 70s in the Indian universities the nineteenth century mostly occupied the time and attention of researchers. He makes a very important observation in the preface of the second book which is still partly true. He writes: "the volume and quality of our critical studies and scholarship have been distinctly disproportionate to the time and energy devoted to it as a popular academic subject (*English Literary Works* v)".Even now in the twenty first century though the volume of research has increased manifold its quality leaves a lot to be desired. In the seventies when Hasan was writing he was concerned with the problem of "wasteful repetition and overlapping" (*Rare English Books* iii). One can agree with his suggestion that "bibliographic projects should be taken up as partial requirement of M Phil and PhD degrees" (*Rare English Books* iii). The problem of repetition and overlapping has become much worse today thanks to the indiscriminate admission policy and the politics of appeasement in our educational institutions and the unholy hurry with which PhD topics are tossed around. Though Hasan's two books, immensely useful in the 70s and the 80s have outlived their utility in our age of information technology, the research issues and the methodology outlined by him in the two books can give some useful tips to the potential researchers even today.

His third venture in this bibliographic series was compilation of work on John Milton available in India. The self-explanatory title of the book *Miltoniana in India:A Select Bibliography Including Translations of Milton's Works in Indian and Other Languages* suggests the range and scope of this work which in all fairness can still be consulted with profit. It gives details of about 500 books, 400 articles and about 360 translations including his translations in many Indian languages like Hindi and Urdu. The book's section titled "Translations and Critical Writings in Indian Languages" is especially very useful at a time when translation is the buzz word. The book has a subtext namely the reception of Milton in India, another useful fact for students of reception theory.

Apart from his books, Masoodul Hasan's many articles and book reviews also distinguish his writing. The most noticeable quality of these relatively short pieces is their variety. Though a bit publication shy—he has more unpublished complete articles than published ones-- he has still published on Rabindranath Tagore, Romantic literary theory, Australian poetry, on individual poems like Keats's *Endymion* and even on contemporary Pakistani-British novelist Qaisra Shahraz. His reviews on books reveal his various interests and as such cannot be reduced to any simplistic pattern. He has reviewed for the *Aligarh Journal of English Studies books* on Spencer, Milton, W.B.Yeats and on dialectical criticism.

WORKS CITED

Hasan, Masoodul. *Donne's Imagery.* Aligarh: Faculty of Arts, AMU, 1958. Print.

— *Francis Quarles: A Study of his Life and Poetry.*Aligarh: Aligarh Muslim University Press, 1966. Print.

— Rare *English Books in India: A Select Bibliography:* Aligarh: Three Men Publisher, 1970. Print.

— *19th Century English Literary Works: A Bibliography of Rare Books Available in India.* Delhi : B.R. Publishing Corporation, 1978. Print.

— *Miltoniana in India: a Selected Bibliography Including Translations of Milton's Works in Indian and Other Languages.* Aligarh : Shalig Ram, 1986. Print.

— *Sufism and English Literature, Chaucer to the Present Age: Echoes and Images.* New Delhi: Adam Publishers and distributors, 2007. Print.

19

Theatricality and Bleak Perspectives in Zahida Zaidi's *Bahut Door Tak Raat Hogi*

Samina Khan

There always crops up an ethical question whether writers should write on the suffering of people. In our age of market capitalism there is another dimension to this question whether writers should make a capital out of the problems of other people. In less sensitive hands the problem rather than being addressed properly can be trivialized. Still, great literary works have come out of the suffering of people. Any major event evokes different responses and response of sensitive souls like creative writers is inevitable. In recent years the terrible scenes of massacre in Gujarat have jolted the conscience of all thinking people in India. The terrible event has been well documented by commentators and journalists. In fact, Siddharth Varadarajan, presently the editor of *the Hindu* but at that time with *the Times of India*, documented these various responses in his now definitive statement titled *Making of a Tragedy* (Penguin India 2002). Fiction and non-fiction writers also handled Gujarat with a lot of sensitivity. Two examples readily come to mind. Rajkamal Jha came out with is novel *Fireproof* (Picador 2007)in which he comes down heavily on the educated and confident urban Indians for their indifference to the suffering of the minority community in Gujarat. Amitava Kumar's *Husband of a Fanatic* discusses at length the life in refugee camps in Gujarat. Kumar's evocative prose shows the bias and prejudice in the minds of the majority community in Gujarat. Among the writers in regional languages, though Vijay Tendulkar made a very angry statement against the perpetrators of violence in Gujarat he fell short of converting it into a play. Gulzar did one better. His play titled *Kharaashein* is about Gujarat massacre. The massacre also resulted in very angry poetry by Urdu poets, regularly recited in public mushairas.

Zahida Zaidi also responded to the tragedy of Gujarat by writing a very sensitive and satirical play titled *Bahut Door Tak Raat Hogi*. Before the play is subjected to a textual analysis it will not be out of place to say a few words why Zaidi felt compelled to write this play. It may be recalled that Zahida Zaidi has been associated with Marxist thought since her school days and she is an important link in the chain of Progressive Writers Movement.A such her art is often devoted to taking up the cause of the poor and the oppressed. Moreover as a sensitive soul she was also shocked by the tales of brutality in Gujarat. Her art is not simply mimetic but it also has an expressive quality. Her writings display both the mimetic and expressive theories of art. This play presents a fine blend of the two. Professor Zahida Zaidi's creative urge to present a sane and comprehensive view of the reality is reflective in her literary, academic and other humanitarian endeavours as a teacher, a writer and an artist. Theatre, being her special area of interest and research, provides her with various modes of communication to offer a blend of the fictional/mythological with the real, the spiritual with the intellectual, and the modern/western with the traditional/Indian.

Bahut Door Tak Raat Hogi, published in 2006 and originally written in Urdu language, brings into focus the victims of Gujarat violence, though in an obliquely artistic manner.The plot of the play is structurally divided into three Acts and twelve scenes. The drama begins and ends in a Khalan (a mythological vacuum) with characters like satan (shaitan) and angels (Farishtey), God's voice (Khuda ki aawaaz). The playwright seems to make a deliberate use of this dramatic situation, i.e., cut out of the real time or place to provide her with an ample opportunity to express her frank and fearless notions about the violations of human rights of the common people in the post-independence secular fabric of the Indian society/ nation.

Zaidi's art consists in her close attention to technique. She experiments with various modern techniques of drama in her plays. This play uses the techniques of the absurd drama where comic is fused with the pathetic and a sense of mutual fear and insecurity is aroused by the absurdities of the thinking patterns that eventually lead to evil. The incidents of the play closely correspond to those of the Gujarat communal massacre, Godhra train incident, mass imprisonments, and struggle for justice in jails, dislocation and displacements of the children, humiliation of women and sufferings of the poor, the old and the homeless. Through this play Zahida Zaidi succeeds in making one believe that theatre not only can transport or involve but can also change people by attempting to turn them into finer and more compassionate human beings who can empathize with the sufferings of the 'others'. Amid bleak perspectives of the lingering darkness, the play infuses the energy to cultivate hope for the better future of humanity. Her art makes an attempt at reshaping an apprehension for the core values of peace and co-existence. In a slightly different context Brustein designates modern theatre as "theatre of revolt", where the modern dramatist's "discontent extends to the very roots of existence", for he says, "...the work of art itself becomes a subversive gesture--- a more imaginative reconstruction of a chaotic, disordered world" (Brustein, 9). Zaidi's protest in this play is against an order in which such brutalities can take place. Her revolt is against the quiet, rather indifferent acceptance of the sufferings of the people.

In the twentieth century the expression of reality underwent a significant change. With the onset of the two World Wars, man began to comprehend his situation in an entirely different way. Experiments with the style of presentation were numerous but some gained a wider acceptance and popularity. Zahida Zaidi's *Modes of Communication* refers to application of many such methods and techniques of modern absurd theatre. According to her, "Absurd drama is not a drama of ideas but a drama of Being... (it) is an attempt to come to terms with the realities of this uncomfortable existence" (Zaidi, 178). *Bohut Door Tak Raat Hogi* briefly summarises the main principle involved in expressionism that determines forms, imagery, language, and syntax.

The term the Theatre of the Absurd was coined by Martin Esslin. The dramatists belonging to the Theatre of the Absurd emphasise man's apparently purposeless role and position in a universe which is imagined to have no discernible existence. The hallmark of the Theatre of the Absurd is that the certitudes of unshakable assumptions of the former ages have been swept away. Zahida Zaidi's play also confirms this idea that man is in an irredeemable exile because it is deprived of memories of a lost homeland. As much as he lacks the hope of a promised land to come, this divorce between man and his life, the actor and his setting, truly constitutes the feeling of absurdity. Zahida Zaidi herself acknowledges, "It is now my purpose to show that the absurd drama is not an eccentric movement, but is in tune with the central quest and intellectual and moral preoccupations of our time, and the image of man emerging from these plays , is a characteristic expression of the modern sensibility and a contribution to the imaginative culture of the contemporary world" (Zaidi, *Modes of communication* 179).

The use of light, sound and music to present the psychological states of mind of the characters in *Bahut Door Tak Raat Hogi* is a manifestation of expressionism and surrealism. The characters are presented as abstractions, not individuals, as types and not as having subjective identity, i.e. Raazdan, Paasban, Darban, Bhagawa Dhoti Waale Aam Log, Subz Kurti Waale Aam Log, Ghareeb Qabaili, Bhagwa Leader. The origin and use of such devices can be traced in Strindberg (*Dream Play*), Ionesco (*Chairs*), O'Neil (*The Iceman Cometh*), Kaiser (*From Morn to Midnight*), where plot is replaced by short episodic renderings of oscillating emotional states. The dialogue is fragmented; it is seemingly incoherent and often the most significant development in the field of modern theatre. The spirit and the structural modalities of the theatre of the absurd are reflective in Zaida Zaidi's play through themes, settings, characters, structural divisions, diction, dramatic devices, and the overall impact.

Absurd drama deals with the elusive experiences of the inner world and themes of permanent validity and universal significance. To quote Martin Esslin, "Ultimately, a phenomenon like the Theatre of the Absurd does not reflect despair or a return to dark irrational forces but expresses modern man's endeavour to come to terms with the world in which he lives." (Esslin, 313) Zahida Zaidi's *Bahut Door Tak Hogi* is an expression of the eternal themes of life, death, time, problems of evil and its eradication, dimensions of justice, metaphysical search for meaningful and dignified existence. Art directly projects images, symbols, dramatic devices, scenes, situations, rhythmic patterns and verbal textures. This drama depends largely on naturalistic, surrealistic, expressionistic and symbolic modes of expressions as realities and experiences which elude the grasp of reason and conceptual thought can be conveyed obliquely through poetic symbols and suggestive use of language.

The characters in *Bahut Door Tak Raat Hogi* are not specifically plot bound, they are rather concepts, and represent various forms of human existence. The traditional notion of characters as an organic unified whole is different from the insight with which the characters are portrayed in the play. Characters bear multidimensional identities i.e. mythological, legendary, contemporary and symbolical. Nameless and complex characters form an environment of an indistinctive unity between the real and the surreal. The plot and action of the play seems to indicate that the playwright deliberately wishes to save it to fall into the form of "closet drama". Ample, consistent and elaborate stage directions appear to establish that Zahida Zaidi wishes to confirm that the action of this play is stage-worthy and the realisation of her intention and the relevance of the theme may hold better and substantial communication with its stage presentation. It may serve as a means to combat communalism and an attempt to ensure social justice in the present Indian socio-political milieu.

The absurd theatre follows the cyclic motion in its structure and the use of locations, settings, devices and justification of manners and moralities. Each end is suggestive of a new beginning as *Bahut Door Tak Raat Hogi* captures a meaningful diversion into negating the possibilities of prolonged gloom and darkness. The interplay of symbolic and factual interpretation of subtle moods and nuances create a highly charged atmosphere for the recipients which enables them to grasp complex and profound ideas and to reach meanings unknown. Zahiza Zaidi herself concludes in her opening chapter of her book Modes of Communication:

> ... drama is not merely a projection of superficial feeling and popular ideas—it is neither mere entertainment, nor a reinforcement of conventional patterns of thoughts and attitudes—but a profound exploration of the self, of the universe and of undefined areas of meanings, and as such, an extension of sensibility. In short, great drama embodies a complex and profound vision of existence and by virtue of its peculiar artistic conditions and with the help of its 'multidimensional language' it can communicate it in an oblique, intense, concrete and compelling manner. (*Zaidi, 30*)

WORKS CITED

Brustein, Robert. *The Theatre of Revolt.* Boston-Toronto: Atlantic Monthly Press, 1962. Print.

Esslin,Martin. *The Theatre of the Absurd.* Harmonds-worth: Pelican Books, 1968. Print.

Zaidi, Zahida. *Bahut Door Tak Raat Hogi (Drama).* Aligarh: Aabshar Publications, 2006. Print.

—*Modes of Communication.* Aligarh: Aabshar Publications, 2005. Print.

20

Asloob Ahmad Ansari's Works in English and Urdu

Amirullah Khan, Sajidul Islam and Shahabuddin Saquib

English Criticism

Books:

1. Ansari, Asloob A. *Arrows of Intellect: A Study in William Blake's Gospel of the Imagination*. Aligarh: Naya Kitab Ghar, 1965.
2. .... Reprint. U.S.A.: The Folcroft Press, 1970.
3. —(ed.) *Essays on Wordsworth: A Bi-century Tribute*. Aligarh: A.M.U. Press, 1973.
4. —(ed.) *Essays on John Donne*. Aligarh: A.M.U. Press, 1974.
5. —(ed.) *Essays on John Milton*. Aligrah: A.M.U. Press, 1976.
6. —(ed.) *Iqbal: Essays and Studies*. New Delhi: Ghalib Academy, 1978.
7. —*William Blake's Minor Prophecies*. Wales (U.K.): Edwin Mellen, 2001.
8. —*Glimpses of Books*. Aligarh: Universal Book House, 2006.
9. —*Shakespeare: The Existentialist*. New Delhi: Sarup Books Pvt. Ltd., 2009.
10. —*Shakespeare and Other Essays*. New Delhi: Sarup Books Pvt. Ltd., 2009.
11. —*A Critique of Time in Shakespeare, Wordsworth and T.S. Eliot*. New Delhi: Sarup Books Pvt. Ltd., 2011.

Articles in *The Aligarh Journal of English Studies:*

1. 'Patterns of Love in *Twelfth Night*', 1:1, 1976.
2. 'The ambivalence of *Caliban*', 1:2, 1976.
3. 'Fools of Time in *Macbeth*', 2:1, 1977.
4. '*Measure for Measure* and the Mask of Death, 2:2, 1977.
5. 'Shakespeare's Allegory of Love', 3:1, 1978.
6. 'The Problem of Identity in *Troilus and Cressida*', 3:2, 1978.
7. 'The Body-Soul Dialectic Marvell', 4:1, 1979.
8. 'The Mockery of art in *The Winter's Tale*', 4:2, 1979.
9. '*Howards End*: The Patterns of Antimonies', 5:1, 1980.
10. '*Much Ado About Nothing* and the Masks of Reality', 5:2, 1980.
11. '*Coriolanus*: The root of Alienation', 6:1, 1981.
12. 'Shakespeare's Existential Tragedy', 6:2 1981.
13. 'No Clock in the Forest of Arden', 7:1, 1982.
14. 'Structure of Correspondence in *To the Light House*', 7:2, 1982.
15. '*Antony and Cleopatra*: Image of Liquification, 8:1, 1983.
16. '*King Lear*': The Vision of Horror', 8:2, 1983.
17. 'Political Man in Shakespeare's History Plays, 9:1, 1984.
18. 'Solitariness of the Victim in *Othello*', 9:2, 1984.
19. 'Marcus Brutus: The Divided Self', 10:1, 1985.
20. '*Women in Love*: Search for Integrated Being', 10:2, 1985.
21. '*The Merchant of Venice*: An Existential Comedy', 11:1, 1986.
22. 'The Protagonist's Dilemma in *Timon of Athens*, 11:2, 1986.
23. '*Cymbeline*: The Design of Harmony, 12:1, 1987.

Articles in *Aligarh Critical Miscellany*:

1. '*Richard III*' and the Irons of Wrath', 1:1, 1988.
2. '*The Family Reunion*: An Assessment', 1:2, 1988.
3. 'Time and History in *Little Gidding*', 2:1, 1989.
4. 'Blake's "Mental Traveller"', 2:2, 1989.
5. 'Blake's "French Revolution"', 3:1, 1990.
6. 'The Power-Nexus in *Richard II*', 3:2, 1990.
7. 'Blake's "Book of Urizon"', 4:1, 1991.
8. 'Iqbal, Islam and the West', 4:2, 1991.
9. 'Northrop Frye on Shakespeare', 5:1, 1992.

10. 'Theme of Love in Shelley's *Prometheus Unbound*', 5:2, 1992.
11. '*Richard III* and *Richard II*: Two Forms of Alienation', 6:1, 1993.
12. '*Edward II* Revisited,' 6:2, 1993.
13. 'Blake's "The Book of Los"', 7:1, 1994.

Articles in *The Indian Journal of English Studies*:

1. 'Sex Symbolism in Blake's Poetry', 1960.
2. 'Interior Landscape in the Odes of Keats', 1964.

Articles in self edited volumes:

1. 'Wordsworth and the Spots of Time' in *Essays in Wordsworth*, 1973.
2. 'Two Modes of Utterances in Donne's 'Divine Poems'', in *Essays on John Donne*, 1974.
3. 'Milton and the Myth of the Garden of Eden' in *Essays on Milton*, 1976.
4. 'An Existential Approach to Iqbal', in *Iqbal: Essays and Studies*, 1978.
5. 'Sir Walter Raleigh's Style' in *Essays on Sir Walter Raleigh*, 1988.

Miscellaneous Articles:

1. 'Iqbal's Relevance to the Present Time' in *Islamic Culture*, Hyderabad. 1976.
2. 'Sir Syed's Views of Rationalism' in *Islamic Culture*, Hyderabad. 1988-89.
3. 'Iqbal, Islam and the West' in *Islamic Culture*, Hyderabad. 1993.
4. 'Iqbal's Conception of God' in *Indo-Iranica*. 1978.
5. 'Iqbal: The Poet of Vision' in *Hindustan Times*. 1978.

Articles in Presentational Volumes:

1. 'The Concept of Time in Eliot's *Four Quartets*' in *President Zakir Hussain Commemoration Volume*. 1968.
2. 'Blake and Kabbalah' in *Essays for S. Foster Damon*. Brown University Press, USA. 1969.

3. 'The Moral Dilemma in *Troilus and Cressida*' in *Malik Ram Presentational Volume*. 1974.
4. 'Time in Shakespeare's Sonnets' in *President Fakhruddin Ali Ahmed Memorial Volume*. 1994.
5. 'The Living World of Hafiz'. Ibid.
6. 'Ghalib: Istefham Ki Sha-ery' in *President Fakhruddin Ali Ahmed Memorial Volume* (Urdu). 1994.

Urdu Criticism

It goes to Asloob Ahmad Ansari's credit that he has developed a fine taste in Urdu literature and for the last sixty years, he has been writing valuable critical articles in Urdu with great regularity and devotion. His critical studies cover a wide range and present a healthy combination of theoretical and practical criticism. He is regarded an authority on Ghalib and Iqbal. He has written two books on Ghalib and five on Iqbal.

Ansari has studied Urdu fiction and poetry in great depth and written a great many articles on these subjects. He is also interested in literary journalism and has edited a quarterly Urdu magazine of immense repute Naqd-o-Nazar for about 20 years with great success and missionary zeal.

A brief introduction of his thirteen Urdu writings is given in the following pages.

1. **"ADAB AUR TANQEED" Allahabad: Sangam Publishers, 1968, pp. 348**

   This is a collection of seventeen articles written by Asloob Ahmad Ansari in which he has thrown light on some basic issues of literary criticism. His comprehensive study of western literature is reflected in these writings. The first seven articles are good examples of theoretical criticism. They are captioned as under:

   a) Poetic truth
   b) Criticism and art of creation
   c) Scientific theory of criticism

d) A few issues concerning literary criticism
e) Values of literature
f) History of literature and literary criticism
g) Style of prose

The other ten articles are concerned with an exclusive study and analysis of contributions of some famous poets and prose writers of Urdu. Among the poets the art of Ghalib, Iqbal, Hasrat Mauhani, Asrarul Haq Majaz and Shaaz Tamkanat has been dealt with. In prose, contributions of Rasheed Ahmad Siddiqi the romantic writer of Aligarh, Rajendra Singh Bedi, a fiction writer, letters of Maulana Abul Kalam Azad addressed to Nawab Habibur Rahman Khan Sherwani titled *Ghobar-e-Khatir* and sketch writings of Maulvi Abdul Haq have been studied and analysed.

2. "ATRAF-E-RASAEED AHMED SIDDIQI" Universal Book House Aligarh, First Edition 1977, pp. 146

Rasheed Ahmad Siddiqi served as a Professor and Head of Urdu Department in Muslim University Aligarh. He was an essayist having his own distinct style. He was a satirist, sketch writer and a famous critic. In Urdu many books highlighting his literary services have been published. But in this book of Asloob Ahmad Ansari, Rasheed Siddiqi's personality opens new avenue of study. It contains a preface and seven articles devoted to a study and analysis of the life and personality of Rasheed Saheb, his humourous writings, sketches, criticism and letters.

3. "URDU KE PANDRAH NOVEL" Universal Book House Aligarh, April 2003, pp. 402

This is partially an anthology of Urdu novels because it extends over the study and analysis of novels written by Deputy Nazeer Ahmad (the first Urdu novelist) and others till the present day novel writer Intizar Husain. Asloob Ahmad Ansari has dedicated this book to two of his close disciples

Abdur Raheem Kidwai and Abdul Mateen. In his long preface (P2 to 21) he has discussed at length the history of Urdu novel, its evolution and artistic characteristics. He has included Mir Amman's Bagh-o-Bahar an Urdu translation of a Persian story "Qissa-e-Chahaar Darwesh" and strictly speaking has not considered it as a novel in this list. About this special consideration he writes, "this story is a landmark in history of Urdu fiction and therefore we can include it in a legendary or romantic category in the words of famous Canadian critic Northrop Frye. In this book quest motif dominates and certain archetypal features create perfect harmony among its different parts".

This book contains study and analysis of the following novels. 1) *Taubatunnasooh* by Deputy Nazeer Ahmad, 2) *Firdaus-e-Bareen* by Abdul Haleem Sharar, 3) *Umraojan Ada* by Mirza Hadi Ruswa, 4) *Maidan-e-Amal* by Munshi Premchand, 5) *Aisi Bulandi Aisi Pasti* by Aziz Ahmad, 6) *Aag Ka Darya* by Quratulain Haider, 7) *Udas Naslen* by Abdullah Husain, 8) *Aangan* by Khudeja Mastoor, 9)Abla Pa by Razia Fasihahmad, 10) *Aiwan-e-Ghazal* by Jeelani Bano, 11) *Rajagidh* by Bano Qudsia, 12) *Karwan-e-Wajood* by NIsar Azeez Butt 13) *Dasht-e-Soos* by Jamia Hashmi, and 14) *Aage Samander Hai* by Intizar Husain.

Most of these articles were published in Ansari's magazine Naqd-o-Nazar and were appreciated by readers. Now they have been compiled in the form of a book.

4. "AINA KHANEY MEIN" University Book House Aligarh, 2004, pp. 192

Asloob Ahmad Ansari carries reputation of being an illustrious critic in English and Urdu languages. But this book presents him as a successful sketch writer. He has written portraits of his ten contemporaries including some of his teachers with the exception of *Malikyah* (an Eminent Delhi based scholar) all others are related to Aligarh. Their names are as under:

a) Dr. Zakir Husain
b) Rasheed Ahmed Siddiqui
c) Khwaja Manzoor Husain
d) Moulvi Zia Ahmad Badauni
e) Dr. Abdul Aleem
f) Syed Hamid
g) Malikram
h) Khaleeq Ahmed Nizami
i) Prof. Al-E-Ahmad Suroor
j) Mukhtar-Uddin Ahmad Arzoo

It is very difficult to write about one's contemporaries and make fair and equitable assessment of their personalities and services. But Ansari has performed well but in some sketches there are touches of aggression and intensity of expression.

On the last pages of this book some letters of Dr. Zakir Husain, Rasheed Ahmed Siddiqui and Khwaja Manzoor Husain addressed to Asloob Ahmad Ansari alongwith footnotes have also been published. Thus the volume contains both sketches and letters.

5. "TANQIDI TABSIREY" Universal Book House Aligarh, Sept. 2004, pp. 592

This is a collection of reviews written by Ansari between 1979 and 2000 A.D. on various books published on different categories of Urdu prose and poetry. Most of these reviews were published in his magazine *Naqd-O-Nazar*. Now these reviews on 90 Urdu books have been published in the form of a book and it is a fine example of fair assessment and criticism.

6. "HARFEY CHAND" Universal Book House Aligarh, 2005, PP. 421

This is a collection of 43 editorials of magazine *Naqd-O-Nazar* edited by Ansari and written between 1979 and 2000. These editorials are related to literary and critical issues, discussions and also include several obituaries which can also be called sketches. Some editorials have also been published in Ansaris' collection of sketches *Aina Khaney Men*. As an appendix an article on Kaleemuddin Ahmad has also been included.

7. "NAQSH-E-GHALIB" Ghalib Academy, New Delhi, Oct. 1970, pp. 142

This is a collection of six articles written by Ansari about contributions of Ghalib to urdu poetry and prose. The author in his preface has stated that his first article 'Kalam-e-Ghalib Ka Ek Rukh' was written in 1952 and was a landmark of his literary career.

This compilation is also significant that Ansari's study of Ghalib's poetry started from its first articles is still going on. The other articles of this book are captioned as under:

a) Kalam-e-Ghalib Ka Ek Rukh
b) Ghalib Ka Fun
c) Ghalib Aur Iqbal
d) Ghalib Ki Farsi Ghazal
e) Abr-e-Guharbar Ka Ek Pahloo
f) Khotoote Ghalib Mein 'Nafs Ki Parchhaiyan'

The third article attempts a comparative study of the thoughts of Ghalib and Iqbal and in the fifth article a Persian Masnavi of Ghalib has been analysed. The articles of this compilation have been published in some other books of Ansari as well.

8. "NAQSH HAAI RANG RANG" (MUTALIAT-E-GHALIB) Ghalib Institute, New Delhi, 1998

This book contains sixteen articles written by Asloob Ahmad Ansari about the thought and art of Ghalib. Professor Nazir Ahmad has written a preface in which he has opined: "This book is an important addition to Urdu's critical literature".

Most of these articles pertain to study of the poetry of Ghalib. Two articles about understanding and comprehension of Ghalib made by two well known critics of Ghalib, Maulana Altaf Husain Hali and Abdul Rahman Bijnori, are also included in this book. In two articles the author has made comparison of Ghalib's poetry to the contributions made by Momin and Iqbal. On Ghalib's Persian poetry a valuable article is also there. In another article the letters of Ghalib have been examined from a literary angle.

Due to its contents the book occupies a significant position in Urdu literary criticism and appreciation of Ghalib's contribution to Urdu literature.

9. "IQBAL KI TERAH NAZMEN" (TANQIDI MUTALIA), Ghalib Academy, New Delhi, 1st Edition 1977, pp 249

This book takes into account the analysis and study of thoughts and poetic art of thirteen poems composed by Iqbal and the actual text of these poems has been appended at the end of the book. The author has dedicated this book to his daughter Iffat Ara. The titles of the poems analysed are as under:

a) Taskhir-e-Fitrat
b) Tanhai
c) Shama Wo Shair
d) Walida Marhooma Ki Yad Mein
e) Khizr-e-Rah
f) Tulooe-e-Islam
g) Masjid-e-Qurtaba
h) Zauq-o-Shauq
i) Saqi Naama
j) La Ilah-Illallah
k) Ek Phalsafa Zada Syed Zade Ke Naam
l) Shoai Ummid
m) Iblis Ki Majlis-e-Shoora

n) "NAQSH-E-IQBAL" Maktaba Jamia Limited, New Delhi, 1st Edition, Jan 1979, pp. 192

In this book there are eleven articles and a preface. These articles revolve round the thoughts and art of Iqbal. The author has tried to present an objective and balanced study of Iqbal because in his view, evaluation of Iqbal's poetry has been biased till now and it suffers from defects of excessive praise or negative criticism. He asserts that some people have tried to degrade Iqbal's poetry on the ground that it projects Islamic thoughts and values.

The articles listed in the book are as under:-

a) Iqbal Ki Maniviyat Hamare Ahad mein (This is Urdu Translation of articles written by Ansari in English)
b) Mutalai-Iqbal Ke Chand Pahloo
c) Iqbal Ka Nazarya-e-Vijdan (theory of Realisation of truth)
d) Iqbal Ke Yahan Tasawwarat Ki Shairi (Poetry of Concepts)
e) Iqbal Ka Tasawwar-e- Faqr (Concept of piety)
f) Iqbal Ki Shairi Mein Dramaee Unsur (Dramatic elements in Iqbal's Poetry)
g) Masjid-e-Qurtaba (Analysis of Iqbals' poem on a Spanish mosque)
h) Zauq-O-Shauq (Analysis of Iqbals' poem)
i) Javed Nama Ka Ek Pahloo (This poetic collection of Iqbal was published in 1932. It has been analysed in this article and at many places it has been compared to Dantes' "*Divine Comedy*"
j) Ghalib Aur Iqbal (Comparison of the two poets)
k) Kalam-e-Iqbal Mein Siasi Shaoor Ki Jhalkian (Glimpses of Political awakening in Iqbal's poetry).

11. "IQBAL KI MUNTAKHAB NAZMEN AUR GHAZLEN" Ghalib Academy, New Delhi 1994

In this book a detailed study and analysis of sixteen poems and ten Ghazals of Iqbal has been made in the context of his thoughts and art. These poems have been selected from three collected works of Iqbal viz *Bang-e-Dara*, *Bal-e-Jibraeel* and *Zarb-e-Kaleem*. Actually this book is an extended form of analysis of contributions of Iqbal assessed by Ansari in 1977 through '*Iqbal Ki Tera Nazmen*'.

Six Urdu Ghazals have been selected from *Bang-e-Dara*, *Bal-e-Jibrael* and *Zarb-e-Kaleem* and two Persian ghazals from Iqbals' Persian work *Payah Mashriq* for study and analysis purposes. For the convenience of readers the actual text of all these poems and ghazals has been given in the last portion of the book.

12. "IQBAL HARF-O-MANEY" Educational Book House Aligarh, 1st Edition 1998, pp. 312.

This is a compilation of 13 articles written by Asloob Ahmd Ansari on he thoughts and art of Iqbal. There is a preface in the beginning of the book. All these articles explain the quatrains, Iqbals' concept of Godhood, his style and expression, Iqbal and Blake; Iqbal, Islam and West, and Iqbal's attitude to fine arts.

13. "IQBAL: JADID TANQIDI TANAZURAT" Universal Book House Aligarh, Feb. 2005, pp. 612.

Ansari has collected and completed valuable articles of several important literary personalities and critics of English and Urdu languages about the thoughts and poetic art of Iqbal. This had made study of Iqbal easy and interesting. It contains two articles written by Iqbal and also two English critics E.M. Foster's article "Iqbal" and A.R. Nicholson's article on Iqbal's Persian collected work '*Asrar-e-Khudi*'. These articles and they have been translated in Urdu by Abdur Raheem Kidwai. This is a valuable addition to the criticism of Iqbal and shows that Ansari is very well informed about the views of Iqbal's critics.

Besides these books the following articles by Asloob Ahmad Ansari can be mentioned here:

A. Articles on Urdu Poetry:

1. Iqbal ka Zehni Irtiqa. Jamia Delhi, 1940.
2. Sheri Sadaqat. Nigar; Lucknow, 1948.
3. Ibsen- Fikr-o-Nazar; Aligarh, 1954.
   Naya Daur; Karchi, 1954.
4. Dagh ki Shairi me Sehatmand Anasir. Nigar; Lucknow, 1954.
5. Iqbal ki Mashrikiyat. Awaz; Delhi, 1977.
6. Iqbal ka Uslub-E-Bayan. Naqd-o-Nazar vol.2; Aligarh, 1979.
7. Lalae Sahra-Ek Tajziya. Naqd-o-Nazar vol.2; Aligarh, 1980.
8. Abdul Rahman, Awwal ka Boya Hua Pahla Khajur Kadarakht-Ek Tajziya. Naqd-o-Nazar vol.2; Aligarh, 1983.
9. Fani ke Kalam me Mutasawffana Rang. Naqd-o-Nazar vol.1; Aligarh, 1981.
10. Kalam e Ghalib ka Ek Pehlu. Ghalibnama; Delhi, 1981.
11. Iqbal ka Tassawar e Khuda. Naqd-o-Nazar vol.2; Aligarh, 1982.
12. Kalaam e Hasrat ka Ek Rukh. Naqd-o-Nazar vol.1; Aligarh, 1982.
13. Ghalib ki Shairi me Isteara ka Amal. Ghalibnama, 1982.
14. Iqbal ki Shairi me Haraki Paiker. Naqd-o-Nazar vol.2; Aligarh, 1983.
15. Iqbal ki Usturi Nazmen. Naqd-o-Nazar vol.1; Aligarh, 1984.
16. Asghar ka Rang e Tagazzul. Naqd-o-Nazar vol.1; Aligarh, 1981.
17. Qahr-E-Ishaq/Antony and Cleopatra. Naqd-o-Nazar vol.1; Aligarh, 1985.

18. Iqbal ki Shairi me Lala ki Alamat. Naqd-o-Nazar vol.2; Aligarh, 1986.
19. Shairi aur Sheri Paiker. . Naqd-o-Nazar vol.1; Aligarh, 1987.
20. Iqbal aur Danish-e- Hazir. Naqd-o-Nazar vol.1; Aligarh, 1988.
21. Hafiz ki Zinda Kainat. Naqd-o-Nazar vol.2; Aligarh, 1988.
22. Masnawi Chirag-E-Dair. GhalibNama; Delhi, 1988.
23. Iqbal aur Blake. Naqd-o-Nazar vol.2; Aligarh, 1989.
24. Jawed Nama me Manzar Nama. Naqd-o-Nazar vol.2; Aligarh, 1990.
25. Iqbal, Islam and Maghrib. Naqd-o-Nazar vol.2; Aligarh, 1992.
26. Irtiqa. Naqd-o-Nazar vol.1; Aligarh, 1993.
27. Masjid-E-Qurtaba. Naqd-o-Nazar vol.2; Aligarh, 1993.
28. Iqbal ki Shairi me Tafakkur ka Unsur. Naqd-o-Nazar vol.1; Aligarh, 1994.
29. Ghalib-Istifham ki Shairi. Naqd-o-Nazar vol.1; Aligarh, 1994.
30. Ghalib ki Shairi me Sholey ka Ramz. GhalibNama; Delhi, 1994.

B. Article on Urdu Prose:

1. Udas Naslen. Guftugu Bombay, 1965.
2. Ghubar-e-Karavan. Ajkal; Delhi, 1970.
3. Rasheed Ahmad Siddiqui. Ajkal; Delhi, 1976.
4. Bagh o Bahar ka Mutala. Naqd-o-Nazar vol.1; Aligarh, 1979.
5. Maidan-e-Amal ka Mutala. Naqd-o-Nazar vol.2; Aligarh, 1980.
6. Hamare Rasheed Sahib. Naqd-o-Nazar vol.1; Aligarh, 1980.
7. Ayena (Jilani Bano) Ek TajZiya. Naqd-o-Nazar vol.2; Aligarh, 1981.

8. Firdaus-e-Bareen Ek Mutala. Naqd-o-Nazar vol.2; Aligarh, 1981.
9. Taubatun Nasooh Ek Mutala. Naqd-o-Nazar vol.2; Aligarh, 1982.
10. Tahrik-e-Jadd wa Jihad Bataur Mauzuesukhan. Naqd-o-Nazar vol.2; Aligarh, 1985.
11. Umrao Jaan Ada Ek Mutala. Naqd-o-Nazar vol.2; Aligarh, 1987.
12. Bijnori Bahsiyaat Naqqad-e-Ghalib. Naqd-o-Nazar vol.2; Aligarh, 1988.
13. Manzoor Husain Khwaja. Fikr-o-Nazar; Aligarh, 1988.
14. Nawab Muzammil Ullah Khan. Fikr-o-Nazar; Aligarh, 1988.
15. Ahmad Nadeem Qasimi ke Afsanae. Lahore.
16. Ghulam Abbas ke Afsanae. Naqd-o-Nazar vol.2; Aligarh, 1989.
17. Ghubar Khatir per Ek Nazar. Naqd-o-Nazar vol.1; Aligarh, 1989.
18. Masood Marhoom. Naqd-o-Nazar vol.2; Aligarh, 1991.
19. Sir Syed ka Nazaria Aqal wa Fitrat. Fikr-o-Nazar, Sir Syed Number; Aligarh, 1992.

21

Zahida Zaidi's Works in English and Urdu: An Annotated Bibliography

Taj Mohammad

Zahida zaidi is a poet, dramatist, critic, translator and novelist. She has written extensively in Urdu and English. She has translated into Urdu the plays of Anton Chekhov, Luigi Pirandello, Jean Paul Sartre, and Samuel Beckett, as well as the poetry of Eugenio Montale, Federico Garcia Lorca, and Pablo Neruda, working from the original French and Italian as well as from English translations.Drawn to Marxist ideology, her creative writing, however, is marked by an existential and mystical strain. As she has a big canvass of writing, her works can be categorized under the heads given below. The list of her works includes most—though not all as many of her creative works and critical articles both in English and Urdu do not figure here—of her important works.

Original and adapted plays

Zahida Zaidi has seven books of drama to her credit. Besides her original plays, she has done translations and adaptations of English, French, Italian and Russian dramatists which are included in her books *Mazdood Rahe* and *Chekhov ke Shahkar drame*. She has also translated Bertolt Brecht's plays *Caucasian Chalk Circle* as *Insaf ka Daira* and free translations by the name of *Alam Tamam Halka-e-Dame Khayal Hai*.

Doosra Kamra (The Second Room)is the first collection of five original plays of Zahida Zaidi published in 1990 by Maktaba Jamia

New Delhi.The plays include *Chattan, Dil-e-Na Saboor Daram, Doosra Kamra, Woh Subah Kabhi to Ayegi,* and *Jungle Jalta Raha.* These plays are highly experimental in nature and by her own admission are influenced by modern American drama, absurd drama in particular. All these plays have been written to be staged and are accompanied by meticulous and detailed stage settings. *Dil-e-Na Saboor Daram* is a surrealistic play. It has a dream like setting and is highly imaginative and poetic in nature. It is symbolic and purely a product of her imagination and has very little to do with real life.

Woh Subah Kabhi to Ayegi (the Dark Night would End into Bright Dawn Someday) Inspired by a real life incident of wife-beating the play expresses the plight of women in India of 1970s and ends with an expression of hope when the protagonist says that "the dark night would end into bright dawn someday".

Dooosra Kamra is highly influenced by the absurd drama. It has traces of "Amedie" by Eugene Ionesco in it where the corpses of the demon of the past of the players keep multiplying in the other room. It is a psychological drama and dwells on the delusions and hallucinations of the lead players where they are trying to exorcise the demons. It borders on paranormal at places and has a disturbing underline tone to it, representing the inner turmoil of the people of that era.

Jungal Jalta Raha (*The Burning Desert*) is a full length family drama in 4 Acts. It is symbolic of the external scenario of troubled and struggling world in a crisis situation and brings out the inner crisis of the people in the play. It, in a way, explores how people react differently to the same crisis situations according to their character complexities and psychological frame of mind.

Sahra-e-Azam is a full length play and is dedicated to those beautiful and majestic cities of Iraq which were destroyed by the American bombardment during the first invasion of Iraq. Published in 1991 by Abshar Publisher in this play, she has used the tamasha technique where there are two sutra dhars or the compares Didi and Gogo borrowed from Samuel Becket's masterpiece *Waiting for Godot* who narrate the story and exit before every Act or Scene starts. She has explored extensively the American politics of distorting the facts, misconstruing them to suit their own means and to justify the means to their end. It is a satirical play and brilliantly exposes the excesses of American nation on the innocent people of Iraq and the destruction of the great historical civilization of Sumaria. The bloody drama of gulf war with its unprecedented violence, whole sale destruction and vast human tragedy had such a harrowing effect on the author's psyche that it resulted into the creation of this extraordinary play. She later translated this play into English by the name of *The Burning Desert*.

Kiyun Kar Us Boot Se Rakhoon Jan Azeez is a satirical play exploring the politics played in literary and cultural circles of universities and intellectual institutions resulting in the erosion of literary values and academic excellence and the high quality of literature giving way to its vulgarization in the name of modernism and uniqueness of expression. It talks of corruption in the form of groupism, character assassination, sycophancy, superficial exhibition of literary prowess and vulgarization of language through overuse of cliché .

Bahut Door Tak Rat Hogi is a play inspired by the tragedy of Gujarat and is dedicated to the victims of Gujarat carnage who continue to be homeless, marginalized and oppressed.

Translation and adaptations of European/ American and English plays

Apart from the above mentioned original plays written by Prof. Zaidi, she has translated and adapted a large number of plays from English language and adapted a lot of them into Urdu. *Anaton Chekhov Ke Shahkar Drame* includes three full- length masterpiece plays of Chekhov *Cherry Orchard* translated as *Charry Ka Bagh*, *Three Sisters* translated as *Teen Behne*, and *Habib Mamoo* which is actually the adaptation of *Uncle Wania*. She has written a very scholarly introduction to this book titled *Anton Chekhov as a dramatist*.

Mazdood Rahei which means blind alleys is a collection of adapted and translated plays of European and American English playwrights and includes such masterpieces as Becket's *The End Game* as *Shehmad*, Ionesco's *Exit the King* and *Chairs* as *Badshah Salamat Khuda Hafiz* and *Kursia*, Sartre's *No Exit* as *Band Kamra* and Pirandello's play *So it is if You Think So*.

Zahida Zaidi as a critic

Zahida Zaidi has touched upon varied subjects in her critical essays which range from critical essays on the poetry of classical poets like Ghalib, Iqbal and Meer Anees to modern contemporary poets like Akhtarul Iman, Faiz Ahmad fiaz,Ali Sardar Jafri and others. Similarly, she has critical essays on novels of very established novelists of her time like Qurratul Ain Haider to the young upcoming novelist like Paigham Afaqi.Her critical essays are complied into five books namely—*Ramooz-o-Fikro Fun, Lazzate Ashanayi*e and *Durd e Tahe Jan* and two books in English including *Modes Of Communication* and *Glimpses of Urdu Literature.*

English Criticism Her book titled *Modes of Communication* has nine essays in it. The first is 'Mode of Communication in Drama' in which she has highlighted the role of drama in fulfilling the need of communication and creative expressions in men.she has discussed the questions of dramatic illusions, the creative approach of some dramatist and the alienation technique of Brechtian drama.The other essay 'Hell in Shaw and Sartre' is the comparative study of concept of hell in the plays of two dramatists belonging to two different genres of play writing.

The essay on Tennessee William traces the evolution of his dramatic form whereas the one on Samuel Beckett traces Beckett's dark vision in his novels and plays. The last essay titled 'Contemporareniety of Prometheus Unbound' is a brilliant study of Shelley's masterpiece as a poetic drama of remarkable originality and his profound vision of life. In this essay she goes on to point out that Shelley's artistic approach to poetic drama has inspired several modern playwrights.

Her English Poetry

Two collections of poetry contain her very sensitive and poignant poetry.The first book titled *Broken Mirror* (1979) was published by Prayer Books, Calcutta.*Beyond Words*, her second collection, came out in 1984 and was published by United Writers, Calcutta.

Her Urdu poetry and Novel

Zahr-e-Hayat (Poison of life) suggests the bitter experiences of her life, her disappointment, disillusionment and dissatisfaction and her struggle in facing vagaries of life. The mood of the book is bitter and sarcastic. The flavor is rebellious. Most of the poems are abstract in form, not rhymed, and are mostly in free verse.

Dharti ka Lams (The feel of earth)-In this collection she comes face to face with reality of life and experiments with the form of poetry called 'Nazm'. She has said much in a few words and most of her poems are abstract in nature.

Sang-e-Jan (stone of life) continues to use symbols of nature like earth, wind and stone in life.She tries to find meaning in absurdity of life, to overcome the vagaries of life and exorcise the demons of her past to find some system in the madness of world, madness which has appeared in the form of Palestinian struggle, Vietnam War, Afghan war and Lebanon crises. Zaidi reflects upon the state of affairs in world, the breakdown of idealism and the defeat of progressive writers' movement and its impact on Indian as well as world literature.

Shola-e-Jan (Flame of life), her fourth collection of poetry, published by Abshar Publication, Aligarh in 2000, is the work of a mature poet at the peak of her poetic creativity. The similes, metaphor and symbolism used in her poetry are by now characteristics of her form of expression. Her poetic idiom is unique and she has introduced many new forms of poetic expression.

Sham-e-Tanhai is the last and final collection of her poems which came in the last years of her life in December 2008 again published by Abshar Publisher along with Bharat offset press, Delhi. Her poems in this collection are philosophical to the point of being spiritual, even religious, where the concept of God and the hereafter enters into her thinking. This is a departure from her earliest works where the communist progressive movement was predominant in her thinking. In these poems written in the evening of her life, she has widely expressed the loneliness of the existence, the wisdom of an ageing poet with a touch of sadness and at times even disillusionment with life. It reflects her preparedness to move on to other life as she herself has expressed in the couplet of one of her lyrical poems.

Inquilab Ka Ek Din is her novel in Urdu. This work is set against the intellectual ethos of a university and can as such also qualify as campus novel. Marxist beliefs are incorporated in the novel in a very obvious manner. Like many debut novels it also has a very strong autobiographical element.

22

English Language Teaching (ELT) at the Aligarh Muslim University: Key Developments and Future Directions

Raashid Nehal

1.0 Introductory

English studies at the Aligarh Muslim University (AMU) has come a long way since the turn of the 19th century up to the present day, making an incredible journey in its mission to educate students in English literature and language. Probably, ELT in AMU is an offshoot of the English studies that can be set against the backdrop of Lord Macaulay's famous 1835 English Education Act. The act unambiguously stated the aims and objectives of teaching English in British India for educating the Indian masses to serve as 'interpreters' and Sir Charles Wood's despatch of 1854 stating that English could be a suitable medium at higher levels of education(Krishnaswamy &Sriraman). Macaulay's Minutes generated continuing expansion of English that brought gradual challenges to the status, role and function of the wider ELT field. As a consequence, Sir Syed Ahmad Khan realized the importance of English studies in establishing the historic Mahomedan Anglo-Oriental (MAO) College at Aligarh in 1875. Sir Syed Ahmad Khan's vision of quality education can be well understood from the fact that the role and function of English became crucial to the cause of education at MAO College and later when it acquired the status of the Aligarh Muslim University.

English studies first began at MAO College in 1876 primarily because it had to play a functional role in facilitating the medium of instruction and examination. The Department of English earned the distinction of having Sir Walter Raleigh, a distinguished literary critic as the Chairman of the Department from 1885-1887 (Dept of English,Platinum plus). In 1885, Sir Walter Raleigh was appointed the first Professor of English at the M.A.O. College, Aligarh and later became the 'first Professor of English studies' at Oxford in 1893. The *Raleigh Literary society* named after him is the oldest of all literary societies in AMU and still continues to organize literary competitions on communication skills to date. Years later, in 1988, A.A. Ansari brought out a volume of *Essays on Sir Walter Raleigh* containing contributions among others from such luminaries as Kenneth Muir, James Ogden, Mary Lascelles, Gabrielle Barfoot, G.Singh and Richard Brinkley.

Sir Syed Ahmad Khan visualised the utilitarian role of English in the courses of studies at MAO College in 1876. Although the purpose was to educate learners through English literature, nevertheless English language and literature were taught with a provision of optional subjects such as Arabic or Persian in the Oriental Dept where English was taught as a second language. The syllabus reflected the teaching the skills of language and the focus was maintained on writing and grammar. Utilitarian purpose of language seemed evident despite that major text selections were from literature.

The texts meant to teach English language served the purpose of making English as an integral subject to courses offered both at the English and Oriental Dept. Prescribed books for different classes were *Grammatical Analysis* by E. Thring, *An English Grammar and Reading Book* by O. W. Rancook (used for language skills, grammar teaching and reading skills and translation portions of the books was used for teaching of writing skills) Howards' *Smaller English Grammar*, Currie's *First Step in Grammar*. In the oriental Dept. Mackay's *Introduction to the English Language*, Nelson's *Senior Reader* and *Advanced Reader* were the texts used for literature teaching.

The Dept. of English is now over 135 years old. From the 1880s to 1940s it had on its staff eminent British Professors for providing English language training to pupils. Professors from England chaired the Dept till 1946 and among those from the UK who taught English were Theodore Beck, T.Morrison, A.A.J.Nesbitt, L.Tipping, F.J.Moss, L.Chase, H.O.Lee and M.Collins (Dept of English 125 years).By the time, the M.A.O. college was accorded the status of University in 1920,English language had seen its proliferation because of British patronage and this was also the time when universities across the country were established, to name a few, at Allahabad, Benaras, Hyderabad, Patna, Mysore. E.C.Dickinson took over as the first Chairman of Aligarh Muslim University's Dept. of English in 1921. The other native teachers who carried this legacy were E.C. Dickinson, Firebrace, Hadow Haris and F. J. Fielden. In addition to, the Department had on its staff D.Humour and F. J. Moss (Ibid).

When MAO College got recognition as Aligarh Muslim University in 1920, English studies got a new face in 1926 as part of degree courses in Arts and sciences. Initially, the general English course was taught as compulsory language course in part one of BA and B.Sc and it acquired a central role in promoting the cause of education in English literature, later in facilitating the cause of the medium of instruction since no literary piece was prescribed(AMU, syllabuses and courses of Studies). Essay writing skills and comprehension questions were the highlights of the first year compulsory English (Ibid.) This reflects the significant role English as a 'compulsory general paper' played later in two years and three years degree courses at AMU. Although later, in the syllabus of 1926 English was primarily tested on the primacy of writing and comprehension skills in part 1 of Bachelor of Arts and Sciences degree and texts for 'poetry, prose and prose fiction and drama 'were prescribed for part II.

The British Council conference held at Mahableshwar in 1950 had seen 'ELT-focused' relationship between the UK and India. The relationship created an opportunity of accessing UK expertise which was considered relevant to the issues and challenges in ELT (Centre for Applied Linguistics, The University of Warwick). Taking advantage of the UK expertise, Professor A. Bose, Chairman of the Department of English, AMU was instrumental in introducing English language teaching and designing remedial courses in the new pre-university course at AMU. ELT became part of three years degree course in 1950.It was during A. Bose's tenure, for the first time in Aligarh, All India English Teachers' Conference was held in 1954. The Dept. hosted it again in 1964 and in 1977. The influence of liberal education was also manifested in making English literature a compulsory subject for all B.A. students till early 1950s. This is best summed up (Krishnaswamy&Sriraman10) as 'the aims and objectives in India were 'basically humanistic, having certain functions that are traditionally associated with literature and liberal education, for instance, *the shaping of gentlemen, the moulding of character, the development of aesthetic sense, the cultivation of ethical thinking*, etc'(italics in original). This was the time around the world, the wider context of ELT was manifested; state schools started teaching English driven by liberal education and structural approach to language teaching figured in the form of Audiolingualism. Though this had knock-on effects for the ELT developments but at the same time school traditions of teaching grammar and Grammar Translation (GT) method continued. The three years degree course at AMU came into effect from 1961 when English became functional with regard to medium of instruction and in examination. Prior to this, A. Bose also took the initiative of introducing research during 1950s and some teachers of the Department gained their research training in language and literature at the leading British and American Universities. This became evident when Badruddin Tayabji Vice-Chancellor, AMU and B.A. Khan, Chairman, Department of English coordinated with the British Council to depute young scholars from Oxford and Cambridge to teach at Aligarh. Helen Bernard took on board the task of material design and restructuring ELT by way of producing need-based remedial materials on English grammar for Pre-University courses at AMU. In addition, Helen Bernard, P. Martin, Robins and Margaret Davies associated with this task served as tutors at the Department.

Prior to the advent of structural method in India, the grammar translation method, was the most traditionally practised method for teaching English in classroom and it continues to this day in some regional language medium schools. At the other end of the spectrum, learning of English was basically associated with the reading of 'classics' and exposure to 'great literature'. However, in the Indian context, the required language competence or needs of the learner or the differences in L1and L2 remained understated in the approach to the literary appreciation of text. This was no less true in the context of Aligarh where English Language Teaching in India was basically modelled on British pattern of curriculum and teaching methodology. A cursory look at compulsory English syllabi suggests that there was little emphasis on listening skills, pronunciation, speaking skills since these skills were not put to test. Born out of an English literary tradition, the post-colonial phase of India and for that matter at AMU, continued to be influenced by the teaching methodology used in Britain. ELT was mainly grounded in literature based text-books at different levels and the language and rhetoric and style of English literature was considered fashionable even for academic and functional English. To this extent, English was not really functional and was restricted to the use of certain structures/phrases which were often drilled. Thus the teaching of English was at the crossroads of language-literature controversy and quite a few seminars, conferences and workshops were held on this issue (Krishnaswamy&Sriraman). Then, English was taught as a compulsory subject at higher secondary school and degree level .

The influence of the behavioural-psychological principles of language teaching culminated into the introduction of structurally graded syllabi in Madras in 1952 by the British Council as Madras English Language Teaching (Prabhu 10 cited in, NFG; Krishnaswamy&Sriraman). This was also associated with the Direct Method having a prerequisite condition of monolingual classroom. Harold E. Palmer's work had a strong influence on the situational based language teaching focussing on oral and direct approach to teaching English. In 1964, under the directives of Kothari Commission, the report of study group of English in India appointed by the Ministry of Education, Government of India supported the structural approach to the teaching of English. This spread in different parts of India. The study group outlined a detailed English language syllabus from class V to XII. The Commission also recommended that the teaching of English be introduced in class V, but this was not possible until class VIII, especially for pupils studying in the rural areas. It advocated adequate command of mother tongue prior to the learning of English as a foreign language. The Commission also recommended that the study of English as a second language should be introduced only after class V. By this time, EFLU(then known as CIE(FL),Hyderabad) had redefined the aims and objectives of teaching English and this influenced a similar exercise at AMU with regard to materials designed as 'functional'. The impact was noticeable in Compulsory English syllabus of 1965 at AMU which featured the prescribed text as *The English We Use* by R.A.Close published from Longman. This included the component of Use of English and Spoken English and a section comprising writing skill in addition to the other prescribed literary texts (AMU, Ordinances). In 1968, the National Policy on Education (NPE) laid special focus on adopting the study of English and other international languages as the medium of instruction for natural sciences and mathematics, which resulted in the rapid growth of secondary and university education, particularly in urban areas. The Committee on syllabus reforms and various study groups were set up by Govt. of India to assess the English language teaching and suggested that English should be taught as a compulsory course for the first and second year degree programmes in Arts, Commerce and Sciences). With the development of applied linguistics and structural teaching, there was a clear differentiation between English used as a functional and literary language. Students offering compulsory English started skipping classes in large number as bazaar notes were easily available on the texts prescribed earlier. Since 1961, the Department of English, AMU started focussing on teacher-prepared remedial materials that provided opportunity to select text, activities and grammar exercises pitched at the exact level of learners and avoiding the problem of one-size-fits-all approach. Further, since 1964, the Dept. of English has been designing intensive, bridge or remedial courses for fresh entrants in association with the British Council for students (Ahmad).

By the late 1970s, dissatisfaction with the *structural* method was felt in the ELT circles. Despite that learners were trained to produce error-free structures and later that was meant to be converted into *skills*, the real point of communication was missing. Excessive attention to form-focussed teaching raised certain vital issues related to function, meaning, notions and communicative potential of the language situated in meaningful contexts. British linguists brought in the concept of *communicative competence* built upon the availability of *grammatical competence*. But this 'communicative revolution' was most successful in English-medium private/government-aided elite schools (Kurrien , cited in NFG 2).Lack of trained teacher in communicative methodology, particularly in rural areas was a major deterrent to the success of Communicative Language Teaching.

This issue also affected the schools of Aligarh and AMU, where ELT at the school level too is a subject of research in the Departments of Education and Linguistics.. However, what seems to be applicable to all situations is that for the majority of our learners, the issue is not so much communicative competence as the acquisition of a basic or fundamental competence in the language (Prabhu13 cited in NFG).

1.1 An Innovative Approach to English Language Teaching (1988)

The new challenges to ELT began with certain probing questions related to the 'needs' of the learners and it demanded the teaching of English to be appropriately pitched at the learner's level. This view, though generalised at the national level, was also put forward in the context of students intake for AMU. Munir Ahmad organised an intensive course for senior secondary students in 1988 and this came to be known as *An Innovative Approach to English Language Teaching* and points out the dismal performance of students in

English language skills:

> The low standards of students in English are a growing problem in colleges and universities in India. Most of our students are unable to write or speak even simple sentences of English. College and university teachers complain that a large proportion of students find it hard to follow lectures in English. They are compelled to deliver lectures partly in English and partly in Hindi. Even those students who came from English medium schools are not able to express their ideas with clarity when it comes to writing a few paragraphs. Four out of five students on leaving secondary school are unable to use English with felicity of expressions. They have no idea of syntax or idiom, not to speak of clarity or precision. This can be seen everywhere-in competitive exams, in interviews of executive posts in admission tests for higher studies (Ahmad 2)

In 1988, Munir Ahmad organised an intensive four week language course for class XII at AMU Aligarh from 18 July to 13 August with an active support from then Vice-Chancellor of AMU, Syed Hashim Ali. Syed Hashim Ali took a keen interest in the Intensive Course and to facilitate this course, 'he suspended the teaching of other subjects' so that students gain an intensive exposure to long duration of 7 hours a day for having 'language bath' (Ahmad 1). This course was in response to XII class learner's needs keeping in view the 'shift in emphasis in approaches to second or foreign language teaching ... to teach the target language as a tool to motivate and monitor the learner's language in action (Ahmad 1)'. This was an altogether a different programme as the title suggested; *An Innovative Approach to English Language Teaching* which had a very focused application of Educational Technology, especially TV/Video, to teach English as a Foreign Language. Large class sizes were avoided and the video lessons on *Follow Me, Follow Through* produced by BBC and *English Telemagazine* produced by Brighton Polytechnic, UK had a tremendous effect on the motivation level of the students and this led to an effective interactive teaching of language skills(LSRW).

The entire course was structured into four units, with an equal emphasis on essentials of English Grammar and exposure to different rules of grammar in different familiar functions and situations, need-based writing practice, oral communication practice on basic stress and intonation patterns in English followed by an integration of skills of speaking ,reading and writing which also included writing simple dialogues, role play or loud reading.

As regards the material preparation and teaching that also included the preparation of Audio Visual materials, faculty members of the Dept.of English, Women's College and senior secondary School were involved. They included Syed Waqar Hussain, Farhtullah Khan, Amina kishore, K.S.Misra and Mujeeb Khan,Kishwar Jabin, Amirullah khan, Asim Siddiqui and others. Students were streamed into two groups- English medium schools and regional medium schools ,with a total of 24 groups in all, each group having a class size of 40 students.

Finally, the post course assessment was conducted to 'suit the different levels of learners' which was a marked feature of a heterogeneous class as it assumed and evidenced two levels of proficiency'(Ahmad,8).

Under the chairmanship of Munir Ahmad, reading, writing and Oral communication skills featured in prescribed texts such as *A Complete Course in English* and *Everyday Dialogues in English* by Robert J.Dixon and *Write Right* by Taya Zinkin. Later, it became obvious that English as a compulsory subject in first year and second year degree courses remained more inclined to the functional purposes and performing the medium of instruction and examination.

The Department undertook the revision of syllabus for the first and second year Compulsory English degree courses in 1994-95 under the chairmanship of S.Wiqar Hussain. Since then teacher-produced text-free materials based on language skills have been in use.

Another significant development in the field of ELT was holding of ELT workshops and lectures under the guidance of Munir Ahmad and S.M.Rizwan Hussain. Some other ELT workshops held later were on the Use of Educational Technology, sponsored by British Council and the UGC, conducted by Brian Hill of Language Centre, Brighton U.K. Workshop on Revision of Language and Literature syllabi *was* conducted by Allen Mailey and much later in 2005,worshops on Effective Use of Materials (2003) and Materials Adaptation under the auspices of Hornby Regional Project: Aligarh Region, sponsored by the British Council's ELT Group, U.K. and Hornby Trust were coordinated by Raashid Nehal and Rizwan Khan. Maximizing Learning and Retention through ELT strategies (2007) was facilitated by Barbara Castelton, and Rajni Badlani. In addition, the first Refresher course coordinated by Mohd.Asim Sidddiqui addressed the issue of the Teaching of English language and Literature in Contemporary perspective. Recently in 2010, two UGC Major Research Projects have been awarded in ELT to Amirullah Khan on 'Developing a Training Course in Spoken English for Teachers of CBSE schools in Aligarh' and to Raashid Nehal on 'Training Needs Analysis of Secondary School English Teachers in Aligarh: Implications for English Language Teacher Education'.

1.2 Rationale for ELT Courses

In the wake of globalization and recent developments in the spread of information Technology, ELT and language courses have assumed utmost professional significance and are considered to have high potential for employment prospects. In view of the challenges discussed in section 1.1, there is an urgent need for developing the communication skills of the AMU students comprising overseas and local, research scholars and teachers on the campus, in addition to the training of human resource for enhancing the language proficiency required for academic and professional competence. English is a mandatory subject in AMU curriculum. Therefore, academic achievement in different disciplines of AMU is significantly correlated with proficiency in English. Besides being an international language of training, instruction and communication, communication skills will be of great help in producing better equipped human resource for greater participation in the social and economic development of the country. This is otherwise not fully possible with the existing literature courses i.e BA(English) MA (English) which have altogether a different concern. The increase in demand for need-based or vocational ELT courses can be inferred from the recent data published in *Outlook, as* the following:

> Sandhya Chitale, Director, Nasscom's Educational Initiative ascribes the rejection rate of 82-83% for non-engineering graduates applying to the IT and IT-enabled sector to the lack of soft skills, including written and oral communication skills .65-75% of applying engineers are rejected for the same reasons. Uma K. Raman, Head, Skills enhancement, HCL BPO reports that the company rejects 92-93% of applications for inadequate command of English (Puri68-69).

2.0 ELT Programmes offered at the Department of English

The Dept. of English runs two specialized programs in ELT: BA (Hons) (Communicative English) and MA in (ELT) in addition to literature-based programmes such as BA (Hons) English and MA (English) in addition to full time residential PhD. programme in English and ELT. BA (CE) is also offered at the Women's College. The Dept. has been offering compulsory English and subsidiary courses which meet the language learning needs of more than four thousand students belonging to different faculties such as faculty of Sciences, Life Sciences, Commerce, Social Sciences, Engineering.& Technology, Law and Theology at first and second year degree level.

2.1 BA (Communicative English)

During the Fifth Five-Year Plan, UGC aimed to make undergraduate courses more relevant to societal and developmental needs of the country and to 'link education with work/field/practical experience and productivity' (UGC: *Vocationalization of First Degree Education*5 cited in Tickoo 93).The CIEFL-UGC Functional English project was an offshoot of this event during the 1990s which was conceived as a job-oriented course by the Curriculum Development Centre(CDC) set up at CIEFL by UGC. The CDC report in 1989 brought out Functional English course, aimed at developing oral and written communication skills in English for graduates seeking entry to professional courses in the University and elsewhere and for employment avenues. Following this, the Dept. of English, AMU along with several universities and autonomous colleges introduced Functional English, also later renamed as Communicative English as a subject in BA programmes in the early 1990s. Initially, this course was funded by UGC for the first 5 years and this serves to this date as a feeder to MA (ELT) program. Initially, the programme was known as a course in Functional English. It was renamed as Communicative English (CE) later. It is offered as three years degree level honours course at AMU. The course aims at applied language skills as it caters to the heterogeneous students belonging to different socio-economic, cultural, linguistic backgrounds, and state and national boards showing varied level of linguistic competence and acquisition environment. Over the years, CE graduates have found this course a passport to gainful employment and entry to professional courses such as MBA, Mass Communications, MFC, MSW, MIB etc. and finally it is seen as stepping stone to enrolment in MA (ELT) program.

2.2 MA (ELT) Program

As to the 'establishment' of MA ELT at the Department in 1997, Munir Ahmad had originally visualized the idea of ELT programmes and courses in the Department. Emeritus Professor Farhatullah Khan,on behalf of the Dept. of English submitted the proposal to the UGC for the establishment of ELT centre at AMU. The proposal highlighted the need for multiple need-based courses for various groups right from the post school to the master's level, in addition to in- service teacher training package and special packages for disadvantaged groups since AMU was seen as nodal agency in a big catchment area of Western UP. It was also proposed that the ELT centre would also provide consultancy services in producing teaching materials for neighbouring school and colleges in addition to meeting the needs of private sector undertakings. Unfortunately ELT centre could not materialize, rather, in the same year, Farhatullah Khan in consultation with RP Bhatnagar Emeritus Professor, University of Rajasthan, Jaipur was instrumental in initiating MA (ELT) programme under the chairmanship of K.S.Misra. This became imminent in the light of the fact that local institutions and practicing teachers of English working in Aligarh and neighbouring areas needed professional training in ELT at different levels.

In India, courses similar to MA ELT run only at few places such as EFLU, Hyderabad, EFLU, Lucknow and HM Patel Institute of English at Vadodra in Gujarat ,Netaji Subhash Chandra Bose Open University and Dept. of English Teaching, Gauhati University. This is in response to growing demand for a trained as well as specialised English teacher in India and overseas in addition to the demand for language certified professionals for training soft skills and written communication skills in MNCs and in various other professional sectors. Because of the professional nature of training provided in communication skills, over the past few years, these need-based courses have earned international and national recognition. Having gained wider acceptance, it is still seen as mostly a job-oriented course. Recently schools have given openings to our ELT graduates and have been seeking consultancy services from faculty members in organizing workshops for teacher training and setting up of language lab in their institutions. So far, over 35-40 MA ELT students have got placements in Universities and Technical colleges of the Kingdom of Saudi Arabia (King Khalid University, King Abdul Aziz University, King Saud University to name a few), Bahrain, Kuwait, Dubai, Oman, Muscat and other neighbouring countries and have been getting placements in professional institutions and schools in the country and in particular in Aligarh. However, in the absence of UGC NET exam in ELT, placements only on the basis of MA ELT in UGC recognised colleges and universities have been next to impossible until a PhD. degree in ELT is obtained.

MA ELT in AMU is now at an interesting evolutionary stage. Currently, the programme has an intake of 25 seats and it started in response to the realization that students graduating from BA in Communicative English and BA in Literature were largely headed for ESL teaching jobs. MA ELT is a specialized teacher training program that has taken care of the shortcomings of English language training programes of the outdated one year B.Ed program which is hardly able to meet the complex challenges of a modern classroom(NFG). The existing B.Ed programme was proving to be inadequate to meet the professional requirements ,particularly in English teaching. The MA (ELT) aims to provide graduates a pre-service professional experience and opportunity to develop a better understanding of ELT at both theoretical and practical level. The courses covered are fundamentals of Linguistics, English Phonology, ELT methodology, Syllabus and Materials Design, Language Testing, Teaching of Grammar, Teaching of Literature, Written Communication and Oral Communication etc. The course is interdisciplinary in nature since it can aid Literature oriented programs to teach language if required at the same time it can also provide inputs to ELT trainees as how to treat literature in language classroom.MA ELT is spread into four Semesters and also includes Project Dissertation and a Practice teaching component. While the project work trains students in future ELT research, it has a strong focus on classroom-based action research. The practice teaching component gives a hands-on teaching experience to our MA ELT teacher trainees as they interact face-to-face with students enrolled for compulsory English at first and second year degree level in AMU.

2.3 Research Program in ELT.

As already pointed out, A. Bose streamlined the introduction of English research studies at AMU.As a result, faculty members utilised the opportunities for receiving training in language and literature from leading American and British Universities. One of the most significant developments in English studies was the launch of *Aligarh Journal of English Studies* in 1976 .This was a journal primarily on literary studies edited by A. A. Ansari, Chairman, Dept. of English, but later it also included contributions to Linguistics, language teaching and literary stylistics. Masoodul Hasan, Chairman, Dept. of English hosted All India Seminar on the Problems of Research in English. Faculty members of the Department of English till date have produced significant publications in the field of ELT and have been supervising research in different areas related to ELT. Research in ELT also has focused on empirical and data-driven studies in the context of Aligarh Muslim University. The National Knowledge Commission constituted by the Govt. of India emphasized that all efforts should be made to attract and retain talented faculty and 'developing a serious research tradition that is globally competitive'. This also implies the development of research infrastructure including the resources to organize workshops, conferences and participate in national and international conferences, and undertake serious need-based and data driven research projects. The ELT research program has to go a long way in developing an institutional research culture that promotes and encourages research in teaching and training. Though funds are available in UGC plan allocation, but a long-term planning and vision is needed for future promotion and growth of ELT. There should be more funds for operating lab-based ELT courses and for developing ELT research projects and related training program. Over the years, owing to paucity of grants and research infrastructure no substantial development has taken place. In spite of all the constraints, the Dept. has produced a sizable no. of PhDs, MPhil dissertation in ELT and published research work in ELT in leading national and international journals. Some of the early publications include *The Teaching of English in Indian Colleges and Universities* by R.A. Naqvi, *Contrastive Syntax* by S.M.Rizwan Hussain, *Uses of English* by Iqbal A. Ansari, *ESP, Vocabulary and Medical Discourse* by Farhatullah Khan, *Language Teaching through Literature* by Syed Asim Ali, *Urdu-English Phonetics and Phonology; A course of Spoken English and Noun Phrase structures of English Urdu* by Asif Shuja, *Translation and Mother Tongue in Language Teaching* by Kausar Hussain, *Schema in Literature: Towards a Model of*

Comprehension Pedagogy by Shagufta Imtiaz, *Policy and Provision for ESL in India's Higher Education; Study Skills* by Mohd.Rizwan Khan, *ESP Vocabulary* by Amirullah Khan (Dept of English, Platinum plus) and *Writing for Audience* by Raashid Nehal. Moreover, one full semester of MA (ELT) is devoted to dissertation in MA (ELT). A sizable section of students have received PhD degrees in ELT and Applied Linguistics from the Dept. of Linguistics and Education as well. There is a big scope for second language learning and teaching and researching teacher training. Research work in this direction has already begun considering the local language learning needs, attitudes, aptitudes, motivation studies related to English Phonetics, Applied Linguistics, language teaching methodology, testing, materials design, teacher training and other areas.

2.4 Faculty Development Programmes through English Access Micro scholarship Programme (EAMP) at the UGC Academic Staff College, AMU, Aligarh

A.R.Kidwai, Director ASC, AMU took initiative to provide language training to young economically backward and underprivileged sections belonging to different schools of AMU Aligarh in the age group of 14-18 years. This has culminated in the ongoing The English Access Micro scholarship Programme which commenced on 14th November, 2007 at Academic Staff College, Aligarh Muslim University. The Programme is sponsored by Regional English Language Office (RELO) of the American Embassy for AMU school students as part of the MoU signed by the Regional English Language Office (RELO), American Centre, New Delhi and Aligarh Muslim University.

As part of the EAMP, RELO, New Delhi has sponsored more than 25 the teacher trainer workshops. These workshops have been facilitated by RELO appointed trainers Amirullah Khan and Raashid Nehal in addition, to name a few, by Prof. Emeritus John C. Miller, Fulbright scholar from University of Colorado, USA, Prof. Emeritus Farhatullah Khan, John Silver, Scott Duarte, ESL Academic specialist from English Language Centre, Michigan State University, USA, Daniel Ringold, Senior English Language fellow, Richard Boyum former RELO and Rosemary Douglas, Qaisra Sheeraz from Ofsted, UK and Rajni Badlani.

2.4.1 AMU Access Representation in India and Abroad

Two Access students Mohd. Ghazi and Hira Sultana from AMU schools got the opportunity to participate in Access Student's Summer 2009 Workshop and 2012 US Summer Alumni(Access plus)workshop respectively .

Syed Faiz Zaidi from Senior Secondary School AMU participated in US English Access Micro-scholarship Teachers workshop at Oregon state University,Corvallis and Washinton D.C,USA july-Aug, 2008. Malik Arshad participated in access teachers' training programme in Austin Texas, US in Nov,2010. Munira T participated in International Visitor Leadership program (IVLP) on 'American Language: Connecting English Teachers to US Society and Culture' from March 19-April 6,2012. As part of her visit Munira T also attended 2012 TESOL conference at Philadelphia from March 28-30.

2.4.2 RELO sponsored Scholarships for online-training course from US Department of state

RELO sponsored Scholarships were awarded to English Access Microscholarship Program teachers for completing an online-training course from the Bureau of Educational and Cultural affairs, US Department of state.

Almost 8-10 faculty associated with the access programme have been awarded RELO sponsored Scholarships for doing ten-week online teacher training course in *Critical Thinking for English Language Teaching (EFL) Curriculum* from the American English Institute, University of Oregon, USA. *Teaching English to Teens (TET)* offered by the English language Centre, University of Maryland,Baltimore County, *ESL Assessment* offered by the University of Maryland, Baltimore County, and Indiana University, USA respectively, *Access*

Teacher Development Online Programme (ATDOP) from American English Institute in the Linguistics Department at the University of Oregon (UO AEI) *Integrating the Internet into the ESL/EFL classrooms.*

In addition, A. R. Kidwai has organised a number of short term training program/workshops at ASC.AMU on Academic *Reading and/Writing Skills* for faculty members of the University, with Raashid Nehal as course coordinator.

3.0 The Need and Scope for English proficiency/ELT Intensive Programs at AMU.

Language proficiency requirement at AMU needs serious attention since students lack basic English proficiency and communication skills. Students coming from non-English medium backgrounds have difficulty in accessing the mainstream education, which has English as the medium of instruction. Acquisition-poor environment and deficit methodologies practised in feeder schools have put newcomers on backfoot and hence there exist gaps between the demands of standardised curriculum and the learner needs. As a result, not enough opportunities are available for the student community at AMU Aligarh to cope with the varied levels of English language competence required later in technical, professional, administrative and managerial sectors. The English proficiency requirement differs from one course to other. There is a range of proficiency level catering to the varied clienteles. Developing appropriate communication skills will provide opportunities to students to prepare for English proficiency tests in high stakes examination such as central and state civil services, defence services, Public sectors, central government jobs and management services in addition to international Testing Exams in English such as IELTS, TOEFL, and management tests including GRE, and GMAT. At the same time, there is an immediate need for capacity building and training in communication skills of Teachers, Principals, non-Teaching Staff, Technical staff, Paramedical and Semi-Professionals. This justifies the launching of need-based

ESP courses in different sectors on priority basis. This will also create ample opportunities for teachers at primary and secondary/senior secondary level, teachers in adult education, DIETS and graduates with relevant teaching experience to enhance their professional expertise and promotion prospects either within their local teaching context or beyond.

There is a persisting concern that challenges facing ELT teacher certification programs and related proficiency courses in the educational context of north India need immediate attention. This propels a growing need for facilitating partnerships between National council for Teacher Education (NCTE) or leading certification agencies and AMU for giving accreditation to teacher certification program in English teaching in addition to the required expertise and training in capacity building and training/orientation of Teachers, Principals and officials and other related administrative functionaries. The context of certification/teaching English in Aligarh in particular, is based on varied levels , need-based programmes and learner-profiling(see 3.1) mentioned below:

1. Certificate/Diploma in Communication Skills in English (for general students)
2. Certificate/Diploma in Proficiency in English Language (CPEL) for Foreign Students
3. Certificate/Diploma in Teacher Communication Skills/ teaching of English (for B.Ed/M.Ed students specializing in ELT)
4. Certificate/diploma in communication skills for faculty/ semi-professionals/non- teaching personnel
5. Courses in academic writing skills for research scholars
6. Certificate in Communication Skills for Students enrolled for technical/vocational/professional Courses
7. Need-based ESP courses

3.1 Learner Profiling

English Language Learners (ELLs) constitute the most rapidly growing diverse and heterogeneous segment of the student population in AMU. Learners have different levels of language exposure, regional backgrounds, community attitudes, socio-economic status and different medium of instruction background at entry points. This calls into question the one-size-fits-all approach to instruction rather there is need to diversify and design different levels of English language curriculum in accordance with UGC's XI and XII plans. More specifically, this requires restructuring of thrust and priorities of ELT intensive program that would take care of inclusiveness and mitigating disparities in terms of the following stakeholders:

(a) English-medium input-rich environments belonging to both public and private schools.
(b) Limited English-medium backgrounds using both English and other Indian languages
(c) Government-aided regional medium schools catering to Urdu and Hindi learners
(d) Madarsa-based vernacular background
(e) Foreign nationals from West Asian, African & South-Asian Countries with limited English proficiency having Arabic & south-Asian Languages as their mother tongue.
(f) ESL learners belonging to remote and far-flung areas of the country such as tribal communities, particularly where there is a wide gap between the urban and rural learner.
(g) ESL learners belonging to socially disadvantaged and marginalized communities
(h) Students of Centre for Distance Education, AMU
(i) Women private students and private teachers for MA and BA courses in the Dept.
(j) Private Students (Adeeb Mahir andAdeeb Kamil) from J&K for English only exam1.

4.0 The Need for Customised Testing Services

Educationists feel that the reasons for failure to deliver English after decades of teaching are simply that the teachers lack training in treating English Language as skill-based subject. For long, English has been treated as content subject. As Rama Mathew,CIE, Delhi University) notes:

> Across states, English exams are content exams. They do not test what a learner can do with the language in a new situation. Memory is tested over proficiency.

English language teaching faces various challenges with regard to different medium of instruction,state and national boards and school typologies across the country. Therefore there is a need to locally develop the Test of English as a Second language Proficiency (TOESLP) rating scales for different proficiency levels in AMU keeping in view the varied requirements. The main objective will be to measure the ability of students in their use of everyday English language skills and will suggest remedial measures to improve it further. There is a strong need to enable the test taker to acquire communicative proficiency in Indian and International context. Developing appropriate testing services for giving opportunity to students to prepare for high stakes examination such as union and state civil services, defence services, Banking services as well as language proficiency tests featuring international testing services.

5.0 Conclusion

There are other factors such as student apathy, lack of funding for courses with increasingly more students per section, lack of classroom space and the increasing workload of teachers. Conventional English courses may not address the basic concern brought about by the perceived shortcomings of academic L2 programs. All this is not possible in teaching compulsory English which is not adequate to meet the multiple and varied needs. This has been articulated repeatedly and it has also drawn the attention of almost every Vice-Chancellor of AMU including the present one, Lt.Gen(Retd.) Zameeruddin Shah expressing concern for students lacking felicity in spoken communication skills. He has initiated measures to rectify it. A similar pilot programme has been initiated in the Dept. of English of Delhi University along with the Institute of Life-long Learning (ILLL).

It is obvious that with the existing staff strength, the total workload of teachers involved in ELT program has been enormous in addition to the normal duties of university and Dept. work. Because of the heavy teaching and evaluation workload, administrative and budgetary constraints, the required attention, expertise, training and facilities in ELT have been negligible and this needs immediate attention. In view of the of heterogeneous learner profile and their varied language learning needs, there is a need to strengthen the infrastructure, funding and faculty support which will be highly beneficial to the different stakeholders and diverse group of learners.

Heavy investments are needed in ESL teacher training with a view to improving the proficiency of the teachers in order to enable the students to attain language proficiency. There is an urgent need for courses that can cater to the communication needs of teachers. This will be similar to the requirements of *English Partnerships* envisioned by the British Council, to train directly or indirectly 7.5 lakh English teachers in India over the next 5 years. In the educational context of heterogeneous and diverse populations entering the ESL classroom, the role of ELT at AMU extends beyond the only English approach since there is a wide cross section of student population who bring in the rich resources and tradition of Urdu, Hindi and other languages, where considerable amounts of code switching and code mixing with Urdu and Hindi take place in informal situations. A few learners arrive at AMU with L1 competence but on the other hand majority of them leave schools with inadequate level of language proficiency in reading comprehension, writing skills and spoken English even in their native language. Nevertheless, the rich legacy of bilingual resource remains otherwise untapped but it can be tapped keeping in view of the positive signals from bilingual pedagogy Studies have shown that multilingualism leads to greater cognitive flexibility and social tolerance (NFG).

Thus the educational context of AMU calls for addressing two main questions:

1. What policy direction on English language education will prevail in the near future?
2. Given the educational context AMU has, what will be the way out for effective bilingual teaching programs?

Research reported by Cummins and Bullock Report (1975) indicate additive bilingual learning-teaching and cross-linguistic transfer of reading and writing showing tangible benefits(as cited in Tickoo, no date). As for English proficiency, the belief is still held among influential section of Indian masses, particularly middle and upper class that English alone is the remedy. This brings a serious disadvantage to those sections that can ill-afford English- medium schooling or those who coming from state-run boards.ELT for them becomes more a subject of elimination compared with those who are favourably placed. Tickoo very well describes this situation that in the recent past 'curriculum designers have been known to favour the adoption of innovative approaches and methods used to teach English which in a way neglects the alternative approach to place ELT in the L1 or mother tongue context. At the same time, it is a reality that a sizable section of state-board students fail to cope with basic language skills and abilities that are required for survival skills and some as feeder to AMU can remain no exception to politicizing of education, growing corruption and falling educational standards.

Acknowledgements:

I have not attempted a documented record of the exact developments of ELT at AMU rather it is a recollection of key events in ELT as they stood out in my mind as part of my shared understanding with my teachers, colleagues and seniors in the Dept. It is based on borrowings, few of which have been acknowledged, however, I do owe myself entirely to inadvertent omissions which might have been found in the write-up.

I am grateful to Prof.Amina kishore, Prof. A. R. Kidwai, Dr. Amirullah Khan and Dr.Mohd Asim Siddiqui whose comments on my paper came in as very handy and constructive.

NOTES

1. the nomenclature English only refers to those students who can earn a Bachelor degree after having passed the stipulated number of papers in one subject such as English.

WORKS CITED

Ahmad,Munir. *An Innovative Approach to English Language Teaching*: Dept. of English ,Aligarh Muslim University,1988. Print.

AMU. *Ordinances and Syllabi.* Aligarh: AMU Press, 1965.Print.

AMU. *Syllabus and Courses of Studies in AMU for examination of 1926.* Aligarh: The Aligarh Muslim University, 1926.Print.

Centre for Applied Linguistics. ELT and The British Council,: Research notes University of Warwick 1934-2009.http://www2.warwick.ac.uk/fac/soc/al/research/collect/elt_archive/research_projects/britishcouncil/

English, Dept of. 125 *years of English Dept.* Aligarh: Aligarh Muslim University, 2002.Print.

English, Dept. of. *Platinum Plus jubliee Celebrations.* Aligarh: Aligarh muslim University, 2003.Print.

Krishnaswamy, N. & T. Sriraman. *English Teaching in India.* Madras: TR Publications ,1994.Print.

Krishnaswamy,N. & T. Sriraman. *English Teaching in India.*Madras: TR Publications, 1994.Print.

National Focus Group (NFG). *Position Paper on Teaching of English.* Delhi: NCERT.2006. Accessed on: 06.20.2010, from: http://www.

ncert.nic.in/new_ncert/ncert/rightside/links/pdf/focus_group/english.pdf

National Focus Group (NFG). *Position Paper on Indian Languages*. Delhi: NCERT. 2005.

NarayananN, R. *et al.*, "English language teaching in India: a theoretical study." *MJAL* (2009): vol 1:1

Puri, A. "English Speaking Curse." *Outlook* 24 March 2008.Print.

Tickoo, M.L. *50 years of English studies at the EFL University An essay in understanding*. Hyderabad: EFL University, 2008.Print

23

Interview with Professor Masoodul Hasan

Mohammad Asim Siddiqui

MAS : All criticism presupposes a theory. How would you define your theory of criticism? Has it changed over the decades? What difference do you find between your early and later criticism?

MH : i) Literary criticism, to my mind, does not necessarily presuppose a 'fixed theory'; for such a presupposition would imply a constrictive, unitary approach to literature, subjecting it to a predetermined formula of assessment. Basically, literature is a multifactor construct, and a strait-jacket theory ill suits its multiple, expansive proportions. The critics' function is to analyse critically, elucidate and assess a work of art from multiple angles – not to judge it by a pre-set code. So, a literary theory is acceptable and valid, but monolithic, mutually exclusive critical theories sound self-serving and extra-aesthetic. We may have miscellaneous approaches to literature, mutually inclusive – not rigid and mutually exclusive (like) the 'institutionalised' critical theories. In 'Frontiers of Criticism' T.S. Eliot warns against the limitations of criticism, which applies still more cogently to the purported critical theories. Helen Gardner's incisive essay 'Business of Criticism' also hints at the self over-valorization of Criticism at the expense of literature proper. Besides, the existing critical theories are not adequately and uniformly applicable to all the genres of literature. So, while an intelligent awareness of various 'Critical theories'/Concepts may be rewarding, making a fetish of any particular theory is likely to under-value the full import of the literary text.

ii) As students, we were not asked to read literature in the light of theories. We were taught older texts on philological points and emendations. Shakespeare was approached triangularly – psychological make-up of his characters, his dramaturgy and his plays as the product of his age, each aspect mainly represented by Coleridge/A.C. Bradley, H. Granville Barker and William Hazlitt. Fiction was studied as a realistic or idealistic transcription of life criss-crossed by fate, chance or individual ingenuity. But as other allied disciplines developed, cross, inter-disciplinary references progressively cropped up – psycho-analytical (Freud, Jung, Adler), socialistic and historical approaches followed almost simultaneously with folklorish, mythical and archetypal perspectives awaiting their debut in the literary curricula in India.

iii) In the 1950s I was drawn to the study of imagery, and in the 60s I got additionally interested in the historical factors, issues of generic influences. This led me to the concept of the holistic criticism (appreciation and analysis of various literary factors together), combining multiple approaches, and currently I believe in appreciating literature as an imaginative and enlightening transcript of culture. In between I had a spell of interest in English literary bibliographies with special reference to India.

iv) I believe that theory-specific study of literature amounts to its fragmentation, and hampers adequate aesthetic appreciation of the text.

MAS : I believe that what teachers of literature often teach in the class is not literature but literary criticism hence the dependence on criticism. And yet teaching literature in a classroom sometimes makes you realize the limitations of literary criticism to explain everything in the text.

MH : I only partly agree with you. I think teachers should infuse appreciation of literature in the class, using multiple relevant critical/ epistemological aids. I am afraid, intelligent use of – not mechanical reliance on – tools is indispensable. Limitations of literary criticism in adequately addressing the texts would multiply if we are obsessed with any particular critical theory. A holistic or, at least, a multi-angular approach in teaching literature would be more meaningful.

MAS : What do you think about Indian literary criticism turned out in India today? Does it share the same virtues and failings as the criticism of the 60s and the 70s?

MH : Frankly, I do not think there is any substantial literary criticism in India today. About three decades ago William Walsh lamented the lack of any Indian school of English criticism despite nearly two centuries of English teaching here. After World War II research in literature is slowly catching up; but invariably theses and articles stem from poor motivation, and are done on 'quick' recipes. In recent years we have had a glut of substandard publications. Our young scholars' exposure to beneficial influences – good library holdings, book stores, literary symposia and seminars is nominal. (I cannot speak about the recent internet/searching facilities because of my own glaring inadequacy in the filed). But about the strictly local scene I am in a position to say a word or two, as I have managed to be in active touch with University library. Students often get cool and discouraging reception in the stack rooms of the central library; and, to top it all, now there is a total ban on the issuance of books more than fifty years old. Reputed journals in the periodical section remain invariably unread. Your departmental library, that used to be the hub of study, has woefully fallen back because of cramped space and declining reading habits.

MAS : Back in the 80s I was asked to read Cassierer, Susan Langer and Northrop Frye. Nobody probably reads them now. They have been replaced by newer voices. Your thoughts on some such figures who were on the reading list of students and teachers of literature but are rarely read now.

MH : I have been out of touch with students for too long now, and so am not in a position to comment on the nature of their studies. I cannot recall off hand some recent titles; but the stacks in the University Library have half-a-dozen *Companions to Literature* (British/American/Third World) that are recent additions. Among the old hats, to my mind, David Daiches, Wilbur Scott, W. Empson and Douglas Bush are still worthy of attention and amply rewarding.

MAS : There have been some critics like I.A. Richards and F. R. Leavis who had a large following. Other critics are not so fortunate in that a lot of criticism published in journals goes unread. Can we say that at the end of the day criticism is largely a matter of self-expression which has an existence independent of any readers. Did you ever have any thought of any readers for your writings?

MH : i) I.A. Richards, F.R. Leavis, Rene Wellek (and their peers) were seminal opinion makers of yester years, and therefore commanded wide and grateful readership. The purportedly "unfortunate" and "unread" writers of India today published in journals are falling by the way not so much because of being published in periodicals as for want of intrinsic worth. Undue haste to publish nascent views spurred by the questionable policy of 'Publish or Perish' may be largely responsible for this 'neglect'.

ii) Personally, I have never been plagued by "any thought of any reader'; for I am a modest scholar and a slenderer scribbler of scholarly distillations. I take literature as an autotelic discipline, untied to any theory or agenda.

MAS : Does it worry you that the concept of the literary has changed drastically from what it was, say, in the 50s and 60s. It has fallen to the left in very uncertain terms. What further changes do you foresee in the study of literature in Indian context? How do you see your own writings on literature now?

MH : i) The concept of literary studies has naturally changed over the years; but the change is unworrying to me, for the world view and literary landscape today are signally different from the old literary scene. English literature is no longer a homogenous product rooted in one soil; and now we have 'Englishes' branded under different rational/regional labels.

ii) Study of English literature in India has become more diversified, and Indian writing in English now legitimately clamours for larger space, though our native product is thin and fragile in the genres of poetry (despite its hydroptic flabbiness), drama and essay. Further, the English literature space is being appropriated increasingly by market-oriented brands of functional English.

iii) Personally, I have no illusions about my own writing on English literature, for I study letters for aesthetic enjoyment and self-edification, and I suspect no harm to literature by my authorial frugality.

MAS : A view is often expressed that familiarity with literature in your mother tongue is essential to appreciate literature in your second language like English. And yet, unlike people of your generation, a lot of Indian academic critics are not so blessed as to have a familiarity, leave alone a thorough grounding, with literature in their mother tongue. In fact, mother tongue has become a problematic concept considering the fact that a great many people are coming from English medium schools. However, they have to carry on the business of literature teaching and literary criticism. The situation is not likely to change in the near future. How do you view the whole issue?

MH : Familiarity with literature in the mother-tongue is decidedly a great help and advantage in the study of a foreign literature, as aesthetic nuances aroused and actuated by one's native literature may easily be applied to the appreciation of literature in another language. Our present generation's inadequate familiarity with Urdu background is a considerable disadvantage indeed, but students in senior English classes may be encouraged to familiarise themselves with Urdu language and its classics through optional, additional courses (as in the case of modern European or South Indian languages). This bilingual orientation may also encourage comparative literary studies, and relieve the existing curriculum of some of its limitations.

MAS : Oriental Studies has gained adherents in the West. With your vast study of Urdu literature how do you compare Urdu literature with the Western literature? How would you comment on Urdu literary criticism particularly about the familiar charge of its being derivative or its being stuck in the 'life and works' mould?

MH : Liberal intellectual activity in the West and the enlarging enlightened Urdu diaspora promises well for the advancement of Urdu studies. Of course, Urdu criticism has been largely imitative so far. In the 1930s and 40s the Halqa-e Arbab-e Zauq sponsored aesthetic/romantic criticism, while the succeeding Progressive Writers' Movement initiated the Marxist vogue, but the boost to formal research studies under UGC's policy has fostered the 'Life and Times' school. This has been overdone, and needs to change – cultural/ thematic/comparative topics offer viable alternatives. So does the translation work.

MAS : Young researchers would like to know about your process of writing. How do you read? How many readings of a book/text do you require before you write on it? How do you formulate an idea and develop it? How do you make notes? Do you revise? In brief, everything about your writing.

MH : I am all for a close study of the text with ample pencil markings on the text (if it is a personal copy); otherwise copious notes may be taken on separate sheets/cards. Subsequently, these notes may be classified caption-wise, and transcribed on fresh sheets/cards. A single close reading may thus provide classified basic material for several chapters or articles. The researcher may also jot down his/her comments on the text. The number of readings may differ from book to book, depending on the level of its difficulty. Suitable paragraphing and revision of the script, and documentation are indispensable.

MAS : Which books/authors you would like all students of literature to read?

MH : I hesitate to recommend the following introductory bibliography for basic study of literary genres lest the titles appear outdated. But, to my mind, they are still rewarding and relevant. I reproduce them from memory:

Scott-James : *The Making of Literature*
Wilber Scot : *Five Approaches of Literary Criticism*
Northrop Frye : *The Critical Path*

W. Empson : *Seven Types of Ambiguity*
Cleanth Brooks : *Understanding Poetry* [I faintly recall that Brooks has done a book each on Novel and Drama on similar lines]
David Daiches : *The Novel and the Modern World*
Marjorie Boulton : *The Anatomy of Drama, The Anatomy of poetry*
James Reeves : *Understanding poetry*

MAS : Finally, what role has literature played in your life? Can you share some moments of epiphany you might have had in your reading of literature?

MH : The final query on the list is a tall order, as it requires a virtual autobiography, especially the references to "Some moments of epiphany" in the course of my reading of literature. But, in brief, the study of literature has largely refined my responses and attitudes to exigencies of life, and it has enriched my understanding of humanistic and ethical values.